Fourth Edition

Consciousness
and
Behavior

Benjamin Wallace
Leslie E. Fisher
both of
Cleveland State University

WAVELAND
PRESS, INC.

Long Grove, Illinois

To our children and wives,
Jacob, Sara, and Roni Wallace
and
Patricia, Gregory, David, Kathryn, and Mary Fisher

For information about this book, contact:
Waveland Press, Inc.
4180 IL Route 83, Suite 101
Long Grove, IL 60047-9580
(847) 634-0081
info@waveland.com
www.waveland.com

CONTENTS

PREFACE

The first edition of this book appeared in 1983. Since then, the psychology of consciousness has continued to evolve. Given the many current research reports dealing with topics in the areas of consciousness, which have changed interpretations of many of the results reported in previous editions of this book, it was time to revise the book and produce this fourth edition.

We were very pleased by the enthusiastic response to our previous editions. We knew that others shared our need for a text that dealt with areas of psychology and behavior that were traditionally not found in most texts, especially in the combined form used in this book. This book has been used as a stand-alone text in a number of courses taught under the name the Psychology of Consciousness, States of Consciousness, or Altered States of Consciousness. It has also been used successfully as an adjunct text in introductory psychology courses, especially in dealing with the topics of perception, cognition, motivation, and, of course, the general field of consciousness. In essence, it appears that in a course dealing with the topics we cover here, our book was the first choice. Needless to say, we are very pleased by this honor.

In the decade and a half that various editions of our text have been in use, a number of professors and students have let us know what they thought was missing from earlier editions or what they would like to see discussed in more or less detail. We have addressed these issues and concerns in the fourth edition.

A number of changes have been made. First, the book has been completely updated in all areas discussed. In addition, we have clarified a number of points that appeared to present problems to both professors and students in previous editions. In brief, the important changes are as follow.

In addition to the well-known, general theories of consciousness discussed in Chapter 1, we have included a brief discussion of Baar's (1997) method of contrastive analysis.

Chapter 2 (The Physiology of Consciousness) continues to present an overview of physiology for students who need this in preparing to study consciousness. In addition, with the increasing use of the electroencephalogram (EEG) and evoked potential measurements in the study of consciousness, we considered it important to include a brief overview of these important measurement tools. Finally, we have added a new section that deals with more advanced research technology in the study of consciousness.

These methods include X-ray techniques, computer-assisted axial tomography (CAT scan), magnetic resonance imaging (MRI), and positron emission tomography (PET scan).

Chapter 3 (Consciousness-Altering Drugs) thoroughly updates the status of many popularly abused drugs that affect consciousness. This edition of the book also presents an expanded discussion of alcohol, cocaine, and marijuana.

Chapter 4 (Hypnosis) now includes a discussion of neurological correlates of hypnosis. Related to this is a discussion of the possible existence of ultradian rhythms during hypnosis. There is also an expanded discussion of the beneficial role of hypnosis in treating the smoking habit and in controlling pain.

Chapter 5 (Biofeedback) has been thoroughly updated. This includes an expansion of the contemporary applications of biofeedback.

Chapter 6 (Meditation) now includes a section on the use of meditation in the treatment of drug and alcohol abuse. There is also a new section concerned with brain-wave activity during meditation and its potential use in treating epilepsy.

In Chapter 7 (Sleep and Dreams), we present an update of the theoretical views and issues discussed in our previous edition, including the latest on Hobson and McCarley's activation-synthesis hypothesis. There is also a new section on sexual fantasies and their role in daydream activity.

Chapter 8 (Sensory Deprivation), the chapter that changed the most in our previous edition, has changed the least in this edition. We have thoroughly updated the literature in this area, but there have been no major theoretical or methodological contributions on this topic since our last edition.

Finally, our discussion of parapsychology in Chapter 9 presents the latest findings on this controversial area of study. This includes an expanded discussion of individual differences and hypnotic influences on parapsychological phenomena. There is also an expansion of the discussion of the near-death experience. Unfortunately, as in previous editions of this book, little has yet been resolved concerning the failure of many researchers to replicate phenomena in this area of research. Nonetheless, many studies continue to appear in the journals, both supportive and critical of parapsychology. This controversy is presented in Chapter 9, replete with contemporary arguments from both sides of the issue.

We hope you will enjoy reading the fourth edition of *Consciousness and Behavior*. We have tried to improve it while retaining the goal of previous editions: to introduce students to those controversial yet popular areas of psychology that are typically neglected or given very little attention in traditional course offerings. We hope to achieve this goal yet keep the presentation of topics at a level that does not necessitate prerequisites for reading and understanding. We hope that we have accomplished this goal in this edition.

ACKNOWLEDGMENTS

We would like to thank Bill Barke, who convinced us in 1980 that there was a need for a text in the psychology of consciousness. We also thank Carolyn O. Merrill for her part in making the fourth edition a reality. And last but not least, as in previous editions, we thank our families for having the patience to put up with us while we prepared and completed this book.

B. W.
L. E. F.

1

INTRODUCTION

The contemporary study of behavior has been greatly influenced by the principles, laws, and theories of behaviorism (Skinner, 1964, 1974; Watson, 1913). Whenever psychologists were interested in studying an aspect of behavior, they generally obeyed certain modes of collecting data, making certain that behavior was observable and, therefore, measurable.

This is not a difficult rule to follow, nor is it necessarily one that we will try to change. However, in being so rigid, data collection in many psychology experiments may be incomplete. If we are concerned only with studying and reporting observable behavior or behavior that can be mutually shared, we may be sidestepping a great deal of human behavior that obviously is not observable. For example, should we ignore totally an individual's thoughts or feelings because they are not directly observable or capable of being mutually shared? Should we fail to study dreams because we cannot share them with the dreamer? Should we fail to study hypnosis or meditation because these phenomena are not directly measurable in the true behavioristic sense?

The answer to these questions, obviously, is *no*. Yet psychology has downplayed the importance of studying some of these interesting phenomena because of a bias still present, to an extent, among many contemporary psychologists. We believe that it is time to do away with the philosophical biases of behaviorism but not yet time to entirely abandon that school of thought, science, and methodology.

Today, the influence of behaviorism is declining, replaced by an interest in cognitive psychology. Compared to the behaviorists, cognitive psychologists have not been as rigid in defining what is permissible in data collection (Kihlstrom, 1994, 1996). These scientists are recovering the tools of psychology that existed before the advent of behaviorism, albeit at a very slow pace (see Banks, 1993).

Although we are well aware that behaviorism emerged as a reaction to the sloppiness and poor experimental control of such processes as introspection (Hamilton, 1880; Malcolm, 1964), it also did away with other ramifications of

1

structuralism (Titchener, 1909). For example, during introspection, a process of self-observation developed by Wilhelm Wundt (1832–1920), subjects were taught to verbalize everything that they experienced during their participation in an experiment. In other words, they were to give a complete phenomeno-logical report of their experiences with a stimulus event and with the environment. This reporting served as a means for the scientist to gain access to a subject's mental episodes.

In agreement with the behaviorists we believe that much imprecision did exist during introspective assessments of experience. However, in reacting against this method of data assessment, behaviorism also reacted against most behavior that was not directly observable or that, at minimum, could not be mutually shared. This tainted the use of individual verbal reports in psychological research (or, for that matter, in all behavioral research). Psychology, as a science, witnessed a considerable decline in the use of such reports in research because they were supposedly not scientific. In fact, many psychology and behavioral science instructors still hold to this belief and try to proselytize their students to the "party line."

This strict adherence to behavioristic philosophy has been at the expense of much important data collection and of hypothesis, law, and theory construction. Not to deviate from strict behaviorism is to accept the dictum that thoughts or mental processes are not scientifically testable. We and contemporary cognitive psychologists (e.g., Eysenck & Keane, 1995; Reed, 1996; Sternberg, 1996) believe that such a view is untenable. All behavior is acceptable for study, whether it is directly observable or is speculated to exist via an individual's verbal report.

One area of research that has made great strides in attempting to assess unobservable behavior through verbal reports and other means, and which therefore falls outside the legitimate realm of study by strict behaviorists, is what is now referred to as the **psychology of consciousness** (Farthing, 1992; Ornstein, 1972, 1986). Although psychologists and philosophers have studied consciousness for many years (see Boring, 1929), it was not until very recently that this area of psychology reemerged as an important area of concern.

What exactly is the psychology of consciousness, and when did the study of this area commence? Why is it reemerging as an area for psychologists to study after being in limbo for nearly three-quarters of a century? Most important, will science gain knowledge as a result of its reemergence? Let us examine these issues.

WHAT IS CONSCIOUSNESS?

Although philosophers have studied consciousness for nearly 400 years (see Natsoulas, 1978b), the psychology of consciousness can trace its beginnings only to the writings of William James (1842–1910). James, who founded the school of functionalism, saw consciousness as a tool that enabled individuals to select their own courses of action. He defined *consciousness* as the "function of knowing" (James, 1890, 1904). To James, knowing or the ability to know was a personal thought; therefore, what one individual knew or thought differed from what everyone else knew or thought.

James also believed that consciousness was forever changing. By this he meant that every conscious state is a function of the entire psychophysical totality and that the mind is cumulative and not recurrent. Implicit in this is the belief that objects can recur but sensations or thoughts cannot. James also urged that consciousness is a continuous process. There are time gaps, such as sleep, but when an individual awakens from sleep, he or she has not become someone or something else.

Finally, James believed that consciousness had the important characteristic of being selective. Only a small part of the potentially effective world of stimuli could come to consciousness. The principle of selecting the effective stimuli was highly dependent upon relevance. That is, we attend to stimuli that are most relevant to us at a given time and place. Thus, consciousness is a highly selective process that is both logical and rational.

From the early thoughts of James we come to more recent considerations of the concept of consciousness. Thomas Natsoulas (1978a, 1987) delineated several separate definitions of consciousness from the *Oxford English Dictionary* (1933). In fact, in a survey of the work of many authors, Baruss (1987) has found 29 separate definitions. We shall limit our discussion to the seven commonly accepted definitions.

The first definition of consciousness deals with the topic as "joint or mutual knowledge." This definition characterizes a kind of relationship between individuals in which they are confidants. To speak of people who are conscious in this sense is to come close to the psychoanalytic definition (Freud, 1913). This school of thought holds consciousness to be an expression, particularly as it is applied to efforts of comprehending what transpires in a patient during psychoanalytic therapy.

The "joint knowledge" definition may also approach the concept as it is conceived by radical behaviorists (e.g., Skinner, 1974). To this group of scientists, individuals must be initiated into the practice of consciousness. Without such practice, people would be unaware of their private events. Since such events are not scientifically measurable unless they can be shared with others, they must be made nonprivate or public. At this point, the event becomes mutual knowledge.

A second definition is that it is "internal knowledge or conviction." This refers to a certain cognitive relation to oneself or to being a witness to one's own behavior. As such, one gains internal knowledge firsthand rather than by hearing about it from someone else.

When James defined consciousness as a function of knowing (1904), he came close to the third definition as delineated by Natsoulas: Consciousness is equivalent to "a state of awareness." Such a state includes a knowledge of unobservable, private events or mental occurrences, as well as a knowledge of external, observable objects or events. Therefore, the concept of consciousness involves the knowledge of being aware of something, generally through sensory confirmation.

Natsoulas described the fourth definition of consciousness as "direct awareness." This is a state or faculty of being conscious as a condition or concomitant of all thought, feeling, and volition, or what John Locke (1690/1975) referred to as what passes in a man's mind. Hunt (1995) views perceptual awareness as the core of consciousness.

In 1987, Natsoulas added to the previous definition by proposing that a person exemplifies consciousness by being aware of, or being in a position to be aware of, his or her perception, thought, or other occurrent mental episode. This fifth definition differs from the previous one in that direct awareness has no involvement with sensory organs or receptors. To undergo a direct awareness is to have a thought that something is happening when there is no sensory confirmation of its occurrence.

Both Natsoulas (1978a, 1978b, 1979, 1987) and the *Oxford English Dictionary* (1933) refer to consciousness as a personal unity. In this sense, consciousness is the totality of the impressions, thoughts, and feelings which make up a person's conscious being. Therefore, all of one's mental episodes might constitute one's consciousness.

The sixth definition, which is the most common, refers to consciousness as a normal waking state. The *Oxford English Dictionary* (1933) says that consciousness is "a general state or condition of the person." Thus, consciousness is a "state of wakefulness with attentiveness to stimuli or to events in one's environment." In this sense this definition of consciousness would best fit that used by cognitive psychologists, who study such topics as language development, reading, arithmetic, and other information-processing tasks. And although it is not our intent to cover the role and nature of consciousness in areas such as language acquisition and reading, the definition of consciousness as used by cognitive scientists is a widely adopted one. As such, we will often refer to it in our discussion of various altered states (Tart, 1972, 1977a), the major theme of this book, or with what Norman Zinberg (1977) refers to as **alternate states**.

The seventh definition of consciousness refers to multiple states of information processing, or what Natsoulas has called **double consciousness**. Since we do not assume a priori that individuals have only a single state of consciousness, we can discuss different levels of consciousness. Individuals may be aware of the presence of some stimulus at one level but not at another. The concept of threshold in perception is a good illustration of how individuals can react to a stimulus situation at different levels of awareness. For instance, if a light source at a very low level of intensity is present and subjects are requested to indicate when they are first able to see it, we notice that they do not give their indication immediately. There are several reasons for this delay in response. For instance, the retinal receptor system may not be physically capable of detecting light at this low level. Or the subjects may think they see the light but are not quite certain; thus, they may choose to be conservative and delay the response, or the delay may be due to a combination of these two reasons.

However, light *is* being emitted from a source, and photons are impinging on the retinal photoreceptors of the subjects' eyes; they simply are not able to detect the light. Does this mean the light is really not present? This question is basically a philosophical one, just like the question Does a falling tree make noise when no one is around to hear it? No, obviously a crash and resultant noise occur physically, but they are not perceived.

In the case of the light we might simply say that, for a given individual at the normal state of awareness and processing, the light was not present because the subject did not perceive it. However, we know that it is physically present, and therefore, it could have been perceived, if not by the subject, by someone else. Thus, the normal waking state of awareness or consciousness may differ from one individual to the next.

At the same time it is also possible for an individual to perceive the light at one level of consciousness and not at another. An excellent example of the existence of such multiple levels of consciousness or awareness is illustrated in the work of Ernest Hilgard (1973, 1976, 1977a, 1977b, 1979), discussed in Chapter 4. Briefly, he showed experimentally that with the aid of hypnosis it is possible to separate out at least two different levels of consciousness. At one level, a subject perceives an event, while at another level, he or she is totally unaware of the event.

The final definition of consciousness delineated by Natsoulas comes closest to ours. We believe that consciousness is the *processing of information at various levels of awareness.* (As you can readily see, we are equating the terms **consciousness** and **states of awareness**.) In fact, we will go one step farther than Natsoulas and Hilgard: Consciousness exists at *many* levels. We define a **level** as one state of awareness that is distinguishable, either empirically or experientially, from another state.

Hilgard has demonstrated two of these levels. However, there is evidence to indicate that more than two levels of consciousness or awareness exist. For example, we can count the several stages of sleep (which are discussed in Chapter 7) as different levels of awareness. Also, as you will see in other chapters, there are different levels of hypnosis (Chapter 4) and meditation (Chapter 6). Many more levels may also exist during other states of consciousness. One of our goals is to deal with consciousness using a multilevel approach. Another goal is to show that we have only begun to touch the surface in our understanding of consciousness, especially of the different levels of consciousness and what takes place in them.

CONTEMPORARY THEORIES OF CONSCIOUSNESS

It is generally not difficult to communicate what consciousness in the normal waking state means. We are well aware of what being awake feels like. We also can describe what we are minimally capable of doing while awake. However, what does it feel like to be in an altered state of consciousness, or not awake? What are we capable of doing in an altered state? Does performance in such a state differ from performance in the waking state?

To begin to answer such questions, it is necessary to enumerate what we believe to be altered states of consciousness or awareness. Then we must decipher existing experimental evidence to determine whether behavior changes or is different in such states. Finally, if behavior does differ, it is necessary to summarize the evidence to formulate laws and theories of cognition, information processing, or neurophysiology that will help to explain the psychology of consciousness.

In the early 1970s, Andrew Weil (1972) attempted to theorize about the concept of consciousness. Although his theory was not formal in any sense of the word, he did elaborate on many observations and hypotheses that ultimately could lead to a formal and comprehensive theory of consciousness. His observations and hypotheses were based primarily on his own personal experiences as well as on laboratory experimentation. The major points Weil made were as follows:

1. The drive to experience modes of awareness other than the normal waking state is innate. In other words, we are born with a desire or urge to experience altered states.
2. Individuals experiment with methods or techniques of changing consciousness. These experimental methods in essence define the topics of the majority of chapters in this book.
3. Altered-state experiences are normal, and individuals spend a certain amount of time each day in such experiences. If you cannot conceive of individuals doing this, just think for example of the last time you had a daydream (perhaps a few seconds ago?).
4. Individuals may not always be aware that they are experiencing or have experienced behavior in an altered state. Again, even if you had a daydream, were you aware of it? Or was awareness something that occurred after the conclusion of the daydream?
5. Altered states form a continuous spectrum from ordinary waking consciousness. That is, altered states are not all or none; they flow naturally from the waking state.
6. Artificial agents (e.g., drugs) may elicit altered states but do not cause them (Weil, 1996). As an example, while many may believe that consciousness-altering drugs (see Chapter 3) produce altered states, Weil

does not believe this to be the case. Rather, the drugs only bring out altered states.

7. It is important to learn how to enter an altered state, because experiences in this state may lead to a more comprehensive understanding of the workings of our central and peripheral nervous systems (see Chapter 2). Such experiences also lead to the realization of untapped human potentials and to a better understanding of the functioning of our ordinary waking state of consciousness. As is evident, Weil believes that altered states are beneficial and that we should learn to make greater use of their potential.

As we will see throughout this book, many of Weil's observations are indeed valid premises for a potential theory of consciousness. However, a great deal more experimentation is necessary to test his hypotheses before these points can constitute an established theory.

In a more formal sense, Charles Tart (1975, 1977a) also proposed a theory of consciousness. He viewed consciousness as a construction or something that requires learning or experience. As such, it is not automatic or given. According to Tart, a number of concepts lead to this construction. These include what he referred to as attention/awareness, structure, the interaction of structure and attention/awareness, and the interaction of structures with structures. Let us examine each of these concepts.

Attention/awareness involves the following: Consciousness begins with a *basic awareness* or some kind of rudimentary ability to know or realize that something is happening (in one's environment, broadly defined). Thus, we are cognizant of being conscious. In addition, we are often aware of being aware, which is what Tart referred to as *self-awareness*. This varies from moment to moment. As a result, there are different degrees of being aware. Further, this attention/awareness can be voluntarily directed to some extent. Thus, we can ask someone to pay attention to our right hand, and attention is focused on that part of the body (although as Tart points out, focused attention is never complete).

Tart (1977a) further stipulates that "attention/awareness constitutes the major phenomenal energy of the consciously experienced mind" (p. 162). **Energy** is defined here as the ability to do work, the ability to make something happen. Finally, the total amount of attention/awareness energy available varies from time to time, but there is probably a fixed upper limit on it at any given moment. On some days, we seem to concentrate or attend well; on other days, we appear incapable of focusing our attention.

Tart's concept of **structure** referred to the idea that consciousness consists of a relatively stable organization of component parts that perform one or more related psychological functions. Such a structure may show variation in the intensity and/or the quality of its activity, but it still retains its basic pattern or quality of organization and its function. And, as such, it remains recognizably the same.

Some structures are essentially permanent. These are biological/physiological givens or the **hardware** of our mental system (some of these are discussed in Chapter 2). Other structures are determined by the individual's developmental history. These are **software,** and they are created by learning and by living within the culture. According to Tart, the essentially permanent structures create limits on what can be done with programmable (software) structures. Thus, in some respects the hardware constrains the software.

An **interaction of attention/awareness and structure** exists because many structures function totally autonomous of attention/awareness. An example is a physiological structure such as the liver. We do not have a direct awareness of this structure; we infer it from other kinds of data.

On the other hand, according to Tart, psychological structures must use a certain amount of attention/awareness energy (1) to be formed or created, (2) to be operable, (3) to have their operations inhibited, (4) to have their structure or operation modified, and (5) to be dismantled. And although Tart postulates that attention/awareness energy is capable of activating and altering psychological structures, this is not always easy. For example, we may be asked to attend to something, but this does not necessarily mean that we do so. Some of you may recall an experience like this when a teacher asked you to pay attention to something and this command went in one ear and out the other without any (or with little) cognitive processing.

Tart also postulates that, insofar as the amount of attention/awareness energy available at any given time has a fixed upper limit, some decrements should be found when too many structures draw on this energy simultaneously. Also, once a structure has been formed and is operating, the attention/awareness energy required for its operation may be tapped automatically.

As for the **interaction of structures with other structures**, individual structures have various kinds of properties that limit and control their potential range of interaction with one another. For example, they may not interact because there is no direct or mediated connection between them. Interaction is also precluded if the codes of output and input information are incompatible or if the output signal from one is too weak. Also, interaction may not occur if the output signal from one overloads the other. Finally, two structures are prevented from interacting if the action of a third structure interferes with them.

Tart also discusses the terms **discrete state of consciousness (d-SoC)** and **discrete altered state of consciousness (d-ASC).** The first concept refers to such phenomena as sleep, dreams, hypnosis, drug intoxication, and various forms of meditation (topics discussed in later chapters of this book). The second concept refers to the difference in observable, and perhaps measurable, behavior between some baseline state of consciousness (waking state) and a d-SoC. Therefore, Tart's views of consciousness are very much in line with the multilevel concept that we advocate in this book. It is true that Tart discusses only two levels of consciousness, but it is certainly a good start toward a theory of consciousness.

In agreement with Tart, Baars (1983, 1988, 1997) has argued that empirical constraints bearing on consciousness involve a close comparison of very similar conscious and unconscious processes. In essence, we can study a phenomenon only if we can treat it as a variable. In the case of consciousness we can conduct a contrastive analysis comparing waking to sleep, attended versus unattended streams of information, recalled versus nonrecalled memories, and so on. Thus, like Tart, Baars compares baseline activity to a d-SoC.

Baars's method of contrastive analysis is much like the experimental method where consciousness becomes, in effect, a variable. However, instead of dealing with only one experimental data set, contrastive analysis involves entire categories of well-established phenomena like those discussed in the remaining chapters of this book.

Perhaps the most controversial theory of consciousness was proposed by Julian Jaynes (1976). On the basis of many laboratory experiments involving brain laterality or hemispheric specialization of the brain (e.g., Galin & Ornstein, 1972; Gazzaniga, Bogen, & Sperry, 1965; Gazzaniga & Sperry, 1967; Gordon & Sperry, 1968; Milner, 1965) and a close reading of existing archeological and historical evidence, Jaynes proposed that people in ancient civilizations could not independently process information or think as we do today. In other words, individuals appeared to be obeying commands that they heard inside their heads. Jaynes (1986a) believed that early peoples interpreted these so-called voices, or possible auditory hallucinations, as commands from the gods that told them what to do and how to behave and basically presented them with everything they needed to maintain their existence. The ultimate source of authority (the voice of the commands of the gods) was tradition. Being so dependent on their gods, people from these cultures were not conscious. According to Jaynes, many examples of obeying these inner voices can be found in both the Old and New Testaments, as well as in writings such as the *Iliad* by Homer.

Because of the catastrophes and cataclysms of many centuries, especially during the second millennium B.C., and because humans were beginning to perform complex activities such as reading and writing, individuals living in those times were forced to become more independent in their thinking and, perhaps to survive, to learn consciousness. Thus, the heart of Jaynes's (1976) theory is that consciousness is a model of the real world composed of words. The model is used to carry out experiments concerning various possible courses of action. The results of these invisible experiments are then used to make decisions and to choose the course of action that appears to be most promising.

More recently, Jaynes (1986b) referred to consciousness in terms of the development of a "mind space." Therefore, consciousness did not evolve in the strict biological sense but was produced via our experiences with history and with different cultures and races. Furthermore, according to Jaynes, conscious-

**FIGURE 1.1   Jaynes's
God-Run Man**

ness is grounded in the physiology of the brain's right and left hemispheres. (We discuss brain laterality and its role in consciousness in Chapter 2).

Three forms of human awareness exist within Jaynes's theory. He refers to these as the *bicameral* or *god-run man*, the *modern* or *problem-solving man*, and the contemporary forms of *throwbacks to bicamerality*. The god-run man was controlled by and within the right hemisphere, which told the left hemisphere (especially the auditory and speech centers of that hemisphere) what to do and how to behave (see Figure 1.1). As civilization became more independent, there was less and less god-run control by the right hemisphere over the left hemisphere. In becoming more independent, people acquired consciousness.

However, Jaynes stipulates that, on occasions, the god-run man reemerges and exhibits himself in what is referred to as throwbacks to bicamerality. These include such states as hypnotism, schizophrenia, and poetic and religious frenzy. As part of these throwbacks, modern humans relegate their consciousness to obey the commands of an individual, group, or higher power who gains control for a period of time (specified, as in hypnosis, or unspecified, as in schizophrenia).

An examination of Jaynes's radical theory suggests that all altered states of consciousness are throwbacks to bicamerality. This suggests further that such states temporarily produce a loss of wakeful and controllable awareness in an individual. If this is the case, then men or women at least temporarily give up some control to another individual. Although this may be true to some extent, we will see in the remaining chapters that this is not as straight-forward as Jaynes would have us believe. For example, an individual who is hypnotized does not really lose control. Similarly, when one meditates or experiences biofeedback, there is no loss of control. Thus, we do not agree with Jaynes's premise that altered states are necessarily indications of a throwback to bicamerality. We will present our case in detail in the various chapters that deal with the different areas of consciousness.

A model of consciousness, which has the potential for ultimately becoming a theory, was recently introduced by Andrzej Kokoszka (1988, 1992). In essence, Kokoszka introduces four types of consciousness: (1) ordinary waking state of consciousness (OWSC), (2) differentiated waking state of consciousness (DWSC), (3) rapid eye movement, or REM, sleep, and (4) slow-wave sleep. For the purpose of a general discussion of consciousness, only the first two types will be discussed here. The latter types are discussed in Chapter 7.

OWSC is characterized by a dominance of mental activity, especially activity from the left hemisphere of the brain (see Chapter 2) and has low reliance on the use of imagery. The OWSC is also characterized by a domi-nance of stimulus reception from the external environment and a dominance of physical or mental action over more internal events such as contemplation or daydreaming. In essence, the OWSC is a state of alertness. As you will see in Chapters 2 and 7, we can actually measure a brain-wave activity that describes the OWSC, the beta wave.

DWSC is characterized by greater restfulness (less mental activity) and relies heavily on the use of imagery. Unlike the OWSC, the DWSC involves a passive state of mind or the dominance of contemplation or other internal activity over action. Some have speculated that many of the activities in the DWSC are controlled by the right hemisphere or at least the right hemisphere seems to show more involvement during DWSC than during OWSC (Bakan, 1969). In addition, DWSC may in some instances be measurable by a change in the wakeful, beta brain-wave activity to a slower wave referred to as alpha. However, there is no universal agreement on the appearance of such brain-wave activity during a DWSC (Springer & Deutsch, 1997).

If one considers consciousness along the lines of Kokoszka's model, it is possible to ultimately describe the various altered states of consciousness in terms of his OWSC and DWSC. As an example, meditation as an altered state (as described in Chapter 6), might be considered a type of DWSC. This is also possible for other altered states. In addition, by fitting these altered states within Kokoszka's model, one can eventually find differences and common-alities among them. This, of course, is one of the ultimate goals of a theory.

In summarizing our sampling of three contemporary theories and one model of consciousness, we can find many commonalities. Consciousness appears to develop through a learning process (defined broadly). Many indi-vidual differences are found in states of consciousness, and many of these dif-ferences help us to learn about the process. Many human potentials can be tapped through knowledge of consciousness and experiencing altered states of consciousness. It is also possible to find commonalities between various states or altered states of consciousness. Finally, states of consciousness are to be considered positive in the development of humankind and civilizations and, as such, can help to improve the quality of life and its accomplishments.

Aside from examining theories of consciousness, we shall also examine or attempt to determine:

1. how an altered state of awareness comes about,
2. how various levels of consciousness or awareness are believed to be operating for a given phenomenon,
3. how these levels can be identified, and
4. how behavior exhibited at each level can be assessed.

Thus, we are not entirely abandoning the positive aspects of science given to us by the behaviorists. To deal with these areas of concern, we need to establish methods of measurement that can be generalized.

This does not mean that we advocate a return to the looseness of introspectionism. However, the study of consciousness requires that we release enough of our rigidity in collecting data to permit the assessment of responses that may not be considered scientifically pure by the radical behaviorist. Thus, verbal responses are permissible and are important in the study of consciousness. Furthermore, by nature, many of these responses may be unable to be shared. Because so many individual differences exist, establishing laws and theories of behavior will be difficult. Yet this must be accomplished, and Weil (1972), Tart (1975), Jaynes (1976), and Kokoszka (1988) are leading the way to doing just that. Not to do so is to relegate the study of consciousness to nonscience. This cannot be permitted if psychology is to seriously consider behavior that occurs during altered states of awareness.

Therefore, the psychology of consciousness, as it is presented here, is a step in the advancement of a study of states and levels of awareness. It is also an attempt to integrate the many diverse areas that define the psychology of consciousness. Many refer to these areas as the peripheral areas of psychology. Yet they are popular areas for discussion by scientists and nonscientists alike. They are also very important areas of study in their own right.

A TAXONOMY OF STATES OF CONSCIOUSNESS

Before beginning an in-depth study of the various states of consciousness as defined in the remaining chapters, we would like to present an organizational theme.

First, from the general theories of consciousness previously presented, it should be clear that states of consciousness contain an element of variability. That is, regardless of any predictions in a theory or in the many experiments that you will read about in the remaining chapters, individual differences will always exist. This is one reason why states of consciousness are so difficult to study. Individual differences are abundant in all the areas we will discuss. Therefore, we cannot generalize as liberally as we would wish about any of the states of consciousness or phenomena that will be presented. There will always be individuals for whom the described results will not seem to fit. Thus, what appears on the surface to be a robust effect may not be nearly so potent. We would hope that the results would be predictive for a large segment of the population.

Second, as you will see throughout the various chapters describing the many states of consciousness, consciousness is not a single state or level. In general, if we equate the concept of consciousness with awareness or alertness, it is possible to form a type of hierarchy of consciousness with *wakefulness* at the top of the hierarchy. Or in terms of Kokoszka's (1988, 1992) model, this would be similar to what he described as the ordinary waking state of consciousness (OWSC). This would be followed by a middle level composed of the various states of consciousness to be described or what Kokoszka termed differentiated waking states of consciousness (DWSC). These include drug-altered states (Chapter 3), hypnosis (Chapter 4), biofeedback (Chapter 5), meditation (Chapter 6), daydreaming and perhaps night dreaming (Chapter 7), sensory deprivation (Chapter 8), and perhaps paranormal experiences (Chapter 9). Finally, in agreement with Kokoszka, the lowest level of the consciousness hierarchy might be sleep (Chapter 7).

Third, within each state of consciousness to be discussed, there exists a further delineation. That is, each state may consist of many levels. As examples, you will see that various levels of consciousness alteration can be produced by the influence of some of the drugs described in Chapter 3. And the effects of one drug may be different for one individual than for another; that is, individuals may experience drugs at different levels of consciousness. Similarly, you will find that hypnosis, meditation, biofeedback, daydreaming, night dreaming, and sensory deprivation can be experienced at different levels of awareness or consciousness.

Fourth, altered states of consciousness must contain an element of pleasure. We believe this because so many individuals (all of us, perhaps) seek to attain altered states, often on a regular basis. These altered states must also be more pleasurable than the waking state. Perhaps Weil (1972) was correct: We have an innate drive to experience modes of awareness. Although the drive may be innate, we must learn to use the drive, perhaps in a manner similar to what Ornstein (1986) described as deautomatization, a detachment from the normal or usual manner by which we experience our environment, a concept we describe in detail in Chapter 6. Thus, altered states can be experienced through experimentation with drugs, meditation, hypnosis, biofeedback, daydreaming, and sensory deprivation. A good night's sleep with a few fantastic dreams might accomplish this.

Finally, many (e.g., Kokoszka, 1992; Springer & Deutsch, 1997) have speculated that altered states of consciousness are dictated by the right hemisphere of the brain or the *right brain*. That is, altered states are somehow related to a shift in electroencephalographic, or EEG, activity from the left hemisphere of the brain to the right hemisphere. Some evidence suggests that this may be correct (Bakan, 1969; Greenwood, Wilson, & Gazzaniga, 1977; Hoppe, 1977; MacLeod-Morgan & Lack, 1982). However, this area is in its infancy, and very little evidence is yet available to solidly substantiate this conjecture. Nonetheless, we are certain that much research to determine the loci and neurological correlates of consciousness will be forthcoming. And perhaps we will discover that many of the altered states of consciousness are right-brain phenomena.

Although consciousness, as a concept, may not have a universally acceptable definition, the area of study is generally definable by the set of phenomena that we will address in the remainder of this book. Most of these were previously enumerated by Farthing (1992), Goleman and Davidson (1979), Ornstein (1986), Tart (1972), and Zinberg (1977). They are also now enumerated and described in almost every introductory psychology textbook, and such coverage generally requires an entire chapter.

What unites all of these phenomena under a single rubric is the notion that each is a tool for demonstrating the possible existence of a state of consciousness or awareness, with accompanying levels of strength, that is discernible from the ordinary waking state of consciousness. Specifically, each phenomenon can potentially show us that humans are capable of processing various types of information at different levels of control. These levels can differ in both their exhibited behavior and the consequences that result from a change from the normal waking state. It is the variability and diversity of this behavior and accompanying experiences that we will explore in the remainder of the book.

FOR FURTHER READING

Baars, B. J. (1997). *Consciousness regained: The new science of human experience.* Oxford, U.K.: Oxford University Press.

Farthing, G. W. (1992). *The psychology of consciousness.* Englewood Cliffs, NJ: Prentice-Hall.

Goleman, D., & Davidson, R. J. (1979). *Consciousness: Brain, states of awareness, and mysticism.* New York: Harper and Row.

Jaynes, J. (1976). *The origin of consciousness in the breakdown of the bicameral mind.* Boston: Houghton Mifflin.

Ornstein, R. (1986). *The psychology of consciousness.* New York: Penguin.

Tart, C. T. (1975). *States of consciousness.* New York: Dutton.

Weil, A. T. (1972). *The natural mind: A new way of looking at drugs and the higher consciousness.* Boston: Houghton Mifflin.

Wolman, B. B., & Ullman, M. (Eds.). (1986). *Handbook of states of consciousness.* New York: Van Nostrand Reinhold.

2

THE PHYSIOLOGY OF CONSCIOUSNESS

With the 1950s and 1960s came tremendous technological advancements that led to a substantive knowledge explosion in physiological psychology. Psychologists were provided with a much better understanding of brain function than had previously been possible. As a result, many psychologists came to believe that the next great breakthrough in understanding behavior would come as a result of neuropsychological research.

It therefore seems strange to report that many psychologists have typically avoided any reference to a potential physiological basis of consciousness, preferring instead to concentrate on behavioral changes as well as means for achieving these changes (often referred to as *altered states*). In part, at least, the apparent lack of interest of many psychologists in the development of a physiological explanation of conscious states can be attributed to historical accident.

In Chapter 1 we learned that the early interest in the psychology of consciousness faded quickly in response to the scientific rigors demanded by behaviorism, the philosophical approach adopted by most physiological psychologists. The research efforts in physiological psychology have been labeled reductionistic, rather than holistic. The physiological psychologist, in his research efforts, views the organism not as an integrated whole but in terms of its component parts: receptors, transducers (those parts of the system that change stimuli energies into neural energy), integrators (the brain and spinal cord in higher organisms such as humans), and effectors. Such a research stance is not conducive to the study of a holistic concept such as consciousness.

Only within the last few decades has there been a rekindling of interest by psychologists in the study of consciousness (Eccles, 1977; Graham, 1990; Ornstein, 1972, 1986). Along with this renewed interest in consciousness has come the realization that our understanding of how changes in consciousness (i.e., altered states) come about and are maintained may be increased by an awareness of their underlying physiological concomitants (Hobson & Strickgold, 1995; MacLennan, 1995; Searle, 1995). Simply not enough time has passed for researchers to mount a concerted effort aimed at developing a physiological explanation of conscious states. Certainly, some research programs pointing to the cerebral hemispheres as possible physiological loci of consciousness have begun, and later in this chapter we will focus our attention on the results of one such research effort that uses the so-called split-brain procedure. First, however, it is necessary that we discuss some microscopic and gross structures and functions of the nervous system, as many of these are ultimately involved in consciousness and are referred to in a number of subsequent chapters of this book.

MICROSCOPIC NEUROANATOMY

The basic anatomical unit of the nervous system is the single nerve cell, often referred to as the **neuron.** There are roughly 12.5 billion neurons in the human adult nervous system. These cells come in a variety of shapes and sizes, but in one form or another they usually have a cell body or **soma, dendrites**, an **axon**, and a **terminal arboration** (see Figure 2.1).

Within the cytoplasm of the cell body the **nucleus** and other **organelles** can be found, which assist in carrying out the life functions of the cell. The nucleus is the central mass of the cell that controls all cellular functions and contains the genetic material, **deoxyribonucleic acid (DNA)**. The most important organelles found in the cytoplasm of the soma and in the axoplasm (the corresponding substance in the axon) are the small, rod-shaped structures called **mitochondria,** which are responsible for the energy-producing reactions of the cell.

The **dendrites** are treelike structures attached to the soma. There may be a single dendrite, as in the case of the **bipolar neuron**, or many, as in the case of the **multipolar neuron**. Dendrites receive information from other neurons and conduct these messages with decrement down their structure to the soma.

While a neuron can have one or more dendrites, it can have but a single axon. That portion of the neuron where the cell body and the axon connect is called the **axon hillock**. It is here that **action potentials**, the neural impulses that are conducted down the axon, are usually initiated. The axon can be covered with a white, fatty substance called **myelin**. The myelin sheath is segmented rather than continuous. The myelin segments are separated by bare spaces called **nodes of Ranvier**. The myelin serves as a kind of electrical insulation preventing crosstalk between myelinated axons. Myelination also results in a more rapid rate of information conduction. At its distal end (the end away from the center, i.e., the soma), the axon divides and branches a number of times. Collectively, these branches are referred to as the **terminal arboration**. On the end of each of these little branches is a rounded swelling called a **terminal button**. The function of these buttons is the storage and, when conditions are right, the release of a chemical called a **neurotransmitter substance**.

FIGURE 2.1 Major Structures and Regions of a Multipolar Neuron

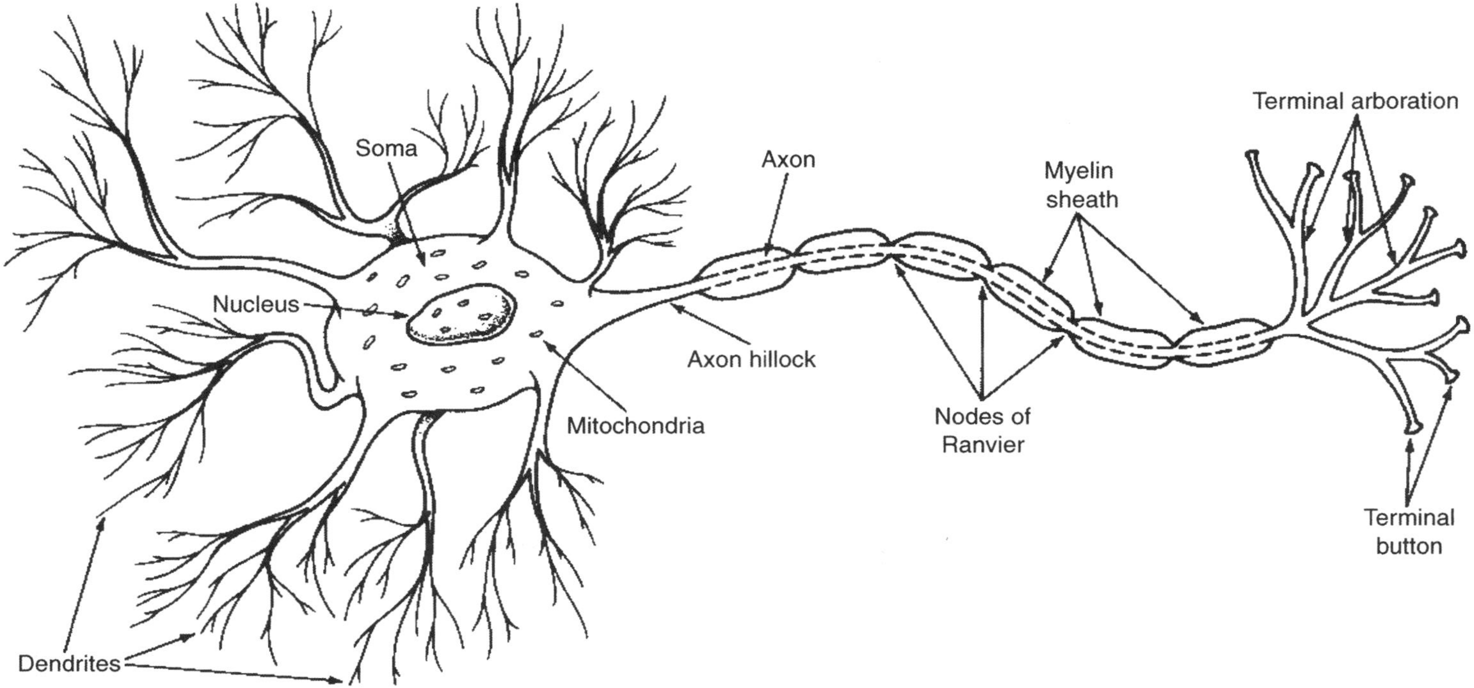

Neurotransmission is accomplished by **neural conduction** and **synaptic transmission**. Since these processes play an integral role in influencing how psychoactive drugs affect consciousness (discussed in Chapter 3), we feel it necessary to present a brief discussion of how they function.

Neural Conduction

Generally, the conduction of information in the form of a neural impulse proceeds in one direction from the dendrite, across the soma, and down the axon to the terminal buttons. Such conduction depends upon the passage of specific charged molecules, **ions**, across the semipermeable membrane of the cell. Conduction along the dendrite is accomplished with decrement. This means that as the graded potential (a potential that varies in amplitude according to the intensity of the initiating stimulus) is conducted along the dendrite, it decreases in strength until it reaches the axon hillock.

In addition to connecting the axon to the soma, the axon hillock is that region of the neuron that has the lowest threshold value. If the strength of an impulse is sufficient to reach or exceed this threshold level, then a full-blown **action** or **spike potential** will be initiated and will be conducted down the axon at full strength and at a rate or speed determined by the neuron. This is the **all-or-none law** of axonal conduction. If the strength of the impulse is not sufficient to reach threshold, then the impulse may summate (add its strength to that of other graded potentials at the hillock), or it may simply die out. When the action potential finally reaches the terminal buttons, the neurotransmitter substance is released and we have the beginning of synaptic transmission.

Synaptic Transmission

The junction between the terminal button of an axon and the membrane of another neuron, muscle, or gland is the **synapse**. The neuron that contains that terminal button is called the **presynaptic element**, and the neuron, muscle, or gland upon which the terminal button synapses is the **postsynaptic element**. Such an anatomical arrangement clearly requires a communication system that differs considerably from that which operates within the neuron.

Synaptic transmission involves a number of separate but interrelated steps. The first of these steps involves the synthesis of the neurotransmitter substance. It is believed that over 20 such chemical molecules serve as neurotransmitters in the human nervous system.

Acetylcholine, norepinephrine, dopamine, and serotonin are the most common of these chemical transmitters. In Chapter 3 we will see that scientists are becoming increasingly convinced that dopamine plays an important role in a broad range of drug addictions (Nash, 1977); in Chapter 7 we will discover the role of serotonin in sleep and dreams.

Generally, the chemical molecule is synthesized from its precursor elements in the presence of an appropriate **enzyme**, a protein molecule that facilitates the biochemical reaction without entering into it. This synthesis typically takes place in the soma of the neuron and is then transported down the axon to the terminal button.

The second step involves the storage of the neurotransmitter substance in the synaptic vesicles located in the cytoplasm of the terminal button. With the arrival of the neural impulse at the terminal button and a sudden influx of calcium (Ca^{++}) into the area from the extracellular fluid, we have the beginning of the third step. These two events must occur before a number of the synaptic vesicles migrate to the presynaptic membrane, adhere to it, rupture, and spill their contents into the synaptic cleft.

Once the neurotransmitter substance is released into the synaptic cleft, it must cross the 200–500-Ångstrom space (a distance measurement with 1 Ångstrom = 10^{-10}m) to the receptor sites on the membrane of the postsynaptic element. This is the fourth step. The fifth step involves an interaction of the transmitter substance with a specific postsynaptic receptor to produce a physiological reaction. This results in a change in the permeability of the postsynaptic membrane with a consequent flow of ions through it and the initiation of a graded potential. Just what this mechanism is and how it works are as yet unknown.

Step six, the final step, is vital if we are to avoid having a postsynaptic element in a continual state of firing. The activity of the neurotransmitter must be stopped. To accomplish this, the system must somehow remove the active transmitter molecules from the synapse. **Enzymatic degradation** and **reabsorption** are the mechanisms employed. In the former case an enzyme is released into the synapse, usually at sites on the postsynaptic membrane. This enzyme destroys the neurotransmitter and renders it ineffective. Reabsorption, or what is also known as the **reuptake process,** is the extremely rapid removal of transmitter substance from the synaptic cleft by the terminal button. The exact mechanism by which reuptake is accomplished is still poorly understood. Any understanding of how drugs in general, and particularly the psychoactive drugs discussed in Chapter 3, produce their effects dependents upon a knowledge of neural conduction and transmission.

GROSS NEUROANATOMY

Together with supportive cells called neuroglia, or simply **glial cells**, neurons combine to form the major structures of the **nervous system**. This system can be divided into two major components: the central nervous system and the peripheral nervous system.

The **central nervous system (CNS)** is the portion of the nervous system housed in a bony skeletal covering, the skull and the spinal column. In turn, the CNS can be divided into two structures: the brain and the spinal cord.

The **peripheral nervous system (PNS)** is the part of the nervous system that lies outside this bony protective covering and allows the structures of the

CNS to communicate with the sensory receptors, muscles, glands, and other organs of the body. The PNS can be divided into two components: the somatic and autonomic divisions.

The **somatic division** of the PNS carries sensory information to the CNS from the skin and musculature and contains motor fibers responsible for body movement. The **autonomic nervous system (ANS)**, the other part of the PNS and the one integrally involved in learning biofeedback (see Chapter 5), is directly involved in the action of those muscles and glands that are not ordinarily under conscious control: smooth muscles, cardiac muscles, and glands. Examples of smooth muscles are those found in the eye that control curvature of the lens for focus size and pupil size during changes in light intensity. Other smooth muscles are found in the skin (associated with hair follicles), in the walls of blood vessels, and in the walls and sphincters of the digestive and urinary system. Cardiac muscles, as is obvious, are found exclusively in the heart.

Studies of the ANS have clearly demonstrated that it has two major branches that appear to be both anatomically and functionally distinct: the **sympathetic branch** and the **parasympathetic branch.** Figure 2.2 shows that these two branches exit and enter the CNS via the spinal cord and brain stem at different levels. Cell bodies that give rise to the fibers of the sympathetic nervous system are located in the thoracic and lumbar segments of the cord, and for this reason the sympathetic nervous system has often been referred to as the *thoracicolumbar system.* Similarly, the parasympathetic nervous system is often referred to as the *craniosacral system* because the cell bodies that give rise to the fibers of this autonomic branch are located in the nuclei of the cranial nerves located in the brainstem and the gray matter in the sacral region of the cord.

The shorter, preganglionic motor fibers of the sympathetic branch exit the spinal cord via the ventral root and shortly afterward pass into the **spinal sympathetic ganglia.** At this point, one of three things can occur. First, the preganglionic motor fibers can synapse on cell bodies that make up the ganglia. Second, they can ascend or descend in the sympathetic ganglia and then synapse. Finally, they can pass completely through the spinal sympathetic ganglia and synapse in one of the **sympathetic prevertebral ganglia.** The longer postganglionic motor fibers then proceed to the **target organ,** the organ that they innervate (see Figure 2.2).

The preganglionic motor fibers of the parasympathetic branch do not synapse in a chain of ganglia but rather synapse on cell bodies that make up ganglia that lie very near their target organs. Thus, the postganglionic fibers that arise from these cells travel only a short distance to reach the organ to be innervated. The preganglionic motor fibers of the parasympathetic nervous system are thus long, while the postganglionic fibers are short. This is in contrast to the situation found in the sympathetic branch, where preganglionic fibers are short and the postganglionic fibers are long.

FIGURE 2.2   Autonomic Nervous System and Target Organs It Serves

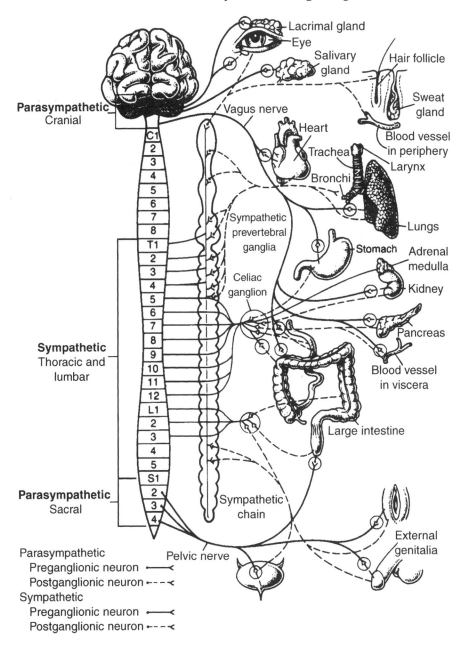

Source: N. R. Carlson (1998). *Physiology and Behavior* (6th ed.). Boston: Allyn and Bacon. Reprinted with permission.

Besides these anatomical differences, a chemical distinction can also be drawn between these two branches of the ANS. Specifically, they use different neurotransmitter substances at the point where they make synaptic contact with the target organ. The preganglionic fibers of both branches are cholinergic. However, most postganglionic fibers of the sympathetic branch are adrenergic, while those of the parasympathetic division are cholinergic. One major exception to this rule involves the sympathetic innervation of the eccrine sweat glands. The sympathetic postganglionic fibers that innervate these glands are cholinergic rather than noradrenergic, as the rule would predict.

Finally, the branches of the ANS differ functionally. Pupil dilation, piloerection (the standing up of hair on the back of the neck), increased blood flow to the skeletal muscles, and the release of epinepherine by the adrenal glands (which produces increased heart rate and a rise in blood sugar levels) are but some of the effects mediated by activation of the sympathetic branch. These effects suggest that the sympathetic branch is involved in *catabolic* or energy-using processes. Among other effects, stimulation of the parasympathetic branch will result in an increased blood flow to the digestive system, decrease in heart rate, increased salivation, and pupil constriction, all of which are energy-conserving or *anabolic* processes. Much more will be said about the ANS in Chapter 5 when we discuss biofeedback.

THE CENTRAL NERVOUS SYSTEM

Earlier in this chapter we observed that the brain and the spinal cord, the two components of the CNS, were the best-protected structures in the nervous system.

The Spinal Cord

Lying within the spinal column, the spinal cord consists of a butterfly-shaped inner core (gray matter) of cell bodies, dendrites, and unmyelinated axons and an outer layer (white matter) of ascending and descending myelinated axons called **tracts**. These ascending sensory tracts and descending motor tracts act as a conduit, carrying information between some of the sensory organs of the body and the brain and between the brain and the body's motor apparatus.

Research Techniques

Advances in X-ray techniques and computers have led to the development of several methods for studying the structure and function of the living brain. For years, X-rays were used to detect changes in the brain as a function of trauma or disease. However, a single X-ray of the brain was extremely difficult to interpret because it presented us with a two-dimensional view of a three-dimensional structure.

What would happen, however, if you could get the X-ray to take many separate pictures through the head at many different angles and then feed these pictures to a computer that could assemble these many pictures into a single composite? Such a marriage of the X-ray to the advanced computers resulted in the development of **computer-assisted axial tomography** in 1973, better known as the **CAT scan.** The word *axial* refers to the procedure of rotating the X-ray around an imaginary axis running through the patient's head. *Tomography* literally means "written in cuts or slices," referring to the fact that this technique creates a pictorial representation of the brain slice by slice (Graham, 1990). The CAT scan provides us with a clear and accurate picture of any particular area of the brain.

An even more detailed view of the brain's structure can be provided by a process called **magnetic resonance imaging (MRI).** Although the MRI scanner resembles the CAT scanner, it does not use X-rays. Instead, the person's head is placed in a strong magnetic field, and radio waves are passed through the brain to reveal the distribution of specific types of atoms within a brain area by using the magnetic properties of the nuclei of the different atoms to make clear pictures of the structures of the brain (Pykett, 1982).

The **positron emission tomography (PET) scan,** which was developed in 1979, allows the researcher to assess the amount of metabolic activity in various parts of the brain. This information, in turn, is helpful in determining brain function. In a PET scan, a radioactive form of glucose, **2-deoxyglucose (2-DG),** is injected into the bloodstream of the subject and is allowed to accumulate in the most active cells of the brain. The individual's head is placed in a PET scanner, and as the radioactive isotopes decay, they emit positively charged subatomic particles called **positrons.** These positrons react with other particles to generate gamma rays, which are detected by a series of detectors in the PET scanner (Li & Shen, 1985). It is the function of the PET scanner to determine from where those gamma rays come. The more gamma rays are detected in a certain area of the brain, the more glucose is being used in that area and the more neural activity is occurring there (Phelps & Mazzietta, 1985). A major emerging research application of the PET scanner has been to provide information concerning two of the most fundamental but least well understood aspects of human behavior, emotion, and consciousness (Reiman, Lane, Ahern, Schwartz, & Davidson, 1996).

Earlier in this chapter we noted that axons produce action potentials and the synaptic vesicles of the presynaptic neuron release neurotransmitters that interact with receptor sites on the postsynaptic neuron to create postsynaptic potentials. In 1929 an Austrian psychiatrist, Hans Berger, discovered that patterns of this electrical activity could be recorded from electrodes placed at various points on the scalps of human beings. The recorded combined electrical activity from large numbers of neurons and synapses was called an **electroencephalogram,** or **EEG.** The instrument used to record such activity is an **electroencephalo-graph.** Electrical activity in the form of a voltage increase produces an upward deflection of the recording pen, and a decrease produces a downward movement. This back-and-forth movement of the pen on a moving paper strip of the electroencephalograph gives these changes the appearance of waves. Today, real-time EEG activity can also be monitored in a paperless environment on a computer screen.

In Chapter 7 we will have much more to say about the electroencephalograph and the typical brain wave activity seen in humans. For now it is sufficient that you understand that what is being recorded is the electrical activity of thousands of neurons and synapses lying in the area below the electrode placed somewhere on the skull. It is also important to point out that brain waves differ in at least two respects: **amplitude** (the height of the wave) and **frequency** (the rate of occurrence).

If an electrode is placed on the skull, perhaps over the auditory or visual cortex, and the subject is presented with an appropriate stimulus, such as an auditory click or a flash of light, we would observe a wave in the EEG record that is distinguishable from the surrounding waves in that it appears just after the stimulus and is of greater amplitude. This large wave is called an **evoked potential.** Had the stimulus been a click and had the electrode been placed over the auditory cortex, the response, called an **auditory-evoked potential**, would represent the voltage changes occurring in the cortex as the burst of impulses enters it from the auditory nucleus of the thalamus.

Similar voltage waves are created by each nucleus in the auditory pathway to the cortex as the stimulus signal travels through the nervous system. The problem with these other evoked potentials is that they are much weaker and remain hidden in the mass of electrical activity reaching the electrode from all simultaneously active brain areas. So while these other evoked potentials existed in theory, it was impossible until recently to observe them.

To solve this problem, electrophysiologists reasoned that while these potentials evoked by a stimulus would always be present, the other potentials in the brain related to other ongoing events were only randomly related to the click-evoked potentials. This would suggest that if the stimulus were presented repeatedly instead of just once and if the results of these repeated records were stored and combined by a computer, the random activity should cancel out, leaving only the click-evoked potentials. The process by which the various records are combined is called **signal averaging** even though it really consists of simply adding the voltages together algebraically. Typically, this process of signal averaging is carried out over a period of 500 milliseconds (msec). The records are termed **averaged evoked potentials** (Carlson, 1998; Graham, 1990). As you can see in Figure 2.3, as more and more records are averaged the random activity does drop out and the smaller potentials are clearly seen. As researchers have become more and more familiar with these evoked potential waves, they have given each its own designation, such as P-300 (the positive

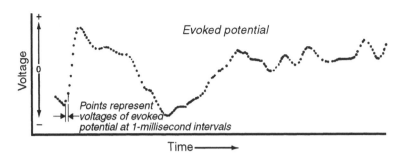

FIGURE 2.3   An Example of an Evoked Potential

Source: N. R. Carlson (1998). *Physiology and Behavior* (6th ed.). Boston: Allyn and Bacon. Reprinted with permission.

wave form that occurs about 300 msec following stimulus onset) or N-80 (the negative wave form that occurs about 80 msec following stimulus onset).

The Brain

The brain is the central character in our continuing story of the biological basis of consciousness. In describing its organization as that part of the CNS that is most integrally involved in consciousness, it would be helpful to include some artificial boundaries. For our purpose it will be sufficient to divide the brain into two parts: the **brainstem** and the **cerebrum**.

If you look closely at Figure 2.4, you will note that the lowest part of the brain retains roughly the shape of the spinal cord, although it enlarges somewhat as you move upward. This part of the brain, from the most inferior level to the superior end of the thalamus, constitutes the brainstem. At this point the tubular form appears to be lost, and the brain becomes greatly enlarged. This part of the brain that lies superior to the thalamus is known as the cerebrum.

In both of these divisions we will find a large number of structures that in turn are composed of **nuclei** (clusters of cell bodies) and **fiber tracts** (groups of axons). As you read the remainder of this section on the brain, you should keep in mind that this boundary between the brainstem and the cerebrum is an artificial one, something that we have concocted but for which nature has little or no regard. One final suggestion to the reader is in order: Refer frequently to Figures 2.4, 2.5, and 2.6 as you read the following section to help you better understand both the structure and organization of the brain.

The Brainstem

Beginning at the most inferior end of the brain and moving upward, the first major structure we find is the **medulla oblongata**. Here, some of the cranial nerves exit and enter the CNS. Here also are located a number of nuclei that regulate many of the life-support systems, including the cardiovascular system,

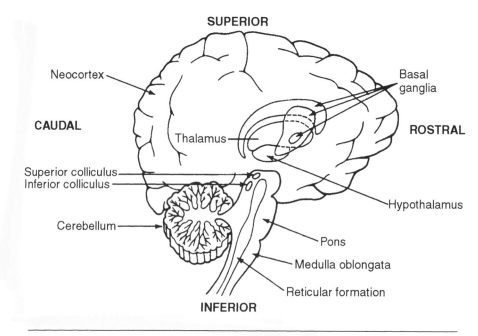

FIGURE 2.4   A Midsagittal View of the Human Brain

the respiratory system, and skeletal muscle tonus (Smith, Ellenberger, Ballanyi, Richter, & Feldman, 1991). From Figure 2.4, it should be clear that all fibers passing between the brain and the spinal cord must pass through this division.

As the motor fibers of the corticospinal tracts, which originate in the motor region of the cerebral cortex, approach the spinal cord, they **decussate,** or cross over to the contralateral (opposite) side. This means that information arising in the left hemisphere (left side of the brain) controls movement on the right side of the body. Similarly, information arising in the right hemisphere controls movement on the left side of the body. We will have more to say about this later in this chapter as we discuss the left-brain/right-brain phenomenon.

Finally, deep in the center of this part of the brainstem lie the beginnings of the **ascending reticular activating system (ARAS)**. Anatomically, it begins as a tight, complex network of nuclei, axons, and dendrites and retains this form until it reaches the tegmentum. At this point, it branches out, sending projections to the thalamus and the cerebral cortex. Functionally, the ARAS is involved with sleep and arousal, selective attention, muscle tonus, and vital reflexes. We will have more to say about the role of the reticular formation in sleep and arousal in Chapters 7 ("Sleep and Dreams") and 8 ("Sensory Deprivation") (Turner & Knapp, 1995).

Immediately rostral (toward the head) to the medulla lies the **pons,** which is exactly what its name implies (in Latin): a "bridge" between the spinal cord, the medulla, and higher brain centers and between the brainstem and the cerebellar cortex. The cranial nerves serving the face also exit and enter the CNS here. Several nuclei that are thought to have a sleep-regulatory function are located in the pons.

Although it forms approximately one-third of the brain volume, the **cerebellum,** which lies dorsal (toward the back) to the pons, does not play a significant role in consciousness. Its function is primarily that of making certain that movements are made smoothly and accurately, with appropriate speed and direction.

Ascending fiber tracts continue to the next major structure, the midbrain, which is usually divided into two parts: the dorsal **tectum** and the ventral **tegmentum.** The principle structures found in the tectum are the *superior colliculi* and the *inferior colliculi.* Collectively, these structures are referred to as the *corpora quadrigemina.* The superior and inferior colliculi function as primitive processing centers for visual and auditory information, respectively. In addition to several important motor nuclei, the tegmentum also contains the superior end of the reticular formation.

As we ascend to the higher levels of the brain, it is clear that the brain expands, losing the tubelike form it had in the lower brainstem and the spinal cord (see Figure 2.4). At this point, the upper part of the brainstem is surrounded by the beginnings of the cerebrum. The **hypothalamus** is located at the base of this region just superior to the pituitary stalk and gland. It is composed of a number of nuclei, and although it is a small structure, its nuclei have been implicated in a wide range of behavioral functions. The *hypothalamus* is important in such diverse behavioral functions as hunger, thirst, maintenance of water and salt balance in the body, temperature regulation, and sexual behavior. Most important, the hypothalamus is central in the study of consciousness, sleep, and waking (discussed in Chapter 7). The hypothalamus also controls, in part at least, the autonomic nervous system (discussed in regard to biofeedback in Chapter 5).

Lying just dorsal to the hypothalamus is the bilobed structure called the **thalamus**. Like the hypothalamus, the thalamus is composed of a number of nuclei. Some of these nuclei receive sensory information from the various sensory tracts and project fibers to the appropriate sensory projection area of the cortex. These are sometimes called *sensory relay nuclei.* Separate sensory relay nuclei are found here for all of the sensory modalities except olfaction, the sense of smell. Other thalamic nuclei receive input from other fibers within the thalamus and project to specific regions of the cortex. Finally, a third type of thalamic nuclei projects diffusely to widespread regions of the cortex and to other thalamic nuclei.

The Cerebrum

Leaving the thalamus and moving upward, we next locate the cerebrum, which is the most highly developed division of the human brain. It consists of three primary structures: the **limbic system,** the **basal ganglia,** and the **cerebral hemispheres.**

The basal ganglia are badly misnamed. Because they lie deep in the brain and are therefore a part of the CNS, they should have been called the basal nuclei. At any rate, the basal ganglia consist of nuclei that are involved in the control of motor responses. The limbic system is also composed of a large number of interconnected structures that are involved in emotional behavior, motivation, and memory. Both the basal ganglia and the limbic system have minimal effects on consciousness.

Earlier, we observed that the entire CNS was essentially bilateral in symmetry. The left and right halves of the brainstem actually do not separate, however, until we reach the level of the thalamus. The cerebrum looks like separate, mirror-image halves connected by bundles of transverse fibers. These halves of the cerebrum are called the **cerebral hemispheres.** The bundles of fibers that serve as connectors between the hemispheres are **commissures**, the largest of which is the **corpus callosum**. The precise role of the cerebral commissures is as yet unknown. Our best guess at this point is that they serve as a communication channel between the hemispheres through which hemispheric function is synchronized and duplication of effort is prevented (Springer & Deutsch, 1997).

The surface of the hemispheres is covered by **cortex,** which in humans is highly convoluted. These convolutions are composed of **sulci** (small grooves), **fissures** (large grooves), and **gyri** (bulges between adjacent sulci or fissures). By using these landmarks, it is possible to divide the surface into

---

FIGURE 2.5   Dominant Lateral Cortical Surface with Lobes

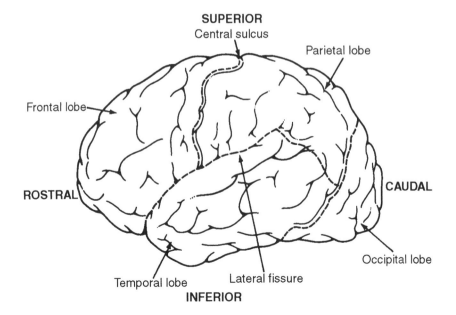

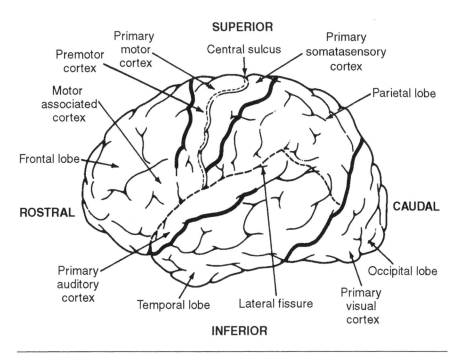

FIGURE 2.6 **Dominant Lateral Cortical Surface with Lobes and Projection Areas**

four lobes: **frontal, parietal, temporal,** and **occipital.** Figure 2.5 shows the division of the surface of one hemisphere. The **central sulcus** or the fissure of Rolando, separates the frontal and parietal lobes. The other major fissure, called the **lateral sulcus** or **Sylvian fissure,** separates the temporal lobe from the frontal and parietal lobes.

Besides looking at the hemispheres in terms of lobes, we can also view them in terms of *projection areas* or *zones*. At least a part of each of these lobes is known to serve a different sensory or motor function. The anterior part of the parietal lobe is associated with a somatosensory function, while the posterior part of the frontal lobe is concerned with motor function. The occipital lobe is a visual center; the temporal lobe is the auditory cortical center (see Figure 2.6).

Not all of the human cortex, however, is committed to the specific senses or to motor function. That part of the cortex not so committed is generally called the *association* or *silent cortex*. Some researchers, such as A. R. Luria (1966), make a distinction between secondary and tertiary association cortex. Found adjacent to the primary projection areas, the *secondary association cortex* areas are higher-level processing centers for the specific sensory information coming into the primary areas. These secondary association areas are believed to be sense-modality specific; thus, damage to one of them produces perceptual disorders restricted to a specific sensory modality.

Sensory modality specificity is lost in the *tertiary association areas,* which are located at the borders of the parietal, temporal, and occipital secondary association areas (see Figure 2.6). Here the various sensory areas overlap, and combinations of sensations become higher-order perceptions such that tactile and kinesthetic impulses are built up into perceptions of form and size and then associated with visual information from the same objects (Springer & Deutsch, 1997). Of more interest to us, perhaps, is the fact that this is the level at which asymmetries in the cerebral hemispheres occur. Such asymmetry may account for the fact that the left and right hemispheres handle different processes.

As the parietal, temporal, and occipital lobes are to the sensory modalities, so the frontal lobe is to the motor system. The posterior (rear) portion of the frontal lobes contains the **primary motor cortex.** Immediately anterior (front) to the primary motor cortex, or **motor strip,** lies the secondary motor area, more generally referred to as the **premotor cortex.** Higher-level motor organization is thought to be the role of this area of the cortex. Clinical support for this theory comes from the fact that damage to the premotor area results in disturbances in the organization of movements. As we will see shortly, damage to a particular part of this premotor cortex on the left side, called Broca's area, produces a disorganization of speech called Broca's aphasia. The remainder of the frontal lobe is often referred to as the **prefrontal area** or **frontal granular cortex.** Clinical findings, by no means conclusive, suggest that this area is involved in intellectual functions, such as the planning and control of actions, and in the control or inhibition of emotional tendencies.

TOWARD A BIOLOGICAL BASIS OF CONSCIOUSNESS

In the beginning of this chapter we noted that psychologists, in discussing the concept of consciousness, rarely refer to its physiological basis. Despite this fact, it has long been recognized that states of awareness or consciousness are products of the brain. Most people who have watched boxing matches, for example, know that a single blow delivered to the head may be sufficient to render the recipient unconscious for several minutes. Medical professionals have observed that severe brain damage, such as might result from an accident or major illness, may reduce the individual to little more than a vegetable—an organism with a series of simple reflexes but with no awareness or consciousness. Finally, more focal damage to specific regions of the brain has been shown to produce a loss of particular functions, abilities, and even some aspects of awareness or consciousness.

HISTORICAL BACKGROUND

To arrive at the point at which a scientist could suggest, without fear of being excommunicated from the scientific community, that "both the structure and function of . . . two 'half-brains' underlie in some part the two modes of consciousness that coexist within each one of us" (Ornstein, 1986, p. 20) has had to await considerable philosophical speculation and scientific endeavor over the years. It would first have to be shown that the assignment of particular mental functions, such as consciousness, to specific regions of the brain, *cerebral localization*, was a scientifically legitimate enterprise. Second, if we assume that two different modes of consciousness are housed in these two cerebral hemispheres, then logic dictates we should see evidence of differences both in function, *cerebral specialization*, and in structure, *cerebral asymmetry*. Time and space do not permit an exhaustive litany of these developments. However, some of the most important advancements in this area can be recounted.

Pinning consciousness to some biological structure has long been a favorite pastime for scientists and philosophers alike. For example, over four centuries ago, French philosopher René Descartes (1596–1650) concluded that the pineal gland, a small gland located at the base of the brain, was the seat of consciousness. His selection of the pineal gland appears to have been based upon a belief in the unity of consciousness and Descartes's anatomical observations that the pineal gland was the only brain structure that was not bilaterally represented as two separate structures.

The concept of cerebral localization, the idea that a particular function could be assigned to a specific region of the brain, began to receive serious attention by the early 1800s. Although he was dismissed as a quack in many scientific circles, Franz Gall (1758–1828), a German anatomist, and his student Johann Spurzheim (1776–1832) were among the first to suggest that specific psychological traits should reside in specific brain locations. More specifically, Gall and Spurzheim proposed that speech was controlled by centers located in the frontal lobes of the cerebrum. What upset the scientific community and eventually led these two scientists into disrepute was their insistence that the shape of the skull reflects the underlying brain tissue and hence the relative strengths of an individual's mental abilities and emotional characteristics. This area was referred to as *phrenology*.

Specifically, it was the work of the French physiologist Pierre Jean Marie Flourens (1794–1867) that spelled the demise of Gall and Spurzheim's phrenology. On the basis of his observations of the behavior of pigeons after the removal of sections of their brain, Flourens held that both common and specific actions are traceable to various portions of the brain, thereby rejecting the notion of exact or precise localization.

This setback to the supporters of the cerebral localization position proved to be only temporary; in 1861, Paul Broca (1824–1880), the noted French surgeon and anthropologist, presented two cases of patients independently diagnosed as *aphasic*, that is, having a loss of articulate speech. Both of Broca's patients had suffered damage to the left frontal part of the brain; the right side of the brain in each case was intact. Broca concluded that the damage to the third convolution of the left frontal lobe, now referred to in the literature as **Broca's area** (see Figure 2.7), had produced the aphasia and therefore was the

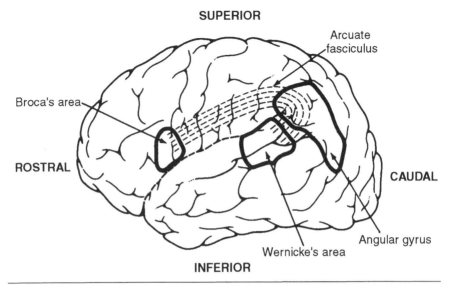

SUPERIOR

Arcuate
fasciculus

Broca's area

ROSTRAL

CAUDAL

Angular gyrus

Wernicke's area

INFERIOR

FIGURE 2.7   Lateral View of Human Brain with Speech Centers Identified

center of articulate speech, at least for right-handed people. Broca's findings served to sway sentiments away from Flourens's position and back to the position of cerebral localization.

Approximately 10 years later, in 1870, Gustav Theodor Fritsch (1838–1927) and Edward Hitzig (1838–1907), German physiologists, provided further evidence to support the cerebral localization position. By applying a very weak current to specific areas of the cortex of dogs, they were able to observe localized muscle contractions of small muscle groups. With this technique, Fritsch and Hitzig were able to develop maps of brain function.

Finally, by the 1930s, to treat epileptic patients who had not responded to drug therapy regimens, Wilder Penfield (1891–1976) and his colleagues at the Montreal Neurological Institute pioneered the use of surgery to remove a brain site where abnormal brain wave activity was initiated. While their technique proved to be successful in many cases, most surgeons were hesitant to use it where brain tissue near the parts of the brain controlling speech and language were involved. After all, why substitute one debilitating syndrome (loss of speech) for another (epilepsy)? Clearly, what was needed was a method for determining with great precision the anatomical centers for these functions. To meet this need, Penfield employed direct electrical stimulation to exposed brain tissue to map the precise location of brain centers which controlled speech and language in a given patient (Penfield & Roberts, 1959).

While it is probably not the first thing you think about when you wake up, you are probably aware that humans have a bilaterally symmetrical body plan. Put another way, if we could pass a knife down your body along the median plane, we would have two equivalent halves: a left side and a right side. You already know that you have two legs, two feet, and so on—one on the left side and one on the right. The human brain also gives the appearance of following this same general body plan; the right and left cerebral hemispheres communicate via the several bands of transverse nerve fibers that cross the median plane.

Are these two cerebral hemispheres identical? In 1868 the British neurologist John Hughlings Jackson (1835–1911) responded to this question in the negative, at least as far as function was concerned (Jackson, 1958). In that year, Jackson proposed his notion of the *"leading" hemisphere,* which has been identified as the intellectual precursor of the concept of *cerebral dominance.* On the basis of the earlier work of Broca, which demonstrated that damage to the left cerebral hemisphere left patients without the ability to speak even though the right hemisphere remained intact, Jackson concluded that rather than the two hemispheres being duplicates, one hemisphere—in most people the left—was the leading side.

In the years following Jackson's pronouncement, research efforts were focused on the localization of function in the leading or left hemisphere of the brain. The German neurologist Karl Wernicke (1848–1905) discovered a language loss that differed from that described by Broca. While Broca's patients were unable to produce articulate speech, those of Wernicke were unable to understand the speech of others. The brain area implicated by Wernicke, the back part of the temporal lobe of the left hemisphere, also differed from that identified by Broca (see Figure 2.7).

Early studies also suggested that the left cerebral hemisphere was involved in certain *apraxias* (ideomotor and possibly ideational). **Apraxia** is the inability to perform certain learned or purposeful movements despite the absence of paralysis or sensory loss (Heilman, Rothi, & Kertesz, 1983; Kimura, 1977).

Most early researchers chose to focus their research efforts on localizing functions in the left cerebral hemisphere, while ignoring the right side, despite Jackson's admonition that such a one-sided view of the localization of function was incorrect. Jackson based his warning on his own clinical observation (Jackson, 1958) of a patient with a right parietal lobe tumor who evidenced great difficulty in recognizing people, places, and things. Still other evidence suggested that singing and general musical ability were controlled by the right hemisphere.

SPLIT BRAIN, SPLIT CONSCIOUSNESS

Although the split-brain procedure was not introduced until the early 1940s, its theoretical effects upon consciousness were being argued as early as the midnineteenth century by such prominent investigators as Gustav Theodor

Fechner (1801–1887), the German experimental psychologist, and William McDougall (1871–1938), the British psychologist and first social psychologist. Fechner argued that such a surgical procedure, were it possible, would result in a doubling of consciousness. Localizing consciousness in the cerebral hemispheres, Fechner argued that the integrity of the brain was necessary to the unity of the consciousness.

McDougall challenged Fechner's position, arguing that the unity of consciousness would remain intact even if the split-brain procedure were performed. To punctuate his point, McDougall offered to undergo such a surgical procedure himself, were he ever to become the victim of some incurable disease. What he hoped to demonstrate by this was that his personality would not be split by such a procedure and that his consciousness would remain intact (Springer & Deutsch, 1997). McDougall never had the opportunity to prove his point, but this was not the last time this argument was to arise.

It was not until the early 1940s that Van Wagenen, a neurosurgeon, performed the first split-brain operations on human patients in a last-ditch effort to control life-threatening seizures in some epileptics (Van Wagenen & Herren, 1940). In the split-brain procedure, the brain is divided into two halves—a left and a right hemisphere. To accomplish this, the transverse bundles of fibers that connect the cerebral hemispheres (the corpus callosum) are surgically severed.

Perhaps the most surprising observation was made by Akelaitis (1941, 1944), who carried out a rather extensive postoperative study of Van Wagenen's patients. Akelaitis observed that these patients evidenced few, if any, deficits in perceptual and motor abilities, and their everyday behaviors appeared to be quite unaltered. Unfortunately for some of these patients, the surgical procedure did little to change the condition that was responsible for the operation in the first place. Van Wagenen soon gave up the use of the procedure with epileptics. It should be noted that Van Wagenen's surgical procedure varied considerably from patient to patient but usually consisted of cutting only the anterior half of the corpus callosum and rarely the anterior commissure (Springer & Deutsch, 1997).

These negative results, however, did not dampen research interest in the split-brain procedure and its effects. Thus, in the early 1950s, Myers and Sperry (1958), using cats instead of human subjects, demonstrated that visual information presented to one hemisphere in a cat that had undergone a commissurotomy was not available to the other hemisphere. Each hemisphere functioned independently, as if it were a complete brain. Myers and Sperry concluded that cutting the corpus callosum had kept the information presented to one hemisphere isolated from the other hemisphere. It was only natural that this initial finding was to open up an entirely new set of research questions concerning the extent of the independence of the two hemispheres and the role of the corpus callosum in the integration of the cerebral hemisphere functions in the intact brain.

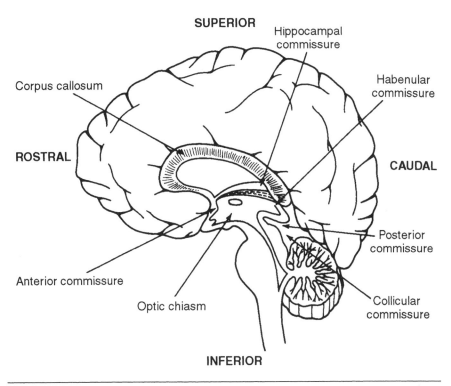

FIGURE 2.8 **Midsagittal View of the Human Brain with Location of Commissures**

Encouraged by the Myers and Sperry animal research findings and the Van Wagenen procedure, two California neurosurgeons, Bogen and Vogel (as reported in Springer & Deutsch, 1997), were led to reevaluate the use of the split-brain surgery in the treatment of epileptics with life-threatening seizures that had not responded to drug therapy. In their surgical procedure, sectioning of the corpus callosum was incomplete, leaving the **anterior, hippocampal, habenular,** and **posterior** commissures intact (see Figure 2.8). This left sufficient, transverse fibers intact to allow for hemispheric communication.

Over the next several years Bogen and Vogel performed some 24 complete commissurotomies on such patients. Postoperative observations demonstrated that, relative to seizure activity, the results of the surgical intervention exceeded expectations. Additionally, the operation appeared to leave the patients' personality, intelligence, and general behavior unaffected. However, when these patients were more closely scrutinized in Sperry's laboratory at the California Institute of Technology, their everyday behavior and their performance on specialized tests devised by the experimenters revealed some very distinct behavioral changes. For this work, Sperry received the 1981 Nobel Prize in Physiology/Medicine.

What were some of these important observations? Sperry and his colleagues observed that these patients showed a strong tendency to favor the right side of the body, which, as you will recall, is controlled by the dominant left half of the brain. Spontaneous activity was frequently observed on the right side of the body but appeared to be lacking on the left side. Additionally, responsiveness to sensory stimulation of the left half of the body was diminished.

More specific tests of sensory function initially suggested that, while the dominant left cerebral hemisphere appeared functionally normal with respect to vision and tactile perception, the right side was severely limited. However, when patients were provided with a nonverbal means of reporting their experiences, their visual and tactile perception controlled by the right side was practically as good as that controlled by the dominant left hemisphere. Clearly, the initial sensory differences observed were due to the fact that the speech centers of the brain are located in the left hemisphere.

Specific tests of motor function in these patients showed that, while the hemispheres exercised normal control over the contralateral (opposite-sided) hand, they had less than normal control over the ipsilateral (same-sided) hand. When a conflict develops between the two cerebral hemispheres, their individual inputs dictating distinctly different movements for the same hand, the hemisphere opposite the hand generally takes charge and overrides any input from the ipsilateral hemisphere.

In examining the effects of such surgery on intelligence, perception, and emotion, these investigators observed that the surgery left each patient with two separate minds—that is, with two separate spheres of consciousness. The dominant left hemisphere showed a clear advantage in both verbal and mathematical tasks. However, the right cerebral hemisphere did not prove to be inferior to the left in all respects. On certain spatial tasks, for example, the right hemisphere showed a clear superiority. Such patients, with right-brain superiority, were able to arrange blocks to match a picture design or draw a three-dimensional cube better with their left hand than their right, which had been deprived of input from the right hemisphere (Sperry, 1996). More recent research has replicated these findings, and taken together, these symptoms have become known as the **disconnection syndrome** (Proverbio, Zani, Gazzaniga, & Mangun, 1994; Reuter-Lorenz, Nozawa, Gazzaniga, & Hughes, 1995; Seymour, Reuter-Lorenz, & Gazzaniga, 1994). Additionally, both hemispheres appeared to be equally capable of independently generating an emotional reaction (Sperry, 1966).

Once again, the argument concerning the effect of physically splitting the brain with respect to the unity of the consciousness was raised. This time, however, the adversaries were able to call upon a considerable body of empirical evidence. Roger Sperry used this evidence to support his position that the split-brain procedure produced a doubling of the individual's consciousness.

Everything we have seen so far indicates that the surgery has left these people with two separate minds, that is, two separate spheres of consciousness.

What is experienced in the right hemisphere seems to lie entirely outside the realm of experiencing of the left hemisphere. (Sperry, 1966, p. 121)

According to Sperry, the unity of consciousness in the split-brain patient is an illusion. This illusion exists because the two cerebral hemispheres share a number of things, including the same position in space, the same sensory organs, and the same everyday experiences (Springer & Deutsch, 1997).

The unity of the mind and consciousness in the split-brain patient remained intact according to Eccles (1977). Eccles distinguished between *consciousness,* which both humans and animals share, and *mind,* which is uniquely human and includes language, thought, and culture. For Eccles, all that can be identified as exclusively human resides in the left hemisphere, where thought and the speech centers are housed and where the brain interacts with the mind. In the intact individual, the right hemisphere, which Eccles referred to as the **minor hemisphere**, is an unconscious part of the brain. Under normal conditions the contributions of the right hemisphere to all perceptions, experiences, and memories are transmitted to the **dominant hemisphere,** the left hemisphere, via the corpus callosum.

Additionally, the minor hemisphere may generate special neuronal activities that provide it with some communication to the self-conscious mind. In the split-brain cases in which the communication system is severed, it becomes clear that the right hemisphere is always an unconscious part of the brain that relies on the linkage through the corpus callosum to receive from and give information to the conscious self (Eccles, 1977).

Having reviewed the extensive body of literature dealing with the role of the right hemisphere in language, Gazzaniga (1983) concluded that the right hemisphere of the normal brain is nonlinguistic. Any indications of linguistic ability in the right hemisphere of split-brain patients can be attributed to early left hemisphere damage resulting in a shifting of language functions to the right hemisphere.

Supporting evidence for this position comes from one of a group of split-brain patients operated on by Donald Wilson of Dartmouth Medical School and studied by Michael Gazzaniga and his colleagues. This patient, identified as Patient P.S., was a right-handed male, 16 years old at the time of his surgery. His preoperative history indicated considerable damage to the left hemisphere at an early age (Gazzaniga & LeDoux, 1978). Because of the normal location of the speech centers in the left hemisphere, the typical split-brain patient is unable to name objects presented only to his right hemisphere. One can imagine the investigators' surprise upon discovering that, by using his left hand to arrange letters selected from a Scrabble game set, Patient P.S. was able to spell the names of objects flashed to his right hemisphere. Initially, P.S.'s right hemisphere could communicate verbally only by spelling with the Scrabble letters. However, further evidence suggested that P.S. was speaking from his right hemisphere as well (Gazzaniga, Volpe, Smylie, Wilson, & LeDoux, 1979).

The importance of this finding lies in the fact that this procedure was also used with this patient to study the right hemisphere's awareness of the world. The researchers' intention was to ask subjective questions of each hemisphere separately and compare the results. To accomplish this, Patient P.S. was asked a question in which the key word (or words) was replaced by the word "blank." Then the missing part of the question was presented visually to the left or the right cerebral hemisphere. For example, the experimenter might ask, "How much do you like 'blank'?" Then the name "Liz" (the name of his girlfriend) would be presented in the left visual field (to the right cerebral hemisphere), and the subject's response was awaited. When the word was presented to the left hemisphere, the subject responded verbally; when it was presented to the right hemisphere, he was allowed to point to a number from 1 ("like very much") to 5 ("dislike very much") or to spell out his answer with the Scrabble letters when the rating scale was inappropriate.

The results of this study clearly demonstrated that P.S.'s right hemisphere was able to respond to the questions asked of it. The answers and evaluations of this hemisphere, however, sometimes differed from those of the dominant left side. For example, the left hemisphere stated that P.S. wanted to be a draftsman when he grew up, yet his right hemisphere spelled out "automobile race" when asked what job it would pick. During the height of the Watergate affair, the widest divergence between the two hemispheres on the like–dislike scale occurred in response to the item "Nixon"; the right hemisphere expressed "dislike," while the left hemisphere expressed "like."

Gazzaniga and LeDoux also observed that the answers to several questions varied in several different testing sessions. The patient seemed to be in a better mood when the opinions and values of the two hemispheres were similar. On the basis of these observations, these investigators concluded that each of P.S.'s hemispheres had a sense of self as well as its own processing system for the subjective evaluation of current events, the planning for future events, the setting of response priorities, and the production of personal responses (LeDoux, Wilson, & Gazzaniga, 1977).

The findings of both the Sperry (1974) and Gazzaniga (1983) laboratories suggest that the split-brain procedure produces some serious behavioral side effects, not the least of which is that the patient evidences behavior of two separate individuals. Recall, however, that in initially describing the results of this surgery, we observed that without the special behavioral tasks devised by Sperry and his colleagues, these behavioral changes might have gone unnoticed. Such patients' everyday speech, language comprehension, personality, and motor coordination remain remarkably intact.

Clearly, some unifying mechanism or mechanisms must exist that explain how the two separate hemispheres in the split-brain patient act as a unit during the individual's everyday activities. As it turns out, a variety of such mechanisms may well compensate for the lack of intact cerebral commissures. Some of these mechanisms have to do with the concept of decussation. Earlier in this chapter we discussed the fact that many of the ascending and descending fiber tracts within the CNS would decussate, or cross over to the opposite side of the body, at some point between origin and terminus. This may involve a complete crossover of fibers or only a partial crossover. In the case of the visual system, half the fibers from each eye decussate to the contralateral (or opposite) side of the brain. This occurs at the **optic chiasma**. The other half of the fibers from each eye remain on the ipsilateral (or same) side and project only to the ipsilateral hemisphere.

VISUAL FIELD

While this seems fairly simple, there is still more, namely, the notion of a **visual field**, which is the surrounding area projecting to the eye and forming an image on the retina. With a subject fixating a point, the part of the visual field to the right of the point of fixation falls on the temporal (toward the side) half of the retina of the left eye and on the nasal (toward the nose) half of the retina of the right eye. At the optic chiasma, the fibers from the nasal half of the retina of the right eye decussate and combine with the fibers from the temporal half of the retina to send information concerning the right visual field to the primary visual cortex of the left cerebral hemisphere. Information concerning the left visual field is projected only to the primary visual cortex of the right hemisphere in the same manner (see Figure 2.9).

Finally, the visual areas of the left and right hemisphere normally communicate through the corpus callosum. If the corpus callosum is cut, however, as it is in the split-brain patient, and if the eyes and head are kept from moving, then each hemisphere would be able to see only half of the visual world. In everyday life, however, how many situations exist in which the head and eyes are not free to move? The conjugate eye movements, combined with the fact that each eye projects to both hemispheres, serve to establish unity of the visual world for the split-brain patient. Thus, even without the communication between the left and right visual cortex, the unity can be maintained, at least in part, as the eye movements initiated by one hemisphere to bring an object into direct view serve to make the information available to the other hemisphere as well.

A study by Levy, Trevarthen, and Sperry (1972) suggests a second mechanism of unity. In this study, an object was placed in the right or left hand of the split-brain patient, who was then asked to identify it on the basis of cutaneous information only. These investigators observed that these patients responded as though they were conscious of stimulation from both sides of space. Touch information, which is primarily responsible for such sensory experiences, is carried principally by the lemniscal tracts, fibers that carry information from the skin receptors to the somatosensory cortex, the part of the cortex that is responsible for processing cutaneous information. Almost but not all of these fibers convey such information to the contralateral hemisphere by decussating at the level of the medulla. The remaining fibers project to the ipsilateral somatosensory cortex; thus, both hemispheres receive touch information.

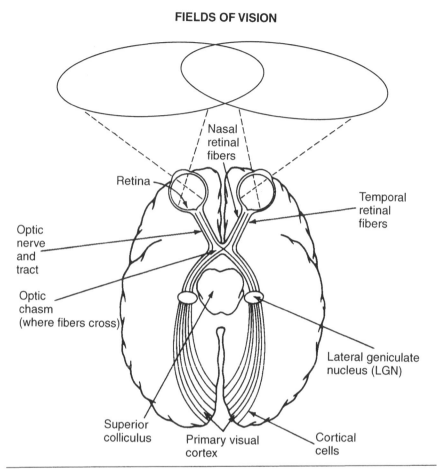

FIGURE 2.9   Primary Visual Pathways to the Brain

Once again, even in the case of the split-brain patient, we have a situation in which both hemispheres receive information from both sides of the body. Because this ipsilateral information is generally incomplete and inadequate, the split-brain patient, who has only that information to work with, is generally unable to identify verbally an object held in the left hand. Nonetheless, these ipsilateral pathways do provide at least partial information.

One final way in which information may be made available to both hemispheres, even in the split-brain patient, is through the commissures located below the cortical level. The commissurotomy severs the transverse fibers that connect the cortical level of the brain. While these are the major fibers connecting the hemispheres, there are other, smaller commissures located below the level of the cortex that connect those paired structures that are a part of the brainstem. Thus, the **collicular commissures,** which connect the superior colliculi of the two halves of the brain, are able to provide each hemisphere of the split-brain patient with information about the location of objects, regardless of where they fall in the visual field.

These mechanisms at least partially help to explain why the split-brain patient's everyday behavior appears to have unity. On the basis of their extensive research, Gazzaniga and LeDoux (1978) would argue that the language system of the left hemisphere be included in any list of unity mechanisms in the normal brain. For these investigators, at least, this is the mechanism that makes most of us feel like single, purposeful individuals.

ALTERED STATES OF CONSCIOUSNESS AND THE SPLIT BRAIN

Up to this point, we have been concerned with finding the physiological underpinnings of consciousness or awareness in the normal waking state. To accomplish this goal, we have relied principally upon studies of the split-brain patient. Can we also learn something about the physiology of altered states by studying them in the individual who has undergone a commissurotomy? In this final section, we will focus briefly on those few studies that have addressed this question.

The two altered states of consciousness that have received the greatest attention from the standpoint of hemisphere differences are dreaming and hypnosis. The association between duality of the brain and dream activity found its origin in anecdotal reports of patients who, after suffering localized brain damage in the posterior region of the right hemisphere, observed that they no longer had dreams (Humphrey & Zangwill, 1951). The notion that the act of dreaming is dependent on the integrity of a particular brain region was certainly a reasonable one, especially in view of the results of the many brain localization studies of that period. Additionally, if you stop and think about how you might describe your own dream world, the conclusion that dreaming depends upon an intact right cerebral hemisphere makes even more sense. Most of us would agree that our dreams are best described as nonlogical, full of visual images and emotional content—terms that have been used to characterize the right hemisphere.

As reasonable as such a conclusion may seem, it is necessary to remember that the database with which we are working is the anecdotal reports of patients who indicated that they did not dream. From the sleep and dream research literature, however, we know that even though the normal person experiences five or six dream periods each night, he or she normally recalls only one or two dreams and often none at all (Rechtschaffen, Verdone, & Wheaton, 1963). A more direct test of this hypothesis would involve the monitoring of both ongoing brain wave (EEG) and rapid eye movement (REM) activity in the sleeping patient to detect a dream episode. The patient would then have to be awakened during or immediately after a dream episode, and a report of the dream content would have to be elicited. Greenwood, Wilson, and Gazzaniga (1977), using precisely this technique, found that split-brain patients do report dreaming and are capable of reporting dream content. According to these researchers, such findings suggest that the left hemisphere does have access to the dream material in these patients.

What about the content of these dreams? Do they differ substantially from the dreams you and I have? Hoppe (1977) executed a psychoanalytically oriented, detailed analysis of the dreams of 12 split-brain patients in an effort to provide answers for these questions. Hoppe found that although these patients were indeed able to recall their dreams, they recalled fewer than normal. He concluded that the isolated, verbal left hemisphere does have access to these dreams. Furthermore, the dreams were not typical. According to Hoppe, they lacked the characteristics of dreamwork; their fantasies were unimaginative, utilitarian, and tied to reality; and their symbolization was concretistic, discursive, and rigid. Hoppe suggested that there may be a lack of communication between the left hemisphere and the source of imagery and fantasy. As Segalowitz (1983) observed, it is very tempting to conclude from all this that the right hemisphere is the seat of the unreal fantasies and images we experience in our dreams. However, until it is clearly demonstrated that the epilepsy these patients had or the major brain surgery they underwent were not responsible for this effect, we must be cautious in making such a generalization.

This is not one of the problems we must face, however, in searching for the physiological concomitants of the hypnotic state. To date, split-brain patients have not been employed in such research. Nevertheless, studies using normal subjects suggest the possibility of differential hemisphere involvement during hypnosis. Research on what contributes to hypnotic susceptibility and the ease with which an individual can be hypnotized or is susceptible to hypnotic suggestions identifies two possible factors: the abilities to become absorbed by a novel event and to concentrate on that event. These are very similar to what is thought to be characteristic of the right hemisphere (Kihlstrom, 1985; Tellegen & Atkinson, 1974). It was but a short step in logic, then, to hypothesize that hypnotic susceptibility is correlated with right-hemisphere activity.

Lateral eye movement studies such as those performed by Bakan (1969), provide some evidence that is consistent with the right-hemisphere hypothesis. In these studies, Bakan found greater hypnotizability in the subjects who had a preference for leftward eye movements. He proposed that the eye movements are related to hemispheric activity, a hypothesis that was based on the well-established fact that eye movements to one side are controlled by centers located in the frontal lobe of the contralateral hemisphere. Bakan suggested that cognitive activity occurring in one hemisphere would produce eye movements to the opposite side, and therefore, eye movements provide the researcher with an index of the relative activity of the two hemispheres in an individual. Later studies (Ehrlichman & Weinberger, 1979; Gur, Gur, & Harris, 1975), however, have cast doubt as to whether lateral eye movements are truly reflective of hemispheric activity. It would be premature, therefore, to assume that the association between hypnotizability and right-hemisphere activation has been conclusively demonstrated.

Again looking for the neurophysiological correlates of hypnotic susceptibility, MacLeod-Morgan and Lack (1982) measured brain-wave activity during the performance of a variety of tasks, including spatial orientation, tonal memory, verbal categorization, and mental arithmetic. These investigators predicted that the spatial orientation and tonal memory tasks would produce greater suppression of alpha activity in the right hemisphere, while the verbal categorization and mental arithmetic tasks would produce greater suppression of alpha activity in the left hemisphere. The highly hypnotizable subjects evidenced a greater shift of cortical activation between tasks than did the lowly hypnotizable subjects, although most subjects in both groups showed a shift in the appropriate direction. These data suggest that rather than high-hypnotic susceptibility being related to greater right-hemisphere involvement, it may involve greater task-specific hemispheric activation.

Little else can be said about the physiology of consciousness at this time. Some investigators argue that humans have a double physiological consciousness; others believe that, physiologically, consciousness is not a dichotomy but rather is a continuum. Unfortunately, the state of the science does not permit us to resolve this controversy.

We also would have been more than pleased to delineate physiological seats of consciousness, or places in the brain that influence or control some of the altered states of consciousness and awareness that we will discuss. However, except for some consciousness-altering drugs (see Chapter 3) and the state of sleep (see Chapter 7), this cannot be done in a concrete way. Yes, we can speculate on right-brain involvement in phenomena such as hypnosis and dreaming, but that is all we can do. We hope that as the study of consciousness grows as an area of interest within psychology, more will be learned about its physiology. We look forward to the discoveries.

FOR FURTHER READING

Carlson, N. R. (1998). *Physiology of behavior* (6th ed.). Boston: Allyn and Bacon.

Ornstein, R. E. (1986). *The psychology of consciousness.* New York: Penguin.

Segalowitz, S. J. (1983). *Two sides of the brain: Brain lateralization explored.* Englewood Cliffs, NJ: Prentice-Hall.

Springer, S. P., & Deutsch, G. (1997). *Left brain/right brain* (5th ed.). New York: Freeman.

3

CONSCIOUSNESS-ALTERING DRUGS

Go to your family medicine cabinet and count the number of different drugs that are stored there. You will probably be as surprised as I was when I recently performed this exercise. Of course, there was the usual family-sized bottle of aspirin for that occasional headache, but that was not all. To begin my count, there was my own medicine for high blood pressure, a barbiturate, and a diuretic. Two bottles of decongestants and several cough syrups (all prescription medications) that had been used last winter in the family's annual bout with the flu were also stored there. A three-year-old bottle of codeine pills prescribed for pain relief following oral surgery, a bottle of muscle relaxants, two containers of antihistamines, and one bottle of ear drops concluded my count. What is your list like?

Clearly, drugs are quickly becoming a part of the American culture. Thus, the hypothetical American businessman, after a weekend of business and social entertaining involving the consumption of many cigarettes and alcoholic beverages, may find that he needs a couple of strong cups of coffee and several aspirin tablets to beat the Monday morning hangover. On his way to the office the traffic is terrible. He arrives too late for an important appointment, his boss is upset with his performance, and his desk is piled high with paperwork requiring his immediate attention. It is little wonder, then, that our junior executive may find himself needing something to calm himself down, perhaps a tranquilizer. After a businessman's lunch that includes at least a couple of drinks, some more work, and a battle with the homeward-bound traffic, our businessman arrives home, greets his family, and collapses into an easy chair with the newspaper and a before-dinner drink. How will he ever get though an evening of bridge with the neighbors? He takes something to "pick himself up," perhaps an amphetamine. The evening over, our friend gets ready for bed, only to find that the amphetamine he took earlier is now preventing him from falling asleep. Finally, in desperation, he goes to the medicine cabinet to get a sleeping pill. Unfortunately, the next morning he wakes with a splitting headache and feeling as tired as he was before he went to sleep. Thus, the vicious cycle begins again.

Traditionally, a **drug** is defined as a compound that, by virtue of its chemical structure, interacts with a specific biological system, perhaps a cell, in ways that change the structure or functions of that system (Ray & Ksir, 1987). The problem with this definition is that it is much too broad and all-inclusive for our purposes. For example, food and water interact with biological systems to produce such changes. Under this definition, then, food and water would have to be considered drugs. However, unless one is on the verge of starvation or dehydration, it would be extremely difficult to argue that food and water have much to do with one's state of consciousness.

Definition is not an insurmountable problem, however; all that is needed is greater specificity about the type of drugs. In the present context we are interested only in those drugs that bring about changes in consciousness or affect mood when they are swallowed, inhaled, or injected. These are the **psychoactive** drugs. Although these drugs vary considerably both in chemical structure and in their effects on awareness and mood, Ray and Ksir (1987) suggest that several basic principles apply to all of them. First, every psychoactive drug has multiple effects. Thus, while the barbiturate user may seek only one of the drug's effects, such as the euphoria (or high), clearly other aspects of consciousness, such as thinking, solving problems, and remembering, are also altered.

Second, the effects of a psychoactive drug depend on the amount of drug the individual has taken. Changes in the dosage level may alter the drug's effects in two ways. Increasing the amount of the drug taken may result in a heightening of the effects obtained at lower drug levels. Also, different dosage levels may change the effect. Many of us are familiar with the fact that, while a few bottles of beer may relax the drinker and produce euphoria, a pint of whiskey may be sufficient to make the drinker pass out.

Third, the effects of a psychoactive drug depend in part on the user's history and expectations. It seems logical to assume that since these drugs change the level of awareness and the ability to process thoughts, any effect that may be produced in an individual would depend on preexisting conditions. Thus, such factors as attitudes, emotional state, previous drug experiences, and physical setting interact with the drug to alter the user's level of awareness. Smith (1964, p. 78) wrote, "If there is one point about which every student of the drugs agrees, it is that there is no such thing as the drug experience per se—no experience that the drugs merely secrete, as it were. Every experience is a mix of three ingredients: drug, set (the psychological make-up of the individual), and setting (the social and physical environment in which it is taken)." In brief, attempting to describe the effects of a particular drug without specifying these factors is an extremely difficult, if not impossible, task.

Finally, the drug itself is neither "good" nor "bad." For example, morphine, when used to alleviate the pain of a terminal cancer patient, is considered good, but the same drug, when used by an addict to feed a drug habit, is labeled bad. Note, however, that it is not the drug, but rather the use to which it is put, that is labeled.

PHARMACOLOGY OF NEUROTRANSMISSION

In Chapter 2 we observed that neurons transmit information to each other at junctions called synapses. Initially, it was believed that this process of information transmission at the synapse was electrical. However, in a brilliant series of studies, Dale (1938) conclusively demonstrated the chemical nature of the process and isolated the neurohumural transmitter substances **acetylcholine** and **norepinephrine**. Following this major research step, there has been a concerted effort to identify other neurotransmitter substances. Although many substances have been proposed as neurotransmitters, conclusive evidence is generally lacking. Hebb (1970) suggested that for a substance to be accepted as a neurotransmitter, it must meet the following criteria:

1. The enzymes necessary for synthesis of the substance should be present within the neuron. (An **enzyme** is a protein that causes a particular chemical reaction to take place without becoming a part of the final product.)
2. Direct application of the substance to the postsynaptic element should be equivalent in effect to stimulation of the presynaptic neuron.
3. Drugs that interfere with synthesis of the substance, or its reaction with the postsynaptic membrane, should block the effects of neuronal stimulation.
4. Drugs that block the enzyme that normally inactivates the substance should lead to a prolongation of its effects and of the effects of neuronal stimulation.

In addition to acetylcholine and norepinephrine, a number of other substances have been identified as potential neurotransmitters. These include **dopamine**, **serotonin**, **glutamic acid**, and **gamma-amino-butyric acid**.

When an adequate stimulus is applied to a presynaptic neuron, the neuron releases one of these substances into the synapse where it diffuses across the **synaptic cleft** (the space between the neurons). Normally, at this point, the neurotransmitter interacts with the appropriate receptor sites on the postsynaptic neuronal membrane to either increase or decrease the likelihood that the postsynaptic neuron will discharge.

Practically all of the drugs that act upon the central nervous system (CNS), and thereby affect consciousness and behavior, do so by somehow influencing some aspect of this neurotransmission process. According to Leavitt (1995), such a drug may interfere with neurotransmission in one of the following ways:

1. It may interfere with the synthesis of the neurotransmitter, thereby decreasing the amount of the neurotransmitter substance available at the presynaptic site.
2. It may interfere with the release of the neurotransmitter substance.
3. A drug may replace the normal neurotransmitter in a presynaptic neuron only to be released later when that neuron is stimulated or in the presence of other drugs. The effects of this **false transmitter** may or may not be similar to those of the normal transmitter.
4. A drug may combine with a postsynaptic receptor site where it may elicit the same effect as the normal neurotransmitter or it may have no direct action at all. In either event, by combining with the receptor, it may prevent the action of the normal neurotransmitter.
5. A drug may lead to the destruction of the neurotransmitter.
6. Most neurotransmitters are inactivated primarily by being taken back up into the presynaptic neurons or into extraneuronal sites. Many drugs act on one or both of these reuptake mechanisms.
7. The drug may produce changes in the sensitivity of the receptor cell.
8. Finally the drug may serve as a neurotoxic agent. A **neurotoxic agent** is a substance that causes the destruction of neural tissue.

BASIC PSYCHOPHARMACOLOGICAL CONCEPTS

To understand the following detailed descriptions of the physiological and consciousness-altering effects produced by a sample of psychoactive drugs, it is necessary that you familiarize yourself with a number of common psychopharmacological concepts.

Drug abuse refers primarily to the recreational, as opposed to the medical or psychiatric, use of drugs. Drug abuse is classified as a disorder by the American Psychiatric Association (APA), which defines it in terms of the resultant maladaptive behaviors that impair social functioning. Also recognized as a disorder by the APA is **drug dependence**, which results from the repeated use of a drug taken in dosages sufficient to elicit a strong desire to continue taking the drug.

Two kinds of drug dependence are recognized: physiological and psychological. The former is frequently referred to as **drug addiction;** this type of dependence is partially or completely organically based. Through the continued use of the drug, the body eventually becomes physiologically dependent on it. Physiological dependence is characteristic of users of such drugs as alcohol, barbiturates, morphine, heroin, and chlordiazepoxide (Librium).

Psychological dependence, sometimes called habituation, is a strong, sometimes overwhelming, desire to continue using a drug. Such dependence is typically caused by the drug's effects on levels of consciousness and mood. The use of such drugs as amphetamines, barbiturates, cocaine, marijuana, and phencyclidine, which relieve anxiety or lead to euphoria, may lead to psychological dependence.

Finally, a pharmacological concept of some importance is that of **drug tolerance.** This is a physiological reaction, which, after prolonged use of a drug, causes the body to require increasingly greater amounts of the agent to experience the same effects. Drug tolerance has been observed in the use of alcohol, barbiturates, amphetamines, and opiate derivatives, such as morphine and heroin. Sometimes the development of tolerance for one drug occurs after the repeated use of another drug. This is known as **cross-tolerance.** Thus, a heroin user may develop a tolerance not only for heroin, but also for morphine.

If our discussion of psychoactive drugs and their effects upon consciousness and behavior is to be coherent, we must adopt some classification scheme. A cursory review of the literature from the many disciplines that are concerned with drugs (chemistry, pharmacology, law, social work, psychology) clearly demonstrates the existence of a number of drug classification models. Having considered the many choices at some length, it seems reasonable to us that from the standpoint of this chapter, the most realistic classification scheme would be the one described by Julien (1997) on how the drugs affect a user's behavior.

Julien's system involves five classes of psychoactive drugs that alter mood and behavior: (1) **sedative-hypnotic compounds** or CNS depressants, (2) **behavioral stimulants and convulsants,** (3) **narcotic analgesics (opiates),** (4) **antipsychotic agents,** and (5) **psychedelics and hallucinogens.**

As Julien observed, even this classification system is not without its limitations. First, the action of psychoactive drugs is seldom restricted to a single functional or anatomical subdivision of the brain. Although there are exceptions, a psychoactive drug will simultaneously affect a variety of processes. This makes the classification process complicated because at different dosage levels, different behavioral actions may predominate.

A second limitation of this scheme has to do with the fact that although a psychoactive drug might have a single effect on a specific neurotransmitter, a variety of effects can be expected because the neurotransmitter is involved in many different functions.

Third, it should be recognized that psychoactive drugs simply modify ongoing behavioral or physiological responses; they do not create new responses.

Finally the classification scheme we have adopted should not be considered rigid and fixed, because different behavioral responses are observed at different dosage levels. The reader must understand that simply classifying a group of drugs does not fully describe their effects on consciousness and behavior. It only serves as a starting point.

With these limitations in mind we have selected one or more representative agents from each of the major groups for a detailed discussion. The exception is that, for two reasons, we will not discuss antipsychotic drugs.

These drugs are typically not drugs of abuse for the purpose of creating an altered state of consciousness. Second, these drugs are typically used to treat individuals who are already exhibiting hallucinations or altered states. Thus, they are used to reduce the magnitude of or to eliminate entirely the altered state so as to permit the individual to return to a normal, nonaltered, waking state of consciousness.

With regard to the remaining four categories in Julien's system, we will examine some representative drugs from these classes and describe their effects on behavior. Unlike the antipsychotic drugs, the compounds or agents in the remaining categories are often drugs of abuse and do bring about changes in levels or states of consciousness.

SEDATIVE-HYPNOTIC COMPOUNDS

Although the sedative-hypnotic compounds are quite varied in their chemical structure, all are capable of inducing varying degrees of reduction in both behavioral output and level of consciousness. The behavioral-depressant action of these compounds appears to result from an action on the arousal centers within the brain: the ascending reticular activating system (ARAS) and the diffuse thalamic projection system (Soulairac & Soulairac, 1965; Stern & Morgane, 1974). Included in this class of drugs are alcohol, chloral hydrate, paraldehyde, the bromides, methaqualone (Quaalude), and barbiturates.

Generally, when we think about the effects produced by the members of this category of drugs, we conjure up thoughts of behavioral sedation and sleep. In truth, however, depending upon drug dosage level, almost all of these drugs are capable of producing any of the behavioral changes along a continuum of behavioral sedation (see Figure 3.1). In this section we will discuss the effects of barbiturates and alcohol on consciousness and behavior.

Barbiturates

In the 1850s a group of new chemical compounds called **bromides** was introduced. These agents gained almost immediate popularity as a sleep-inducing preparation. However, with this popularity came abuse and the realization that excessive use of bromides results in consciousness-altering effects such as delusions, hallucinations, and a variety of neurological disturbances. The toxic psychosis caused by bromide abuse proved to be a major cause of admissions to mental hospitals for some time (Jarvik, 1967).

Participating in the search for a sleep-inducing drug with fewer dangerous side effects, Adolf von Bayer (1835–1917) in Munich, Germany, succeeded in combining urea with malonic acid to produce a new compound called barbituric acid (Sharpless, 1970). Von Bayer's 1862 creation was not a CNS

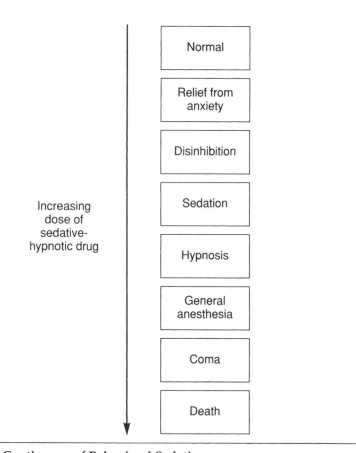

FIGURE 3.1   Continuum of Behavioral Sedation

depressant; however, the many barbiturates that came to be derived from barbituric acid proved to be excellent CNS depressants. The first barbiturate to be used clinically, barbital (Veronal), was introduced in 1903.

The medical uses of barbiturates include, but are not limited to, sleep induction, daytime sedation, treatment of epileptic seizures, induction of anesthesia, preanesthetic medication before surgery, and the treatment of anxiety and neurosis. The medical uses for these drugs, however, have declined considerably over the past 20 years primarily because of newer compounds that have less toxicity or dependence liability (Harvey, 1985). At present, the only real advantage of the barbiturates is their low cost, which has come about because they are no longer protected by patent. Social and recreational uses include euphoria and relief from anxiety (Julien, 1997). Despite this, barbiturates have proven to be extremely dangerous and are commonly associated with both physiological and psychological dependence as well as fatalities from overdose.

There are more than 2,500 barbiturates, and they are usually classified on the basis of the duration of their activity (Martindale, 1967). It is the short-acting agents, such as pentobarbital (Nembutal) and secobarbital (Seconal), that are abused. These barbiturates are likely to produce the initial euphoric high within 15 minutes after ingestion. The duration of their action is typically between two and three hours. Tolerance to barbiturates develops gradually, and the dosage must be increased periodically to maintain a constant effect. However, the lethal dosage remains the same. Thus, as tolerance develops, the difference between these two levels becomes dangerously small. Nearly one-third of accidental drug-related deaths are due to barbiturate overdose (Julien, 1997).

Once the individual requires a daily dosage level of about 400 milligrams, he or she will probably experience some withdrawal symptoms if barbiturate use is temporarily interrupted. Traditionally, barbiturate dependence has been associated with an emotionally maladjusted individual seeking relief from the stresses and strains of life. More recently, the introduction of the "all new and greatly improved" diet pill has provided a new cause of barbiturate addiction. The old diet pills helped the user to shed unwanted pounds of fat but produced a bad case of "jumpy nerves." This was because the old diet pills contained only amphetamines.

To counteract this unwanted side effect, the new pills contain fixed-ratio combinations of amphetamines and barbiturates. Unfortunately, both types of drugs are highly addictive, when used either separately or in combination. Also, since the addition of barbiturates may make the amphetamines more tolerable, addiction-prone individuals may increase their pill intake rapidly, thus increasing the possibility of addiction to both drugs (Harvey, 1985).

While this fact may help to account for the increase in barbiturate abuse among middle-aged people, it does little to explain such an increase among teenagers. Cohen (1971), testifying before a U.S. Senate subcommittee to investigate juvenile delinquency, noted that "For the youngsters barbiturates are a more reliable 'high' and less detectable than 'pot.' They are less strenuous than LSD, less 'freaky' than amphetamines, and less expensive than heroin. A school boy can 'drop a red' and spend the day in a dreamy, floating state of awayness untroubled by reality. It is drunkenness without the odor of alcohol. It is escape for the price of one's lunch money."

Teenagers have also discovered a distinctly different effect that is obtained by combining barbiturates, amphetamines, and alcohol; this effect has been described as a controlled hypersensitivity. Because barbiturates and alcohol potentiate one another, one very real possible effect of such a combination is barbiturate overdose and death.

It is generally agreed that barbiturates tend to decrease the excitability of neurons throughout the nervous system (Harvey, 1985). The inhibitory influence of barbiturates is thought to be due to enhanced GABA activity at its receptor cites (Skolnick, Noncada, Barker, & Paul, 1981). It has been suggested that the inhibitory effects of barbiturates may also be due to increases in the conductance of potassium ions across the neural membrane (O'Beirne, Gurevich, & Carlen, 1986). The overall decrease in brain activity probably can best be accounted for by the fact that the pathways of the ascending reticular activating system are among the first of the major brain centers to be affected by barbiturates.

Shortly after dropping some "rainbows" (Tuinal) or "red devils" (Seconal), the individual experiences feelings of relaxation, some behavioral stimulation, and a euphoric high. It is also possible that the individual will exhibit some aggressive behavior, as if he or she were fighting the inevitable drowsiness and sleep. This is especially the case if the barbiturate used is secobarbital (Tinklenberg & Woodrow, 1974). These effects on the user's consciousness level are then replaced by a sense of confusion and cognitive impairment such that problem solving and decision making seem to require great effort; the individual is usually aware that his or her thinking is, at best, "fuzzy." Memory and concentration may also be impaired. Emotionally, the user is likely to be extremely labile, ranging from the euphoric high to severe depression. Finally, loss of motor coordination is reflected in the person's slurred speech, depressed motor activity, and staggering gait (Wesson & Smith, 1971). At dosages between 100 and 200 milligrams, secobarbital and pentobarbital have a hypnotic or sleep-producing effect; therefore, they are often employed in the treatment of certain sleep disorders, including insomnia. This will be discussed in some detail in Chapter 7. It is sufficient here to note only that these drugs do not bring about a normal sleep in that rapid eye movement or REM sleep is suppressed (Dement, 1972).

In addition to the behavioral effects described, barbiturates also produce psychophysiological effects suggestive of parasympathetic arousal, including pupillary constriction, decreased heart rate and blood pressure, and depressed respiratory rate. Excessive dosages are lethal because they result in paralysis of the respiratory centers of the brain.

Cessation of barbiturate administration causes withdrawal symptoms to appear. At normal dosage levels, withdrawal symptoms are not typically serious or life-threatening. Among the symptoms is a rebound increase in rapid eye movement (REM) sleep, which causes sleep difficulties. The individual may be quite irritable for days or even weeks after discontinuing the barbiturate. At higher dosage levels, removal of the drug may lead to serious and even lethal withdrawal symptoms, chief among which is convulsions. Associated with these convulsive episodes may be periods of hallucinations, restlessness, and disorientation. Obviously, this is even more serious in the case of the epileptic patient who is already prone to severe convulsions.

Alcohol

Although few of us probably view alcoholic beverages as drugs in the same way as we do heroin, barbiturates, amphetamines, and tranquilizers, the fact remains that alcohol (more properly, ethyl alcohol) does fit our initial definition of a drug in that its chemical structure interacts with a specific biological system. What is important here is that alcohol alters both the mood and the conscious state of the user. Thus, it is also a psychoactive drug which is every bit as powerful as the more notorious drugs. Although alcohol has all of those qualities, psychological and physical dependency, social disruptiveness, toxicity, and lethality, that our drug-conscious society has deemed unacceptable with respect to drugs, it is so accepted in our culture that it is one of the most widely used and abused drugs known. It has been estimated that alcoholics alone represent about 20 percent of all the patients seen in psychiatric facilities (Guze, Cloninger, Martin, & Clayton, 1986).

From a historical standpoint, it would appear that alcohol has been with us for a very long time. Mead, which is made from honey, is probably the oldest alcoholic beverage, and some authorities (Ray & Ksir, 1987) suggest that it first appeared as early as about 8000 B.C. Beer and berry wine were known and used about 6400 B.C. Grape wine first made its appearance about 300–400 B.C. Cambyses, king of Persia in the sixth century B.C., holds the dubious distinction of being one of the first alcoholics on record. His drunken episodes apparently were associated with periods of uncontrollable rage. He behaved much like "a madman not in possession of his senses" (Whitwell, 1936, p. 38). It is reported that on one occasion, without making any plans for feeding his troops, Cambyses set out to thrash the Ethiopians, who had angered the king by referring to the Persians as "dung eaters." Because of his lack of planning, King Cambyses and his troops were forced to retreat to Memphis, where, much to his anger, he found his people celebrating the feast of Apis. Perceiving in his drunken state that the people were rejoicing at his failure, he ordered the entire citizenry taking part in the feast to be executed.

The list of other celebrities, poets, painters, authors, musicians, and leaders who are known to have used alcohol excessively would be endless— Samuel Butler, Lord Byron, Edgar Allan Poe, Ulysses S. Grant, John Barrymore, and Ernest Hemingway, to name a few.

The basis for all alcoholic beverages is a process called **fermentation.** Certain yeasts act on sugar (glucose) in the presence of water so that the yeast recombines the carbon (C), hydrogen (H), and oxygen (O) of the sugar and water into ethyl alcohol and carbon dioxide ($C_6H_{12}O_6 + H_2O \xrightarrow{yeast} C_2H_6O + CO_2$). Glucose is readily available in most fruits, including grapes. The limitation of this process lies in the fact that yeast generally has only a confined tolerance for alcohol. Thus, when alcohol concentration reaches approximately 15 percent, the yeast cells die and the fermentation process is terminated.

Cereal grains are also used in the production of alcoholic drinks, but here the process is somewhat different. To begin with, grains contain starches, not sugars. Therefore, before fermentation can take place, it is necessary to convert the starches to sugars by the use of enzymes during a process called **malting.** The grain is placed in water and allowed to sprout; afterward, it is dried slowly to kill off the sprouts but preserve the enzymes that formed during the growth. The dried, sprouted grain is then crushed, and when mixed with water, the enzymes convert the starch to sugar. Once yeast is added, fermentation can begin.

However, what if concentrations of alcohol stronger than the 15 percent that can be obtained by fermentation are desired? In this case, it is necessary to resort to a second process called *distillation*. During this process, an alcohol-containing solution is heated; the resulting vapors are then collected and condensed once more into a liquid form. Because the boiling point of alcohol is lower than that of water, the distillation process produces a much higher concentration of alcohol in the distillate (the condensed liquid) than was present in the original solution. While there are any number of variations in the processes leading to the end product (e.g., charcoal fire brewing, storing and aging in special barrels), it is the process of fermentation and distillation that determines the beverage's alcoholic content. In the United States, the alcoholic content of a distilled beverage is indicated on the label by the term **proof.** When a friend gives you a gift bottle of 90-proof rum, you are really getting a distillate from the fermentation of sugar cane molasses, which now contains 45 percent ethyl alcohol. In brief, the percentage of alcohol by volume is one-half the proof number indicated on the label.

Because of the widespread use and frequent abuse of alcohol, it is safe to assume that during your lifetime, many of you have had some personal contact with one or more of the many alcoholic beverages available. These experiences may range from a sip of beer or wine "just to see what it tastes like" to a more dangerous "lost weekend" or (most probably) something in between these two extremes. By comparing your experiences with those of your friends, you may have discovered that alcohol, like most other drugs, produces a variety of behavioral effects.

Some of these effects are general and are experienced by most people; others are peculiar to the individual and may well result from an interaction of the individual's mental set, the setting, and the alcohol. Thus, while some of the behavioral effects are due to pharmacological effects, a large number of the "effects" of alcohol are due to set and expectancy (Critchlow, 1986; Cutter, O'Farrell, Whitehouse, & Dentch, 1986; Hull & Bond, 1986).

It is apparent that there is a gender disparity concerning the ease with which women and men become intoxicated. Because of differences in the content of their stomach enzymes, women absorb alcohol into their bloodstreams more rapidly than men can (Frezza et al., 1990). Remember that it is not really a matter of how many drinks you have but rather how much alcohol reaches your brain. Take these two facts and then add the fact that women tend to have a lower volume of fluids in their bodies than do men of equal weight, so the alcohol in women may be more concentrated. York and Welte (1994) suggest that this may explain, in part at least, why women generally become intoxicated more easily than do men.

Alcohol is a consciousness-limiting drug that appears to attack and numb the higher brain centers. See what happens to a fictitious friend, Joe College, whose fraternity pledge class has decided to hold its annual weekend "house-cleaning-and-keg" party. By Friday evening, the fraternity house is spanking clean, the older members have gone their various ways, and now the kegs and other assorted bottles are brought from their hiding places; the party has officially begun. Depending on how tired he is, when he ate last, his body size, his mood, and a host of other factors, the first drink or two may have little effect on Joe's state of awareness. However, with a couple more drinks, Joe's alertness is decreased, and he begins to experience good feelings—feelings of expansiveness, warmth, and well-being. All the unpleasantness, tensions, and worries of the real world begin to melt away. His feelings of self-worth are greatly increased, and everybody is Joe's friend.

With a few more drinks our friend's judgments and other rational processes become impaired, and his self-control diminishes. With the diminution of restraints, more primitive emotional responses are very likely to occur (e.g., the lamp shade on the head, crying, and even aggression), responses that under more normal circumstances he would have kept under control. Most of us are familiar with the crying or belligerent drunk. There are now convincing data that alcohol intoxication, with its resulting disinhibition, also plays a major role in aggressive behavior and violent crimes (Gunn, 1979; Hindman, 1979).

By now, the alcoholic content in Joe's bloodstream has reached or exceeded 0.1 percent, and he is quickly approaching intoxication. Because alcohol is an emetic, users vomit once the blood alcohol level reaches about 0.12 percent. Vomiting is a safety device that may not function if the critical level is approached slowly. Fatal amounts of alcohol may then be ingested. Should our friend decide to return to his room and his studies, he would find the learning process most difficult; learning is impaired in alcoholics and in normal subjects who have had too much to drink (Goldman, 1983; Parker, Chelune, Hamblin, & Kitchens, 1984). On the other hand, some evidence suggests a facilitating effect of small doses of alcohol on difficult intellectual tasks (Keller, 1966).

Chronic alcoholism often leads to severe memory deficits. Evidence suggests that alcohol produces considerable impairment in the ability to convert information from short-term to long-term memory (Nelson, McSpadden, Fromme, & Marlatt, 1986). Until a few years ago, it was pretty much agreed that intoxication resulted in a disruption of the encoding operations involved in attempting to store new information, whereas retrieval of previously learned information was unimpaired. Recent data, however, suggests that retrieval from long-term memory may be affected by acute intoxication and that this effect may be greater for females than for males (Haut, Beckwith, Petros, & Russell, 1989). Depending on the circumstances, memory processes may be so affected that the person experiences blackouts (i.e., complete amnesia for the events that took place during much of the period of intoxication).

It should also be noted, however, that there is some evidence that when alcohol is given immediately after the learning of new information, it may actually facilitate its retrieval at a later time (Hashtroudi, Parker, Yablick, DeLisi, & Wyatt, 1981). Once the blood alcohol level reaches 0.15 percent, Joe is legally intoxicated (according to the laws of most states). His motor coordination is now beginning to show some signs of impairment. This, combined with slowed reaction times and impaired judgment, means that the time has come for one of Joe's sober friends to hide the keys to his car. Should Joe and his motor deficits decide to go for a ride at this point, he would be a menace, not only to himself but also to anyone else on the road. Drivers with a 0.10 percent or greater blood alcohol level are often arrested and removed from the road (Langenbucher & Nathan, 1983; Smith-Donals & Klitzner, 1985).

As the drinking continues and the alcoholic content of Joe's blood increases, his ability to sense pain, cold, and other discomforts is also severely diminished. Alcohol dilates peripheral vessels, so increased amounts of blood circulate through the skin. One consequence is that alcoholics often have red noses. The increased blood flow promotes a feeling of warmth but also leads to a loss of body heat (on cold days, peripheral blood vessels normally constrict so that flow to the skin, and hence heat loss, are minimized). Perhaps you know someone who took a flask of the spirits to a football game or on a winter hunting expedition to help keep warm, only to suffer frostbite or worse because of an inability to sense accurately the severity of the cold weather. Additionally, because of the heat loss caused by blood vessel dilation due to the alcohol, the individual may also have suffered hypothermia, a severe loss of body heat.

Certainly by this point, the clumsiness, staggering, and unsteadiness in standing and walking, all symptomatic of impaired motor coordination and vision, are very apparent. Joe's speech is now badly slurred, and his judgment of his own condition and ability is extremely disturbed. His moral judgments become even more immature, and any qualms Joe may have had about driving while drinking have left him. At this point, even if Joe were given a Breathalyzer test and told that he was dangerously intoxicated, he would probably still insist on driving (Denton & Krebs, 1990; MacDonald, Zanna, & Fong, 1995).

When Joe's blood alcohol reaches approximately 0.5 percent, his entire neural balance is upset, and he slowly slides out of his chair, then under the table, and passes out. As blood concentrations above 0.55 percent are considered lethal, it is generally agreed that this lapsing into a state of unconsciousness is simply the body's way of protecting itself. An unconscious drinker is not likely to take another drink, at least for a while. Had Joe College's bout with the demon spirits gone this far, he probably would awaken the next day with an upset stomach, fatigue, headache, thirst, depression, anxiety, and an overall bad feeling, the classic **hangover.** Many experts believe that this is a sign that a physical dependence has developed (Cicero, 1978). The fact that reexposure to alcohol can cure the hangover supports this belief.

Exactly how alcohol produces these effects is not yet clear. However, at a cellular level, the best evidence to date suggests that alcohol acts directly on the membrane of the neuron, altering its basic semisolid structure to make it more fluid (Chin & Goldstein, 1977). This may have the effect of inhibiting the movements of the sodium and potassium ions across the membrane. This would interfere with the nerve cell's ability to produce electrical impulses and render it unable to process information normally. Alcohol may also change synaptic activity directly. It has been found to depress both excitatory and inhibitory postsynaptic potentials while potentiating presynaptic inhibition. There is also some recent evidence to suggest that alcohol enhances the activity of the neurotransmitter GABA at its receptor cites (Suzdak et al., 1986). Specifically affected, at least initially, are nerve cells that comprise the ascending reticular activating system. Depression of the activity of this system leads in turn to a disruption of cortical activity and the changes in behavior and arousal observed in the drinker.

Should Joe drink himself to sleep, the sleep induced will be abnormal. Slow-wave and REM sleep stages are greatly reduced, and stage shifts occur more frequently than under normal conditions (Ritchie, 1985; Zarcone, 1973). During periods of very heavy drinking, sleep patterns may be profoundly disturbed. Greenberg and Pearlman (1967) note that during withdrawal, sleep is of extremely poor quality, with REM sleep predominating.

Finally, suppose that this is not the first time that Joe C. has used alcohol. Instead, Joe has been using alcohol since his last year of high school, and although he was only a moderate drinker, the "clean-up party" and the hangover the next day have convinced him that it is time for him to give it up. If he were truly a moderate drinker, one or two beers a day, about the only withdrawal symptom he would experience would be limited to prolonged disturbances in brain wave patterns during sleep.

On the other hand, had Joe been consuming larger quantities of alcohol over that period of time he would probably experience a high degree of arousal associated with weakness, tremor, anxiety, and elevated blood pressure, pulse rate, and respiration rate. Very heavy drinkers, those who consume a pint or more of pure ethyl alcohol daily over a protracted period of time, are likely to experience convulsions and a toxic psychosis, commonly referred to as **delirium tremens,** or the DTs. It includes such symptoms as rapid pulse rate, severe anxiety, headaches, and even death. Vivid hallucinations, especially of small, quickly moving insects or animals, also occur and can heighten the individual's anxiety. The hallucinations may be due to REM rebound, since alcohol suppresses REM; when alcohol is withdrawn, a great deal of REM returns. These together with irritability, headaches, fever, nausea, agitation, confusion, and visual hallucinations complete the picture (Grilly, 1998). These withdrawal symptoms can occur even when there is still a fairly high level of blood alcohol (Ritchie, 1985). A second long-term consequence of alcohol use is *Korsakoff's syndrome,* a severe brain impairment characterized by the inability to remember recent events or to learn new information.

BEHAVIORAL STIMULANTS AND CONVULSANTS

Drugs such as caffeine, strychnine, pentylenetetrazol (Metrazol), amphetamine (Benzedrine), and cocaine differ widely in their molecular structure and mechanisms of action. However, they share at least one common property: They all excite the CNS, which in turn results in an increase in the user's behavioral activity and in the production of a heightened level of arousal. Additionally, these stimulants, including caffeine, can be addictive (Silverman, Evans, Strain, and Griffiths, 1992). This section discusses one of the major abused behavioral stimulants: cocaine, a definite consciousness-altering drug.

Cocaine

Cocaine is a natural plant product derived from the leaves of *Erythroxylum coca,* a plant that thrives on the slopes of the Andes Mountains of Bolivia and Peru where the annual rainfall is more than 100 inches (Ray & Ksir, 1987). Research indicates that as early as A.D. 500, the native inhabitants of these areas, as well as those of Columbia and northwestern Argentina, chewed on the leaves of this tree to increase their physical stamina (Guerra, 1971).

Before the invasion led by Francisco Pizarro (1476–1541) in the 1500s, the Incas had built a well-developed civilization in Peru. The coca leaves played an important role in Inca culture, functioning initially as a part of the religious ceremonies and later, by the time the Spanish under Pizarro had arrived, as a medium of exchange. The conquistadors also adopted this custom and paid the native laborers in coca leaves for mining and transporting gold and silver. The leaves probably gave the workers an increased sense of strength and endurance and at the same time decreased their appetites (Ray & Ksir, 1987).

While historians, through their early writing on Inca civilization, had made available to Europeans the knowledge of the unique properties of the coca leaves, no real interest in the plant was manifested there until the later part of the nineteenth century (Taylor, 1949). Three individuals have been suggested as having played prominent roles in introducing cocaine to Europe (see Ray & Ksir, 1987). One was the French chemist Angelo Mariani, who first made coca leaves available to the general public by using their extract in a series of products, including coca tea, coca lozenges, and his famous Mariani coca wine. Uplifted spirits, freedom from fatigue, and an overall good feeling were the major benefits consumers derived from Mariani's coca leaf extract products, which proved so satisfactory that Pope Leo XIII presented Mariani with a medal of appreciation.

The second member of this trio was Sigmund Freud (1856–1939), the founder of psychoanalysis. In the early 1900s, while suffering from a bout of depression and fatigue, Freud read an account of the isolation of cocaine and was determined to experiment with this "new" drug. He found that it not only relieved his own depression and fatigue, but also seemed to provide him with newfound energy to continue his work. It is clear that his personal experiences with the drug, combined with the results he achieved using it in his practice, made Freud an early advocate of cocaine. In his papers on cocaine written in 1885, Freud recited a litany of the drug's supposed therapeutic benefits, which included effectiveness as a local anesthetic, production of exhilaration and aphrodisiac properties, usefulness in treating asthma and digestive disorders of the stomach, and its role in the treatment of alcohol and morphine addiction (Freud, 1970). In regard to the last benefit, Freud wrote:

> *It was first discovered in America that cocaine is capable of alleviating the serious withdrawal symptoms in subjects who are abstaining from morphine and of suppressing their craving for morphine . . . . On basis of my experiences with the effects of cocaine, I have no hesitation in recommending the administration of cocaine for such withdrawal cures in subcutaneous injections of 0.03 to 0.05 grams per dose, without any fear of increasing the dose. On several occasions, I have even seen cocaine quickly eliminate the manifestations of intolerance that appeared after a rather large dose of morphine, as if it had a specific ability to counteract morphine. (Freud, 1970)*

So convinced was Freud of cocaine's effectiveness in this connection that he used it in the treatment of the morphine addiction of a close friend, Dr. Fleischel. What transpired clearly was not anticipated. Freud found that as treatment progressed, increasingly larger doses of the drug were needed, until finally a cocaine-induced psychosis was precipitated. This experience was more than adequate to change Freud's initial attitudes toward cocaine (Jones, 1953–1957).

Finally, in 1890, it was made public that the world's foremost fictitious detective, Sherlock Holmes, advocated the use of cocaine as a means of relieving the boredom of day-to-day existence (Grilly, 1998). In *The Sign of the Four* (Doyle, 1938), the fictitious Dr. Watson describes the effects of cocaine use on the master detective:

> *"It is cocaine," he said, "a seven-percent solution. Would you care to try it?"*
>
> *"No, indeed," I answered brusquely. "My constitution has not got over the Afghan campaign yet. I cannot afford to throw any extra strain upon it."*

He smiled at my vehemence. "Perhaps you are right, Watson," he said. "I suppose that its influence is physically a bad one. I find it, however, so transcendently stimulating and clarifying to the mind that its secondary action is a matter of small moment."

"But consider!" I said earnestly. "Count the cost! Your brain may, as you say, be roused and excited, but it is a pathological and morbid process which involves increased tissue-change and may at least have a permanent weakness. You know, too, what a black reaction comes upon you. Surely the game is hardly worth the candle. Why should you, for a mere passing pleasure, risk the loss of those great powers with which you have been endowed?" . . .

He did not seem offended. On the contrary, he put his finger tips together, and leaned his elbows on the arm of his chair, like one who has a relish for conversation.

"My mind," he said, "rebels at stagnation. Give me problems, give me the most abstruse cryptogram, or the most intricate analysis and I am in my own proper atmosphere. I can dispense then with artificial stimulants. But I abhor the dull routine of existence. I crave for mental exaltation." (pp. 91–92)

In the United States, use of cocaine for both medical and quasi-medical purposes was widespread around the turn of the century. Traveling salesmen sold their "snake oils," "elixirs of life," and patent medicines, all of which supposedly contained a secret ingredient to bring long life, a sense of exhilaration, and well-being to all its users. Very often, the so-called secret ingredient was cocaine. In fact, cocaine was also at one time an ingredient in cola soft drinks. With the passage of the Harrison Act of 1914, use of cocaine was forced underground, where it was to remain until the emergence of the drug subculture in the late 1960s. Since 1969, use of cocaine in the United States has shown a substantial increase.

Cocaine acts both as a local anesthetic and as a CNS stimulant. The ability of cocaine to numb the area to which it has been applied topically was first discovered in 1860 by Dr. Carl Koller, a Viennese eye surgeon, who used it as a local anesthetic in the eye. Low concentrations of cocaine used in this manner appear to block neural conduction when brought into direct contact with sensory nerve fibers. The drug's ability to increase the user's awareness levels represents the CNS function of cocaine. All available evidence would suggest that the initial central effect occurs at the level of the cerebral cortex, although it is possible that this effect may be mediated by subcortical activity.

The increase in CNS arousal is closely associated with the action of cocaine at noradrenergic synapses—that is, synapses at which norepinephrine serves as the transmitter substance. It is generally accepted that cocaine inhibits the active reuptake of norepinephrine in the brain and the peripheral nervous system. This blockage increases the amount of norepinepherine available in the synaptic cleft, which means that the transmitter will be in contact with postsynaptic receptor sites at higher concentrations and for longer periods of time than would normally be the case.

The gross physiological responses to cocaine are essentially sympath-omimetic. During cocaine use, the heart accelerates, the respiration rate increases, the pupils dilate, and blood pressure increases, often to dangerous levels. Sweating and dryness of the throat may also be observed.

Actually, cocaine not only stimulates the sympathetic nervous system, it also suppresses the parasympathetic nervous system, a fact that may help to explain why it can put enough stress on the heart to kill an otherwise healthy young person with just a single use (Cowen, 1990). Use of cocaine can also cause brain atrophy, a form of damage in which the brain actually shrinks (Pascual-Leone, Dhuna, Altafullah, & Anderson, 1990). Despite these functional changes, until the 1980s there was some question as to whether or not cocaine produces psychological dependence (Jaffe, 1985; Petersen, 1979). Studies during the 1980s suggest that, particularly when administered intravenously or by free-basing (smoking), cocaine can induce a very strong psychological dependence (Perez-Reyes, Guiseppi, Ondrusek, Jeffcoat, & Cook, 1982). Dackis and Gold (1985) suggest that several major biochemical events play a role in cocaine dependency, not the least of which is the fact that cocaine inhibits dopamine reuptake by the presynaptic neuron. This has the effect of prolonging the amount of time that substantial amounts of dopamine are available in the synapse. This biochemical effect seems to be the key to the rewarding property of the drug (e.g., euphoria).

Cocaine, also referred to as coke, flake, snow, gold dust, blow, nose candy, and Bolivian marching powder, is a white, translucent, flaky substance. It takes more than 200 pounds of coca leaves to produce a little over 2 pounds of pure cocaine, which is distilled into a paste and mixed with hydrochloric acid before being exported for further processing. Importers cut the potency in half by adding agents like procaine, amphetamines, or even strychnine. Before it gets to the street, local dealers and handlers have cut it further, usually with a sugar substance.

About 11 percent of Americans above the age of 12 have used cocaine at least once (U.S. Department of Health and Human Services, 1994), although the number of users has declined since the 1980s. The availability of cocaine has not changed significantly, but perceptions of cocaine's risk and disapproval of its use appear to have increased (Bachman, Johnston, & O'Malley, 1990).

Coke is very convenient to use (Ashley, 1976). In the United States, cocaine is most frequently inhaled, or **snorted,** into each nostril (see Figure 3.2). The drug is absorbed from the mucous lining into the bloodstream, reaching the brain almost instantaneously. The **oral method** is another way of ingesting cocaine, although it is often assumed to be ineffective. Van Dyke and his colleagues compared the intranasal and oral rates of ingestion and found that three of four volunteers experienced more intensive highs after oral administration (Van Dyke, Jatlow, Ungeru, Barash, & Byck, 1978). How-

**FIGURE 3.2   Inhaling
Cocaine**

ever, the latency of onset was more rapid after snorting. Another, more dangerous method of ingestion is intravenous injection, or **mainlining.**

A typical single dose of cocaine (approximately 30 milligrams) ingested in the most preferred manner (i.e., snorting) usually precipitates a state of euphoria that peaks in a matter of a few minutes. The high typically lasts between 20 and 40 minutes, generally with little or no discernible aftereffects (Ray & Ksir, 1987). Thus, the effects of cocaine are quite similar to those of amphetamines but of shorter duration. A single moderate dose works for about 30 minutes, compared to several hours for amphetamines. The effects are also more subtle and less physical (Julien, 1997).

This altered state of consciousness, however, may be preceded by headache, dizziness, and restlessness. Feelings of fatigue and sleepiness vanish and are replaced by those of exhilaration, newfound energy, and excitement. The individual may have a sense of increased self-confidence, which may be a product of the feelings of enhanced mental abilities. Cocaine has been viewed as a social drug, one that has recreational properties; that is, instead of turning inward, the user becomes talkative and seeks the company of others. The cocaine user's sleep is profoundly affected; both REM sleep and total sleep are greatly reduced. Finally, it has been reported that cocaine may enhance the user's sex drive and sexual experience. At least one study (Resnick, Kestenbaum, & Schwartz, 1977) has produced results that suggest a biphasic effect of cocaine—that is, an initial state of euphoria followed by dysphoria. Six of the subjects in this study reported that, following an initial high, they experienced "postcoke blues" or "crashing," which was characterized by feelings of anxiety, depression, fatigue, and a desire for more cocaine.

Crack

Probably the most serious drug problem today is the smoking of a compound produced with cocaine known as crack. **Crack** consists of cocaine and baking soda mixed with water. The mixture is allowed to dehydrate to form a crystallinelike hardness which then is cracked and broken into small pieces. The term *crack* derives from the cracking sound that is heard when the drug is mixed with these chemicals and heated (Langton, 1991). These pieces are then heated to degrade the compound, and the result is smoked in a pipe.

Unlike cocaine, which produces a slow euphoria that lasts for several minutes, crack produces a fast euphoria that lasts only seconds. As a result, to continue the euphoric feeling, abusers end up using more crack than cocaine to attain a high. This creates a dangerous situation, and abusers easily overdose on crack, doing damage to the cardiovascular system and often producing death.

Cocaine is also sometimes mixed with tobacco, marijuana, and even heroin and is heated, then smoked in a pipe. Because cocaine hydrochloride is volatile only at extremely high temperatures, during which it is degraded, it must be chemically converted back to to its alkaloid state for it to be effective when it is smoked. This is generally referred to as **free-basing** (Jacob, Jones, Benowitz, & Shulgin, 1989; Nelson, 1987). Whatever method of ingestion is selected, the rate of absorption into the system is very rapid (Jeffcoat, Perez-Reyes, Hill, Sadler, & Cook, 1989). Clearly, factors such as how cocaine is ingested and what dosage is used will play a major role in determining both the physiological and the psychological effects of the drug (American Society for Pharmacology and Experimental Therapeutics and Committee on Problems of Drug Dependence, 1987; Resnick, Kestenbaum, & Schwartz, 1977).

As was alluded to earlier, most users do not habitually take high doses of cocaine (Post, 1975; Siegel, 1985), unless it is the crack variety. However, when coke is chronically abused, it produces a toxic syndrome that is typified by an enhanced sense of physical and mental capacity; loss of appetite; grinding of teeth; stereotyped, repetitive behavior; and paranoia. The addict often carries weapons to use against alleged persecutors. Two very commonly reported perceptual changes that occur with cocaine use are the appearance of "cocaine bugs," technically called **formication,** and "snow lights" (Jaffe, 1985). Formication is a tactile disturbance in which the user feels a sensation like bugs crawling under his or her skin; the sensation may become so great that he or she may resort to a knife to cut them out. The physiological basis for this phenomenon is probably drug-induced stimulation of free nerve endings in the skin (Ellinwood, 1969). Snow lights are a visual disturbance in which the user perceives bright flashing lights in his or her visual field.

Until recently, there was some question as to whether tolerance occurs with cocaine use. There were conflicting reports regarding the development of a tolerance to cocaine. Spotts and Schontz (1976), for example, found some support for the then majority view against development of tolerance when their group of habitual users did not increase dose levels over time. The users did, however, experience a kind of temporary tolerance, in that when they administered cocaine several times in a single day, they had to use increasingly larger doses to achieve the same effect.

Today, however, there is considerable evidence that tolerance does develop to many of the physiological and subjective effects of cocaine, especially crack, and in some cases it develops very rapidly (American Society for Pharmacology and Experimental Therapeutics and Committee on Problems of Drug Dependence, 1987; Fischman, Schuster, Javaid, Hatano, & Davis, 1985; Wood & Emmett-Oglesby, 1986). Whether tolerance or sensitization occurs with chronic cocaine use appears to depend on many factors, only some of which are known (Grabowski & Dworkin, 1985).

Withdrawal symptoms following continued high dose use are not dramatic or life threatening. However, cocaine users do experience withdrawal symptoms after extensive cocaine use. Furthermore, the symptoms occur in several phases (Gawin & Kleber, 1986). During the first few hours after heavy use, the cocaine user feels depressed and agitated, lacks an appetite, and experiences high cocaine craving. In the next several hours or days, the user experiences extreme hunger, although cocaine craving is absent. In some individuals there is also a strong abhorrence for cocaine during this time, and the need for sleep is overwhelming. During the next several days the user's sleep patterns and mood return to normal, and there is little cocaine craving.

Subsequently, the user experiences anxiety, a lack of energy, an inability to enjoy normal activities, and high cocaine craving that is enhanced by environmental cues previously associated with cocaine use, such as a particular room, a party, or other friends who also use cocaine. After several weeks, the user's mood and pleasure response return to normal, and he or she experiences only episodic cocaine craving, which again is most common in the presence of specific environmental cues. If the person begins taking cocaine again, he or she generally returns to the first phase of withdrawal.

Although Wetii and Wright (1979) have suggested that only in rare cases does chronic abuse of cocaine prove fatal, today's sports enthusiasts have become tragically aware that cocaine use can be deadly. Obviously, one might predict that extremely high dosage levels of cocaine in pure form would cause problems, but one has to wonder how it is possible that a moderate dose of this drug could kill a world-class athlete such as Leonard Bias of the University of Maryland or Donald Rogers of the Cleveland Browns, who had no known physical weaknesses, while others are able to chronically abuse the drug with no fatal effects. Medical authorities seem to be divided in their explanations of fatal reactions to cocaine but one hypothesis offered by Dr. Grinspoon, a cocaine expert at Harvard University, revolves around the fact that cocaine is a drug. We are all aware of the fact that some people are extremely sensitive to certain drugs (e.g., aspirin, caffeine, penicillin) and cannot take them without severe consequences. Dr. Grinspoon contends that there are some individuals who are especially sensitive to even recreational doses of cocaine and cannot ingest it without suffering severe consequences (Leo, 1986).

Cocaine use may cause sudden death because of cerebral hemorrhaging (Lichtenfeld, Rubin, & Feldman, 1984), convulsion induction (Ellinwood, Kilbey, Castellani, & Khoury, 1977), or acute myocardial infarction (sudden insufficiency of blood to the heart muscles), which can occur even in individuals with no preexisting arterial dysfunctions (American Society for Pharmacology and Experimental Therapeutics and Committee on Problems of Drug Dependence, 1987). While the exact mechanism behind sudden deaths is still obscure, recent evidence suggests that even low doses of cocaine can lead to inflammation of the muscular walls of the heart in some individuals (Grilly, 1998).

NARCOTIC ANALGESICS (OPIATES)

The **opiates** and their derivatives including opium, heroin, morphine, codeine, Percodan, and Demerol, together with their antagonists (e.g., nalorphine) make up the class of consciousness-altering drugs also referred to as **narcotic analgesics** or **strongly addictive analgesics.** Opiates are any natural or synthetic drug that acts upon the body in a way similar to that of **morphine,** which is one of the most powerful analgesics derived from the opium poppy plant, *Papaver somniferum* (see Figure 3.3). The use of the term **narcotic** by law enforcement agencies, medical personnel, and the general public has led to a proliferation of meanings for this term. However, here it will be used to refer to those drugs that have both a **sedative** (sleep-inducing) and an **analgesic** (pain-relieving) action. This definition restricts the term to the opiates.

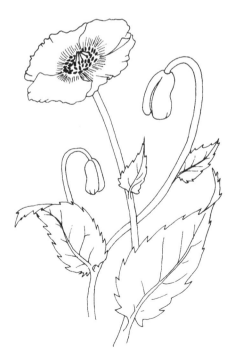

FIGURE 3.3   Opium Poppy Plant (*Papaver somniferum*)

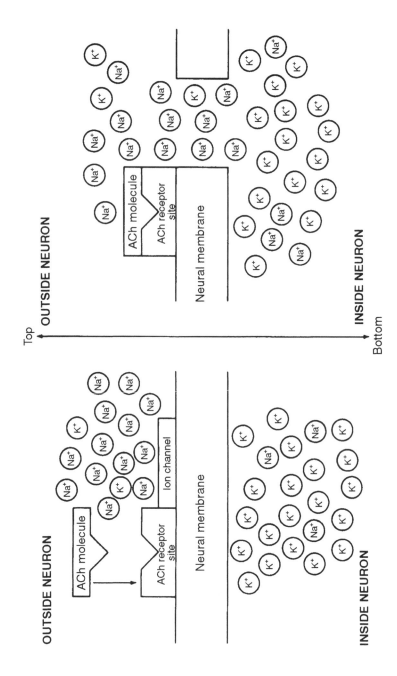

FIGURE 3.4 A Lock-and-Key Mechanism

The primary medical uses of these drugs include the relief of pain, the treatment of diarrhea, and the relief of a cough. Of course they are also quite capable of inducing sleep. However, because of the euphoria associated with the use of these drugs, which may lead to their abuse, they are seldom, if ever, used for this purpose.

It is hypothesized that the opiates may produce their analgesic effects by interacting with receptor sites for "natural opiate substances" called **endorphins** (Leavitt, 1995). The way the opiate drug acts on these sites is suggested to resemble a lock-and-key mechanism (see Figure 3.4). Thus, the receptors are specific nerve cells that serve as locks into which the appropriate opiate drug (the key) fits.

Pert and Snyder (1973) were the first to provide experimental evidence that such receptor sites actually exist. They first injected radioactively tagged naloxone into each of their animal subjects. (Naloxone is a drug whose chemical substance so closely resembles morphine that its molecules fit the same receptor locks. Thus, it acts as an opiate antagonist and competes for the same receptor sites.) This afforded the investigators the opportunity to observe the distribution of radioactivity and thus the distribution of opiate receptors. Their findings suggest that the opiate receptor sites are to be found in especially large numbers in the amygdala, the caudate nucleus, the substantia nigra, the medial nuclei of the thalamus, and the periventricular and periacqueductal gray matter that immediately surrounds the ventricles in the lower portion of the brain. Other investigators—Simantov, Goodman, Aposhian, and Snyder (1976)—discovered that only vertebrates possess receptors of this type. However, the degree to which opiate receptors appear to be constant varies among all vertebrates, from the most primitive to the most advanced.

Another reason for suspecting that the opiates may operate on specific receptor sites in the brain was best expressed by Restak (1977). Restak suggested that the existence of a lock strongly suggests the existence of a key or keys in the brain. Stated differently, if there are opiate receptor sites in the brain, then there should also be opiumlike substances that are manufactured in the brain. In 1975, Hughes, Smith, Kosterlitz, Fothergill, Morgan, and Morris announced their discovery of two short-chained peptides called **enkephalins,** which are produced in the brain and distributed in the same locations as the receptor sites. These results were confirmed in other laboratories (Akil, Watson, Sullivan, & Barchas, 1978). Today, we recognize three distinct families of these opiatelike substances in the brain; in addition to the enkephalins there are the **endorphins** and the **dynorphins** (Akil et al., 1984). Each family is derived from different precursor polypeptides (Marx, 1984).

Such advancement in the understanding of the physiological mechanisms that underlie opiumlike drug activity led Snyder (1977) to offer a theory of opiate addiction. According to Snyder, under normal conditions, opiate receptors are exposed to a certain basal level of enkephalin. If an opiate drug is administered to the individual at this time, the drug molecules will proceed to bind the usually unoccupied receptor sites. The net effect is a potentiation of the analgesic effects of the enkephalin system. If the administration of opiates is continued, the opiate receptor sites are soon overloaded with opiatelike material, causing them to transmit a message, probably by some hypothetical neuronal feedback loop, to the enkephalin neurons to cease firing and releasing enkephalin. Once this occurs, the receptor cells are exposed only to the opiate, and they can now tolerate more of it to make up for the enkephalin they are no longer receiving. When the administration of the opiate is terminated, the opiate receptors find themselves with neither the opiate nor the enkephalin. Snyder believes that this lack initiates a sequence of events that result in withdrawal symptoms.

The opiates produce a depression of neural activity in the respiratory and cough centers of the brainstem, along with a depression of neural activity in the cortex. It also appears that they have an excitatory effect on the neural elements that make up the vomiting center of the brainstem.

Heroin is the most frequently abused narcotic. Horse, Harry, Smack, Stuff, Junk, and just plain H are but a few of the many street names by which this drug is known. The name of the drug is derived from the Greek god Heros, who was the savior of humankind. In a real sense, this is probably how many initially viewed heroin after its discovery in 1874 by Heinrich Dreser. Another opium derivative, morphine, had been used before Dreser's work, both as an analgesic and in the treatment of alcoholism. However, it proved to have one serious side effect: Its use often led to addiction. Dreser, searching for a non-addictive opiate, found that by treating morphine with an inexpensive and readily available chemical called acetic anhydride, he could produce a drug much more potent than morphine without the addictive properties, or so he thought. The new drug rapidly replaced morphine as a painkiller, and by the early 1900s, heroin was being used in the treatment of alcoholism and morphine addiction. Soon it was found, however, that heroin was not only more powerful than morphine but also more addictive. Since 1914 the Harrison Act and subsequent laws and court decisions have progressively restricted the legal use of heroin; today, its use for any purpose is considered illegal.

Opium is derived from the sticky resin produced by the opium poppy plant. Approximately 75 percent of the weight of a given quantity of opium is composed of nonpharmacological organic agents, including oils, sugar, proteins, and resins. The remaining 25 percent includes **morphine,** the major pain-relieving drug found in opium and codeine. Heroin does not occur naturally but is a semisynthetic derivative produced by a chemical modification of morphine, which leads to an increase in the end product's (heroin's) potency. Thus, heroin is approximately three times as potent as morphine (Snyder, 1977). What you might not suspect, however, is that this increase in potency of heroin over morphine has nothing to do with increased activity at the receptor sites in the nervous system, but rather is due to the fact that heroin crosses the blood-brain barrier much more rapidly than does morphine. This allows it to accumulate in the brain much more quickly. Once in the brain, heroin is metabolized into morphine, but because it gets there so rapidly, it exerts effects that are much more rapid and intense than those of morphine (Grilly, 1998).

Manufacturers and distributors of street heroin take little care in its production and cutting. Quinine, milk sugar, and talc are commonly used to cut the drug (Duvall, Locke, & Brill, 1963). According to Hoffmann and Hoffmann (1975), the heroin content of packets seized by police generally ranges between 1 and 5 percent. As we will see shortly, many of the substances and dilutents are directly harmful.

Heroin is usually introduced into the body by smoking, snorting, eating, skin popping, or mainlining. Oral ingestion leads to a slower and considerably less complete high than that produced by other routes. Mainliners experience a **rush,** an immediate and intense pleasure seconds after the drug is injected into the bloodstream. Current thought suggests that heroin does not reach the brain that quickly and that this rush is most probably due to a powerful action on the peripheral nervous system or on the cardiovascular system. Some of the cutting agents are poorly soluble in the injected solution, and an intravenous injection of incompletely dissolved substances may cause a fatal reaction (Eiseman, Lam, & Rush, 1964). In the case of skin popping, the liquefied heroin is injected just beneath the surface of the skin. Such a technique can lead to the development of severe multiple ulcerating lesions. These lesions most likely are caused by the quinine or other agents used to cut the heroin, and they create a most favorable environment for the development of tetanus (Hirsch, 1972).

Upon ingesting heroin, the user experiences a restriction of awareness and an almost immediate and intense feeling of pleasure in the abdominal area, which typically lasts about one to five minutes and is often described as resembling a whole-body orgasm (Leavitt, 1995; Mathis, 1970). This brief euphoric spasm, called a "rush," "bang," or "kick," is followed by a sense of euphoria and contentment that may last from four to six hours. During this high period, the heroin user is able to escape reality and experiences the predominantly pleasant feelings of relaxation, euphoria, and reverie. The user feels sedated—"nods"—during which time there may be vivid visions and dreams. Since the heroin user no longer cares about much of anything, he or she does not seem to be bothered by tensions and anxieties. Everything looks rosy and harmonious, at least until the drug effects wear off. As one might predict, heroin has a dramatic effect on pain perception and the response to it. The major effect on pain, however, is not so much to raise the pain threshold as to simply change the response to pain. Heroin makes the pain more bearable.

Along with these behavioral and consciousness-altering effects, heroin also produces some physiological effects. These reactions include pupillary constriction (pinpoint pupils), changes in body temperature, constipation, nausea, and vomiting (Julien, 1997). Clearly, not all of these reactions are pleasant. However, the negative physiological effects seem to be overridden by the euphoria and the escape from reality. As one might expect, individuals vary widely in their reactions to the drug. Thus, for some, the introduction to heroin is anything but pleasant. Such "experimenters" may only experience the discomforts associated with heroin use.

Intermittent use of heroin may be continued indefinitely by some people, who eventually quit without difficulty (Chien, Gerard, Lee, & Rosenfeld, 1964). Continued use of heroin results in the development of both a psychological dependence and a tolerance and physiological craving for the drug. After frequent and repeated administration of smack for two or three weeks, a tenfold tolerance can easily develop. Although the actual time necessary to establish a drug habit varies considerably from individual to individual, it has been estimated that continued use over one month or longer is sufficient to develop a physiological addiction (Grilly, 1998). The definition of addiction is complicated by the fact that most heroin addicts have tried, and sometimes regularly use, other drugs, including alcohol, amphetamines, barbiturates, and cocaine. When people consume more than one drug, it is hard to classify them as addicts of one drug or another (Istvan & Matarazzo, 1984). The addicts find that the high is followed by a negative phase that produces a desire for more of the drug. If for some reason the drug supply is cut off for even a short time, the heroin addict enters into a phase of withdrawal, during which he or she becomes physically ill. Within four to six hours after stopping, withdrawal discomforts are felt, which turn into agonies by 12 to 16 hours after the last dose. Sweating, shaking, vomiting, running nose and eyes, chills, aching muscles, abdominal pain, and diarrhea are common (Julien, 1997). However, withdrawal from heroin does not cause death.

PSYCHEDELICS AND HALLUCINOGENS

The drugs included in this class are a highly varied group of chemical compounds, all of which have the ability to induce visual, auditory, somesthetic or other **hallucination,** a sense perception for which there is no appropriate external stimulus. For this reason these agents have been called **hallucinogens.** These drugs may also produce disturbances in the individual's thoughts and perceptions and in some instances may produce behavioral patterns that have described as being similar to the components of psychotic behavior. Because they are thought to be able to mimic psychoses or induce a psychotic state, they are often referred to as **psychotomimetic drugs.**

Since both of these terms focus on a single pharmacological action of these drugs rather than their full range of actions, they seem inappropriate. Additionally, there is some question concerning the accuracy of the use of these terms in referring to this category of drugs. For example, these drugs most frequently distort rather than produce sensory images. Thus, the user sees and hears what is going on in his or her world but in very strange and different ways. Additionally, a careful analysis of the effects of these drugs suggests that they are really unlike the behavioral patterns observed during psychotic episodes. Osmond (1957), observing that all of the drugs in this category had the ability to alter sensory perception and therefore may be considered mind-expanding, proposed the term **psychedelic drugs** as a label for this group of chemical compounds (Julien, 1997).

As we suggested at the beginning of this section, the category contains a number of drugs that vary considerably in their chemical structure. Like most of the drugs we have discussed to this point, many of these agents produce their effect by changing the synaptic transmission process. Thus, *physostigmine* and *diisopropyl fluorophosphate (DFP)* increase the amounts of *acetylcholine (ACh)* available at the synapse by blocking *acetylcholinesterase's* ability to terminate achetylcholine's transmitter action. Other psychedelic drugs block the neurotransmission activity of ACh. This is the case with both *atropine* and *scopolamine*. *Muscarine's* effect at the acetylcholinergic synapse is that of directly stimulating the ACh receptor sites on the postsynaptic neuron. Together, these drugs constitute the **acetylcholine psychedelics.**

Norepinephrine psychedelics are those psychedelics that alter synaptic transmission at the norepinephrine synapses. Many of these drugs are closely related in structure to norepinepherine and are thought to exert their effects through changes of transmission at norepinephrine synapses.

A number of the psychedelic drugs, including *dimethyltryptamine (DMT)*, *bufotenin, psilocin, psilocybin, lysergic acid diethylamide (LSD)*, and *diethyltryptamine*, have been found to be structurally similar to the neurotransmitter substance *serotonin* (5-hydroxytryptamine) and are thought to produce their effect by changing the synaptic transmission process at serotonergic synapses.

The **psychedelic anesthetics,** including *phencyclidine (PCP), Sernylan*, and *ketamine (Ketalar)*, represent a unique grouping within this category; they do not resemble structurally any of the known neurotransmitters. This has made it particularly difficult to determine the sites and mechanisms of the action of these drugs.

The final grouping, the **cannabis drugs,** includes *marijuana* and *hashish*. While we have known about the cannabinols for a long time, we have yet to determine exactly how and where these drugs produce their effect. In this section we have selected marijuana and lysergic acid diethylamide (LSD) as representatives of this category.

Marijuana

The earliest known record of marijuana use dates back to 2737 B.C. A description of the drug was found in a book of medicines belonging to the Chinese emperor Shen Nung. Its use as an intoxicant spread to India, where it became a favorite ingredient in Indian cookery. During the nineteenth century,

English ladies visiting India enjoyed their afternoon tea, which was often served with teacakes containing marijuana. From India the use of this drug spread to North Africa and then to Europe. It is believed that one of the major factors involved in this later extension was the return of Napoleon's troops to France after the Egyptian campaign.

Although it had been known in South and Central America for centuries, marijuana did not appear to any significant extent in the United States until about 1920 (Grinspoon, 1969). Snyder (1971) observed that a century ago, cannabis (the common hemp plant from which marijuana comes) was used for medical reasons, much as aspirin is today. It could be found in almost any drugstore, could be purchased without prescription, and was commonly prescribed by physicians for many common medical problems such as ulcers, headaches, cramps, and tooth decay.

In the 1920s the press decided that marijuana was a societal evil that was being used and spread in this country by the underworld element. Claiming an association between marijuana and the increase in crime, a New Orleans newspaper called for outlawing the drug. Shortly thereafter, laws were passed in Louisiana to rid the state of this agent of evil. This push to have marijuana declared illegal was spearheaded by the then Commissioner of Narcotics, Harry Anslinger, who had a strong interest in encouraging the states and the Bureau of Narcotics to enforce rigorously the laws against the drug. His position that marijuana was a narcotic, an agent responsible for crimes of violence, and a great danger to public safety was popularized in the news media. Eventually, this led to the passage of a federal law in 1937, which outlawed marijuana completely. By 1940 the country was convinced that marijuana was a "killer weed" that drove people to insanity and violence. Nevertheless, it became widely used during the 1960s and 1970s. Since 1979 its use has declined, largely because of growing disapproval and concern about perceived risks (Bachman, Johnston, O'Malley, & Humphrey, 1988). However, marijuana use may be on the rise, especially among individuals aged 12–17 (Chalsma & Boyum, 1994). An estimated 70 million Americans aged 12 and older have used marijuana at sometime in their lives (U.S. Department of Health and Human Services, 1994).

Technically, marijuana is not a drug but rather the leaves and buds of the hemp plant, *Cannabis sativa*, which grows in Jamaica, Mexico, India, the Middle East, and most of the United States (see Figure 3.5). These leaves and buds contain over 400 different chemicals called *cannabinoids*, most of which are probably not psychoactive even in high doses. The major psychoactive chemical in marijuana is delta-9-tetrahydrocannabinol (THC), a compound that was first synthesized in Israel in the 1960s and is very expensive to manufacture (Grilly, 1998; Grinspoon & Bakalar, 1993). In its naturally occurring form, it is concentrated in the sticky resin of the flowers and seeds of the female plant and, to a much lesser extent, in the leaves and branches of both male and female plants. Besides THC, there are two other cannabinoids, cannabi-

FIGURE 3.5
Cannabis Sativa Leaf

nol and cannabidiol, which may be active at high doses, though not at the levels found in street marijuana. However, Karniol and Carlini (1972) have found that cannabinol and cannabidiol interact with THC to modify its effects; this may help to explain, in part at least, why users experience different effects with different varieties of marijuana grown in different localities. Finally, Stephens (1987) has shown that the concentration of THC in marijuana has slowly increased during the last decade from an average of less than 1 percent before 1974 to an average of nearly 2 percent in samples taken between 1974 and 1979. More recently, some samples with 4 to 5 percent THC have been observed (Grilly, 1998).

Exactly how marijuana produces its effects is not clear. Our lack of understanding of these mechanisms is due to some unique characteristics of THC (Martin, 1986). First, it is highly soluble in lipids (fat) and therefore is absorbed in high concentrations in practically all of the body tissues. Second, it alters just about every biological system in which it is found. Precisely what the significance is of these effects, especially in light of THC's psychoactive properties, is very difficult to determine. However, several investigators have called attention to the many behavioral and pharmacological similarities between the effects of marijuana and those of the anticholinergic drugs (Miller & Branconnier, 1983). The latter block activity in a part of the brain called the hippocampus, and it has been argued that marijuana acts via the same mechanism (Campbell, Foster, Hampson, & Deadwyler, 1986).

As evidence for this position, the effects of marijuana, anticholinergics, and hippocampectomy were compared on various behaviors. All three produced decrements in both the acquisition and performance of maze behaviors, impaired sequential behaviors, and impaired short-term memory. They also interfered with the ability to concentrate, reduced conditioned emotional responses, increased resistance to extinction, and produced state-dependent learning. Additionally, many of the physiological effects of marijuana, such as dry mouth and increased heart rate, are the same as those produced by anticholinergic drugs.

Finally, in 1992, a natural marijuanalike compound was found in the mammalian brain (Devane et al., 1992). Researchers had known for some time that there exist brain receptor sites that attract the THC of marijuana, but most believed that these receptors had evolved to serve as receptors for a natural brain compound, not a plant derivative. Devane and his colleagues called this new substance *anadamide,* from the Sanskrit *ananda,* which means "bliss." When purified, the natural substance is a little less powerful than THC. It appears that anandamide plays a role in the regulation of mood, memory, pain, movement, and other activities (Dworetzky, 1997).

The physiological effects of marijuana closely resemble those produced by the sympathetic nervous system when it is mildly stimulated. Small to moderate doses of THC usually lead to feelings of well-being and euphoria; large doses can cause paranoia, hallucinations, and dizziness (Fackelmann, 1993). The most common physical effects of THC are an increase in heart rate and a reddening of the eyes. However, attention, short-term memory, and coordination can be impaired (Block, Farinpour, & Braverman, 1992; Block & Ghoneim, 1993; Grinspoon & Bakalar, 1993; Leavitt, 1995). Additionally, gastrointestinal symptoms, such as diarrhea and nausea may occur (Brown, 1971, 1972). Cardiovascular effects include an elevated systolic blood pressure and an increased pulse rate. No change in respiration rate, pupil size, or blood-sugar level is observed (Hollister, 1971; Rossi, Kuehnle, & Mendelson, 1978). The eyes may be bloodshot. Certain spinal reflexes may be elicited more easily than normally, suggesting a lower sensory threshold.

How does the inhalation of marijuana alter the user's awareness? First, it should be noted that the subjective experiences reported by "pot" smokers vary considerably, and it now seems clear that an *expectancy effect* does operate in this situation. In fact, an expectancy effect appears to operate for subjective reports of all consciousness-altering drugs (Barber, 1970). This means simply that the smoker often describes what he or she thinks the experience ought to be. When compared with some of the other drugs discussed in this chapter, marijuana takes effect fairly slowly, and the subjective experiences may take as long as 10 minutes to occur after the user has inhaled the smoke, even longer when the drug is ingested. It is quite possible, however, that these experiences may persist for considerable periods of time. This is because marijuana is metabolized slowly and its half-life in humans has been estimated to be as long as 48 hours (Ray & Ksir, 1987).

According to Tart (1972), perhaps the most striking experiences reported by subjects are changes in perception. They observed physical objects to be clearer than they were before using marijuana. They examined shapes and colors very carefully. Their auditory perception underwent a similar change, sounds being more vivid and musical notes being more pure. Some subjects reported that listening to music became a "total experience." Touch, taste, and smell also appeared to be similarly enhanced. Users generally reported increased appetite and appreciation for the flavor of food (Foltin, Brady, & Fischman, 1986).

Marijuana users also regularly report perceptual distortion of space and time. They may judge distances inaccurately and overestimate the passage of time. It is these perceptual changes that may account, at least in part, for the findings reported by Petersen (1977, 1979) and Klonoff (1974). These investigators suggest that smoking the amounts of marijuana that are commonly used is detrimental to performance in automobile driving, whether it is measured in the laboratory or on the road. Miller, McFarland, Cornett, Brightwell, and Wikler (1977) found that marijuana causes a change in attention span, combined with an impairment of driving skills. Whatever the cause, this decrement in driving skill has been firmly established as a contributor to automobile fatalities (Sterling-Smith, 1976). It is interesting to note that over the last several years there has been a significant change in the recognition of these effects by the general population and marijuana users in particular. Before 1975 the majority of marijuana users denied that marijuana impaired driving skills, whereas since 1975 there has been a growing recognition by these individuals that driving skills are impaired by the substance (Grilly, 1981). Hollister (1986) also demonstrated that after getting high on marijuana, airplane pilots evidence a marked decrease in performance in flight simulators.

Sexual pleasure seemed to be increased, although this apparently is due in large part to generally heightened perceptual awareness. In any event, there is little concrete evidence that sexual performance is improved; indeed, with large doses it is likely to be significantly impaired. Recent animal model studies as well as some human studies have demonstrated that prolonged exposure to marijuana exerts significant harmful effects on the male reproductive system, including the development of abnormal sperm cells (Husain, 1989; Husain & Patra, 1989).

Drowsiness and sleep may occur if the marijuana user gets high alone. However, if taken in the presence of others, the drug is more likely to induce a euphoric mood. Feelings of detachment and happiness and preoccupation with simple and familiar things are likely to dominate the individual's conscious awareness. Sometimes the user experiences a paranoid state in which he or she is keenly aware of others watching. If the surrounding company seems unpleasant, the user typically withdraws rather than resorting to antisocial behavior. Marijuana users exhibit antisocial behavior only rarely. While prolonged and regular use of the drug does not bring about the development of a physical dependency, it may result in a feeling of apathy, especially in adolescence; this is often referred to as the *amotivational syndrome*. Such a phenomenon has not been observed in the general population, however.

Marijuana disrupts memory formation, both long-term and short-term. This is found to occur with both verbal and graphic material. The effect on long-term memory recall is more prominent than with recognition. Much of the memory disruption seems to be due to increased imagery and thought flow due to the intrusion of irrelevant associations (Hooker & Jones, 1987). The drug also interferes with immediate recall of information learned only a few

... before. Finally, such cognitive effects outlast the period of smoking (Pope & Yurgelun-Todd, 1996; Smith, 1995). It would appear that being stoned is not conducive to learning.

For decades, policymakers have debated whether to legalize marijuana. Many people, scientists and nonscientists alike, have tended to consider marijuana a relatively benign substance—a recreational drug—compared to drugs such as heroin and cocaine. Moreover, it has recently been demonstrated that this agent also has some therapeutic uses, such as in the treatment of the eye disorder glaucoma (Jaffe, 1985) and alleviating the nausea and vomiting caused by chemotherapy in the treatment of cancer as well as the treatment of such ailments as asthma, seizures, and spastic conditions (Grinspoon & Bakalar, 1993; Relman, 1982). Melzack (1990) argued that people typically do not become addicted when using drugs medically. Contrary to this popular view, Wickelgren (1997) reports that there is now new evidence that suggests that the effects of marijuana in the brain is quite similar to those of such hard drugs as cocaine and heroin.

Lysergic Acid Diethylamide (LSD)

Last Friday, April 16, 1943, I was forced to stop my work in the laboratory in the middle of the afternoon and to go home, as I was seized by a particular restlessness associated with a sensation of mild dizziness. On arriving home, I lay down and sank into a kind of drunkenness which was not unpleasant and which was characterized by extreme activity of imagination. As I lay in a dazed condition with my eyes closed (I experienced daylight as disagreeably bright) there surged upon me an uninterrupted stream of fantastic images of extraordinary plasticity and vividness and accompanied by an intense kaleidoscope-like play of colors. This condition gradually passed off after two hours.

Thus wrote Albert Hofmann (Hofmann, 1971, p. 23), the Swiss chemist, who in 1938 first extracted d-lysergic acid diethylamide (LSD-25). He was describing his experiences following the accidental ingestion of a small amount of this substance. As we noted earlier, acid, sugar, big D, trips, or micro-dots, as LSD-25 is called in the language of the streets, is an extremely potent hallucinogen. The average dosage that produces changes in the individual's state of awareness or consciousness—what Barron, Jarvik, and Bunnell (1964) called the **psychomimetic effects**—is approximately 0.5–1.0 micrograms of LSD per kilogram of body weight.

What is even more amazing is the fact that, if such a dosage is taken orally, only about 1 percent of it will ever reach the brain (Freedman & Halaris, 1978). While it is generally agreed that the use of LSD probably does not produce either physical or psychological dependency, the user does develop a tolerance for the drug very quickly. After three or four days of use,

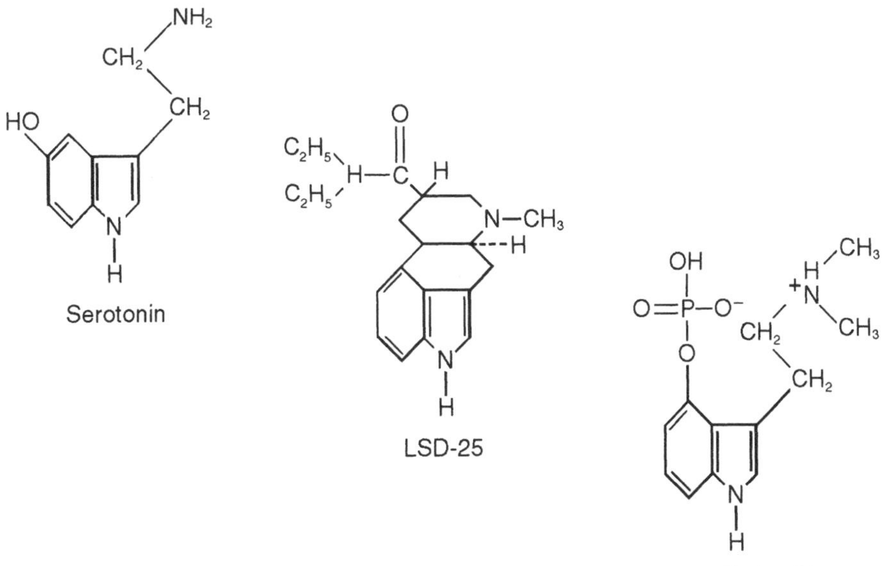

FIGURE 3.6   Indole Ring

previously effective dosage levels become ineffective. However, this tolerance appears to be lost after an equal period of abstinence.

Chemical analysis of this white, tasteless, odorless powder reveals that structurally, LSD-25 is composed of a lysergic acid and a diethylamide portion. The former is a natural product of the ergot fungus that can be found growing on grains, especially rye. The latter component is related structurally to certain other drugs that are commonly employed as smooth-muscle relaxants. Perhaps the most interesting chemical feature of the LSD molecule, however, is the existence of what chemists refer to as an indole ring. As you can see in Figure 3.6, the indole ring is characteristic, not only of LSD and psilocybin, but also of the neurotransmitter substance serotonin (Sepinwall & Cook, 1980).

At present, exactly how the LSD-25 molecule exerts its effects on an individual's state of consciousness is not completely understood. However, current theory suggests that LSD acts as a blocker of activity of serotonergic neurons in the brain, possibly by activating the serotonergic autoreceptors directly on cell bodies (Rech & Commissaris, 1982; Rech & Rosecrans, 1982). The most recent evidence suggests that LSD induces the majority of these behavioral effects postsynaptically, by acting as agonist at a specific subtype of serotonin receptor (Cunningham & Appel, 1987; Jacobs, 1987). Large numbers of these receptors are located in neocortical, limbic, and brainstem areas. The brainstem consists of two centers in the reticular activating system called the dorsal and medial raphe nuclei. Mokler and his colleagues have demonstrated that these two areas are likely candidates for many of LSD's effects, since microinjections of LSD into these areas produce the most pronounced LSD-type effects in animals (Mokler, Stoudt, Sherman, & Rech, 1986).

What types of changes in consciousness might one expect to experience after ingesting an average dose of LSD? A psychology professor at Harvard University during the height of the drug culture, Dr. Timothy Leary, described his experiences with the drug as being religiouslike. Admitting to having used LSD on hundreds of occasions, he believed that the drug made him more creative and gave him insights into daily life, religion, and philosophy that would otherwise not come about. He even advocated to his students that they should try this drug. This got him into trouble with his university, and shortly thereafter he was relieved of his academic responsibilities.

The experiences that individuals report with the abuse of LSD vary from individual to individual. And such variables as the user's mental set, the environmental setting, and the drug itself often contribute to the variety of experiences reported. However, some of the more typical experiences with LSD will now be described.

After LSD is applied to a sugar cube and this is then ingested, there is generally a period of 30 to 45 minutes during which no effects occur. This is followed by a period of 8 to 10 hours during which the individual goes through changes in sensory perception, lability of emotional experiences, and feelings of depersonalization and detachment. These changes in awareness typically peak between the second and fourth hour of the LSD experience.

Chief among these experiences are the changes reported in sensory perception. Katz, Waskow, and Olsson (1968) observed that while there is a feeling of perceptual sharpness, perceptions of the outer world take on an unreal quality. Vision appears to be the sense that is affected most profoundly (Levine, 1969). Illusions develop initially as both objects and people in the environment appear to change color, shape, and perspective (Lingeman, 1974). Walls and other objects may become wavy and appear to move; colors seem brighter and more intense. Bizarre shapes and designs that have no basis in reality may be seen (Siegel, 1977). Generally, awareness of time is also affected to the point at which the individual cannot distinguish among past, present, and future. Often, the LSD user reports the visual perception of music or the "warmth" of red and the "icy" feeling of blue. This curious phenomenon, which involves the translation of one type of sensory experience into another, is called **synesthesia.** Such distortions in consciousness, when combined with an emotional state of euphoria, are descriptive of what was labeled a "mind-expanding" trip during the LSD craze of the 1960s.

Many of the early, prominent proponents of the drug, such as author Aldous Huxley (1894–1963), as cited by Ray and Ksir (1987), suggested that its use allowed them to achieve a degree of personal insight, increased their sensitivity, produced mystical experiences, and helped them to develop an understanding of their place in the universe that they could not have achieved in any other way. Lilly (1972) observed that the LSD experience may lead not only to mystical or transcendental adventures, but also to profound insights. It has been suggested that LSD experiences can bring about an enhancement of creative activity. One of the problems with relying on a drug for creative production is that the drug does not provide "the checks and balances between intuition and analytic reason required for genuine creation" (Grinspoon & Bakalar, 1979, p. 267). During the drug experience, you are unable to communicate your new insights, partly because of the drug's effects on motor abilities. After taking LSD, users do not show any more creativity than they did beforehand (Dusek & Girdano, 1980).

In addition to altering the state of awareness, LSD produces a number of physiological effects. Ataxia, or loss of muscle coordination, and spastic paralysis are frequently observed. Autonomic effects include an elevated heart rate (tachycardia) and blood pressure, faster and more erratic breathing, excessive amounts of sugar in the blood (hyperglycemia), elevation in body temperature, and pupillary dilation.

Not all LSD experiences can be described as pleasant, mind-expanding trips. In fact, some experiences, referred to as "bad trips," can be extremely harrowing and traumatic. Although the problem has been addressed experimentally (Blacker, Jones, Stone, & Pfefferbaum, 1968), exactly what determines whether a trip will be pleasurable or nightmarish remains unknown. As in the pleasurable trip, hallucinations constitute a dominant feature of the bad LSD experience. Objects and people in the environment, as well as one's own body image, may become so distorted that they are perceived as grotesque and threatening. These perceptions may seem so unreal that they produce a feeling of detachment from the real world. Strange and bizarre thoughts and emotions may creep into consciousness, and the user may have mental experiences causing him or her to feel completely out of control. Such thoughts may represent a major break with reality—a belief that one can fly, walk on water, or perform some other amazing feat. Depression and feelings of acute anxiety or panic are often a part of the bad trip. Occasionally, these feelings may lead to extremely dangerous self-directed behavior, including suicide.

Smith and Rose (1967–1968) observed that a feeling of paranoia may also develop in which the individual fears not only strangers but friends and relatives as well. Because of the fear that accompanies bad LSD trips, Tinklenberg and Stillman (1970) believe that the user's resorting to assaultive behavior would be highly unlikely and that, should it occur, it would be poorly executed. Although these acute effects dissipate within 6 to 12 hours after the ingestion of LSD, a very small minority of individuals continue to experience mental confusion, perceptual distortions, and poor concentration beyond this time—in some cases for days or weeks. In extremely rare cases, individuals have complained about mental and emotional disturbances several years after being exposed to LSD (Jaffe, 1985).

Finally, some individuals experience the phenomenon of flashbacks. The flashback is a spontaneous, involuntary recurrence of perceptual distortions or hallucinations that may follow LSD use weeks or even months later. Abraham (1983) has observed that one of the most common precipitants of these episodes is entering a dark environment. Flashbacks may produce changes every bit as vivid as those experienced during the original trip. However, since the individual is completely unprepared for such an experience, he or she is likely to react to it with fear, anxiety, and, in some cases, psychotic behavior (Brecher and the Editors of Consumer Reports, 1972; Horowitz, 1969; National Institute of Drug Abuse, 1992).

Cohen (1981) has suggested that flashbacks represent some type of learning phenomenon that occurs in predisposed individuals during acute stress. Studies of individuals who have experienced flashbacks suggest that these individuals had strong tendencies to fantasize and were highly suggestible before their LSD use (Silling, 1980). Thus, it is possible that, after an LSD experience they may encounter a situation that reminds them of the experience and elicits a small, conditioned response that they are able to elaborate on and interpret as a druglike experience. Others have hypothesized that some flashbacks are a product of visual seizures (Abraham, 1983).

To summarize, many drugs have been, or are being, abused by adults as well as by children as young as four or five years of age. Whenever a "new" drug becomes available, there are individuals who will try it and find that it produces a new consciousness-altering experience. This person will describe the experience to his or her friends, and they may proceed to try it. Thus, we have the makings of a new drug of abuse. Very little can be done to protect society from such abuse except to prohibit the use of the drug totally, even for beneficial medical purposes. This is impractical, however; besides, it would not halt the abuse of drugs any more than Prohibition stopped the use of alcohol in the United States. As was mentioned in Weil's (1972) theory in Chapter 1, many humans have a drive to experience altered states of consciousness. Unfortunately, this drive may exhibit itself in the abuse of certain drugs such as the ones described in this chapter. Our list is by no means comprehensive or all-inclusive. We have chosen to discuss what we consider the most abused drugs. We hope that this list will not grow with the continued development of the study of consciousness in the the years to come. However, in all likelihood, it will, because people inevitably choose these drugs to express their drive to experience different states or levels of consciousness.

As we have seen, drugs affect behavior and have dramatic and immediate effects on consciousness. As human beings ingest drugs, they alter their states of consciousness in profound ways. Sometimes the changes are mild and produce only states of relaxation. At other times the changes are profound and long-lasting and produce anywhere from mild to serious changes in mood, temper, personality, and behavior. When psychologists study such changes in behavior, they are studying the effects of how drugs alter consciousness. They have studied particularly carefully both how various dosages of various drugs affect consciousness and the relationship between drug dosage and changes in states or levels of consciousness. If we consider consciousness as a state of awareness, drugs clearly alter that state in significant ways.

FOR FURTHER READING

Grilly, D. (1998). *Drugs and human behavior* (3rd ed.). Boston: Allyn and Bacon.

Jones-Witters, P., & Witters, W. L. (1983). *Drugs and society: A biological perspective*. Belmont, CA: Wadsworth.

Julien, R. M. (1997). *A primer of drug action* (8th ed.). San Francisco: Freeman.

McKim, W. A. (1997). *Drugs and behavior: An introduction to behavioral pharmacology* (4th ed.). Englewood Cliffs, NJ: Prentice-Hall.

Milkman, H. B., & Shaffer, H. J. (Eds.). (1985). *The addictions: Multidisciplinary perspectives and treatments*. Lexington, MA: Lexington Books.

4

HYPNOSIS

Hypnosis has long been a popular topic of discussion by both psychologists and nonpsychologists. Many individuals' only exposure to hypnosis has been the most stereotyped version, namely, stage hypnosis. In this form of entertainment, audience members are hypnotized and then asked to perform all sorts of strange acts. Some may be made to sing the "Star-Spangled Banner"; others may be asked to act like a turkey and gobble about on stage. It appears to the audience that the hypnotist has complete control over the participant's behavior.

As a result of the popularity of stage hypnosis, the fear of losing control by potential hypnosis subjects, and the many misconceptions concerning the reality of hypnosis and its usefulness off stage, hypnosis has received an inordinate share of bad press. Furthermore, people often ask whether hypnosis is a real manipulation or is simply an act performed by entertainers. If it is a bona fide phenomenon, what is it? Why is it that some people can be hypnotized readily while others cannot? What does it feel like to experience hypnosis? Is hypnosis an altered state of consciousness? These questions and many others will be addressed in this chapter as we consider hypnosis as an area of study in the psychology of consciousness.

In the scientific investigation of hypnosis, a clear definition of the phenomenon has still not been produced. However, several attempts have been made to describe some of the processes that underlie hypnosis. Some have identified hypnosis as a trance state or as an altered state of consciousness (Hilgard, 1965, 1979). Others assert that hypnotized individuals do not behave as they do because they are in a trance; rather, they are striving to enact the role of a hypnotized subject as it is defined by the hypnotist and society in general (Coe, 1978; Coe & Sarbin, 1977; Sarbin & Coe, 1972, 1979). Still others have described hypnosis as a normal state of awareness or consciousness involving the holding of positive attitudes, strong motivations to perform a suggested task, and positive expectancies of the hypnosis situation (Barber, Spanos, & Chaves, 1974). Regardless of how hypnosis is defined, we do know that it is a manipulation that can often affect or alter behavior.

Before discussing the contemporary applications of hypnosis in science and behavior, we need to elucidate the role of hypnosis in the study of consciousness. A brief historical overview of this manipulation will then be presented, along with a discussion of the various theoretical explanations of what hypnosis is and is not, in light of existing experimental evidence.

HYPNOSIS AND CONSCIOUSNESS

As we stated in Chapter 1, our definition of consciousness is synonymous with the concept of awareness. To be aware of an event is to be fully conscious or cognizant of its occurrence. When we are not aware of an event, this generally indicates that the information from its occurrence either is not processed or is being processed at a level below consciousness.

It appears that a different level of awareness operates during hypnosis than during the nonhypnotic state. When individuals are hypnotized, they may or may not feel sleepy, although they usually do feel a bit more relaxed than usual. They report experiencing behavior that differs from their normal state of consciousness or awareness (Hilgard, 1977b, 1987). While hypnotized, individuals have an increased susceptibility to suggestions. They also experience enhanced imagery and imagination, including the availability of visual memories from the past, although many of these memories may be distorted (Loftus, 1979). Hypnotized individuals also experience a loss of initiative and lack the desire to make and carry out plans of their own. This change from their normal state of consciousness is only relative, for the hypnotic subject retains the ability to initiate or terminate actions. In other words, the popular belief that a hypnotized individual experiences a total loss of control is simply not true. People cannot be made to commit certain acts against their will.

There is also a reduction in reality testing for hypnotized subjects. For example, they accept falsified memories, they may show a change in their own personality, they may modify the rate at which they process time, and they may experience the presence of an object that is physically not present or they may not perceive an object that is present.

Because of the nature of the behavior exhibited by hypnotized subjects, hypnosis is considered to be an integral part of the study of consciousness. Studying the phenomenon of hypnosis may help to unravel many of the mysteries of how, and at what level, information is processed. Furthermore, we will see how hypnosis can be employed to help focus or refocus the processing of information for modifying behavior that is not as easily shaped or changed in the normal state of awareness or consciousness.

HISTORICAL DEVELOPMENT

The earliest reference to the use of a manipulation resembling hypnosis most probably can be traced (Shor, 1979) to a Viennese physician, Franz Anton Mesmer (1734–1815). In the latter part of the eighteenth century, Mesmer demonstrated that behavior could be affected with the use of magnetic plates that would induce so-called cosmic fluids to react in individuals. He called this reaction *animal magnetism*. Animal magnetism was demonstrated by placing magnetized metal bottles of water in a large wooden tub called a baquet. Beneath the bottles in the tub was a surface of powdered glass and iron filings. The tub was subsequently filled with water and covered with a top containing openings through which iron rods were passed. The rods were then applied to a subject's body. Since the tub was, in reality, a crude form of battery, the applications of such rods produced a mild electrical charge.

The *mesmerist* (as early hypnotists were called) would then apply his hands to the subject's body. The result of this was the induction of convulsions and seizures, which in all likelihood were produced by the electrical current. This process was known as **mesmerism**. Afterward, the subject often reported an alleviation of minor aches and pains. In some instances, more severe afflictions, such as blindness and deafness, were reported to have been successfully treated. As you can imagine, the treatments that Mesmer provided were highly controversial and met with considerable disfavor from the medical and scientific communities.

In 1784 a commission headed by Benjamin Franklin, historically referred to as the Franklin Commission, was organized to pass judgment on the value of animal magnetism; this commission disaffirmed the existence and value of the technique. This conclusion did not represent the personal views of Franklin, who believed that mesmerism did have some curative powers (McConkey & Perry, 1985). Other Franklin contemporaries, such as the Marquis de Lafayette and George Washington, also believed that mesmerism had some value.

The Marquis de Puysegur (1751–1825) also saw some promise in the mesmeric demonstrations. Unlike Mesmer, and in agreement with the Franklin Commission, the Marquis did not believe that the results reported and observed were due to the production of seizures and convulsions. Rather, he felt that the presence of a trancelike state was the major reason for the ability to treat afflictions with mesmerism. In such a state, the subject could respond to suggestions made by the mesmerist. For example, since Mesmer performed his "cures" in a darkened room while going from patient to patient and touching each of them, this could suggest to patients that "magnetism" was being transferred from Mesmer to them. Owing to such a belief, patients would have instilled in them the indirect suggestion that a cure was taking place. Such a suggestion was likely a reason why many of Mesmer's patients felt that they had been helped with their various afflictions. As such, animal magnetism was superfluous in the treatment of Mesmer's patients.

With the focus of mesmerism shifted toward a trancelike manipulation and away from the mystical concept of animal magnetism, John Elliotson (1791–1868), a British physician, tried to gain consent to teach mesmerism at University College Medical School in London. Unfortunately, he failed. As a matter of fact, this suggestion met with such furor that he was subsequently forbidden to practice his trade within the confines of his affiliated medical school hospital. As a result of his futile effort, Elliotson resigned his position at the medical school and established the first journal devoted to the study of mesmerism, the *Zoist*.

During the same period, James Esdaile (1808–1859) was making considerable use of mesmerism in India. Mesmerism did not receive the scorn in India that it had in England. As a result, mesmerism became an acceptable manipulation in hospitals during Esdaile's time, especially as a means for inducing analgesia, or anesthesia, during surgery. The first documented case of the use of hypnosis as surgical anesthesia was reported on April 12, 1829, when Jules Cloquet performed a mastectomy in Paris (Gravitz, 1988).

Also during Elliotson's time, James Braid (1785–1860) introduced a very important theory that advanced the historical development of hypnosis (mesmerism). He recognized that certain mesmeric phenomena were genuine, but he rejected, as did the Marquis de Puysegur, the influences of external or cosmic forces. Contrary to Mesmer's mystical explanation of animal magnetism, Braid advanced a naturalistic, physiological theory to account for the results of mesmerism. This theory was based on the production of eye-muscle fatigue during a mesmeric induction. Braid observed that subjects who fixated on a bright object for a given period demonstrated a gradual lowering of the eyelids or a closing of the eyes. He postulated that this closure was the result of a general exhaustion of the nerve centers. In other words, an important characteristic of mesmerism was an induced state of relaxation or "near sleep."

In addition to demonstrating this important characteristic of behavior during the process of mesmerism, Braid wanted to remove as much of the stigma associated with the concept as possible. To help with this, he changed the name of mesmerism to **neurhypnotism**. The prefix was later dropped. Braid is credited with coining the term **hypnotism** in 1826. However, it should be pointed out that some credit Étienne Felix d'Henin de Cuvillers (1755-1841) with coining the term *hypnotism* in 1821, before Braid (Gravitz, 1993; Gravitz & Gerton, 1984).

A few years before Braid changed the name of mesmerism to hypnotism, José Custodi di Faria (1756–1819) advocated a psychological explanation of the phenomenon. Basically, he stressed that "lucid sleep," his term for hypnosis, was produced solely by the subject's heightened expectations and receptive attitudes. Since the subject wanted to be hypnotized and expected something to result from this manipulation, the expectations were, in fact, realized. With the emphasis on psychological factors during the hypnosis process, Faria developed what might be called a standard procedure for inducing lucid sleep. He used a series of soothing and commanding verbal suggestions while the subject was in the receptive hypnotic state. Faria then realized, as did others many years later—for example, Ambroise August

Liébeault (1823–1904) and Hippolyte Marie Bernheim (1837–1919)—that verbal suggestion played a major role in hypnosis.

After Faria's discoveries became known and well publicized, Braid extended Faria's ideas and developed a concept he called **monoideism**. Basically, this term refers to a process of focused attention or concentration on a single idea or image during a state of relaxation. Thus, during hypnosis a subject's attention is focused only on this thought while all other thoughts are attenuated, or "put on the back burner." This concept is comparable to what is referred to today as **selective attention** (Haber & Hershenson, 1980; Treisman & Geffen, 1967). According to Braid, the ability to attend readily to a single idea or thought was limited to about 10 percent of his subjects.

Thirty years later, Jean Martin Charcot (1825–1893) described hypnotism as a process involving physiological reflex actions, including eye-muscle relaxation. Although there was, and still is, no evidence that hypnosis has a physiological basis, the eminence of Charcot as a leading authority on neurology gave considerable credence to the phenomenon of hypnosis.

Sigmund Freud (1856–1939) also must be mentioned as having played an important role in the historical development of hypnosis. Actually, some of his early theoretical conceptualizations of psychoanalysis were formalized with information he obtained from his patients while they were hypnotized. For example, he observed that, on awakening, patients did not recall many suggestions given to them during hypnosis. As a result of this demonstration of hypnotic amnesia, Freud believed that many human behaviors were the result of unconscious thoughts or motivations. Freud also discovered that many pent-up emotions and feelings could be uncovered with the aid of hypnosis. With hypnosis it was possible to tap information from the so-called unconscious or subconscious. Freud eventually abandoned the use of hypnosis because he believed that it allowed access to repressed feelings too quickly, suppressed symptoms too easily, and swayed individual responses toward what he perceived the hypnotist wanted.

As you can see, hypnosis has had a controversial historical development (Shor, 1979). However, without the brave experiments and applications of hypnosis by Elliotson, Braid, and others, hypnosis would be only a quaint relic of the past and not an important manipulation in science and medicine.

ASSESSING HYPNOTIC SUSCEPTIBILITY

Because hypnosis is a scientifically valid and reliable tool, it has become possible to determine how susceptible given individuals are to this manipulation. In determining whether a subject can be readily hypnotized or is readily susceptible to hypnotic suggestions, several standard tests and nonstandard procedures have been employed. Each standardized test is administered to subjects by beginning with an induction of hypnosis followed by suggestions that represent hypnotic experiences. The standard tests include the **Stanford Hypnotic Susceptibility Scale** (Weitzenhoffer & Hilgard, 1959, 1962), the **Barber Suggestibility Scale** (Barber & Glass, 1962), and the **Harvard Group Scale of Hypnotic Susceptibility** (Shor & Orne, 1962).

The Stanford Hypnotic Susceptibility Scale

The Stanford Hypnotic Susceptibility Scale (SHSS) appears in Forms A, B, and C. The first two emphasize compliance with motor-related suggestions; they are also parallel, permitting test-retest reliability. This means that, for example, Form A can be used interchangeably with Form B. Form C emphasizes cognitive components of hypnotic susceptibility and has become the standard against which all other scales are compared.

Form A of the Stanford Scale consists of 12 parts and is administered to each subject individually. That is, only one person at a time is tested for susceptibility to hypnotic suggestion. The 12 parts of the test are arranged in order of difficulty; the first few parts or tasks are easier, and the last parts the most difficult in terms of subject compliance. Thus, most subjects are capable of performing the first few tasks easily, while only a small number of subjects are capable of performing the last ones.

The first and easiest task on the Stanford scale is referred to as *postural sway*. In this portion of the test, the person giving the test asks the subject to close his or her eyes, after which the test administrator suggests that the subject is slowly falling backward.

The second item is called *eye closure*. In performing this task, subjects, with their eyes wide open, are given the suggestion that their eyelids are becoming very heavy, so heavy that they can no longer keep them open.

Hand lowering is the third item on the scale. Subjects are asked to extend one of their arms out in front of their body. They are then made to feel that their hand is becoming very heavy, so heavy that they can no longer keep their arm from falling.

The fourth item is referred to as *arm immobilization*. This task is, in essence, the opposite of the third task. Instead of the administrator suggesting to subjects that their arm is falling, they are told that their arm is becoming so heavy that they cannot lift it from the original position.

The fifth task on the Stanford scale is the *finger lock*. To perform this, subjects are instructed to interlock the fingers of both hands. They are then told that their fingers have become a solid mass and they will not be able to separate them. Individuals are then challenged to separate their hands.

Arm rigidity is the next item on the scale. This task requires subjects to extend their arm out straight in front of their body and then to make it as rigid as possible. Following this procedure, subjects are challenged to bend their arm.

The seventh task is concerned with *hand movement*. Here, subjects are required to move their hands together. To perform this task, individuals first separate their hands, palms facing inward, about 12 inches apart. They are then requested to imagine that a strong, magnetic force is attracting their hands together.

Verbal inhibition is the eighth task on the scale. For this situation the administrator suggests that when a subject is asked his or her name, the subject will be unable to verbalize it.

The next task is perhaps one of the most difficult on the Stanford scale. It is called the *fly hallucination* suggestion. The individual is asked to imagine a fly buzzing about his or her body. The subject is further told that the fly is becoming more and more annoying and that he or she will want to shoo it away. The test administrator tells the subject to get rid of the fly so that it will no longer be a disturbance.

The tenth scale item is called *eye catalepsy*. While the individual's eyes are closed, the administrator suggests that the subject will feel as though his or her eyes have been glued shut and the subject will not be able to open them. Subjects are then challenged to open their eyes.

The next-to-last item is a *posthypnotic suggestion*. Subjects are told that after the testing session is over, to determine their hypnotic susceptibility level, they will, for some reason, feel like changing chairs upon hearing a tapping noise. After the test administration, a tapping noise is sounded.

The final task item on the Stanford scale is the testing for *hypnotic amnesia*. After completing the susceptibility scale items, subjects are first required to enumerate the tasks they remember. Failure to recall more than three such tasks is considered adequate evidence that hypnotic amnesia was successful.

After the Stanford scale has been completed, hypnotic susceptibility level can be determined by adding the total number of task items with which subjects successfully complied. Generally, if they complied with nine to twelve suggestions, they are considered highly susceptible to hypnotic suggestion. If they complied with three or fewer suggestions, this is taken as evidence that they will be difficult to hypnotize and, as such, are considered low in the attribute of hypnotic susceptibility. A score between five and eight is considered to indicate moderate hypnotic susceptibility. Most individuals taking the test fall within this range. The particular items that the subjects successfully complete are not as important as the total test score. However, it is rare to find subjects who successfully complete the most difficult scale items and not the easiest ones.

As a side note, it should be pointed out that a score obtained on a standardized hypnosis test tends to remain stable. That is, on a repeat administration, the subject is likely to score about the same. In fact, a recent study by Piccione, Hilgard, and Zimbardo (1989) reports that in a 25-year follow-up, hypnosis scores remained stable. While in the short term, hypnotic susceptibility is modifiable (Diamond, 1974, 1977), without intervention procedures, hypnotic susceptibility level seems to be determined by the first administration.

The Barber Suggestibility Scale

Like the Stanford test, the Barber Suggestibility Scale (BSS) is administered on an individual basis. However, unlike the Stanford scale, the Barber scale consists of only eight tasks. Three of the eight items are comparable to items on Form A of the Stanford scale—*arm lowering, hand clasp,* and *verbal inhibition.* The remaining five items are *arm levitation, extreme thirst suggestion, body immobility, posthypnotic response,* and a *selective amnesia.* More recently, Spanos and his colleagues (Spanos, Cross, & De Groh, 1987; Spanos, Radtke, Hodgins, Bertrand, Stam, & Dubreuil, 1983; Spanos, Radtke, Hodgins, Stam, & Bertrand, 1983; Spanos, Radtke, Hodgins, Stam, & Noretti, 1983) introduced a new scale based on the Barber scale. This is called the Carleton University Responsiveness to Suggestion Scale (CURSS). Unlike the Barber scale, it consists of an induction and only seven items.

The Harvard Group Scale

The third standardized test to determine hypnotic susceptibility level is the Harvard Group Scale of Hypnotic Susceptibility, Form A (HGSHS:A). This test was based on Form A of the Stanford scale. Unlike the Stanford and Barber scales, however, this test is administered in a group setting. Also, subjects taking this test score themselves for their level of hypnotic susceptibility. This is not the case for the Stanford or Barber scales, in which the test administrator does the scoring. Numerical scoring for hypnotic susceptibility on the Harvard scale is comparable to that on the Stanford scale. A score between nine and twelve indicates high susceptibility to hypnotic suggestion; a score below three is considered low susceptibility.

In addition to the standardized techniques for assessing hypnotic susceptibility, investigators have reported several "quick" methods of assessment. One such technique is the **Hypnotic Induction Profile,** or **HIP** (Spiegel, 1979a;

FIGURE 4.1   Eye-Roll Test

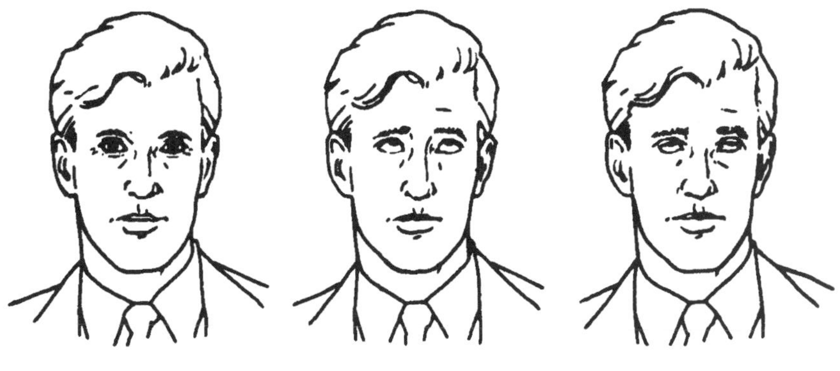

Stern, Spiegel, & Nee, 1979). This test consists of the controversial eye-roll test (Spiegel, 1970) accompanied by a very brief hypnotic induction and test. In the eye-roll test (see Figure 4.1) subjects are requested to open their eyes as wide as possible. They are then instructed to roll their eyes to the top of their eyelids and to lower their eyelids very slowly over their eyes without moving their eyes from the upward position. Subjects' ability to perform this simple task is considered as evidence of their susceptibility to hypnotic suggestion.

Although the eye-roll test appears to be a reasonable assessment of hypnotic susceptibility for some subjects (see Frischholz, Spiegel, Trentalange, & Spiegel, 1987), it is far from being a reliable and valid measure (Eliseo, 1974; Orne, Hilgard, Spiegel, Spiegel, & Crawford, 1979; Switras, 1974; Wheeler, Reis, Wolff, Grupsmith, & Mordkoff, 1974). For example, Wheeler et al. (1974) found a very weak relationship between hypnotic susceptibility as assessed by the standardized scales described previously and the ability of a subject to perform the eye-roll procedure. Therefore, the eye-roll test cannot be considered a reliable or valid substitute for the standard testing procedures (Kihlstrom, 1985).

CORRELATES OF HYPNOTIZABILITY

Cognitive Correlates

A number of investigators have reported cognitive and perceptual correlates of hypnotic susceptibility. For example, Wallace and colleagues (Wallace, 1978b, 1979, 1988; Wallace & Garrett, 1973; Wallace, Garrett, & Anstadt, 1974; Wallace, Knight, & Garrett, 1976) found a relationship between level of hypnotic susceptibility, as assessed by the Harvard scale, and frequency of perceiving various visual illusions (see Figure 4.2). Generally, the more susceptible a subject is to hypnotic suggestions, the greater is his or her susceptibility to visual illusions, especially those involving a frequency report such as viewing the Necker cube, the Schroeder staircase, and the autokinetic effect (the illusory movement of a stationary light source).

Such correlates have been theorized to exist because subjects who are judged high in hypnotic susceptibility generally are better able to selectively

---

FIGURE 4.2   Examples of Reversible Figure Illusions

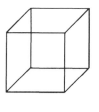
Necker cube

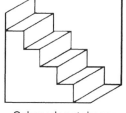
Schroeder staircase

attend to a stimulus situation in which there is competition for attention. Thus, when presented with an illusion, high hypnotic subjects are better able than low hypnotic subjects to concentrate on the elements that create the illusion. Their attention is not drawn away to other competing stimuli. As a result, they report a stronger illusory response.

Because of the difference between high and low hypnotics in their response to various illusions, and because this has been reported in a number of independent laboratories (e.g., Crawford, Brown, & Moon, 1993), it might be possible to use such a tool for assessing hypnotic susceptibility. Perhaps in the future, responses to various visual illusions will, in fact, be incorporated in tests of hypnotic responsiveness.

Hypnotic susceptibility has also been found to correlate with a high capacity for absorption or involvement in imaginative activities outside of hypnosis (Kumar & Pekala, 1988; Snodgrass & Lynn, 1989; Tellegen & Atkinson, 1974), with focused attention (Graham & Evans, 1977; Karlin, 1979), with the production of vivid mental images or other fantasies (Priebe & Wallace, 1986; Sheehan, 1979, 1982), and with fantasy proneness (Lynn & Rhue, 1986; Rhue & Lynn, 1989). Crawford (1981, 1982, 1983) has argued that what links these correlates is the ability of a hypnotizable subject to use synthetic or holistic thinking. This has been demonstrated in the performance of Gestalt closure tasks (Crawford, 1981) and in tasks requiring subjects to perform a visual search for a hidden letter (Wallace & Patterson, 1984) or object (Priebe & Wallace, 1986).

Personality Correlates

Many people wonder whether hypnotic susceptibility is related to any personality variables. Unfortunately, hypnotizability has not been found to significantly correlate with most of these types of variables. As examples, it does not correlate with test results on the Minnesota Multiphasic Personality Inventory (MMPI) or the California Personality Inventory (CPI) (Hilgard, 1979). However, some support was found for a relationship between greater hypnotizability as assessed by the Harvard scale and relative mental health as assessed by the Rorschach ink-blot test (Zlotogorski, Hahnemann, & Wiggs, 1987).

Physiological Correlates

Gur and Gur (1974) have also argued that hypnotizability is correlated to right-brain processing. This conclusion was reached from a body of evidence that has indicated, for example, that hypnotizable subjects are more likely than low-susceptibility subjects to show reflective eye movement shifts to the left. Also, Graham (1977) and Graham and Pernicano (1979) reported that hypnosis led to increases in autokinetic movement to the left, compared to when subjects were not hypnotized. In addition, Sackeim, Paulus, and Weiman (1979) reported that when hypnotizable individuals are asked to find a seat in a room, they tend to find chairs in the right portion of the room. However, Monteiro and Zimbardo (1987) failed to replicate this finding.

Pagano, Akots, and Wall (1988) reported that in a dichotic listening task there was a greater left ear monitoring advantage during hypnosis. A similar finding has been reported by Frumkin, Ripley, and Cox (1978), although there has been difficulty in replicating the effect (Crawford, Crawford, & Koperski, 1983; Levine, Kurtz, & Lauter, 1984).

Pagano et al. also reported an increased respiration rate and a decreased heart rate during hypnosis. Spiegel and Barabasz (1988) and Spiegel, Bierre, and Rootenberg (1989) also reported finding changes in cortical event-related potential amplitude (see Chapter 2) during hypnosis. These evoked potentials are electrical changes in the brain that are typically produced by a stimulus, such as a sound or light source or, in the case of the Spiegel et al. studies, by hypnotic induction.

Related to the previous studies, MacLeod-Morgan and Lack (1982) reported an apparent shift in cortical activation, as measured by alpha EEG activity (see Chapter 7), from the left to the right hemisphere when individuals are hypnotized. Also, London, Hart, and Leibovitz (1968) found that subjects who were judged to be highly responsive to hypnotic suggestions tended to show more alpha wave activity during the waking state than did subjects with low responsiveness to hypnotic suggestions.

Graffin, Ray, and Lundy (1995) also found that high- and low-hypnotic-susceptible participants displayed a differential pattern of EEG activity during a baseline period, characterized by greater theta brain-wave activity, instead of alpha activity, in the more frontal areas of the cortex for the highly susceptible individuals. During the baseline period and after a standard hypnotic induction, low-susceptible participants displayed an increase in theta brain-wave activity, whereas highly susceptible individuals displayed a decrease. Finally, during the actual hypnotic induction itself, theta brain-wave activity increased significantly for both groups in the more posterior areas of the cortex, whereas alpha activity increased across all sites.

Although the results reported by MacLeod-Morgan and Lack differ from those reported by Graffin et al., the implications include the possibility of psychophysiological measures offering a stable marker for hypnotizability. We hope that these results will be replicated by others (see DePascalis, Silveri, & Palumbo, 1988).

Interestingly, DePascalis et al. did report that highly hypnotizable subjects exhibited significantly higher alpha brain-wave amplitude (see Chapter 7) compared to low hypnotizable subjects. Also, Leskowitz (1988) has found some evidence that the reason the eye-ball test, as part of the Hypnotic Induction Profile (Spiegel, 1979a), may be predictive of hypnotic susceptibility for some subjects is because of optimum pituitary gland function.

Hypnotic susceptibility has also been considered as a function of when it is assessed and whether this may be related to the possible existence of ultradian rhythms (regular peaks and valleys in activity). Wallace (1993) and Wallace and Kokoszka (1995) have reported that individuals who are judged to be most alert during daytime hours (day people) show greater susceptibility to hypnosis during the day. Similarly, individuals who are judged to be most alert during late afternoon or evening hours (night people) show greater susceptibility during these period. In a related study, Mann and Sanders (1995) have reported that subjects who reported the greatest alertness in the morning achieved greater trance depth in the morning than in the evening, whereas those who reported greater evening alertness reported deeper trance depth in the evening than in the morning. However, in assessing hypnotic susceptibility and hypnotic depth, evidence for the presence of ultradian rhythms was not found (see Rossi, 1982).

Thus, a number of physiological/biological correlates of hypnotic susceptibility and hypnosis appear to be emerging. In the mid-1980s (Kihlstrom, 1985) it was concluded that there were no reliable, physiological correlates of hypnotic susceptibility or hypnosis. This conclusion appears to be changing.

HYPNOTHERAPY

Habit Control

Regardless of what hypnosis is or is not, and what variables are associated with hypnotic susceptibility, hypnosis can be a useful tool in dealing with certain behavioral problems, such as the control of an unwanted habit. Hypnosis has been used extensively in dealing with obesity, smoking, stress, and the control of other types of potentially debilitating habits. This application is possible most likely because hypnosis enables individuals to deal with their habit at a level of awareness or consciousness that varies from their normal state of consciousness. In the normal waking state, an individual's habit is in full force and is difficult to alter or reshape. However, at a different level of awareness, at which subjects are more susceptible to suggestions of changing their habit, and thus, perhaps, are more inclined to do so, reshaping or altering becomes easier. Hypnosis, then, is a useful tool for reshaping behavior that can be generalized beyond the altered state to the normal waking state of awareness.

Stanton (1975) has found hypnosis to be a useful technique in the treatment of obesity. Specifically, he employed five procedures to help patients with weight-control problems, all with the aid of hypnosis. These included direct suggestions relating to amount and type of food to be eaten in the future; ego-enhancing suggestions to help patients live their lives more pleasantly; mental imagery to establish a desired goal; self-hypnosis to reinforce the therapist's suggestions; and audiotapes to provide additional support after the completion of formal treatment. Stanton reported that the combined use of these techniques had a marked effect on weight loss as reported by patients who completed the entire process. In other words, hypnosis was a successful procedure in the treatment of obesity.

One factor that appears to be very important in determining whether hypnosis will be successful in treating obesity is hypnotic susceptibility level. Andersen (1985) reported a positive association between degree of hypnotizability and success at weight reduction. Subjects who had scored high on the Stanford Hypnotic Susceptibility Scale, Form A (previously described), were aided more by a treatment program designed to help individuals lose weight through hypnosis than were those who had scored in either the medium or low parts of the scale.

Hypnosis has also been successful in the treatment of smoking, sometimes requiring no more than one session (Williams & Hall, 1988). However, unlike the treatment of overeating or obesity, smoking control does not require that the person score in the upper range of hypnotizability to achieve success (Holroyd, 1980; Perry, Gelfand, & Marcovitch, 1979; Perry & Mullen, 1975).

Spiegel (1979b) employed a competing-response technique using hypnosis to help individuals stop smoking. After a subject had been hypnotized, he or she was asked to concentrate on three points: (1) that cigarette smoking is a poison to the body, (2) that life is not possible without the body, and (3) that life is possible only if one respects and protects one's body (i.e., by not smoking). These suggestions, administered under hypnosis, were then put in a type of competition with the life process, since Spiegel made it clear that a subject could not maintain both life and the smoking habit. As such, life could be reinforced only if the individual was willing to stop smoking. Thus, smoking became a destructive force in maintaining life.

When subjects were confronted with the life-versus-smoking dilemma, it was up to them to make a choice. They could choose smoking, and thereby decrease life, or they could choose life by abandoning the smoking habit. With the aid of hypnosis and the suggestions, Spiegel reported a 20 percent success rate in the termination of the smoking habit. Although this is not a high percentage, one must keep in mind that subjects received only a single treatment session. With an increase in the number of hypnosis sessions, Hall and Crasilneck (1970) reported a 75 percent cure rate. Jeffrey, Jeffrey, Greuling, and Gentry (1985) reported a success rate of 63 percent in a five-treatment program that combined the use of hypnotic, cognitive, and behavioral interventions. Also, Powell (1980) showed that individuals who had stopped smoking through hypnosis and who subsequently returned to smoking were helped to become more permanent nonsmokers with a flooding of hypnosis and systematic desensitization sessions. It appears, then, that the smoking habit can be controlled with the help of hypnotic suggestions.

How does hypnosis compare to other techniques as a means of dealing with a smoking habit? In a recent survey, West, Fellows, and Easton (1995) asked professionals to respond to questions about the effectiveness of hypnosis as a therapy. Smoking was seen as one of the habits that was least successfully treated by hypnosis. However, others disagree. Barkley, Hastings, and Jackson (1977) compared hypnosis to rapid smoking as a method for treating the smoking habit. In rapid smoking, an individual is made to smoke a large number of cigarettes in a short time. Hypnosis was found to be an effective treatment method, although the rapid smoking technique proved slightly more effective. Unfortunately, one must question this advantage because rapid smoking produces severe effects, such as explosive nausea (vomiting) and loss of appetite.

Thus, it appears that hypnosis can play an important role in the treatment of overeating and smoking. However, one must ask whether the cure is long-lasting. The follow-up data on the treated subjects indicate that some individuals return to their old eating or smoking habits. This was true especially when relatively few hypnosis sessions were employed to treat the habit; that is, hypnosis ceased to serve as a strong motivator to control the habit. Thus, although it has been a successful method of treatment for some individuals, hypnosis alone probably is not a likely method of treatment for control. However, when it is used as an adjunct to behavior modification or cognitive techniques, it appears to be fairly successful (Dengrove, 1976; Jeffrey et al., 1985).

Phobias

With regard to phobia control, if an individual shows an irrational fear of some type of object, event, or environment, a popular method of treating this fear is to use hypnosis along with a process called **systematic desensitization** (Wolpe, 1969). This process creates a hierarchy of stimuli that provoke different levels of fear of the event. For example, if someone is fearful of nonpoisonous snakes, the hierarchy might consist of a series of fear levels ranging from fright on hearing the word "snake" to severe fear of direct contact with a snake. If the hierarchy consists of several steps, desensitization would involve a process of giving the subject muscle relaxation therapy at each step of the hierarchy and continuing this therapy until the subject no longer feared the snake at that level. Thus, the therapist would first try to reduce the fear of hearing the word "snake." Once this was accomplished, the therapist would continue to reduce fear at more, increasingly intense levels until fear at all levels of the hierarchy had disappeared.

Although systematic desensitization is a successful treatment therapy by itself (Carson, Butcher, & Coleman, 1988; Costin & Draguns, 1989; Wolpe, 1969), it can be even more successful when used in conjunction with hypnosis (e.g., Lang & Lazovik, 1963), especially since phobic patients appear to be relatively highly hypnotizable (Frankel & Orne, 1976; John, Hollander, & Perry, 1983). This is because, once a level of fear has been established for a phobic individual, hypnotization before the start of actual desensitization therapy increases the efficacy of the therapy. The irrational fear probably developed at a subconscious level of awareness; hypnosis may help to reinstate this level of consciousness and allow the fear to be treated at the same level of awareness at which it was created.

An example of the joint use of hypnosis and desensitization in the treatment of a phobia is illustrated in an experiment by Lang and Lazovik (1963). The investigators were interested in the success of systematic desensitization in treating people who have a phobia of nonpoisonous snakes. Using the technique illustrated earlier, they found that asking subjects under hypnosis to imagine the fear situation at various levels of the established hierarchy was conducive to producing relaxation and vivid imagery. Therefore, the individual could overcome the fear of snakes through imagery. Thus, the dual use of hypnosis and desensitization can be a potent means of treating phobias.

This treatment procedure sounds fairly impressive, and the results reported are equally impressive. However, what is even more important is that the success reported with imagery held true in actual situations. That is, individuals who used this procedure to overcome fear of snakes under laboratory conditions also showed a diminution or elimination of the fear when they actually encountered a snake. Lang and Lazovik reported that the therapy maintained its effectiveness after six months.

Sexual Dysfunctions

Another successful use of hypnosis teamed with systematic desensitization is in the treatment of sexual dysfunctions. One such dysfunction that has been treated successfully in this way is vaginismus (Fuchs, Hoch, & Kleinhauz, 1976; Fuchs et al., 1973; Oystragh, 1988). **Vaginismus** is a disorder in which the vaginal opening is constricted so as not to permit entry of the penis. One case involved a 23-year-old woman who had never had sexual intercourse with her husband because her vagina was too constricted to allow his penis to enter. After it was determined that the woman's problem was not physiological in origin, the investigators treated the vaginismus as a fear of pain associated with sexual intercourse. They employed a treatment similar to that used by Lang and Lazovik in the treatment of snake phobia. That is, the woman was taught to relax and to produce vivid imagery under hypnosis. In addition, a fear hierarchy of pain was developed for her. She subsequently was given the hierarchy of events to imagine under hypnosis in order from the least to the most anxiety provoking. The hierarchy ranged from imagining herself going home with her husband and resting with him (least anxiety provoking) to imagining herself having sexual intercourse with him (most anxiety provoking). The therapy continued until the woman felt relaxed imagining the final level of the fear hierarchy.

When the patient no longer felt fearful of having intercourse with her husband (as witnessed by overt signs of relaxation, such as muscle relaxation, and her statement that she felt relaxed), she was asked to try to have intercourse with him. She reported that the treatment had been successful and that, for the first time in two years, her husband had been able to penetrate her vagina. Thus, as with snake phobia, the fear of sex can also be successfully treated with the dual use of hypnosis and systematic desensitization.

Hypnosis has also been successfully used in the treatment of premature ejaculation. Milton Erickson (1973), a pioneer in the use of hypnosis in psychotherapy, reports the case of a 38-year-old who, after trying countless remedies, decided to find out whether hypnosis could help him with his problem. In a number of sessions with the patient, a posthypnotic suggestion was given to him that no matter how hard he tried and no matter how long coitus endured, an ejaculation would not occur for many minutes. Erickson reported that this technique proved successful and the man no longer experienced his former problem.

In addition to the use of hypnosis in the treatment of sexual problems, it has been found useful in the treatment of other psychological disorders. As examples, it has been used in the treatment of bipolar affective disorders such as manic-depression (Feinstein & Morgan, 1986); bulimia, or the purging of food (Hall & McGill, 1986), and other eating disorders, such as anorexia nervosa (Baker & Nash, 1987; Yapko, 1986); and multiple-personality disorders (Kirsch & Barton, 1988; Kluft, 1988).

It appears, then, that hypnosis is a useful manipulation in the treatment of many psychological problems. Surgeons and dentists also have used hypnosis as an analgesic or an anesthetic. The next section of this chapter considers the use of hypnosis in the relief of pain.

HYPNOSIS AND PAIN CONTROL

Before we discuss the role of hypnosis in the control of pain, two terms need to be defined: **analgesia** and **anesthesia**. The former refers to the removal of existing pain; the latter is the prevention of pain that is not currently present.

As was mentioned earlier in this chapter, in the 1800s, Esdaile and others successfully employed hypnosis to create an analgesic effect during surgery. As a matter of fact, hypnosis was used as a means of eliminating pain before chemical agents were discovered. Before Esdaile's important work in this field, surgery without analgesia or anesthesia was so painful that 40 percent of all patients who underwent surgery for the removal of tumors died not long afterward. However, with the advent of hypnotic anesthesia, this rate was reduced to about 5 percent (Fromm & Shor, 1979).

When chemical anesthetics, such as chloroform and sodium thiopental (Pentothal), appeared for use in surgery, hypnosis was effectively eliminated as a procedure to reduce experienced pain, since chemical agents induced an anesthetic effect faster. This development was most unfortunate for several reasons. First, although time-consuming to administer, hypnosis was a successful procedure for reducing pain. Second, hypnotic anesthesia was far safer to use than chemical anesthetics, since the latter were associated with several side effects, including respiratory depression, myocardial depression, cardiac arrhythmias, and prolonged somnolence.

Why does hypnosis play an important role in reducing pain? Mostly because hypnosis helps to dissociate the experience of pain into two levels of awareness (Hilgard, 1973). At one level, the patient is aware of feeling the pain. However, during an altered state of awareness such as hypnosis, the patient does not experience the pain (Hilgard & Hilgard, 1994; Malone, Kurtz, & Strube, 1989). In fact, Crawford, Gur, Skolnick, Gur, and Benson (1993) have provided evidence via PET scans (see Chapter 2) that during hypnosis there is increased cerebral blood flow in the frontal cortex to reduce the magnitude of experienced pain. Thus, hypnotic analgesia seems to produce a change in how the brain processes and ultimately reduces the pain experience (see Crawford, 1996).

Surgeons who use hypnosis in their practice today do so primarily when a patient shows allergic reactions to chemical anesthetics or when the surgeon wishes to reduce the dosage of the chemical agent (Fredericks, 1980; Hogue & Hunter, 1988). Regarding the latter concern, many surgeons believe that there really is no need to rely totally on chemical agents as anesthetics during surgery. Therefore, they might reduce the dosage of the anesthetic by employing hypnotic anesthesia as an adjunct. The more effective the hypnotic anesthesia, the lower the dosage of chemical anesthetic. The dual use of chemical and hypnotic anesthesia effectively reduces many of the drug-related risks mentioned earlier (Nathan, Morris, Goebel, & Blass, 1987).

Unfortunately, not all patients can benefit from the use of hypnotic anesthesia or analgesia. Many are not highly susceptible to hypnotic suggestions and are not readily capable of dissociating various levels of experienced pain. For such patients there is usually no choice but to use a chemical anesthetic or analgesic. Although hypnotic susceptibility may, at least in the short term, improve with practice (Diamond, 1974, 1977; Spanos, 1986), the time required to train individuals to be more hypnotically susceptible becomes a great obstacle to normal operating procedures, both before and during surgery. As a result, relatively few surgeons employ hypnotic anesthesia as either an alternative or an adjunct to chemical agents.

Besides the use of hypnotic anesthesia in surgery, this pain-reducing procedure has been employed in the field of obstetrics. The use of hypnotic anesthesia and analgesia in childbirth is not new; it was used as a means of reducing childbirth pain more than a hundred years ago (Kroger, 1977). As with hypnotic anesthesia in surgery, it is necessary first to determine whether the patient is sufficiently susceptible to hypnotic suggestions. If the expectant mother is susceptible, she can be trained to accept suggestions for hypnotic anesthesia before and during parturition. However, relatively few patients (about 20 percent) can be taught to reduce pain effectively without the aid of some chemical anesthetic or analgesic.

There are some obvious advantages for patients who can profit by the use of hypnotic anesthesia during childbirth. These include a reduction in postoperative side effects that would be present with chemical anesthetics, a reduction in postchildbirth pain, and the elimination of danger to the baby from the administration of a chemical agent to the mother (Kroger, 1977). However, while hypnotic techniques are beneficial during childbirth, procedures for natural childbirth (e.g., the Lamaze technique) are as beneficial as hypnosis (Davenport-Slack, 1975; Weishaar, 1986). Perhaps this is because both procedures enable women to alter their state of awareness temporarily and thus escape the level of pain they would normally experience during the waking state. Additionally, natural childbirth procedures do not differ much from self-hypnosis procedures. During self-hypnosis an individual can temporarily induce an altered state of consciousness. Thus, hypnotically induced pain relief and natural childbirth procedures are equally effective in helping a mother to alter her state of consciousness during childbirth.

Hypnosis has also been employed as a means of dealing with pain during dental procedures. However, hypnosis is rarely used as an anesthetic or analgesic in dentistry. Rather, it is used as a tool to help reduce tension and fear of pain and to allow the patient to become more relaxed (Forgione, 1988). The result of this, of course, is to reduce the magnitude of experienced pain. In general, as with the use of hypnosis in surgery, its use in dentistry is not common. It is time-consuming to administer, and only a limited number of patients can profit by its use. Therefore, neither surgery nor dentistry make considerable use of hypnosis in dealing with experienced pain.

As an analgesic, hypnosis has been used in the treatment of headaches. Generally, two procedures have been tried in treating this type of pain: glove anesthesia and the hand-warming technique. **Glove anesthesia** (Barber & Adrian, 1982; Kroger, 1977) is a procedure whereby the patient's hand is anesthetized hypnotically. The person is then taught to apply the anesthetized hand to the portion of the head that hurts. The result is to transfer the anesthetic effect to the head. In this manner, individuals can be taught to eliminate or control headaches. Naturally, for this procedure to be maximally beneficial, the individual must be taught self-hypnosis so that he or she can learn to anesthetize the hand to apply it to the head.

The second procedure, **hand warming,** was developed by Sargent, Green, and Walters (1973); it utilizes hypnosis as well as biofeedback (see Chapter 5). In this technique, patients are taught to achieve passive concentration and to relax their entire bodies with hypnotic procedures. Then they receive instructions concerning the use of temperature in the control of pain. Patients are instructed to visualize temperature changes in their hands while watching a temperature trainer, a feedback mechanism by which they can determine whether their hand temperature really has changed. Thus, they think about making their hand warm, and, in fact, it becomes warm. Then they apply the warm hand to the head; in this way the severity of the headache is reduced or the headache is totally eliminated. The principles underlying this phenomenon are discussed in Chapter 5.

Success has been reported in the treatment of headaches with the use of both glove anesthesia and hand warming (Andreychuck & Skriver, 1975; Graham, 1975). Therefore, hypnosis can be a beneficial substitute for the chemical agents (e.g., aspirin, buffered aspirin, acetaminophen) that are commonly used to relieve headache pain. Another method for treating headaches is the sole use of biofeedback (see Chapter 5) in a manner similar to the hand-warming technique.

Finally, and related to pain control in subjects who are hypnotizable, a number of investigators (Hagemann-Wenselaar, 1988; Hilgard & LeBaron, 1982, 1984; Smith, Barabasz, & Barabasz, 1996; Wall & Womack, 1989) have reported that hypnotizable children who have cancer and are undergoing chemotherapy show significantly more pain control and reduction during bone-marrow aspirations than do those who are not hypnotizable. However, even children who are judged to be low in hypnotic susceptibility benefit by the use of distraction techniques (Smith et al., 1996).

HYPNOSIS AND MEMORY

With regard to memory, investigators have sought to determine whether hypnosis can induce amnesia and hypermnesia. **Amnesia** is defined as a loss of memory. **Hyperamnesia** is concerned with improving an individual's memory for events experienced in the past.

You may recall that on the Stanford and Harvard scales, amnesia through hypnosis is used as a criterion for establishing susceptibility. As such, investigators believe that amnesia can be induced through hypnosis. However, hypnotic susceptibility aside, how effective is this induction in the laboratory? Basically, it appears that hypnotically induced amnesia affects episodic memory (defined, for example, as the ability to recall a word list that was memorized during hypnosis) but not semantic memory. (The ability to use the same word list items as responses on word association tasks would be semantic memory.) This has been demonstrated in a number of experiments (Evans, 1979b; Kihlstrom, 1980; Spanos, Radtke, & Dubreuil, 1982).

With regard to hypermnesia, or improving an individual's memory, several experiments have shown this to be possible through hypnosis (Dhanens & Lundy, 1975; Dywan & Bowers, 1983). There have also been reports in real-world situations of witnesses to a crime providing useful information while hypnotized. For example, in 1976 in Chowchilla, California, a bus filled with children on a field trip was kidnapped. The bus, children, and driver were buried beneath the ground and were to be kept there until a ransom was paid. As the car being driven by the culprits left the scene of the crime, the bus driver observed it. However, he had difficulty remembering important details that would lead to the arrest of the kidnappers. Under hypnosis he was able to recall the license plate of the car. This information ultimately led to the arrest of the kidnappers.

Unfortunately, not all attempts at recovering information from an eyewitness are so successful. Many recall attempts appear to be associated with increases in inaccurate recollection or confabulation (Sheehan, 1988; Worthington, 1979). Thus, in theory, although individuals can recall so-called forgotten information through hypnosis, one cannot be certain that what is being recalled is fact or fiction (McConkey, 1988; Perry, Orne, London, & Orne, 1996). Needless to say, this has presented problems, legal and otherwise, for the use of hypnosis in the courtroom as a means of establishing information about a crime that an individual witnessed (Gianelli, 1995; Laurence & Perry, 1983; Putnam, 1979; Sanders & Simmons, 1983; Sheehan & Tilden, 1983; Zelig & Beidelman, 1981). Despite its problems, hypnosis continues to be a useful tool in forensic psychology and is used as a means of helping witnesses to a crime recall some of the detail that they may have forgotten. Yes, there have been instances of confabulation, but there have also been instances in which valuable information has surfaced that has led to the solution of a crime (Beahrs, 1988; Sloan, 1981).

Hypnosis has also been used in an attempt to help individuals remember information about their childhood, information that is normally not available for recall. Examples of such studies are those by Walker, Garrett, and Wallace (1976), Wallace (1978a), and Nash, Johnson, and Tipton (1979). In each of these studies, hypnotically induced age regression was used to help individuals recall or reconstruct information that was no longer available to conscious retrieval. **Hypnotic age regression**, as you might guess, involves taking a subject back in time. For example, an individual might be taken back to the age of five to recall events that happened then. He or she might be asked to remember what happened, for example, at a birthday party.

In the Walker et al. study, **eidetic imagery**, or what is popularly referred to as photographic memory, was being investigated. As the researchers noted, this phenomenon is very rare in adults (Stromeyer & Psotka, 1970) although it can be found in about 8 to 10 percent of children around the age of seven to eight (Haber, 1979; Haber & Haber, 1964). The investigators reasoned that a good test of hypnotic age regression would be to recreate the process of eidetic imagery in adults who are regressed to the age at which this process is most visible. They also reasoned that if age-regressed adults displayed eidetic imagery in an experimental paradigm in which results could not be faked, they would find evidence to suggest that hypnotic age regression is a valuable tool for investigating the processes involved in memory.

The task that was used was a difficult one and not easily faked. Subjects were asked to perceive, in a binocular fashion, half of a 10,000-dot stereogram for sixty seconds (Julesz, 1971). Immediately after the removal of the first half, they were asked to perceive the second half. Presentation of either half produced a meaningless, unidentifiable composite of dots. Subjects were then asked to combine the memory of the first half with the observed dot composite of the second half and to identify the object formed by such a combination. From a sample of 20 hypnotically age-regressed subjects, two (10 percent) were capable of demonstrating eidetic imagery. This study has been replicated by Wallace (1978a) and Crawford, Wallace, Nomura, and Slater (1986). Spanos, Ansari, and Stam (1979) failed to replicate the phenomenon, but given the rarity of its occurrence in age-regressed adults, this is not surprising. Also, Raikov (1980) believes that some experiments with hypnotic age regression have failed because of the nature of the hypnotist's suggestion and the subject's depth of hypnosis.

It should be mentioned that the concept of hypnotic age regression is controversial. While phenomena with its use have been demonstrated (e.g., rudimentary, childlike handwriting or speaking in a child's voice), thus leading us to believe that it is real, there are many instances in which hypnotic age regression could not be experimentally substantiated as a bona fide event (Ascher, Barber, & Spanos, 1972; Barber, 1962; Fisher, 1962; O'Connell, Shor, & Orne, 1970). Yet experiments, such as those by Walker et al. (1976) demonstrate that while subjects are age regressed, they exhibit behavior that differs from their behavior when they are not regressed. This could, of course, simply be an indication that subjects process information differently when they are asked to be "adults" than when they are asked to be "children." And such processing differences may illustrate age regression in action. However, this issue remains unresolved, and we cannot cite definitive evidence that hypnotic age regression is real. Undoubtedly, an answer to the question of whether hypnotic age regression is real or not will be a fruitful area for future research.

HYPNOSIS AND PERCEPTION

As with the study of memory, hypnosis has also been used to study various perceptual effects. Some of the more dramatic reports include those by Graham and Leibowitz (1972) and Sheehan, Smith, and Forrest (1982), who found that hypnotic suggestions led to improvements in visual acuity in myopic (nearsighted) subjects. That is, hypnosis can be used, at least temporarily, to help improve a nearsighted individual's vision. This improvement takes place without requiring the subject to wear corrective lenses.

The induction of hypnotic deafness has also been reported to affect auditory sensitivity (Crawford, MacDonald, & Hilgard, 1979) and auditory interference on visual choice-reaction time (Blum & Porter, 1974). Thus, hypnosis can temporarily be used to produce a type of artificial deafness, especially for some sound tones. As a simple example, subjects might be taught to selectively attend to the voice of an instructor in a college course while attenuating the distracting voices of fellow students who happen to be conversing during the lecture.

Also, hypnotic anesthesia has been employed in a number of perception experiments. Wallace and his colleagues (Garrett & Wallace, 1975; Wallace & Fisher, 1982; Wallace & Garrett, 1973, 1975) have reported that anesthesia disrupts the ability of individuals to localize visual objects in the environment or to coordinate parts of the body (e.g., arm, leg) with those objects after wearing displacing prisms. Hypnotic anesthesia has also been shown to disrupt the normal ability of subjects to localize their nose when asked to find it with their eyes closed (Wallace & Hoyenga, 1980). Although Spanos, Gorassini, and Petrusic (1981) replicated this latter finding, they failed to replicate the formerly described effect of displacing prisms. However, this failure has been tied to an inadequate control of conditions that would lead to the findings reported by Wallace and his colleagues (Wallace & Fisher, 1982, 1984).

The anesthesia studies imply that hypnosis helps scientists to isolate the factors involved in coordinated motor activities. By doing so, hypnosis gives us some clues about what is going on when, for example, a person suffers a stroke and cannot perform normal (or any) motor activity in a given limb. By isolating the components involved in normal motor functioning, techniques might be devised to more quickly rehabilitate an affected limb or body part in stroke victims.

Hypnosis and hypnotic susceptibility have also been shown to affect performance on the Stroop effect (Sheehan, Donovan, & MacLeod, 1988). The Stroop effect occurs when subjects are asked to name the ink color of an incompatible color word (e.g, the word *yellow* is printed in *blue*) and they show strong interference from the word. When provided with an attention-focusing instruction under hypnosis, highly hypnotizable subjects sharply reduced the Stroop effect, whereas less easily hypnotized individuals decreased it slightly.

From the perspective of either a scientist or a student, one can appreciate the usefulness of hypnosis in the study of behavior. Although there is, and will continue to be, controversy concerning the phenomenon of hypnosis, it has proven itself to be a useful tool for scientific research. Hypnosis can be used in a variety of experiments and in professional therapies for habit control, phobias, obsessions, compulsions, and sexual dysfunctions. It can also be used beneficially in the control of pain and in the recall of information that cannot be extracted in the normal waking state of consciousness.

Now that we have seen how hypnosis is measured and used, how has this phenomenon been explained? In other words, what theories describe the phenomenon of hypnosis?

CONTEMPORARY THEORIES OF HYPNOSIS

Today, three theoretical approaches predominate in explaining the phenomenon of hypnosis. These were mentioned very briefly at the beginning of this chapter. They include the trance theory of hypnosis (Conn & Conn, 1967;

Fromm & Shor, 1979; Hilgard, 1965, 1973, 1977b, 1979), the sociological role theory (Coe, 1978; Coe & Sarbin, 1977; Sarbin & Coe, 1972, 1979), and the task-motivation theory (Barber, 1969; Barber, Spanos, & Chaves, 1974; Spanos, 1982).

The **trance theory** postulates that hypnosis is a process that involves an altered state of consciousness, or a trance, during which the subject is in a heightened state of susceptibility or responsiveness to suggestions or commands. Therefore, in hypnosis an individual must either be temporarily dissociated from the normal waking state of awareness or consciousness or be minimally capable of performing some tasks with hypnosis that are not as easily accomplished or even possible to accomplish at all without hypnosis.

Hilgard (1973, 1979) has presented evidence that a subject is in a special state of consciousness during the reception of hypnotic instructions. In dealing with the perception of pain, Hilgard produced pain by applying extreme cold to a subject's arm. Such application produces what is referred to as *cold-pressor* pain. Hilgard found that hypnotically suggested analgesia can reduce considerably the felt pain sensation associated with the cold pressor. However, if a subject reports feeling no pain and is then asked to write down his or her felt experiences, he or she does indeed report experiencing pain. Therefore, though the subject did not orally report pain, a "hidden part" of the person may report the true level of pain experienced. This "hidden part" has been referred to as the *hidden observer* (Hilgard, 1973; Hilgard, Morgan, & MacDonald, 1975; Knox, Crutchfield, & Hilgard, 1975).

Sometimes, this true level of pain is reported through *automatic writing*, in which it can be suggested to subjects that the hidden observer can communicate with the hypnotist through writing. Subjects orally report no pain but, through this writing, report that they are experiencing pain. Therefore, according to Hilgard, a subject experiences pain at two levels. One level is consciously cognitive; at this level, hypnotic analgesia clearly affects the severity of experienced pain. The subject indicates a cessation or diminution in the level of pain.

However, at the second level the subject does experience pain and reports this via automatic writing. On the basis of these results, Hilgard developed a neodissociation theory of pain reduction in hypnosis. This theory specifies that, at some cognitive level, the subject has experienced the cold and can report its intensity even though the suffering may be reduced. Since Hilgard's theory obviously implies cognitive control of a stimulus event, it suggests that a trance or altered state of consciousness appears to be operating during hypnosis.

Hilgard's neodissociation theory focuses on cognitive changes that occur following hypnotic suggestions. A second theory, by Sarbin and Coe (1972, 1979), focuses on the social context in which hypnosis takes place. Unlike the trance theory, the **sociological theory** does not propose that hypnotized individuals behave as they do because they have undergone a change in the state of consciousness. Rather, it proposes that hypnotized subjects behave as they do because they are striving to enact the role of a hypnotized subject as it is defined by the hypnotist and society in general. Sarbin and Coe have described a number of variables that appear to be important to the success of this role enactment (Kihlstrom, 1985). These include the location of individual participants in their proper roles, perceived congruence between self and role, accuracy of role expectations and sensitivity to role demands, possession of role-relevant skills, and the influence of the audience. Depending upon the degree to which these factors are favorable, the subject is capable of giving a performance that is as convincing to observers as to oneself.

Related to Sarbin and Coe's theory, Barber (1969) has suggested that hypnosis does not require a trance or a trance state for the phenomenon to be demonstrated. In other words, according to this **task-motivation theory,** hypnosis is not an altered state of consciousness. Rather, it is a predisposition in a normal state of awareness to attend to commands and suggestions from a hypnotist. Barber believes that most of the phenomena that are purported to come about as a result of hypnosis can be demonstrated in a nonhypnotic, wakeful situation as well. Thus, nonhypnotized subjects are capable of performing tasks that supposedly are possible only under hypnosis. A subject who has positive attitudes about hypnosis, who is sufficiently motivated to perform a given task, and who expects that a given task is possible with hypnosis can perform hypnotic feats without being in an altered state of consciousness.

Some examples of experiments in support of Barber's theory include those by Spanos, Ham, and Barber (1973) and Johnson, Maher, and Barber (1972). In the experiment by Spanos and associates, subjects were asked to hallucinate the presence of an object that in reality was not present. Three conditions were employed in this study. In the first condition, subjects were asked to hallucinate the presence of an object without any special instructions. In the second condition, subjects received task-motivational instructions in which they were told to try as hard as they could to imagine the object. The third condition involved the standardized induction of hypnosis, in which the hallucination of an object was suggested via so-called hypnotic instructions.

The result of the study showed that 98 percent of the control subjects (i.e., those given the first condition) reported imagining the object either vaguely or vividly, but they really did not *see* it. However, 8 percent of subjects who were given either a hypnotic-induction procedure or task-motivational instructions reported actually seeing the object. This percentage did not differ as a function of receiving hypnotic-induction procedures or task-motivational instructions. Therefore, the investigators concluded that task-motivational instructions were as effective as actual hypnotic-induction procedures in producing a visual hallucination. This finding appears to indicate that a trance or an altered state is not necessary for the production of a phenomenon that theoretically is possible only under a hypnotic trance.

Johnson and associates (1972) reached a similar conclusion. In their experiment they investigated a phenomenon referred to as *trance logic*. Trance logic (Orne, 1959) refers to the use of a special form of reasoning in which it is totally plausible for an individual to report seeing a hallucinated image in a room and at the same time see the same object in another room. Or a person may see a person in one part of the environment and at the same time see a hallucinated image of that person in another part of the environment.

This supposed ability of objects or people to be in two places at the same time does not appear illogical to hypnotized subjects; hence, the term trance logic. Accordingly, it appears, as Orne postulates, that a special trance state exists for a subject to be able to perform trance logic. However, Johnson and associates found that nonhypnotized subjects gave the same kind of reports with the same frequency as subjects who were judged to be deeply hypnotized. Therefore, it appears that the phenomenon of trance logic is possible both for subjects who appear to be in a hypnotic trance and for others who are not hypnotized but who are asked to imagine this form of hallucination under task-motivational instructions. Again, this type of experimental evidence led Barber to postulate that hypnosis is not a trance state, but rather is the result of positive attitudes, positive motivations, and positive expectancies toward the hypnosis-related task.

It appears that, at least for some situations, Barber has found sufficient evidence to support his theory. However, many experiments support the trance theory, so Barber's theory cannot be considered the sole explanation of hypnosis (see Bowers, 1976, and Fromm & Shor, 1979, for reviews of this literature). Also, many experiments have shown that positive attitudes, motivations, and expectancies toward hypnosis may not always be sufficient to produce hypnosislike results (see Krauss, Katzell, & Krauss, 1974; Walker et al., 1976; Woody, Drugovic, & Oakman, 1997).

It is without question that Barber's research has added considerable information to the study of hypnosis. However, for the nontrance approach to be more acceptable, results such as those obtained by Walker et al. (1976) and Wallace (1978a) in the restoration of eidetic imagery through hypnosis (which, incidentally, could not be produced solely with Barber's conditions) will have to be explained in terms of positive attitudes, motivations, and expectancies. At present this has not been accomplished.

As you can see, the definition or theory of hypnosis is as controversial as the phenomenon itself. Each theory has its advocates and its opponents. In addition, available experimental evidence appears to support, at least to some extent, each side of the argument. To help resolve the controversy, it may be necessary to accept a position similar to that expressed in Hilgard's description of the two levels in hypnotically controlled pain. That is, with regard to the phenomenon of hypnosis, at one level, individuals become cognizant of hypnosis, and at another level, they experience hypnosis.

Thus, it is possible that, at one level, individuals have positive attitudes, motivations, and expectancies concerning their ability to be hypnotized. At this level, hypnosis becomes possible even though the individual is still in a normal waking state. At the second level, however, a subject must assume an altered state of consciousness for a hypnotic feat (e.g., hypnotic analgesia) to become effective. With this dual approach to hypnosis, perhaps we can come a bit closer to defining the phenomenon. In fact, something similar to this was proposed by Sheehan and McConkey (1982).

Ultimately, we may discover that hypnosis involves many more levels of consciousness than even Hilgard describes. For example, we know that some hypnotized subjects can be in a so-called light trance at one point and in a deep trance at another. Whether these trance states are actually different levels of awareness or incremental differences in the same level is not known. However, such speculation can be fruitful only if scientists are encouraged to pursue an answer to this possibility.

One unfortunate aspect of the study of hypnosis is our failure to understand fully what it is. We also do not know why some individuals are readily hypnotizable while others are not, although many clues are emerging that were previously discussed. Furthermore, we do not know what triggers a state of hypnosis. We think we know that hypnosis is not controlled physiologically, but that idea does not tell us what *does* control hypnosis.

Despite the theories that purport to explain the phenomenon, hypnosis is still a controversial area of study within psychology and medicine, although not nearly as much so as during the days of Mesmer. Only the passage of time, a proliferation of experiments, and an understanding of the general role of hypnosis as an altered state of consciousness will help to place this important scientific tool in the forefront of investigations in the behavioral sciences and medicine. And, at least according to a survey conducted by Nash, Minton, and Baldridge (1988), this is exactly what is happening. There is more scientific interest today (as witnessed by the sheer number of articles in dental, medical, and psychological journals) in hypnosis than there has been since the resurgence of the study of consciousness in the late 1960s and early 1970s. With this increased interest, it is likely that many of the questions surrounding hypnosis may, at least to some extent, be answered.

FOR FURTHER READING

Bowers, K. S. (1976). *Hypnosis for the seriously curious*. New York: Norton.

Edmonston, W. E., Jr. (1986). *The induction of hypnosis*. New York: Wiley.

Hilgard, E. R., & Hilgard, J. R. (1994). *Hypnosis in the relief of pain*. New York: Bruner/Mazel.

Kunzendorf, R. G., Spanos, N. P., & Wallace, B. (Eds.). (1996). *Hypnosis and imagination*. Amityville, NY: Baywood.

Naish, P. L. N. (Ed.). (1986). *What is hypnosis? Current theories and research*. Philadelphia: Open University Press.

Olness, K., & Kohen, D. P. (1996). *Hypnosis and hypnotherapy with children*. New York: Guilford.

Wallace, B. (1979). *Applied hypnosis: An overview*. Chicago: Nelson-Hall.

5

BIOFEEDBACK

Our bodies have many physiological responses of which we are normally not aware. Some of these include our heart rate, muscle tone, blood pressure, skin-surface temperature, and brain activity. However, through a process called biofeedback, it may be possible to train ourselves to become aware of such involuntary responses. In other words, through biofeedback, we may be capable of learning to attend to responses that normally we cannot control consciously.

Very simply defined, **biofeedback** is a behavioral technique that, by use of instrumentation, is meant to increase an individual's level of awareness of his or her biological condition. Such awareness may help people to bring a physiological response (e.g., muscle tone, heart rate, blood pressure) under conscious control. As an example, this might help an individual gain some control over hypertension. The increased level of awareness or consciousness is brought about as the biofeedback instrument detects the physiological activity of the responses in question and simultaneously provides this information to the subject in the form of visual or auditory feedback. Using this feedback, the subject can then manipulate and control the physiological response.

In this chapter we will attempt to explain the relatively simple and basic principles underlying biofeedback. We will also describe the historical development of the manipulation and the basic components of the technique as it helps us to gain access to bodily information of which we are normally unaware. Finally, we will assess the importance and validity of biofeedback as a means of helping us bring to consciousness physiological information that we can use in dealing with behavioral and medical problems.

BIOFEEDBACK AND CONSCIOUSNESS

To explain the process of biofeedback, we will first illustrate a basic principle of learning through general feedback. Try to recall the very first time you went bowling. Remember when you picked up the ball and discovered how heavy it seemed? Remember how far away the pins appeared and how awkward you felt as you approached the foul line and released the ball for the first time? Finally, remember the embarrassment of watching the ball roll down the gutter or, at best, of leaving all but one or two pins completely unscathed?

If, after all this, you were still determined to continue bowling, you probably found that with time and experience, the ball seemed a bit lighter than before, your feelings of awkwardness as you approached the foul line diminished substantially, and rather than dropping your ball two or three feet to the alley or hurl it into the gutter, you actually released it correctly. As a consequence of these improvements, gutter-ball frames became much less frequent as more and more pins fell victim to your ball.

In large part, these improvements in performance were made possible by learning through sensory feedback. Imagine what your improvement would have been had you been forced to wear earplugs and a blindfold each time you went bowling. Lacking visual and auditory input, you would have been completely unaware of your successes and failures, your need or lack of need for correction. For any given frame, your score would be pretty much a function of blind luck. In short, without such feedback, learning to bowl, as measured by improvements in pin count, would be virtually impossible.

Instead of bowling, suppose that you wanted to learn to increase or decrease your heart rate at will. An obvious similarity between the bowling task and the heart rate task is that both involve bringing certain muscles or muscle groups under conscious control. On the basis of the bowling example, you might predict that any improvement in performance (i.e., increasing or decreasing heart rate as desired) would depend, in large part, on your reception of adequate sensory feedback. Herein lies the problem. The human body simply is not designed to provide any but the most rudimentary feedback concerning internal physiological states. As you read this page, you are probably not aware that your heart is beating at a rate between 65 and 75 beats per minute.

At this point, guess what your heart rate is, note the number in the margin, and then take your pulse. (The simplest method of taking one's pulse is to count pulse beats for a 15-second period, multiply this value by four, and express the answer in terms of beats per minute.) Note your actual pulse rate in the margin and circle it. How accurate was your guess?

Suppose for a moment that our systems were constructed so that we did not receive constant feedback concerning their level of physiological activity and that each system was under voluntary control. If this was the case, our consciousness would be bombarded constantly with information concerning the physiological state of each organ of the body. Simply to stay alive, all our conscious efforts would have to be directed toward making certain that each system functioned properly. Imagine the sensory overload that would occur. With our attention so focused, we would have little or no awareness of our external environment and little or no time to respond to changes in it. As we have already noted, however, under normal conditions our bodily systems continue to function well, despite our lack of awareness of such functioning.

Does this mean that we are never aware of the biological state of an organ system? The answer to this, obviously, is no. From previous experiences at the doctor's office or in a gym class, almost everyone is familiar with the fact that hopping up and down on one foot for one minute produces a perceptible increase in heart rate. However, we are aware of an increase in heart rate under these conditions because the number of beats per minute has almost doubled.

Now stop reading for a minute and check your pulse rate in the same manner as before. When you compare this new value with the one circled earlier, you will probably observe a change of several beats per minute, even though, in all likelihood, you were not aware of any such change because it was so small. Unfortunately for us, at least in terms of the heart rate task, it is these minute changes that are the most valuable as feedback in permitting us to achieve conscious control over the response.

The process of biofeedback training places the individual in a closed feedback loop with an instrument that continually provides information about subtle changes in bodily processes. In turn, the individual or subject who is undergoing biofeedback continually adjusts, corrects, and modifies responses as more and more information is received. The training is continued until it is determined that some final, generally predetermined goal (set by a trainer or clinician after lengthy discussions with the patient) has been achieved (Hart, 1967).

The biofeedback procedure, as it exists today, is a relatively new technique, but one that has substantial historical roots. To place biofeedback in its proper historical perspective, we will now examine some of the most important factors that have led to its present state of development.

HISTORICAL DEVELOPMENT

Many centuries ago, Plato (427–347 B.C.) observed that humans possessed a "superior rational soul" located in the head and an "inferior soul" located in the heart and liver. Plato believed that the superior rational soul, which he equated with reason, controlled the voluntary responses of the striated musculature, while the inferior soul controlled the responses of the nonstriated muscles and glands. Plato equated the inferior soul with emotions. This dichotomy between reason and emotion, between voluntary and involuntary responses, was to prove both troublesome to later theorists in the area of learning and extremely persistent in psychological thought.

In the seventeenth century this dichotomy once again gained prominence when M. F. Bichat (1771–1802), a French neuroanatomist, distinguished between the cerebrospinal nervous system, which he labeled the "great brain," and the spinal cord and sympathetic ganglionic chains, which he referred to as the "little brain." To the former, he attributed control of the voluntary skeletal responses; to the latter, he attributed control of the emotional and involuntary visceral or autonomic responses.

The twentieth-century manifestation of this dichotomy was expressed by the European investigators Miller and Konorski (1928). They distinguished between what they called Type I (classical) and Type II (instrumental) conditioning. More important for our discussion, however, is that they proposed, for the first time, that involuntary responses were not subject to instrumental conditioning. The subsequent acceptance of this stance by some of the most prominent psychologists of the day—e.g., Schlosberg (1937), Mowrer (1938), and eventually Skinner (1953)—turned the exclusion of autonomic responses into psychological dogma (Kimmel, 1974). Neal Miller suggested that both classical and instrumental conditioning followed similar laws and that a common mechanism might be found that actually controlled both. As we will see shortly, this hypothesis was at the center of Miller's early research, in which he employed paralyzed animals to determine whether these animals could learn to control their cardiovascular activity for reward or punishment (Dienstfrey, 1991).

This is not to suggest that there were no dissenters. Several independent groups of investigators had begun research programs designed to demonstrate that human involuntary responses could be modified to obtain a desired result. In the Soviet Union, for example, Lisina (1965) attempted to condition at will the dilation and constriction of the blood vessel in a single finger. Initially, this investigator employed electric shock as a negative reinforcer, but such training failed to change blood vessel activity in either direction (constriction or dilation). When Lisina combined electric shock with a visual feedback display of the subject's vasomotor activity, however, she was able to demonstrate operant conditioning of dilation in the blood vessel.

Meanwhile, in the United States, Harwood (1962) and Shearn (1960) were engaged in attempts to modify heart rate responses using operant learning techniques. Using rats as subjects, Harwood obtained what essentially were negative findings for both acceleration and deceleration of the heart rate. Shearn was somewhat more successful in that he was able to condition an increase in heart rate for human subjects to whom such an increase would postpone the delivery of an electric shock.

Finally, Mandler and colleagues at the University of Toronto and Kimmel and colleagues at the University of Florida were interested in determining whether the galvanic skin response (GSR), or sweat-gland activity, could be operantly conditioned. The results that Mandler, Preven, and Kuhlman (1962) obtained forced these investigators to report negative findings with respect to the possibility of operant autonomic conditioning. However, these results could be considered suggestive; when the workers reviewed the results, subject by subject, they found that six of their nine subjects produced a significantly greater number of GSRs during the training session than they did during the extinction period when behavior was no longer reinforced.

Kimmel and Hill (1960) used pleasant odors as positive reinforcers and unpleasant odors as negative reinforcers in a study designed to detect methodological problems in operant autonomic responding. These investigators obtained results that, at best, only suggested operant modification of the conscious ability to control autonomic responding. Refining the procedures used in the initial study and employing a more conventional reinforcer (a dim white light), Fowler and Kimmel (1962) were able to demonstrate the effects of instrumental conditioning during both the acquisition and extinction phases of the study.

Having demonstrated that autonomic responses were indeed subject to instrumental techniques, contrary to the 1928 dictum of Miller and Konorski, the next logical step was to replicate, refine, and advance this pioneering research. Kimmel (1967), in reviewing the research literature in this area, found that a number of different laboratories had focused on this task and that, in general, they had produced supportive findings. Therefore, Kimmel observed that the operant modification of autonomically mediated responses had been adequately demonstrated.

Kimmel's conclusion was almost immediately challenged by Katkin and Murray (1969) and Katkin, Murray, and Lachman (1969). These authors raised the question of skeletal mediation. To explain the hypothesis of skeletal mediation, we can return to the heart rate task that appeared earlier in this chapter. One of the ways in which you might have increased your heart rate would have been to adopt a strategy for altering your respiration. You might want to test this by first taking your pulse rate, next breathing deeply for 30 seconds, and finally taking your pulse rate again. You should observe a sharp increase. According to the Katkin and Murray mediation hypothesis, you have not directly altered your heart rate, over which you had no control before you adopted the breathing strategy. Instead, you actually modified a skeletal-muscle response (i.e., depth of breathing), over which you already had voluntary, conscious control, to produce or mediate the visceral response (the increased heart rate).

Similarly, it could be argued that subjects in the previous operant conditioning studies, who had demonstrated appropriate changes in autonomic responding, had learned to produce those changes not directly, but rather by manipulating the appropriate voluntary-muscle mediators. Of all the studies Katkin and Murray reviewed, they contended that none had employed experimental control procedures that would have eliminated the effects of potential skeletal mediators. They argued that these researchers could not conclude with any degree of certainty that their subjects had learned to operantly modify an autonomic response by manipulating a voluntary response.

A way of achieving experimental control for potential skeletal-muscle mediation is to use the drug curare (d-tubocurarine). The injection of curare at relatively low dosages blocks the action of acetylcholine at the skeletal neuromuscular synapse (Chagas, 1959) while leaving the autonomic nervous system essentially unaffected (Miller & Dworkin, 1974). Such a preparation leaves the subject limp and motionless, so that artificial respiration is needed.

Actually, the problem described by Katkin and Murray was already being addressed in a series of animal studies begun in the laboratories of Neal Miller. In these laboratories, Trowill (1967) was the first to employ deep curarization, which he coupled with electrical stimulation of the pleasure center of the brain as a reinforcer to operantly condition heart rate changes. Using rats as subjects, he was able to demonstrate heart rate increases for 15 of the 19 subjects that were rewarded for fast heart rates and decreases for 15 of 17 subjects that were rewarded for slow heart rates. It should be pointed out that while these average changes were statistically significant, the amount of change was quite small.

In a subsequent study, Miller and DiCara (1967), again using curarized rats, attempted to replicate the Trowill results while, at the same time, attempting to increase the magnitude of these changes by progressively shifting rats to a more and more difficult criterion after they learned to meet the easier one. Using a discrimination conditioning procedure, these investigators were able to demonstrate remarkable results. Not only were they able to replicate the Trowill results, but after demonstrating achievement of the easy criterion of a small change, their subjects in both the increase and the decrease conditions went on to show significantly larger changes, in the range of 100 beats per minute, as a result of the shaping procedures. It was also clear from the results that the rats had learned to respond discriminatively to the stimuli signaling that cardiac response change would be rewarded.

Black (1966) suggested that even though the subjects in these studies were deeply curarized, it was conceivable that they still might show evidence of action potentials in electromyographic (EMG) recordings. EMG recordings are simply recordings of the electrical activity taking place in the muscles. The implication was that while skeletal-muscular activity had been interrupted by curare, the activity of the motor cortex of the brain was not, and there might be conditioned motor cortex responses that mediated the instrumental conditioning of the autonomic nervous system (ANS).

Miller (1972) reasoned that if such instrumental conditioning of the motor cortex impulses had occurred, the effects would be general rather than specific to a single autonomic response. He then set out to demonstrate that it was possible to instrumentally modify one response independent of other closely related autonomic responses. This study compared the effect of rewarding either heart-rate changes or spontaneous intestinal contractions on the rate of response of both systems in deeply curarized rats. He observed that the subjects that were rewarded for increased or decreased intestinal contraction showed progressive changes in the appropriate direction but that heart rate did not change. Conversely, rats that were rewarded for high or low rates of heartbeat learned to change rates appropriately but showed no changes in intestinal contraction. These findings eliminated Black's alternative explanation.

Other studies from the Miller labs showed that animals could exert specific control over a variety of very subtle responses. Miller and DiCara (1968) demonstrated instrumental learning of urine formation independent of other physiological responses. DiCara and Miller (1968) also successfully trained rats to blush in one ear and not the other. It should be pointed out that blushing is brought about by the vasodilation of blood vessels. It was concluded from these studies that there was greater specificity of action in the sympathetic part of the ANS than had previously been attributed to it.

With such experimental success achieved, the idea that operant conditioning of specific autonomic responses could occur independent of skeletal or cognitive mediation gained wide acceptance from the scientific community. Even Katkin and Murray (1969) were willing to accept these findings as adequately controlled examples of operant conditioning of autonomic responses. However, they were not willing to take the necessary next step to conclude that similar processes were involved in human autonomic conditioning.

To date, investigators have failed in attempts to replicate the results of these curare studies. Miller and Dworkin (1974) and other investigators (Hothersall & Brener, 1969; Slaughter, Hahn, & Rinaldi, 1970) have attempted such replication but have reported great difficulty in replicating the large response changes reported in the earlier curare studies.

Actually, one of the studies of operant conditioning that Katkin and Murray reviewed had employed curare with a human subject. After a baseline period and six normal training sessions, an immobilizing but subparalytic dose of curare was administered to the senior author, and only subject, in an electrodermal study reported by Birk, Crider, Shapiro, and Tursky (1966). Although Birk was able to produce more skin-potential responses during the curarized seventh session than during the baseline control period, the results were inconclusive because he was conscious and only partially paralyzed.

In a critical response to the mediation position, Crider, Schwartz, and Shnidman (1969) suggested that Katkin and Murray should identify some of the mediators they had so frequently invoked to discount the earlier examples of human autonomic operant conditioning. It soon became clear, even to Katkin, Murray, and Lachman (1969), that the controversy they had begun was of little more than theoretical importance. From any applied or therapeutic standpoint, how a subject produces an increase or decrease in response magnitude, frequency, or likelihood of occurrence is not nearly as important as the fact that it has been accomplished.

Following some very early training experiments with alpha brain waves in the late 1950s, which became widely known despite the fact that they were not formally published, Kamiya (1968, 1969) turned his attention to a determination of whether subjects could exercise control over the alpha brain wave patterns on command. For this work, many credit Kamiya with initiating the study of biofeedback. Also in 1969 the Biofeedback Research Society, now called the Biofeedback Society of America, was formed at a scientific meeting held in California.

THE BIOFEEDBACK TRAINING PROCESS

Today, biofeedback training is the procedure by which a subject is made aware of what was previously an unconscious physiological activity and learns to use this information to gain control over an involuntary process. Because biofeedback training often differs from one laboratory or clinic to another, we need to examine the actual procedure more closely. This variability is probably due to a number of factors, not the least of which is the comparative newness of the technique and consequent lack of much-needed methodological research. Another factor that contributes to the differences in biofeedback training is the many different applications that have been found for the procedure. Despite the great variability in biofeedback training, however, at least four common elements can be extracted: (1) the trainee, (2) the trainer, (3) the instrument, and (4) the training sessions. To help answer some of the questions you may have about the biofeedback process itself, we will consider each of these elements.

The Trainee

The **trainee** is the subject of a biofeedback experiment or the client who seeks biofeedback therapy. In brief, the trainee is the individual who will actually experience the biofeedback process. The selection of a volunteer to serve as a subject in biofeedback research is based primarily on the match between the individual's characteristics and the characteristics demanded by the nature and design of the study. For example, the trainer needs to be aware of how the biosocial characteristics of the subject's race, gender, and age might affect the efficacy of the biofeedback procedure (Roberts & McGrady, 1996). On the other hand, the biofeedback client is someone who has concluded, through either reading, study, or consultation with a physician or other primary-care source, that biofeedback may be helpful in dealing with a particular symptom.

Typically, both the biofeedback therapy client and the research subject are requested to submit current health information about themselves. The reasons for this become clear when we recall that the eventual goal of biofeedback training is to increase the trainee's awareness of an involuntary physiological activity to learn to bring the physiological response under voluntary control. Does the trainee have any health problems that might contraindicate the use of biofeedback? Obviously, one would not want to include a patient with hypertension (high blood pressure) in an experimental group being trained to increase blood pressure.

Perhaps less obvious is the need to consider the trainee's mental health as well. Sterman (1973) and Fuller (1978), however, have observed that the use of biofeedback is contraindicated if the client suffers from a mental illness in which the biofeedback instrument may become a component of a delusional framework or in which existing feelings of dissociation may be increased by biofeedback-induced relaxation. Biofeedback is also contraindicated for individuals who suffer from depression.

Another reason for obtaining health information is to determine whether the trainee is currently taking drugs, either prescribed or nonprescribed, that might affect performance in biofeedback training. Finally, the biofeedback therapist must be aware of the client's current state of health if he or she is to select the biofeedback technique that will be most effective in dealing with the client's present symptoms.

In Chapter 4 we described several standardized tests for determining whether a subject could be readily hypnotized. Although such tests would be of great value in biofeedback, their development remains a task for future investigators. Clearly, however, a highly motivated individual with a positive attitude toward biofeedback has at least two personality characteristics of a potentially successful trainee. Assessment of these factors ought to be considered a necessary feature in any such test designed to predict success or failure in biofeedback training.

The Trainer

The **trainer** is the individual who is responsible for administering the biofeedback training process. In addition to being well trained in his or her area of expertise (e.g., medicine, psychology, physical therapy), the trainer must have a firm understanding of the nature of the physiological processes as they are related to biofeedback training. He or she also should have a working knowledge of biofeedback instrumentation and techniques.

In the biofeedback training process, the trainer and the trainee form the elements of a social dyad. On the basis of research findings in related areas, such as psychophysiology (Christie & Todd, 1975; Fisher & Kotses, 1973) and social psychology (Deutsch, Canavan, & Rubin, 1971; Rosenthal, 1966; Sattler, 1970; Winkel & Sarason, 1964), we might logically predict that the characteristics of one member of the dyad, the trainer, may affect the performance of the other, the trainee.

Until recently, biofeedback research had failed to address this problem. Recently, however, using chronic headache patients, Borgeat, Hade, Larouche, and Gauthier (1984) obtained data that suggest that psychophysiological measures, such as those collected in biofeedback research and clinical applications, are indeed sensitive to therapist variables. These investigators' results also suggest a need for further biofeedback research related to the therapist-client or trainer-trainee dyad, since they may well affect trainee performance. Gaarder and Montgomery (1977) suggest that the trainer who brings to the training process a cheerful, positive, friendly, and encouraging attitude should have a positive influence on the trainee's performance. Finally, it is essential that the trainer, clinician, and researcher have carefully considered their own beliefs as well as those of their colleagues concerning ethical practices in domains such as limits of confidentiality, informed consent, and dealings with minors (Percival & Striefel, 1991).

The Instrument

We noted earlier that the human body is not designed to provide its owner with the subtle information concerning internal states that would be necessary to develop conscious control over a physiological response. To make the trainee aware of these changes in activity, the biofeedback instrument mirrors the response and feeds the information back to the subject in the form of a tone, lights, meter display, and the like.

Three basic types of instruments are used in biofeedback training (Paskewitz, 1975). The first of these is the **biomedical polygraph**, or electroencephalograph (EEG), combined with certain logic modules and some type of feedback display. (The EEG is discussed in Chapter 2.) These instruments are highly accurate and reliable and have the capacity to monitor more than a single response at one time. They also provide the trainer with a permanent record of the monitored response systems. Besides cost, the only disadvantages of such instruments are their size and complexity. Many investigators who are engaged in basic research in the field of biofeedback still rely on such equipment.

Major advancements in electronic technology have made possible the development of another class of instruments designed to meet the needs of clinical therapists and applied researchers. These instruments are what we generally think of when we hear the term *biofeedback machine*. As well as being considerably less expensive than the first class of instruments, the biofeedback machines are more compact and simpler to operate. Additionally, today's machine sacrifices little, if any, reliability and accuracy. The major drawback of such instruments is that only one signal from one site can be monitored at any given time. This problem has been answered recently, in part at least, by the development of the *multichannel data-acquisition system*. Such systems are composed of several biofeedback instruments monitored simultaneously by an automatic printout device. As you might expect, however, such systems are much more expensive than the single biofeedback machine.

As researchers began to find more and more applications for biofeedback, and as these applications began to receive popular media coverage, the public demand for a private, home-use model increased. The machines that were developed to meet this demand constitute the third class of instruments. The use of these devices ranges from home practice of therapy to exploration of self-awareness and meditation. In the production and development of these machines, accuracy and reliability are often sacrificed to reduce their cost.

Despite the great differences in outward appearance, all instruments operate on similar basic principles. First, the physiological activity must be picked up by electrodes or a transducer attached to the surface of the body. When this activity is a bioelectric signal, electrodes are employed. Examples of such responses include muscle tonus, brain waves, and skin response. In instances in which the signal takes some other form of energy (e.g., mechanical, thermal, photoelectric), a transducer is employed to translate the signal into an electrical event. Monitoring of responses such as blood pressure, respiration, and skin surface temperature call for the use of a transducer.

In either case the signal detected is very small and may contain not only the signal of interest, but other electrical activity (noise) as well. Thus, signal refinement is the next step necessary in the biofeedback loop. Signal refinement involves boosting or amplifying the raw signal and then filtering it. This is accomplished with a series of complex electronic circuits that make up a preamplifier and amplifier. Finally, the energy of the refined signal is converted by the signal display into some type of varying stimulus that is made available to the subject; this is the feedback.

The Training Sessions

Because the physiological changes that occur during biofeedback training are usually beyond the level of conscious experience, it is necessary that in the initial stages of training, the trainee work with a biofeedback machine that is designed to monitor subtle physiological changes in the system, refine the biological signal, and make the trainee aware of this activity by some type of feedback display. This is the external feedback loop illustrated in Figure 5.1. This increased awareness will enable the trainee to accomplish two major tasks.

The more immediate of the two tasks is to respond to the feedback in ways that will alter the physiological activity of the system in a desired direction. Often, the trainee is instructed to develop, or develops independently, a kind of strategy (e.g., imagining feelings of warmth, calm, and peace) to bring about these changes. Early in the training process, performance may be extremely variable as the trainee attempts first one strategy and then another. A more constant, desirable performance is achieved as the trainee receives more and more positive feedback showing that the physiological changes are in the desired direction) and settles on the particular technique that works best. As the trainee practices the strategy, it is hoped that he or she will become aware of the relationship between the psychological activity and the physiological changes that occur.

The second task that the trainee must accomplish during these sessions is to learn to produce the desired response change without the aid of the machine. Until this point in the training process, the trainee has depended

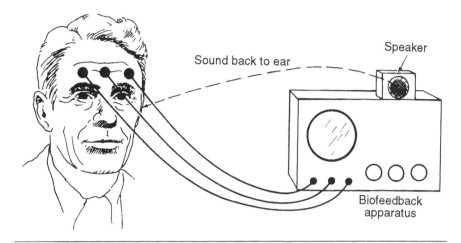

FIGURE 5.1   Biofeedback Loop

almost exclusively on external feedback. Now, he or she must become aware of internal sensory cues that provide information about the overall physiological state and the relationship between this state and the external feedback. Once these links have been established, the information from the internal sensors can replace the external feedback, thus establishing the internal loop.

The actual biofeedback training process can be broken down into a series of training sessions, the number and nature of which vary considerably, depending on the goal of the investigator or therapist. There are four major types of training sessions: (1) the baseline sessions, (2) the shaping and reinforcement sessions, (3) the test sessions, and (4) the follow-up sessions.

The goal of the initial baseline sessions is to obtain a representative sample of the internal system's activity before training. Measurements obtained during these sessions are used to set training goals and to compare pretraining and posttraining performance levels. If the sample is to be considered truly representative, measurements should be taken during more than one baseline session.

The shaping and reinforcement sessions follow the initial baseline sessions. During the baseline session, with the aid of feedback, the trainee learned to bring about voluntarily a desired change in the physiological activity of a system of which he or she was previously unaware and over which he or she had no control. Because the desired change usually occurs involuntarily and at the unconscious level, the probability of its occurrence is generally very low. Often, the trainer must rely on small spontaneous changes in the response system that represent remote approximations of the desired change and reward their production when they occur. As the trainer rewards progressively better approximations of the desired response, the response eventually can be shaped into occurring. Once the trainee has learned to produce the desired response, reinforcement in the form of feedback will occur more and more frequently.

To determine whether the trainee has been able, during these sessions, to replace the external feedback loop with a newly developed internal loop, the trainee is subjected to a test session in which he or she is required to produce the desired physiological changes without the aid of external feedback.

In many respects, follow-up sessions are similar to the test session. The subject must again attempt to produce the desired change in activity without the aid of external feedback. Instead of being administered immediately after the final shaping and reinforcement session, however, follow-up sessions are usually executed some time later. The results of these sessions provide the trainer with information about how well such training holds up over time.

BIOFEEDBACK APPLICATIONS

How can we use increased awareness of the activity of an internal response system gained with the biofeedback training process? From almost the inception of this technique, applied research has focused on finding answers to this question. As an example, if people's levels of awareness and consciousness are altered through biofeedback, they may be able to better their lives in some important ways. The applications to be considered in this section fall into three broad categories: (1) clinical therapy, (2) exploration of meditative processes, and (3) research.

The obvious potential of biofeedback training to alleviate symptoms has produced a substantial flurry of research activity. To date, biofeedback has been successfully used to treat depressive disorders (Kumano et al., 1996), hyperactivity (Denkowski, Denkowski, & Omizo, 1984; Shouse & Lubar, 1977; Whitmer, 1978), learning disabilities and attention deficit disorder (Carter & Russell, 1985; Linden, Habib, & Radojevic, 1996), stress-induced urinary incontinence in the elderly (Burns, Clesse-Desotelle, Nochajski, & Pranikoff, 1990), epilepsy in children (Dahl & Melin, 1989; Kay, Shively, & Kilkenny, 1978), and irritable bowel syndrome (Radnitz & Blanchard, 1989; Schwartz, Taylor, Scharf, & Blanchard, 1989).

Researchers have also applied biofeedback techniques to treat speech disorders (Craig & Cleary, 1982; Davis & Drichta, 1980), the acquisition of fine motor movement (French, 1980; LeVine & Irvine, 1984), the control of sexual arousal (Hatch, 1981; Hoon, 1980; Palace, 1995), alcohol dependency (Saxby, 1995; Schneider et al., 1993), essential hypertension (Achmon, Granet, Golomb, & Hart, 1989; Cornish, Blanchard, & Wittrock, 1989; Jurek, Higgins, & McGrady, 1992; Latha, 1991), Raynaud's disease (Freedman, Ianni, & Wenig, 1985; Freedman, Lynn, Ianni, & Hale, 1981; Stroebal & Ford, 1981); stress-induced hyperhydrosis, or excessive sweating (Nigl, 1981), and painful menstrual symptoms (Belick, Elfner, & May, 1982), to name but a few. This section will provide only a sample of the many applications of biofeedback.

Headache

Headache is one of the most common disorders known to humankind and was one of the first medical problems to be diagnosed and treated by physicians of early civilizations (Nigl, 1984). Most often headache is related to stress and other benign conditions; however, it may also be due to serious, even life-threatening disorders.

Appenzeller (1973) suggested that over 80 percent of all headache sufferers treated in headache clinics have *tension headaches*. According to Budzynski (1978), the estimates of the number of people in the United States who suffer from tension headache ranges from 50 million to 100 million. While one must be careful in interpreting such data, it is clear that most professionals consider tension headache to be the most prevalent pain disorder today.

According to a 1962 report by the Ad Hoc Committee of the National Institute of Neurological Disease and Blindness (NINDB), tension headache is described as having the following characteristics (as reported by White and Tursky, 1982):

1. A gradual onset.
2. A variable duration that may last hours, days, or even months.
3. Steady, nonpulsating pain, often described as being like a vise or a band tightening around the head; also there is soreness and a sensation of the skin drawing tight.
4. The headache is bilateral in the occipital, suboccipital, or posterior cervical area, radiating to the temples and to the frontalis region.
5. The patient frequently awakens with the headache, and it gradually becomes worse and more intense as the day progresses.
6. The pain is aggravated by exposure to the cold. It can be relieved by massage, heat, or stretching of muscles.

The primary underlying physiological mechanism of tension headache has been identified as the sustained contraction of skeletal muscles in the scalp, face, shoulders, and neck, combined with ischemia (less than the required or normal blood supply) in the affected muscles (Friedman, 1979). These muscles are identified in Figure 5.2. Contrary to the statement by the NINDB Ad Hoc Committee, which proposed that the vascular constriction was diagnostic of migraine but not of tension headache, a number of studies have demonstrated that it is both of these physiological events, occurring concurrently, that lead to the development of a tension headache (Budzynski, 1978).

Although the bulk of the empirical evidence suggests that both muscular contraction and vasoconstriction of the cephalic arteries and arteries carrying

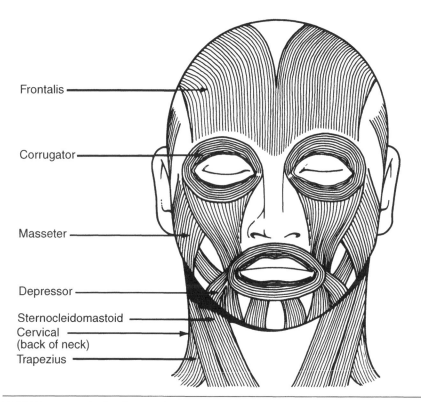

Frontalis

Corrugator

Masseter

Depressor

Sternocleidomastoid
Cervical
(back of neck)
Trapezius

FIGURE 5.2   Skeletal Muscles in the Scalp, Face, Shoulders, and Neck

blood to the affected muscles are necessary to trigger the tension headache, biofeedback techniques have focused primarily on decreasing the activity of cervical, frontalis, and other muscles of the shoulders, neck, and head.

The initial studies were carried out in the laboratories of Budzynski (Budzynski, Stoyva, & Adler, 1970; Budzynski, Stoyva, Adler, & Mullaney, 1973). Rather than attempting to relax specific muscles or muscle groups that are thought to cause the symptom, however, these researchers, as well as many others, have employed a general relaxation process, which we will call **electromyographic** (EMG) feedback-assisted relaxation (Fridlund, Fowler, & Pritchard, 1980).

In this process, the trainee is made conscious of the activity level of a small pair of muscles located near the center of the forehead. These are the frontalis muscles (see Figure 5.2). The subject's task is to reduce the activity level, and thus the tension, of these muscles. The rationale underlying this approach is that, by relaxing this muscle pair, biofeedback training will generalize the relaxation to the untrained muscles, and they, too, will show a decrease in tension.

In reviewing the results of these earlier studies, Budzynski (1978, 1979) observed that subjects who received frontalis EMG biofeedback treatment had significantly lower frontalis EMG levels than did subjects who received noncontingent feedback (feedback that is not related to the muscle activity) or no feedback at all. Additionally, subjects who received contingent EMG biofeedback and relaxation therapy significantly reduced headache activity beyond baseline compared with the subjects who received noncontingent feedback and relaxation. Finally, he found substantial reductions in headache activity for most subjects within an eight-week period involving two EMG feedback sessions a week.

Since Budzynski's studies in the early 1970s, some 40 or more additional studies have been published that have employed some form of biofeedback, usually frontalis muscle activity, in the treatment of tension headache. In reviewing many of these studies, Budzynski (1978) stated that "the evidence appears strong that the use of EMG (primarily frontalis) feedback is effective in the alleviation of tension headaches" (p. 147).

In a study typical of the earlier research efforts in this area, Kondo and Canter (1977), employing EMG-feedback-assisted relaxation and a noncontingent feedback control group, found that after 10 training sessions, the 10 tension headache patients who received the contingent feedback from the frontalis muscles reported a significantly greater decrease in headache frequency than did the 10 tension headache patients who received the noncontingent feedback. Careful analysis of these results suggests that the improvement in headache frequency directly resulted from the EMG biofeedback training and not from expectancy of therapeutic value or attention.

Finally, one year after this treatment, follow-up reports demonstrated that while four of five contingent subjects indicated continued reduction of headache frequency, only two of five noncontingent subjects reported any such reduction. Similar findings have been reported by numerous investigators (Borgeat, Hade, Larouche, & Bedwant, 1980; Hart & Cichanski, 1981).

In the first half of the 1980s, research in this area raised a number of serious questions, including the following: Is EMG-feedback-assisted relaxation more effective than other forms of behavior therapy? Are there certain individual characteristics that might affect the efficacy of biofeedback in the treatment of chronic tension headache?

Concerning the latter question, Friedman (1979) suggests that while most tension headache patients clearly have some emotional problems that are intricately involved with their headache symptoms, few researchers have studied the effects of personality factors on chronic tension headache. Although biofeedback is accepted by most psychiatrists, it is perceived as an adjunct to psychotherapy, not as a primary mode of treatment.

This position seems to have been supported by a study (Levine, 1984) of 48 patients who were given forehead/posterior neck biofeedback therapy for 20 weeks. Half these patients had depression either with or without a previous history of head trauma. Levine reported that headache activity was lowered more for the nondepressed patients than for those who suffered from depression. These findings suggest that there is a probable need for the separation of depressed and nondepressed patients in headache treatment as well as a need for the treatment of the depression itself, aside from the headache.

Another personality variable that has been found to be significant in the treatment of chronic tension headache using biofeedback is introversion-extroversion, or whether one is reserved or outgoing (Merkel, 1979). The results of this study force us to agree with Beaty and Haynes (1979) that far more research and clinical attention be given to who can best benefit by the application of EMG biofeedback to headaches.

As to whether EMG biofeedback is more effective than other forms of behavioral therapy, most reviewers of the research in this area suggest that EMG biofeedback is no more effective than relaxation in reducing headache activity (Silver & Blanchard, 1978; Turk, Meichenbaum, & Berman, 1979; Yates, 1980). Assessing the efficacy of three procedures—relaxation therapy, frontal EMG biofeedback, and thermal biofeedback—in the behavioral treatment of 250 chronic headache patients, Blanchard, Andrasick, Evans, Neff, and Appelbaum (1985) found that relaxation alone led to improvement in 41 percent of the tension headache patients, while the combination of relaxation and thermal biofeedback therapy accounted for the improvement observed in 52 percent of the migraine and combined migraine and tension headache patients. One major dissenting position has been published by Budzynski (1978), who stated that "research indicates that EMG biofeedback can result in greater decreases in EMG at a faster rate than nonbiofeedback relaxation training" (p. 430).

Migraine Headache

The incidence of the second type of chronic headache, the migraine headache, is reported variously as being between 5 and 8 percent in the U.S. population (Schnarch & Hunter, 1980). Unlike what most nonsufferers think, migraine is not just one kind of chronic headache. Actually, migraine headache comes in several different flavors. To be more precise, Schnarch and Hunter (1980) were able to identify four different classifications of migraine headache:

1. *Classic migraine* has two phases, a preheadache, or prodromal, phase and a headache phase. The prodrome is characterized by such symptoms as flashing lights, strange odors, blind spots, tingling or numbness in the limbs, muscular weakness, emotional changes, and dysphasia or disturbances of language function (Olton & Noonberg, 1980). It is generally believed that this prodrome, which has both a sudden onset and a sudden end, is caused by a functional disturbance of intracerebral circulation, which in turn leads to the neurologic disruptions.

2. The *common migraine* is characterized by the absence of the prodrome and may be bilateral, whereas the classic migraine is most often unilateral.

3. *Cluster headaches* are briefer than classic migraines, lasting only 10 to 20 minutes, whereas classic migraines typically last for hours but appear in groups over a time period. Some authorities argue that despite the similarities in both mechanism and subjective report, these headaches should not be included in a migraine classification.

4. *Hemiplegic* or *ophthalmoplegic migraine* is the last type of migraine headache. It leaves those who have it with neurological symptoms still present after the pain is gone. Because of the significance of organic factors in this migraine, it is quite probable that behavioral therapies would be of little consequence.

Migraine is classified as a vascular headache because of the cerebrovascular dysfunction which results in head pain. Theoretically, a migraine is initiated by a complex, intracerebral vascular process that includes excessive vasoconstriction of arteries and arterioles, followed soon after by rebound, excessive vasodilation. Excessive vasodilation, in turn, results in supranormal pulsation and stretching of muscles and elastic fibers within the vessel wall (see Figure 5.3). The corresponding stimulation of stretch receptors surrounding the vessel walls results in pain (Nigl, 1984).

According to Olton and Noonberg (1980), four characteristics of migraine are most often mentioned in the literature:

1. The head pain initially is typically unilateral.
2. The head pain is often relieved, or attacks prevented, by vasoconstricting drugs such as ergotamine tartrate.

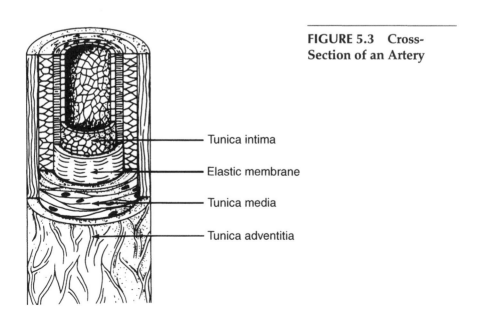

FIGURE 5.3   Cross-Section of an Artery

Tunica intima

Elastic membrane

Tunica media

Tunica adventitia

3. Migraine is often accompanied or succeeded by gastrointestinal distur-
    bances including nausea, vomiting, diarrhea, or constipation.
4. An aura or prodrome, caused by neurologic disturbances, precedes the
    migraine attack, except in common migraine.

Olton and Noonberg (1980) indicated that empirical research has not demonstrated a clear-cut dichotomy between migraine and tension headache.
Raskin (1980) suggested that both tension and migraine headaches are quan-
titatively different manifestations of the same phenomenon—instability of
vasomotor regulation.

The use of hand temperature biofeedback in the treatment of migraine was
discovered by accident when a group of investigators (Schultz & Luthe, 1969)
at the Menninger Clinic, in an effort to improve the outcome of autogenic training, combined such training with EMG, alpha brain-wave, and temperature
feedback. The encouraging results prompted Sargent, Green, and Walters
(1973) to carry out a more extensive pilot project. In this project they combined
autogenic phases and temperature feedback in the treatment of 19 patients with
migraine headache. After their training, all the patients were evaluated clinically by an internist and two psychologists. All three researchers considered 12
of the 19 patients treated to have improved and 3 not to have improved. The
researchers did not agree on the clinical evaluation of the remaining four subjects. These successful findings have been confirmed by a number of other
investigators (Engel & Rapoff, 1990; Johnson & Turin, 1975; Reading & Mohr,
1976; Stambaugh & House, 1977; Wickramasekera, 1972).

Although the Menninger research stimulated the development of clinical
techniques employing skin temperature biofeedback to treat migraine, the
findings have been subject to considerable criticism. Some of these methodological inadequacies were corrected in later studies that also obtained successful findings regarding the use of skin temperature biofeedback to treat
migraine headaches (Boller & Flam, 1979; Drury, DeRisi, & Liberman, 1979;
Fried, Lamberti, & Sneed, 1977); Kewman & Roberts, 1980).

A review of the various research studies suggests that biofeedback methods such as skin temperature and cephalic blood volume feedback are able to
reduce headache symptoms effectively for individuals suffering from
migraine. Overall, the results of several large-scale follow-up studies suggest
that 60 to 80 percent of migraine patients can be expected to show significant
improvement with skin temperature biofeedback combined with autogenic
training (Aloe, Collings, Wauqwer, McGrady, & Gerard, 1994; Diamond, Diamond-Falk, & Deveno, 1978; Sargent, Green, & Walters, 1977).

Nigl (1984) suggests that a closer look at this body of research literature
forces the conclusion that migraine treatment with biofeedback can be
viewed in one of two ways, depending on the reviewer's point of view. On
the one hand, follow-up studies on large numbers of patients suffering from
migraine and mixed migraine-tension headache strongly support the efficacy

of skin temperature biofeedback combined with autogenic training. This is what Nigl calls the *clinical perspective*. This point of view is best represented by the work of Green and Green (1979) and Diamond, Diamond-Falk, and Deveno (1978). While these studies lack something in experimental rigor and control, they do employ large sample sizes, long-term follow-up, and clinical expertise and thoroughness of treatment. Finally, the methods used by these and other applied research groups more closely reflect the type of treatment given to migraine patients in the clinic, hospital, and offices.

On the other hand, we have well-designed and well-planned experimentation using selected groups of patients. This research has compared the efficacy of biofeedback with relaxation or combinations of treatments, and results suggest that there is no advantage to using biofeedback methods instead of simpler, less expensive relaxation procedures. This position may be referred to as the *experimental perspective*; it is best represented by the work of Blanchard, Ahles, and Shaw (1979); Silver, Blanchard, Williamson, Theobald, and Brown (1979); and Kewman and Roberts (1980, 1983). The experimental procedures and statistical analysis that these investigators use are generally quite sophisticated and rigorous. Although these studies meet or exceed applied research design standards, the sample sizes are small, and the treatments are somewhat deficient with respect to the duration of the treatment. The problem is that these studies simply do not adequately reflect the standard treatment practices used by most experienced biofeedback clinicians under real-life clinical conditions (Steiner & Dince, 1981).

Asthma

Recently, biofeedback has been applied in the treatment of asthma. Despite tremendous research efforts, *asthma*, a respiratory disease that affects from 2 to 5 percent of the population, remains a puzzling disorder and the subject of considerable controversy. One of the few points of agreement that has been reached to date concerns the objective characteristics of the asthmatic's breathing patterns. An asthmatic episode appears to be characterized by a changed sensitivity of the bronchial mucosa (mucous membrane lining) and musculature, which in turn produces increased resistance in the airways. Edema (swelling) of the bronchial mucosa, secretions, and spasms of the bronchial muscles finally lead to a constricture or severe narrowing of these airways. The severe bronchial spasm can be a life-threatening event. The relative contributions of the autonomic and central nervous system to these changes are still a matter of some dispute (Yates, 1980).

A review of the literature suggests that asthma is a complex of factors involving allergies, stress, endocrine changes, genetic disposition, and psychological traits. The role of psychological factors in asthma seems to be well established. For example, Weiner (1977) has demonstrated that dependency and fear of separation or rejection are present in a significant number of asthmatics, as well as a wide range of defenses employed to deal with anxiety and the symptoms. For a fuller treatment of the role of psychological factors in asthma, we encourage the reader to read Knapp and Wells (1978).

To date, two distinct biofeedback procedures have been employed in the treatment of asthmatics: skeletal-muscle feedback and direct airways feedback. Yates (1980) suggests that these two approaches are based on divergent views as to the role of anxiety in the asthma attack. The assumption of those employing skeletal-muscle feedback appears to be that asthmatics are characterized by high levels of anxiety and that training in relaxation will help to reduce the severity of an attack after it has begun. On the other hand, those who favor a direct airways approach assume that it should be possible to control the events associated with impairment in the control of breathing so that either an attack is less likely to occur or, if it does occur, it can be controlled better. An excellent critical review of both applications and the research in this area can be found in Kotses and Glaus (1981). Our discussion here will be limited to skeletal-muscle, feedback-assisted relaxation.

In a recent series of studies the relationships between changes in muscular tension and respiratory measures in both normal adults and asthmatic children were examined (Glaus, Happ, & Kotses, 1976; Glaus & Kotses, 1976; Kotses, Glaus, Bricel, Edwards, & Crawford, 1978; Kotses, Glaus, Crawford, Edwards, & Scherr, 1976). The results of these studies demonstrated the following:

1. Tension changes in different muscles are not the same insofar as their effects on *peak expiratory flow rate* (PEFR) measures are concerned. PEFR is the maximum flow rate of air in liters per second during the first 0.1 second of a forced expiration. Tension changes in the facial musculature reliably influence PEFR, whereas limb muscle tension changes do not (Glaus, Happ, & Kotses, 1976).

2. Facial muscle tension changes are inversely related to PEFR behavior, so increases in facial muscle tension result in PEFR decreases, whereas PEFR increases result from decreases in facial muscle tension (Glaus, Happ, & Kotses, 1976; Glaus & Kotses, 1976; Kotses, Glaus, Bricel, Edwards, & Crawford, 1978; Kotses, Glaus, Crawford, Edwards, & Scherr, 1976).

3. Muscle tension changes do not influence respiratory activities in a general manner. Changes in PEFR due to changes in facial muscle tension are not correlated with respiratory rate changes (Glaus & Kotses, 1976).

4. Both clinical (asthmatics) and nonclinical (normal) subjects exhibit comparable changes in PEFR as a function of facial muscle relaxation (Glaus, Happ, & Kotses, 1976; Glaus & Kotses, 1976; Kotses, Glaus, Bricel, Edwards, & Crawford, 1978).

5. Finally, the effects of facial muscle tension change on PEFR can be observed after a single muscle tension training session of relatively short duration (Glaus & Kotses, 1976).

On the basis of these findings, Kotses and Glaus (1981) conclude that the relationship between facial muscle tension and PEFR is mediated by a physiological mechanism, the action of which is fairly specific. Although the precise nature of this mechanism is unknown, Glaus, Happ, and Kotses (1976) argue that it may be convenient to think of this mechanism as a neural reflex. It is assumed that the neural components of such a reflex would include a trigeminal afferent pathway and a vagal efferent pathway. The trigeminal and vagus nerves are cranial nerves whose point of origin lies in the pons and medulla of the brainstem (see Chapter 2). Trigeminal and vagal pathways are known to participate jointly in several protective reflexes involving airway resistance changes. This suggests that trigeminal afferent activity is capable of altering airway resistance through modification of vagal efferent activity (Tomori & Widdicombe, 1969).

Further support for a neural reflex mechanism mediator between facial muscle tension and peak expiratory flow rate comes from studies reported by Harver, Kotses, Segreto, and Creer (1984). In the earlier study, healthy adult subjects who evidenced operantly conditioned increases in facial muscle tension also showed increased airway resistance, whereas facial muscle relaxation resulted in decreased airway resistance. Conditioned increases and decreases in limb tension, on the other hand, did not produce such changes in airway resistance. In addition to ruling out general muscular events, this latter finding also weakens the position of possible alternative explanations employing metabolic agents altered or released by muscle tension change.

Harver et al. (1984) provided further evidence that supports the specificity of the relationship between facial muscle activity and pulmonary function. They monitored changes in peek expiratory flow rates (PEFR), respiration rate (RR) and heart rate (HR) while the subjects underwent either facial muscle training or limb muscle training. Increases in facial muscle tension resulted in the predicted decreases in PEFR but produced no related changes in either HR or RR. Increases in limb tension had no such effect.

Harver et al. (1984) also examined the effectiveness of facial muscle biofeedback-assisted relaxation training on asthmatic symptomology in 40 asthmatic children. Each of these children was randomly assigned to one of three treatment conditions: biofeedback training for frontal muscle EMG decreases, biofeedback training for maintaining frontal EMG activity at baseline levels (placebo control), and quiet sitting (no treatment). Children in the first group did reduce frontalis muscle tension as a function of training. The self-reported improvements in asthma severity and in psychological measurements were greater in this group than in the control groups.

It has been clearly demonstrated that biofeedback training for facial muscle relaxation improves short-term pulmonary function in asthmatic individuals. More recently, Tibbetts and Pepper (1989) combined both facial EMG relaxation and incentive inspirometer feedback to encourage slow diaphragmatic breathing while decreasing muscular efforts in a group of asthmatic subjects. All subjects were able to increase inhalation volumes and decrease EMG levels. These subjects also reported a 69.4 percent reduction in medication use, a 73 percent increase in sense of control, and 64 percent fewer emergency room visits. Research to date, however, still leaves us with a number of unanswered questions. Chief among them are the following: What are the long term effects of such therapy? What influence does this treatment have on asthma-related variables other than pulmonary function (Kotses, Hindi-Alexander, & Creer, 1989)? We cannot endorse relaxation assisted by biofeedback of facial muscles as a treatment for asthma—at least not without qualification.

As is evident, biofeedback is a useful technique for permitting individuals to attend to psychophysiological responses of which they are normally and consciously not aware. Awareness and control of these responses can lead to many useful applications. However, in the case of biofeedback therapy there has been a tendency to make enthusiastic claims that often exceed the results shown in published research data. That is, there may be little relationship between research findings in biofeedback and the clinical practice of such. Simply put, clinical psychologists may be using biofeedback on patients or clients when, in fact, there is little if any laboratory evidence to determine whether biofeedback actually works. In fact, Roberts (1985), in reviewing the current literature on biofeedback, has reached that very conclusion, and he has support from a number of biofeedback studies (e.g., Adams, Brantley, & Thompson, 1982; Beatty, 1982; Guglielmi, Roberts, & Patterson, 1982; Kewman & Roberts, 1980, 1983). As a result, Roberts concludes (in agreement with Katkin and Murray, 1969) that there is still no convincing evidence that the autonomic nervous system can be taught by operant methods independent of mediation of the striate muscles.

So does biofeedback really work, or is it being used with no research substantiation? This question is not easy to answer. As with the historical controversy between Kimmel (1967) and Katkin and Murray (1969) that we previously discussed, the controversy still rages despite claims that it has been resolved. Although there is difficulty in replicating many biofeedback experiments, clinical psychologists continue to use biofeedback to treat a variety of problems. While Roberts (1985) has questioned whether success is really achieved through the use of biofeedback in a clinical setting, a large body of literature seems to indicate that it is useful (see Schwartz & Beatty, 1977; White & Tursky, 1982; Wickramasekera, 1976). But a number of studies seem to arrive at the opposite conclusion (Adams, Brantley, & Thompson, 1982; Surwit, 1982). Thus, the controversy continues and probably will do so for a long time to come.

BIOFEEDBACK AND THE
PRODUCTION OF ALTERED STATES

In addition to being used as a therapeutic technique, biofeedback has been employed as a procedure to alter or change the conscious state indirectly through the manipulation of brain-wave patterns. For example, while the use of alpha biofeedback as a therapeutic technique has met with only limited success to date (Gannon & Sternbach, 1971; Glueck & Stroebel, 1975; Melzack & Perry, 1975), the "alpha state" has received a considerable amount of popular attention. Much of this enthusiasm can be attributed to the early studies of Nowlis and Kamiya (1970) and Brown (1970). These studies suggest that bringing the amount of alpha rhythm to a particular level can produce in the subject a state of meditativeness, serenity, and even happiness. This positive subjective state associated with alpha enhancement led to speculation that the "alpha experience" represented an altered state of consciousness.

Interestingly, those who supported this view also pointed to findings of consistent physiological changes, including alpha wave and occasional theta wave activity, during the practice of certain meditation techniques, as reported by Anand, Chhina, and Singh (1961a); Kasamatsu and Hirai (1969); and Wallace, Benson, and Wilson (1971). These observations are discussed more fully in Chapter 6. Finally, the fact that alpha wave activity of the occipital is seen to increase as the individual enters the sleep state (Dement & Kleitman, 1957) has been cited as further support for the notion that the alpha experience represents a state of consciousness that differs from wakefulness, sleep, or dream activity.

Despite these observations, many investigators were skeptical. To begin with, the alpha state simply does not exist. The use of such a term suggests that the brain is an undifferentiated mass of tissue that produces a single brain-wave pattern at any given time. This is not the case. Typically, alpha feedback training involves becoming aware of and learning to increase the amplitude of 8–13 Hz activity reported from the back of the skull immediately superior to the occipital cortex. However, there are several ways of increasing the strength of occipital alpha waves without the aid of feedback training. These include relaxing, defocusing, and closing the eyes.

The oculomotor adjustment that is related to occipital alpha wave production has been demonstrated in the laboratory. In an extremely creative study, Dewan (1967) taught subjects to send Morse code by using their brain waves, which they learned to modify simply by focusing or defocusing their eyes. Defocusing the eyes produced the occipital alpha rhythm, which in turn produced an audible tone. Production of a dot or dash depended on how long the alpha signal was maintained. More recently, Plotkin and Cohen (1976) designed a study to ascertain the extent to which the strength of occipital alpha waves is related to five subjective dimensions most commonly associated with the alpha experience.

The investigators found that visual processing and degree of sensory awareness were involved in control of occipital alpha waves, while the degree of body awareness, deliberateness of thought, and pleasantness of emotion state were not. These findings support the notion that the pleasant, quasi-meditational state of consciousness known as the alpha experience is not associated directly with an increase of alpha wave strength and that the occipital alpha wave strength is a direct function of oculomotor adjustment.

Such findings cast serious doubts on those of earlier alpha feedback studies. First, a close reading of the early studies reveals that only about 50 percent of the subjects actually reported feelings of pleasantness and relaxation associated with alpha wave production. These findings suggest that factors other than alpha wave manipulation may have been operating in these studies. Suggestion, in the form of instructional set, has been considered to be theoretically relevant to alpha feedback because of its demonstrated role, both in hypnosis and in other altered states of consciousness similar to the alpha state (Barber, 1970; Lynch & Paskewitz, 1971; Orne, 1959; Weil, Zinberg, & Nelson, 1968). To observe the individual and combined effects of alpha activity and instructional set, Walsh (1974) paired both alpha and no-alpha feedback with alpha-expectancy and neutral instructions. The alpha-expectancy instructions that were used in this study induced subjects to expect "a special state of consciousness known as the 'alpha state'; a calm, contemplative, dreamlike, or 'high' state." The results showed that for an alpha experience to occur, both alpha activity and alpha set are necessary and neither alone is sufficient.

The findings of meditation studies that are often cited in support of the existence of an alpha experience are also equivocal. The EEG findings of the Kasamatsu and Hirai (1969) study of Zen monks suggest that these monks were, in fact, very much aware of the external environment. In short, although they were in a meditative state, the monks produced brain-wave rhythms that were not alpha. Overall, the research results to date that support a correspondence between an increase in alpha-rhythm production through alpha biofeedback and the alpha experience certainly have been less than convincing.

RESEARCH AND BIOFEEDBACK

It is clear that much of the research in biofeedback and biofeedback therapy is of a pioneering nature. Many investigators appear to have been attracted by the exciting possibility of finding new applications for biofeedback and by biofeedback's potential as a means of helping to understand our states or levels of consciousness. Unlike hypnosis, however, biofeedback enables the subject to perceive directly and rather quickly the physiological consequences of the altered state. Because of this feature, biofeedback is deemed a very useful therapeutic technique as well. It is hoped that the future will lead to even more uses of biofeedback in the treatment of behavioral and physical problems. Biofeedback should also enable us to learn more about humans' capability to control and manipulate involuntary and unconscious responses. Thus, biofeedback at present is one of the most interesting and research oriented areas in the psychology of consciousness.

FOR FURTHER READING

Gatchel, R. J., & Price, K. P. (1979). *Clinical applications of biofeedback: Appraisal and status.* New York: Pergamon Press.

Schwartz, G. E., & Beatty, J. (1977). *Biofeedback theory and research.* New York: Academic Press.

Schwartz, M. S. (Ed.). (1995). *Biofeedback: A practitioner's guide* (2nd ed.). New York: Guilford.

White, L., & Tursky, B. (Eds.). (1982). *Clinical biofeedback: Efficacy and mechanisms.* New York: Guilford.

6

MEDITATION

S ome individuals known as *yogis*, from such Eastern countries as India or Tibet, claim they are able to perform some rather unusual feats. They say that they are able to stop their heart from beating; they show how they can walk on burning coals or sleep on a bed of nails. They demonstrate these abilities, and we watch with amazement and even awe. Have these people really found the secret of controlling pain? Can they really stop the heart from beating? When asked how they can perform these seemingly impossible feats, yogis report that as a result of meditating for many years, they have so learned to control pain that they experience none during such activities. That is, meditation has taught them to concentrate on relaxation, and they do not experience the sensations that you and I might if we were to perform these foolhardy tasks. Has meditation really done this? Can meditation help to achieve such control over bodily functions and sensations? Or are these claims exaggerated? Let's consider these questions.

In many respects, meditation, as a process for altering experiences of consciousness, is very similar to hypnosis. In both processes, subjects report being in a very relaxed state, far more relaxed than in their normal or waking state of consciousness. Also, meditation and hypnosis both require a form of concentration or attention to a stimulus event.

However, unlike hypnosis, which appears not to have reliable physiological correlates (Evans, 1979a; Kihlstrom, 1985), proponents of meditation claim that it can control physiological events, including brain-wave activity, electrical resistance of the skin, oxygen consumption, and blood-lactate level. Some of these claims have been experimentally verified (Wallace & Benson, 1972). In this respect, meditation appears to be similar to biofeedback; it enables the subject to become aware of and control behavior he or she is not capable of controlling during a normal, waking state of consciousness.

Also, many have assumed that meditation, unlike hypnosis, is associated with religion or religious practices. Specifically, meditation is often believed to be something to do while praying. Thus, it is thought to be something done in a church, synagogue, mosque, or home but not in the laboratory. Because of this association, the lay community (and even some scientists) either look at meditation negatively or at best accept it as an area of study in the physiology of consciousness but relegate it to nonscience. This type of attitude has resulted in a serious lag in the scientific study of meditation.

At this point we need to elaborate on the role of meditation in the psychology of consciousness and to consider the historical roots of the practice. We also will examine the possibility of using meditation as a means of helping to control behavior and of tapping human potentials that are not usually accessible during the normal, waking state of consciousness or awareness.

MEDITATION AND CONSCIOUSNESS

As we mentioned, many forms of meditation are similar to hypnosis. In both situations an individual must concentrate on a stimulus, thereby blocking external interference. In hypnosis the stimulus to which an individual attends is typically the voice of the hypnotist. In meditation the stimulus is either a visual object of regard, a physical motion of the body, or a chant.

However, it is possible to induce an altered state of consciousness by hypnotizing oneself. This process is called **autohypnosis** or self-hypnosis. Individuals concentrate on a stimulus of their own choosing, and the net result is a very relaxed feeling. In fact, the behavior exhibited in self-hypnosis approximates that observed in meditation, especially the Zen variety of meditation. Thus, self-hypnosis does not usually involve suggestions of the type discussed with hypnosis induced in other ways (see Chapter 4). Self-hypnosis is also reported to involve less steady and less focused attention (Fromm et al., 1981; Johnson, 1981; Kihlstrom, 1985; Orne & McConkey, 1981). Kihlstrom (1985) has described self-hypnosis as emphasizing relaxation and reverie.

Like self-hypnosis, meditation is a procedure a person must learn. The ability to hypnotize oneself or to meditate does not come instantly or easily. It must be practiced repeatedly over a period of time to concentrate effectively on a situation while attenuating potential sources of disturbance. Typically, initial attempts at self-hypnosis and meditation meet with failure because (1) it is difficult to concentrate on only one thing for more than a few minutes and (2) most people have never had to do this or anything like it before. Because the situation is novel to us, we initially resist it. However, with time, the ability to concentrate on a stimulus situation and to isolate ourselves in our environment becomes easier and easier. Eventually, the task does not appear difficult at all. In fact, we start to enjoy it because it helps us to relax and to escape the world as we experience it in our normal, waking state of consciousness. These effects provide reinforcement, and the result is that we have learned to meditate.

Where did meditation originate? What do we have to do to learn how to meditate? What are the different styles of meditation? What benefits can one achieve through meditation? These are some of the questions we will address in this chapter. To understand better how the process of meditation relates to altered states of consciousness, let us examine closely how meditation has developed over the decades and why psychologists view it the way they do.

HISTORICAL DEVELOPMENT

Meditation as an area of psychological study does not have a formal historical development comparable, for example, to hypnosis. No prominent figures in the history of psychology have introduced important methodological or theoretical facets to the study of meditation. Therefore, to search for some of the roots of meditation, we must look to the various Eastern religions and religious practices.

Since many such religions actively encourage the practice of meditation, it is not difficult to understand why many individuals automatically associate meditation with religion. In fact, for many, this association is so strong that to admit to meditating is akin to admitting membership in a strange religious cult. Obviously, this need not be true, since many people who meditate are neither members of cults nor, for that matter, religious in any sense of the word. They simply practice meditation for its beneficial psychological effects (e.g., altering their state of consciousness) or its beneficial physical effects (e.g., reducing tension, anxiety, and blood pressure).

The popular forms of meditation in Western countries—Zen, yoga, and transcendental meditation (TM)—are clearly grounded in, and can trace their origins directly to, Buddhism and Hinduism. Buddhism, founded by Siddhartha Gautama (563–483 B.C.), stressed that suffering is caused by desire and that individuals must destroy this desire in order to achieve peace. Eight paths were described to win freedom from desire, one of these being meditation. Through meditation a person could achieve *nirvana*, or passionless peace. But nirvana could be achieved only if the meditator had reached perfect self-control, unselfishness, knowledge, and enlightenment. It is, in part, through meditating that these goals could be achieved.

In the fifth century the Buddhist monk Buddhaghosa described meditation in his *Visuddhimagga* (a textbook of Buddhist philosophy and psychology) as a "path to purification" (Goleman, 1988; Nanamoli, 1964, 1976). Such purification eventually would lead to an altered state of consciousness, or what was previously referred to as *nirvana*.

Visuddhimagga describes the basic process of meditation, including the various exercises that must be performed to achieve a state of relaxation and eventually the state of nirvana. It details how one learns to focus attention on a specific object or thought and how to begin to attenuate possible sources of interference that can detract from, or prevent achievement of nirvana. As such, *Visuddhimagga* can be considered the first handbook or guide to the practice of meditation.

According to *Visuddhimagga*, meditation consists of breaking with the normal state of awareness or consciousness through absorption, or *jhana*. The book describes eight jhanas, or levels of absorption, ranging from a simple attenuation of thoughts, which occurs during the normal state of consciousness, to total absorption away from normal consciousness to a state of nirvana. Therefore, meditation is not a single altered state of awareness that differs from the normal state of consciousness. Rather, it is a multilevel process involving a continual and progressive change in awareness.

Hinduism also has played an important historical role in the development of contemporary meditation (Goleman, 1988). Hinduism emphasizes a oneness of Brahman, the Supreme World-Soul, or Spirit. To become one with Brahman, it is necessary to discipline one's mind and body. This is accomplished through *yoga*. The Bhagavad-Gita, a devotional poem, describes three ways of reaching Brahman, one of which is the way of thought, or philosophy and meditation.

In the Hindu tradition there is an emphasis on the *mantra*, or the chanting of a harmonious word or phrase on which to concentrate. Such concentration helps a person to become absorbed in the phrase (or, according to Hindu tradition, to become one with the universe or Brahman) and thus to meditate effectively. Although the mantra is not unique to Hindu meditative practices, it is stressed as a means of helping the meditator become aware of his or her thoughts and attenuate external sources of interference. Today, the mantra is an important part of many meditative styles. (This topic will be discussed in the next section.)

Christianity and Judaism have also played a role in the historical development of meditation. In these religions, prayer often involves a process that resembles meditation. It is not unusual during prayer to fix one's thoughts on an object or action to aid concentration and to lessen interferences from the materialistic world and the normal state of consciousness. In Christianity a person may fixate upon a cross or an image (real or visualized) of the Christ figure. Roman Catholics often use a rosary, or chain of beads, which they manipulate in their hands to count prayers and to attenuate thoughts that might interfere with prayer. In Judaism a prayer book and the Torah serve as objects of fixation. Also, Orthodox Jews may perform a forward-and-backward swaying action during prayer to help them concentrate. The objects of fixation and the movements performed in Judaism and Christianity are very similar to actions performed in many Eastern religions and various meditative styles. Therefore, all major religions appear to have played an important role in the development of contemporary meditation.

Probably the most important figure to introduce meditation (in a secularized and popularized form) to the Western world was the Maharishi

Mahesh Yogi. He became known to the West through his writings (Maharishi, 1963) and through publicity from visits by the British rock group The Beatles, who, for a while, acclaimed the Maharishi to be a source of inspiration. This belief spread in popularity with the Beatles' music. In fact, many of their recordings included Eastern instruments (e.g., the sitar) and chants (e.g., "Hare Krishna"). Other Eastern traditions, including meditation, became known to the West along with the introduction of Eastern music and chants. Soon the Maharishi was on tour in most Western countries, and many Westerners began to meditate and to join various meditation societies. These societies flourished, and many still exist with followings as strong today as they were during the 1960s and the 1970s.

In fact, the Maharishi helped to found Maharishi International University in Iowa, which offers a nontraditional curriculum with emphasis on meditative styles and other areas of consciousness. Some of the most controversial claims of meditators have come from professors at this university, including claims of the ability to walk through walls and fly as a result of having meditated. Various psychology and medical journals contain work by professors, and researchers there also claim that world events can be controlled, to some extent, through practicing TM. This is discussed in more detail later in this chapter.

MEDITATIVE STYLES

Concentrative Meditation

Many of the popular forms of meditation require restricting one's attention to achieve the desired state. In essence, meditators concentrate on something while ignoring all else around them. Ornstein (1986) has referred to this as *one-pointedness of mind*. Such activity has also been referred to as *selective attending* (Treisman & Geffen, 1967).

The four most popular forms of concentrative meditation are Zen, yoga, TM, and Sufism. **Zen** is the most classical form of meditation and is often referred to as classical Buddhist meditation (Ornstein, 1972), since it has its origin in the Buddhist religion. In this meditative form, an individual is given instructions to perform several acts. The first is a breath-counting exercise. The meditators count their breaths from one to ten, over and over again. If they lose count as a result of inattentiveness, they must start over.

Once they have mastered this exercise in attention, indicating that they are now able to concentrate on a stimulus event (in this case, breaths), they are given a more advanced attention exercise. This time, instead of counting breaths, they concentrate on the breathing process itself. They are requested to concentrate on nothing but their breathing activity and to attend to the movement of air as it fills their lungs via the air passages through the nose and mouth. This exercise enables them to concentrate on their breathing rate,

FIGURE 6.1 Example of the Lotus Position

and such activity produces a monotonous, repetitious, rhythmic behavior pattern that enables them to begin meditating.

Some more advanced Zen meditation exercises require the meditators to remain motionless as they sit in the *lotus position* (Figure 6.1). This position entails sitting with the legs crossed and the back as straight and erect as possible. While sitting in this position and attending to their breathing, they are expected to meditate on a *koan,* a type of riddle or thought-provoking question given to them beforehand. The koan is designed to be either very difficult or impossible to solve or respond to by rational thought. A few examples of koans, as mentioned by Ornstein (1986), include "Show me your face before your mother and father met" and "What is the sound of one hand clapping?" The basic idea behind the koan exercise is paradox: Concentration is used as a vehicle to shatter, and thus transcend, rational thinking. To solve the koan, meditators must focus their attention on the koan and on nothing else.

In other words, during Zen meditation, individuals perform a type of selective attending (Treisman & Geffen, 1967). Such attending enables them to remove themselves temporarily from their normal state of consciousness or awareness to an altered form. Actually, the ultimate goal of Zen meditation is to attain a *permanent* altered state of consciousness, not a temporary one. In short, living itself becomes a form of meditation.

Yoga is another popular form of meditation, with origins in the Hindu religion. This meditative form differs considerably from Zen or Buddhist meditation. In fact, **yoga meditation** is more closely related to biofeedback training (see Chapter 5), though it does not use elaborate electrical/physiological equipment. Individuals who practice yoga attempt to alter their state of consciousness by regulating involuntary or autonomic physiological processes, such as heart rate, blood pressure, blood flow, digestion, and smooth muscle activity. During yoga meditation the practitioner usually assumes a lotus position and gazes on a visual stimulus known as a *mandala* (see Figure 6.2). This object may take one of many forms, such as a circle, a square, a hexagon, or an octagon. The form of the

FIGURE 6.2   Example of a Mandala

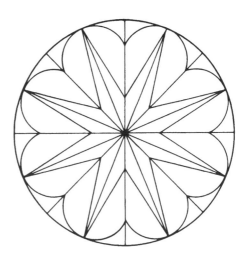

mandala is not as important as its presence. The mandala serves a function similar to that of the mantra: By focusing their thoughts on a single stimulus, practitioners are better able to concentrate and to attenuate external forms of noise or interference. Such focusing becomes more and more elaborate throughout the concentration process. The meditator first focuses on the periphery of the object and gradually moves closer to the center. This technique is a more advanced method for helping the individual concentrate.

In yoga meditation exercises a **mantra** is commonly used. As was mentioned in the section entitled "Historical Development," a mantra is a word or a set of words that helps meditators to concentrate on a stimulus event. As a result, they are able to attend to the mantra selectively while they attenuate all other forms of information, such as external noise. Thus, in yoga meditation the mantra serves the same function as does breath counting in Zen meditation. Also, as with Zen breath counting, the mantra must be repeated over and over for the individual to attain a state of consciousness that differs from his or her normal, waking state.

Another visual technique for meditation that yoga practitioners use is the **tratakam**, or steady gaze (Ornstein, 1986). This is very similar to the mandala, except that anything can serve as an object of a tratakam. For example, one may use a vase, a light from a candle, a star in the sky, the moon, or a flower in a garden. The exact form of the object is not as important as the act of concentrating and focusing on it. As we discussed earlier, Western religions rely on a tratakam during prayer (e.g., the cross in Christianity, the Torah in Judaism).

In addition to the use of a mandala and a tratakam, yoga meditators may also practice **mudra**. Mudra consists of repetitive physical movements of the body. The body parts usually used are the arms, the legs, and the fingers. Individuals perform some type of bodily movement on which they are to concentrate. This movement, then, serves the same function as the mandala, the mantra, and the tratakam: It enables the meditator to focus attention on some event and ignore all other sources of stimulation. Some yoga meditators even combine some concentrative stimuli during their practices. For example, one may combine a mudra with a mandala or with a tratakam. Again, the exact form of a concentrative stimulus is not as important as the fact that it enables the practitioner to concentrate.

The stimulus also must be sufficiently salient to prevent the practitioner from redirecting attention to another, interfering source of stimulation. When such interference occurs (as it usually does for most beginning meditators and even for some advanced ones), the task is to bring attention back to the original concentrative stimulus. Attentiveness to a concentrative stimulus and then to an interfering object or event indicates that, in fact, the meditator is moving from one level of awareness or consciousness to another and back again. The goal is to prevent such shifting of consciousness; that is where meditation becomes difficult to master.

Transcendental meditation, or **TM,** is the third form of meditation. In reality, TM is a form of yoga meditation. As in all forms of yoga meditation, TM requires the practitioner to have a mantra on which to meditate silently over and over. Meditators practice this for about a half hour twice a day, although they can meditate more often. Unlike the traditional form of yoga meditation, TM does not require a specific posture. The practitioner may assume any comfortable position. While in this position, individuals are to concentrate intently on the mantra, focusing all of their thoughts on it. Should their thoughts wander to something else, they are to concentrate on bringing them back to the mantra. Thus, the stimulus serves both as an anchor to which one returns when thoughts drift elsewhere and as a medium on which one concentrates to help keep thoughts from wandering.

Sufism is the final concentrative, meditation form we will discuss. This type of meditation is probably the least known in the United States and the rest of the Western world. There are several reasons for its relative obscurity. First, the exercises for inducing a meditative state in Sufism are quite different from those of the three types of meditation we have discussed so far. Second, the principles and styles of Sufi meditation are usually not made public. As a result, even if people with a strong interest in Sufi meditation wished to develop it, they would not be able to do so merely by reading about it. They would have to join a Sufi meditation society and, as members, would be held responsible for keeping the secrets of the society from the general public.

However, on the basis of what is known from writings about Sufi meditation (Goleman, 1988; Ornstein, 1986; Shah, 1970), we do discover some reasons for the secretiveness of Sufi practices. Sufi meditators believe that public knowledge of their practices may lead to faulty applications of the exercises. They are most concerned about this because, to Sufi meditators, meditation exercises vary as a function of time and place. Thus, one Sufi exercise may be appropriate for one individual in a given place and time but totally inappropriate for a different individual at the same place and time. Also, an exercise that is appropriate for a given individual at one time becomes inappropriate at another time. The reasons for these beliefs are neither known to Westerners nor discussed for lay consumption.

Despite the seemingly disparate methods of Sufi meditation and the Sufists' unwillingness to make public their exercises, Sufi meditation exercises share some common features. One exercise calls for the meditator to move in circles. This whirling action is somewhat similar to an individual simply turning about in circles over and over again. On the surface, it would appear that this exercise might make the practitioner nauseous at worst and dizzy at best. However, these sensations are eventually overcome and are replaced with a state of relaxation. This state or level of awareness appears to be different from what one experiences in the normal, waking state of consciousness.

The whirling action by some Sufi meditators, most notably the Maulavi, or whirling dervishes of Turkey, is performed as a type of dance that is generally accompanied by the repetition of phrases or sounds, called *zikr* (Goleman, 1988). These sounds begin as oral repetitions and later become silent ones. They are monotonous in tone and are believed to induce an altered state of consciousness.

Because of the vast degree of individual differences in meditative technique used by Sufi meditators, it is only natural that not all such meditators perform the whirling exercise. In fact, many Sufi meditators use exercises that appear to be very similar to those used in the other types of meditation (e.g., the lotus position, chanting a mantra). Other Sufi meditators simply sit in a comfortable position and chant a sound to produce a relaxed or concentrative state.

Since so many differences exist within the Sufi exercises, it seems obvious that Sufi is a nonstandard form of meditation. However, regardless of the types of exercise performed, the goal of all Sufi meditators is the same: to achieve a state of awareness or consciousness that differs from the normal, waking state. This altered state enables meditators to concentrate on a given stimulus situation or environment while effectively blocking all other thoughts and feelings during meditation. Such concentration enables them to achieve a type of bliss or escape from the troubles of the real world.

Opening-Up Meditation

In addition to concentrative meditation, Robert Ornstein (1986) describes a style he refers to as **opening-up meditation**. Here the focus is not on something upon which the meditator concentrates. In fact, this form of meditation does not require individuals to isolate themselves nor to fix their gaze upon anyone or anything.

Ornstein describes a form of opening-up meditation in the Zen tradition, which is called *shikan-taza*. In essence, opening-up is a more advanced form of meditation compared to the concentrative forms previously described. After the meditator has mastered concentrative meditation, for example counting breaths, it is possible to achieve a state in which awareness of the external environment is increased. The meditator not only learns to attend to a given object or person of regard, but at the same time pays attention to other things or people around him or her. In this manner, the meditator has expanded his or her horizon or environmental dimensions so that a panorama of stimuli from the environment can be cognitively processed.

An example of opening-up meditation at work might be illustrated by the abilities of a good quarterback in a football game. He must simultaneously concentrate on the position of all of his teammates and the players on the opposing team before, during, and after the snap of the ball. Since the quarterback has decided a play in advance, he may simply rely on what had previously been planned. If all goes as planned, the play is successfully executed. However, we are all aware of the fact that many times things do not go as planned. Therefore, the quarterback has contingencies. He fixes his attention not only on the preplanned actions but also on alternatives. This requires that he open his panoramic horizons to the players who will be rushing him from the opposing team as well as to the position of the members of his own team and, of course, the snap of the ball. When the ball is ultimately snapped, a quick decision must be made. But that decision requires an advanced form of information processing, or an opening-up form of meditation. Such meditating does not and cannot endure for long. But it is necessary to accomplish the desired goal, a successfully executed play.

We need not delve into what would happen if the quarterback were to concentrate only on the ball. The likely outcome would be that he would be tackled or that the play would not be executed properly. By opening up his dimensions and processing multiple actions simultaneously, the quarterback's chances for success are greatly improved.

While the example we have chosen to use to illustrate opening-up meditation may not seem traditional, it is an appropriate example of opening-up meditation at work. (Ornstein [1986] cites other examples.) In any case, opening-up meditation is, by nature, of short duration. To concentrate for a prolonged period of time (greater than 30 minutes) is possible with concentrative meditation. However, to expand one's horizon of attention for a prolonged period is not possible with opening-up meditation. Thus, opening-up meditation usually lasts only a few seconds; it can last longer in situations that permit longer endurance. Needless to say, football or other sport activities do not permit prolonged periods of opening up.

In summary, concentrative meditation requires a limiting of input to achieve the goal of attaining a meditative state; opening-up meditation requires an expansion of input. However, regardless of type of meditative style employed, the goal of *all* meditators is the same: to temporarily alter the state of consciousness or awareness. And by doing so, it is hoped the meditator will achieve some predetermined goal.

CONTEMPORARY THEORIES OF MEDITATION

The most recent theories or theoretical models concerning the process of meditation are those of Deikman (1966, 1971), Ornstein (1972, 1986), Welwood (1977), Washburn (1978), and Walsh (1981, 1982). Although these theories or models have much in common in their explanations of the meditation process, they also differ from one another in their manner of explaining what happens during meditation and how a meditative state of consciousness can be achieved.

Deikman and Ornstein

Arthur Deikman and Robert Ornstein explain meditation in terms of a bimodal concept of consciousness. Briefly, the model distinguishes two modes of consciousness: an active mode and a receptive mode.

The *active mode* is concerned with focusing awareness on an object in the environment and distinguishing or isolating the object from the context in which it is found. In addition, the active mode is analytic, sequential, and discursive in nature. According to Deikman and Ornstein, it is the active mode that is involved in concentrative meditation.

The *receptive mode* permits the meditator to be open to experiences in the environment. In other words, rather than concentrating on an object, the meditator eventually (or in some instances, immediately) comes in contact with experiences of the senses. In the receptive mode, the meditator sees parts as they relate to wholes. He or she uses intuition and is not aware of the passage of time. This mode is at work during opening-up meditation.

According to Deikman and Ornstein, we automatically shift from one mode of processing consciousness to another. However, the automatic process can be changed, and we accomplish this through another process called **deautomatization**. Through this process we no longer automatically shift from one mode of processing to another. The principal mode for learning deautomatization is meditation. When we achieve this process successfully, our awareness opens up in a way similar to escaping the bounds that determine our behavior. Instead of being selective about what we attend to or concentrate on, we permit ourselves, in a way, to start from the beginning in the processing of information. Rather than reacting to situations in a learned, automatic fashion, we allow learning to start anew. By doing so, we become more receptive to various stimuli or sensory-input information. This receptivity enables the active mode to take a brief vacation (Ornstein, 1972) from the old, learned, familiar environment of our everyday existence. Afterward, we can return or *dishabituate* to the normal environment and to the normal, waking state of awareness or consciousness fully refreshed and ready to go again (an experience very similar to the relaxed feeling subjects report after hypnosis).

Welwood

Another theory of meditation was proposed by John Welwood (1977), who sees meditation as a means for making ourselves aware of experiences that we do not consciously notice. To explain how meditation helps us become cognizant of previously unnoticed behavior or experiences, Welwood proposes four levels of awareness:

1. the *situational ground*, which Washburn (1978) translates roughly as corresponding to the concept of the preconscious;
2. the *personal ground*, or the conceptualization of an individualized environment;
3. the *transpersonal ground*, in which an individual recognizes that an object of regard is merely an object within a larger and more complex environment; and
4. the *basic ground*, in which an object stands by itself in isolation (e.g., the object *is* the environment).

These four levels form a system whereby meditation becomes an effective tool for helping an individual become aware of information, potentialities, and abilities that previously had existed at an unconscious level.

In this sense, Welwood's theory is comparable to the Deikman-Ornstein theory; that is, meditation helps to diffuse information so that we become aware of previously unnoticed elements or objects in the environment. However, Welwood goes further by stating that such diffusion is a continuous process; we diffuse to become aware of new information. This information is then diffused further, progressively and repeatedly, until the basic elements in the environment are uncovered for comprehension. Thus, in stepped fashion, meditation enables individuals to become more and more aware of their environment. According to Ornstein (1986), this is exactly what happens in opening-up meditation. Thus, on a conceptual basis, Welwood's theory, and that of Deikman and Ornstein, do not appear dissonant.

Washburn

Michael Washburn (1978) has pointed out several weaknesses in Welwood's theory. First, Welwood's theory artificially assumes a single, general unconscious, which may not be the case. Second, his theory postulates that diffusion is a sufficient rather than a necessary condition for bringing information and knowledge from the unconscious state to awareness. In light of these criticisms, Washburn has proposed a three-level theory of meditation. These levels include (1) defocalization, (2) reduction of the intensity threshold of awareness, and (3) immobilization of psychic operations.

Defocalization is quite similar to Welwood's concept of diffusion. However, Washburn stipulates that defocalization is a means of focusing on awareness, but in a manner opposite to the process inherent in various forms of concentrative meditation (e.g., yoga, Zen). In concentrative meditation, attention is selective and is restricted to a single object, thought, or action. For a short period, selective attention rules out awareness to all other sources of stimulation in the environment. According to Washburn, such attenuation prevents the meditator from reaching the unconscious, further preventing a tapping of the receptive mode.

In Washburn's theory the second level is a *reduction of the intensity threshold of awareness* by meditation. In the normal waking state, consciousness operates with a relatively high-intensity threshold. Meditation reduces this threshold by "calming the storm on the surface of consciousness" (Washburn, 1978, p. 54), thus permitting the contents of the unconscious to reach awareness. When this occurs, a new threshold is established that is lower in intensity than that of its predecessor. Continued meditation thus becomes progressively easier because it is no longer necessary to reach the previous high threshold. This process is comparable to Welwood's progressive process of diffusion.

The third factor in Washburn's theory, *immobilization of psychic operations*, is the state of complete, motionless attention to the totality of experiences that arise during the meditative process. Through this operation, contact with the unconscious is secured and brought to conscious awareness by interfering with functions of the normal, waking state. This process is automatic; as a result, meditators are unaware that it is happening.

Walsh

In what appears to be a merging of the philosophies of behaviorism and consciousness, Roger Walsh (1981, 1982) has proposed a *stimulus-response*, or *S-R*, model of meditation. In this, Walsh perceives the meditative practice as representing a stimulus (S) event. This event elicits responses (R) that are considered to be mediated by a variety of psychological, physiological, and chemical mechanisms. The psychological mechanisms include relaxation and global desensitization (Goleman, 1971), deconditioning, behavioral reactivity, heightened awareness (Walsh, 1977), dehypnosis (Walsh, 1982), behavioral self-control skills (Shapiro, 1980), and facilitation of psychological development and maturation (Wilber, 1980, 1982). The physiological mechanisms include reduced arousal, hemispheric lateralization (Earle, 1981; Pagano & Frumkin, 1977), and EEG resonance and coherence or intrahemispheric and interhemispheric synchronisms (Glueck & Stroebel, 1975). Although Walsh (1982) speculates that chemical mechanisms may also be involved in mediating meditation, no such chemicals have to date been discovered. Walsh thus perceives of meditation as being multidetermined and within an S-R framework. In this manner, meditation is perceived as the conscious training of attention aimed at modifying mental processes so as to elicit enhanced states of consciousness and well-being. Or quite simply, meditation, whether of the concentrative or opening-up variety, is something that one learns and that is helped along by psychological, physiological, and possibly chemical mechanisms.

Theories Compared

In a comparison of the theories discussed, one commonality is evident. The goal in all the discussed approaches is to tap the receptive mode of consciousness. Deikman and Ornstein specify that this comes about through the initial concentration on a stimulus object, thus tapping the active mode. After continual practice with a concentrative meditation exercise, the active mode is replaced eventually by the receptive mode. On the other hand, Welwood, Washburn, and Walsh do not see the need for a concentrative exercise to stimulate the active mode before yielding to the receptive mode. Rather, they see meditation as a response of the receptive mode; concentrative exercises simply detract or interfere with reaching this mode.

Unfortunately, there is no experimental support for these theories. To date, their predictions have not been tested. However, there is some support for the dishabituation concept of Deikman and Ornstein.

Habituation and Dishabituation

Before discussing dishabituation, we should briefly discuss **habituation**. This phenomenon occurs as a result of continual exposure to a stimulus situation. When we first come in contact with a novel stimulus, we attend to it readily. This produces what Sokolov (1963) referred to as an *orienting response*. As exposure to the stimulus continues, its novelty dissipates and the orienting response disappears. The result is an eventual tuning out of the stimulus event. For example, you may live in an environment where traffic noise is readily apparent. When you first moved to your habitat, the noise probably bothered you; it kept you from sleeping at night or performing your daily activities in an undisturbed manner. After a while, however, you became accustomed to the noise and no longer noticed it, until a friend commented about how noisy it was in your house. Getting used to the noise in this situation is an example of habituation.

Dishabituation means not becoming accustomed to the stimulus (noise) or becoming accustomed to it through some procedure such as meditation. An experimental example of dishabituation through meditation was illustrated in a study by Anand, Chhina, and Singh (1961a, 1961b). A yoga meditator was shown a novel stimulus; his EEG (brain-wave) activity was recorded at this time. During meditation the subject produced alpha brain waves. There was no interruption of this wave production upon presentation of an external, novel stimulus. Such an interruption would normally occur for a nonmeditator. Also, when the subject was not meditating, the presentation of a novel stimulus did not produce the typical habituation effect. Thus, we can say that in this study, the meditator had successfully dishabituated.

In a study by Kasamatsu and Hirai (1966), habituation to a stimulus was tested on a larger sample than that of Anand and associates. Zen masters and controls (nonmeditating subjects) were exposed to a repeated clicking sound every 15 seconds; their EEG activity was recorded during this time. The control subjects showed the typical habituation to the sound source, and their brain-wave activity indicated reception of the stimulus. After repeated presentations of the sound, brain-wave activity no longer responded to the sound source; that is, habituation had taken place. This was not the case with the meditators. Their brain-wave or EEG activity remained constant throughout a five-minute exposure period.

Thus, it appears that, at least for advanced Zen meditators, dishabituation, as defined by Deikman and Ornstein, does take place. Whether this occurs via the route suggested by Deikman and Ornstein or by the route suggested by Welwood, Washburn, or Walsh is not known. It is hoped that future research will give us the answer to this question.

CORRELATES OF MEDITATION

Psychological Correlates

A number of investigators have sought to determine what variables appear to be associated with meditation. Some of these were mentioned earlier in a discussion of Walsh's (1982) S-R model of meditation. In addition to those previously mentioned, meditation has been reported to reduce nonspecific anxiety and anxiety neurosis (Girodo, 1974; Shapiro, 1976). It has also been shown to be a helpful intervention in treating specific phobias, particularly those related to fear of enclosed places, examinations, and being left alone (Boudreau, 1972).

Meditation has also been reported as useful in dealing with drug and alcohol abuse. A number of investigators (Gelderloos, Walton, Orme-Johnson, & Alexander, 1991; Kus, 1995; Walton & Levitsky, 1994) have shown that dependence on chemical substances was reduced after learning how to meditate. Beneficial effects of meditation have also been reported in enhancing confidence, self-esteem, self-control, empathy, and self-actualization (Hjelle, 1974; Kelly, 1996; Nidich, Seeman, & Dreshin, 1973).

Several studies have also shown that meditation has psychosomatic benefits and is thus useful in rehabilitation following myocardial infarction (Tulpule, 1971), bronchial asthma (Honsberger, 1973; Wilson, Honsberger, Chiu, & Novey, 1975), and insomnia (Miskiman, 1977a, 1977b; Woolfolk, 1975). Others have reported that hypertension, or high blood pressure, has been reduced following instruction and practice in meditation (Benson, Rosner, & Marzetta, 1973; Benson & Wallace, 1972; Blackwell et al., 1975; Dixit, Agrawal, & Dubey, 1994; Michaels, Huber, & McCann, 1976; Patel, 1975; Sudsuang, Chentanez, & Veluvan, 1991). Still others have reported that meditation seems to be beneficial in releasing stress (Dillbeck, Assimakis, Raimondi, Orme-Johnson, & Rowe, 1986; Miller, Fletcher, & Kabat-Zinn, 1995), in leading to better health (Orme-Johnson, 1987), and in enhancing psychological development (Gelderloos, 1987).

In summary, it appears that meditation is a useful manipulation or intervention in the treatment of a variety of psychologically related problems. However, meditation has also been shown to be effective in influencing physiological responses of the body, as well. We shall now examine some of these.

Physiological Correlates

As we mentioned at the beginning of this chapter, practitioners of meditation have long claimed that they are capable of inducing many changes in their physiological responses to events. For example, they claim they can voluntarily stop their heartbeat temporarily and that they can alter their normal breathing pattern. Are such feats possible? According to a growing body of scientific literature, some physiological changes can be induced with meditation.

As might be expected, most experiments on physiological controls of behavior during meditation have employed well-experienced meditators as subjects. One such study is by Sugi and Akutsu (1964), who used Zen monks from Japan. The researchers found that during meditation the monks were capable of decreasing their consumption of oxygen by 20 percent, which subsequently reduced their output of carbon dioxide. Anand, Chhina, and Singh (1961a, 1961b) reported a similar finding with their yoga meditator.

Changes of brain-wave activity have also been noted in well-practiced meditators. Kasamatsu and Hirai (1963) found that Zen monks were capable of producing a predominance of alpha activity with their eyes half open. This brain-wave pattern is usually present only when subjects are very relaxed and have their eyes closed. The Zen monks were also capable of controlling the amplitude and frequency of the alpha brain waves. For example, they demonstrated the ability to slow the frequency of the waves from the normal 8–13 Hz, to 7 or 8 Hz. This seemingly voluntary control of alpha wave production and activity also produced rhythmic theta waves of 6–7 Hz.

There have also been reports of the control of brain-wave activity in drug-resistant epileptic patients. Deepak, Manchanda, and Maheshwari (1994) showed that with training in meditation, patients showed a significant reduction in seizure frequency and duration, an increase in the dominant background EEG frequency, and a reduction in slow-wave activity in the range of 0.7–7.7 Hz. With continued meditation practice, these patients experienced improvement in their ability to control their seizures. (See Chapter 7 for a detailed description and explanation of various brain-wave patterns produced during relaxation and sleep.)

Perhaps one of the most comprehensive investigations of the effects of meditation on physiological control was undertaken by Wallace and Benson (1972). Using practitioners of TM as subjects, the researchers were able to support many of the long-standing claims made by meditators. They found that TM practitioners were capable of reducing oxygen consumption as well as carbon dioxide elimination during meditation. The investigators also found a high correlation between TM and a marked reduction in blood-lactate concentration, a rapid rise in the electrical resistance of the skin, an increase in the intensity of alpha brain waves, a slowing of the heartbeat, and an overall decrease in respiratory rate and volume of air breathed. In other words, the results reported by Wallace and Benson substantiated and replicated some of the earlier experiments performed by other investigators with Zen monks and yoga meditators.

Also, as Wallace and Benson pointed out, there is little or no resemblance between the physiological changes noted in meditators and those found in hypnotized or sleeping subjects. For example, whereas after meditation there is a marked drop in oxygen consumption for about five to ten minutes, there is no such drop during hypnosis. Also, decreased oxygen consumption during sleep occurs over several hours.

In light of the results reported by Wallace and Benson and a number of other investigators (Jevning, Wallace, & Beidebach, 1992; Orme-Johnson, 1973) showing that physiological variables are affected by meditation, some have suggested that these effects can be demonstrated with other self-control strategies such as simply resting (Holmes, 1984). Specifically, Holmes suggested that there is nothing unique about meditation and that what can be achieved with it can be achieved by simply teaching an individual proper techniques of relaxation through resting.

In making his case, Holmes has examined three types of meditation investigations: case studies, own-control studies (in which the effects of meditation versus simply sitting quietly are compared on the same subject), and experimental control studies (in which one group of subjects meditates while another group simply sits quietly). In general, Holmes concluded that simple resting was just as effective as TM and related forms of meditation in achieving control over heart rate, electrodermal activity, respiration rate, systolic blood pressure, skin temperature, oxygen consumption, electromyographic (EMG) activity, and blood flow.

In response to the report by Holmes, a number of investigators criticized his conclusions on several grounds. Benson and Friedman (1985) believed that Holmes misinterpreted much of the meditation literature; in fact, if we examine earlier research, there appear to be consistent and reproducible physiological differences in measures of somatic arousal between subjects who practice relaxation-meditation techniques and those who attain relaxation by simply resting. Also Shapiro (1985), while agreeing that relaxation and control over somatic arousal can be attained by simply resting, thought that Holmes underplayed the role of meditation as an important intervention in the treatment of stress and related problems. While meditation may not be a unique form of achieving relaxation or of dealing with arousal, it is an effective tool and should not be dismissed as valueless simply because other self-control procedures (e.g., deep-muscle relaxation, self-hypnosis, simply resting) produce equivalent results. Shapiro asserted that "there is an important benefit that can be gained from the proper use of meditation as a clinical self-regulation strategy for arousal reduction, as well as an altered state of consciousness for psychotherapy and personal growth" (p. 721).

Also, Dillbeck and Orme-Johnson (1987) noted that a number of studies appearing after the study by Holmes (1984) reported that TM was associated with a significantly greater effect than resting with eyes closed. They considered basal skin resistance, respiration rate, and plasma lactate (Delmonte, 1984; Gallois, 1984; Wolkove et al., 1984).

Thus, the controversy concerning whether meditation is more useful and beneficial than other techniques for achieving relaxation and gaining somatic control goes on. We will not try to resolve this issue here. It should be stated, however, that meditation can help individuals to achieve a state of relaxation and that relaxation has been shown by parties on both sides of the controversy to be integrally involved in attaining control over a variety of somatic responses.

However, control over somatic responding is not the major reason individuals learn to meditate. The major reason is that certain benefits, especially relaxation and control over stress or other situations (e.g., Morrell, 1986), appear to result from meditation. In addition, many forms of meditation are rather easy to learn and are relatively undemanding.

As Holmes (1984) pointed out, a subject does not need to learn to meditate to reach a state of relaxation, which can be achieved through sitting quietly or self-hypnosis. However, for avid meditation practitioners, relaxation will be achieved, and this will result ultimately in a reduced level of tension (Carrington, 1978). The decrease in tension level is manifested by a lessening of anxiety, disappearance of inappropriate startle responses, increased tolerance for frustration, improvement in psychosomatic conditions (e.g., headaches, asthma, hypertension), and a reduced need for psychotropic medication (Carrington, 1977).

With the continued practice of meditative techniques, there also appears to be a heightening in energy level, an improvement in self-esteem, and an elevation and stabilization of mood state (Carrington, 1978). Further, individuals who have meditated for, say, a few weeks at minimum, report that they experience strong feelings of pleasure, sadness, anger, love, and other emotions that they suppressed previously (Glueck, 1973). As a result of the various benefits of practicing meditation, Carrington (1978) advocated incorporating meditation in psychotherapy as an intervention to help individuals with some of the problems mentioned.

Also, Walsh (1978) elaborated on some additional changes that occur during, or as a consequence of, meditation. One such change is in sleep habits.

Intensive meditation over time effectively reduces the need for sleep to about four hours per day—a dramatic reduction from the eight hours a nonmeditator usually needs. Since meditation is, in fact, a very relaxing experience and relaxation of the body is one of the consequences of sleep, the decrease in the amount of sleep required by a meditator is not surprising.

Other Correlates

A number of investigators have reported that when a group of individuals are collectively involved in meditation, specifically TM, some interesting phenomena seem to occur. For example, a significant improvement in the quality of life was found during a three-month period during which a small group of TM participants in Rhode Island collectively meditated. The improvements included drops in the rates of crime, auto accidents and fatalities, and deaths due to cigarette smoking and alcohol consumption (Dillbeck, Cavanaugh, Glenn, Orme-Johnson, & Mittlefehldt, 1987). Similarly, collective meditation sessions were reported to have reduced the number of hostilities in a Lebanese war (Abou Nader, Alexander, & Davies, 1992; Davies & Alexander, 1989) and other international conflicts including acts of terrorism (Orme-Johnson, Dillbeck, & Alexander, 1989).

Can it really be that when a group of individuals gathers to meditate in a trouble spot somewhere in the world that, in fact, hostilities and other undesirable behaviors decrease? The investigators would argue yes. However, we should not confuse *correlation* with *causation*. While it is interesting that significant correlations have been found between collective meditative sessions and reductions in violence and other undesirable acts, remember that these are only correlations and not causal relations. Also, we must be careful to interpret studies that purport to demonstrate causality when other interpretations are also possible (e.g., lulls in a war, time of meditation versus time of hostilities, insufficient control techniques and groups). Nonetheless, the correlations that have been reported are interesting.

In summary, it appears that many psychological, physiological, and other changes can occur during and as a consequence of practicing meditation. Thus, meditation is another useful tool for helping us to understand our state of being and to identify various levels of consciousness and awareness. Also, with extensive and intensive practice in meditation (especially yoga and TM), we can become adept at altering many responses under the control of the autonomic nervous system.

This is not to imply that meditation is the only procedure for achieving these results. Simple resting (Holmes, 1984), progressive relaxation (Jacobson, 1938), and biofeedback (see Chapter 5) are also beneficial tools for accomplishing this task. In fact, biofeedback and most nonmeditative relaxation procedures do not require as much time to learn, nor does one need to become as adept at them as at meditation. However, conscientious meditators may practice their art or skill for a lifetime and therefore use it in their every-day experiences. This is not the case with biofeedback and other self-control procedures, which are generally employed to treat specific problems at specific times. Thus, meditation can be regarded as a slow, cumulative, long-term procedure for producing an altered state of consciousness.

As far as we know, compared with the use of drugs (see Chapter 3), meditation is a relatively safe procedure for bringing about an altered state (see Naranjo & Ornstein, 1976). Many lifelong meditators claim that the "high" they achieve with meditation is as fulfilling as any they could achieve with drugs. In fact, they refer to meditation as a "natural high." If, as Weil (1972) suggested, we have a drive to experience modes of awareness other than the normal waking state, then meditation appears to be a safe outlet for satisfying that drive.

FOR FURTHER READING

Goleman, D. (1988). *The meditative mind: The varieties of meditative experience.* New York: G. P. Putnam's Sons.

Odajnyk, V. W. (1993). *Gathering the light: A psychology of meditation.* Boston: Shambhala.

Shapiro, D. (1980). *Meditation: Self-regulation strategy and altered states of consciousness.* New York: Aldine.

Shapiro, D., & Walsh, R. (Eds.). (1984). *Meditation: Classic and contemporary perspectives.* New York: Aldine.

West, M. A. (Ed.). (1987). *The psychology of meditation.* New York: Oxford University Press.

7

SLEEP AND DREAMS

If you are an average, healthy individual, it is estimated that you will spend about one-third of your life asleep. Thus, when you reach the age of 60, like Washington Irving's Rip van Winkle, you will have slept about 20 years of your life. Moreover, during your 20 years of sleep you will have spent approximately four years dreaming.

While sleep and dreams represent a dramatic departure from our normal state of awareness, they are, at the same time, a state of consciousness that each of us has experienced directly. Perhaps this familiarity with sleep and dreams has fostered questions about these phenomena.

Our current state of knowledge concerning sleep and dreams represents the combined research efforts of investigators working in such areas as clinical psychology, physiological psychology, and, more recently, psychophysiology. There are several reasons why psychologists and other behavioral scientists have studied sleep and dreams so extensively. Besides the fact that we spend a great portion of our life in the altered states of sleep and dreams, we also often drift into sleep, daydream, and enter states of consciousness in which we are not fully asleep yet not fully awake. And we do so quite frequently. As a result, it is relatively easy to study these phenomena and to collect a wealth of data about them through introspective reports.

Furthermore, we all have experienced sleep and dreams, while many of us have not experienced altered states, such as hypnosis, meditation, and drug experiences. And it is not considered odd to discuss sleep and dreams with friends, professors, and other acquaintances. Before we survey the results of research efforts in sleep and dreams, let us examine the role of these phenomena in the psychology of consciousness.

SLEEP, DREAMS, AND CONSCIOUSNESS

In terms of our taxonomy of consciousness described in Chapter 1, **sleep** is the lowest level of consciousness. However, a quick return to the highest level

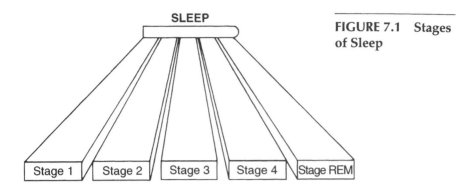

FIGURE 7.1 Stages of Sleep

of our hierarchy is possible when an appropriate stimulus is present, such as the sound of an alarm clock or your mother's voice calling you.

With the advent of modern electroencephalography, Loomis, Harvey, and Hobart (1937) noted that brain-wave recordings could be used to distinguish different stages of sleep. On the basis of electroencephalographic (EEG) records, the investigators were able to identify five distinct stages, ranging from awake to deep sleep. These stages, represented in the Dement-Kleitman (1957) system, are presented in Figure 7.1.

Dreams occur primarily during the stage in Figure 7.1 referred to as Stage REM. We will describe this and other stages of sleep in more detail later in the chapter.

It is important now to identify some of the most significant scientific contributions that have led to our current understanding of the phenomena of sleep and dreams. What has history taught us about sleep and dreams? To help us answer this question, let us examine the historical attempts to study these states of consciousness.

HISTORICAL DEVELOPMENT

Because sleep and dreams are such common human experiences, it is probably safe to conclude that these phenomena have been of interest since the dawn of humanity. Early humans imbued dreams with magical and mystical properties and viewed them as coming from outside themselves and containing omens of the future. Old Testament references to dreams provide clear examples of these beliefs. Joseph, through Pharaoh's dreams, was able to foretell a time of drought in Egypt, and Daniel was able to predict a period of madness in the life of King Nebuchadnezzar through the king's dreams.

The early Greeks and Romans were also extremely interested in sleep and dreams. In his collection of monographs on the biopsychological characteristics of animals, titled *Parva Naturalia*, Aristotle (384 B.C.–322 B.C.) devoted five chapters to dreams and predictions derived from dreams. On the basis of his own naturalistic observations, Aristotle concluded that dreams were not divine or supernatural but rather followed the laws of the mind. Lucretius (94 B.C.–50 B.C.), the Roman poet and philosopher, suggested that the little movements he observed animals making while asleep were somehow related to dreaming.

According to Webb (1973), surprisingly little scientific inquiry into the nature of sleep and dreams was initiated until the late 1800s. Until that time, most of what was accepted concerning these phenomena had been forged from natural observations, anecdotes, opinions, and a smattering of scientifically based knowledge pertaining to human physiology. It is little wonder that Webb, in describing this "dark age of sleep," refers to this time as an era during which "sleep and dreams were almost exclusively the property of poets and dream diviners" (p. 3).

Much of the early research in the quest for a brain sleep center took the form of clinical anatomical evidence. Gayet in France, in 1875, and Mauthner in Austria, in 1890, worked independently on finding the pathological cause of lethargy syndromes. Both noted the importance of a rostral midbrain lesion. On the basis of his observations, Mauthner proposed one of the earliest sleep center hypotheses. He located this center in the gray matter of the brainstem that forms the walls and floor of the fourth ventricle.

From 1916 through 1926 a worldwide epidemic of encephalitis lethargica developed. More commonly called "sleeping sickness," encephalitis lethargica is a degenerative inflammation of the brain that is thought to be virally produced. The disease is characterized by fever, lethargy, or hypersomnia, and general motor symptoms, such as tremors and body spasms (Marcus, 1972). The search for the pathological basis of this disease led von Economo, in 1929 (Marcus, 1972), to conclude that not one, but two brain centers were involved in the control of sleep. A *waking center* served to turn off sleep when properly stimulated and was located in the posterior hypothalamus and mesencephalic tegmentum (the floor of the midbrain). The brain center, which turned on sleep when properly activated, was thought to be located in the basal forebrain structures. This was labeled the *sleep center.*

The late 1930s and the 1940s proved to be a most productive period in the search for the brain centers that controlled the sleep/waking cycle. Partially responsible for this progress was the decision by many investigators to use animals to allow more direct and controlled experiments. Two major research techniques were used. The first involved damaging specific neural structures, then observing changes in behavior (Bremer, 1937). The second technique (Sheer, 1961) involved exciting or activating a specific neural site by applying a series of electrical pulses, then noting changes in the sleep/waking pattern. The pulses were low in voltage and of short duration. Such pulses are not painful.

Bremer believed that sensory input to the cerebrum was responsible for keeping the brain "awake." His argument was based, at least in part, on the effects of lesions that interrupted sensory input via the sensory cranial nerves. He discovered that severing the brainstem at the midbrain level would eliminate all cranial-nerve sensory input to the cerebrum except for vision and olfaction. On the other hand, the more caudal transection would leave all the cranial-nerve sensory input intact.

In studying the effects of various brain lesions on the sleep/waking cycle of the rat, Nauta (1946) found support, not only for the presence of a waking center at the junction of the midbrain and hypothalamus, but also for the existence of a sleep center in the basal preoptic region. Nauta demonstrated that lesions in this area were followed by complete insomnia, motor hyperactivity, and finally, within several days, death.

By the mid-1940s, then, scientists appeared to be on fairly sound footing in proposing the existence of a neural center located somewhere near the rostral midbrain, probably in the posterior hypothalamus, that served as a waking center for the intact organism. More questionable, however, was the notion of a corresponding sleep center. The existence of a sleep center located in a thalamic nucleus, the *massa intermedia*, was suggested by the pioneering study with electrical stimulation reported by Hess (1944). Electrical stimulation of this center in cats induced a state of drowsiness or sleep with all the appropriate behavioral characteristics.

The 1940s closed with the studies of Moruzzi and Magoun (1949), who found that electrical stimulation of the reticular formation in a cat's brainstem produced an EEG pattern of desynchronization and other signs of wakefulness. In the same year, Lindsley, Bowden, and Magoun (1949) provided additional evidence implicating the reticular formation. They showed that midbrain lesions that interrupted the ascending fibers of this structure resulted in a constantly stuporous or sleeping animal. These findings provided an experimental basis for assuming the existence of both sleep centers and waking centers in the brainstem.

As the 1950s came to a close, it was generally accepted that regions necessary for both sleep and waking existed in the parts of the brainstem referred to as the pons and the medulla. It was also evident at this point, in contradiction to Bremer (1937), that sensory input to the brain was not a necessary condition for an organism to demonstrate behavioral signs of wakefulness.

The study of the electrophysiology of sleep and dreams actually originated with the English physiologist Richard Caton, who discovered in 1875 that the brain continually produces low-voltage electrical fluctuations or waves. Using a galvanometer and recording from the exposed cerebral cortex of rabbits, Caton observed these brain-wave activities and noted that they ceased upon the animal's death.

Caton's observations went virtually unnoticed by the scientific community until 1929, when the German psychiatrist Hans Berger, using human subjects, reported on a technique he had developed for recording the electrical activity of large populations of cortical neurons lying beneath the intact skull. Berger accomplished this by attaching surface electrodes to the scalp and forehead. This development signaled the advent of modern electroencephalography (EEG). The early 1930s saw the development of EEG as a clinical tool (Gibbs,

Davis, & Lennox, 1935; Walter, 1936), but it remained for Loomis, Harvey, and Hobart (1937) to demonstrate that Berger's technique could be used to measure levels of consciousness. As we observed earlier, in the section "Sleep, Dreams, and Consciousness," these investigators showed that cortical brain waves exhibited distinct changes in dominant frequency and amplitude with the onset of sleep and continued to change throughout the sleep period. Loomis and colleagues devised a system for classifying these EEG patterns into five distinct stages, ranging from wakefulness to deep sleep. (See Figure 7.1).

What little understanding scientists had before the 1950s of the nature of dreams was based almost exclusively on clinical observations. Two of the most influential psychoanalysts of the period, Sigmund Freud (1856–1939) and Carl Gustav Jung (1875–1961), paid particular attention to the dreams and dreaming behavior of their clients. Freud referred to the dream as the "royal road to the unconscious." He believed that an understanding of a patient's dreams could provide the therapist with helpful clues as to what the client actually thought and felt. Freud's *The Interpretation of Dreams*, published in 1900, is still regarded as one of the most influential books on the topic. Jung, one of Freud's earliest disciples, eventually separated from Freud and set about developing his own system, which included his own theory of dream interpretation. Both theories will receive a more thorough treatment later in this chapter.

In 1892, Ladd speculated that a sleeper's eyeballs moved during dreaming (Aserinsky & Kleitman, 1953). Unfortunately, Ladd failed to pursue the observation, so it went unnoticed for more than 50 years. While carrying out some sleep studies, Kleitman and his graduate student, Aserinsky, noted that periodically during the night, the eyes of the sleeping subject moved rapidly in a generally horizontal fashion. Aserinsky and Kleitman (1953) were able to demonstrate that dreaming occurs during these periods of rapid eye movement (REM). However, before discussing REM activity any further, let us look at the various brain-wave patterns, or EEGs, that commonly accompany sleep and dreams.

SLEEP, DREAMS, AND THE EEG

It has been estimated that the human brain consists of as many as 100 billion neurons (Hubel & Wiesel, 1979). These neurons are constantly involved in receiving information about the environment (sensory input), processing such information, and sending neural messages to the muscles and glands of the body so that the individual can respond appropriately (motor output). In carrying out these functions, voltages of the nerve-cell membrane and electrical activity at the synapses are in a state of constant fluctuation. The combined electrical activity from large numbers of neurons and synapses, called *brain waves*, can be recorded by placing electrodes in contact with the scalp and with an instrument called an **electroencephalograph**. The resultant

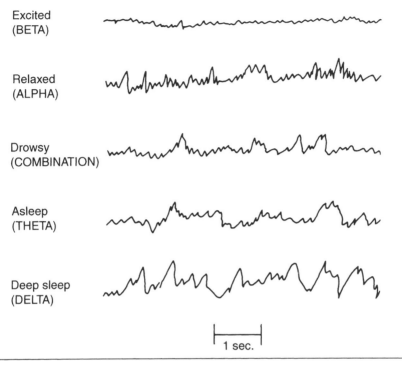

Excited
(BETA)

Relaxed
(ALPHA)

Drowsy
(COMBINATION)

Asleep
(THETA)

Deep sleep
(DELTA)

1 sec.

FIGURE 7.2   Human Brain-Wave Activity

recording of the gross electrical activity of the brain (examples are illustrated in Figure 7.2) is called an **electroencephalogram (EEG)**.

Brain waves differ with respect to at least two major characteristics: *amplitude* (the height of the wave) and *frequency* (rate of occurrence). Much of the pattern of electrical activity in a typical EEG recording can best be described as irregular, low-amplitude activity with no particular pattern. Such activity is described as *desynchronized.* At other times, distinct, very regular patterns of brain waves that are approximately of the same amplitude and occur with a regular frequency can be detected on the EEG. This is called *synchronous* activity. On the basis of the number of waves per second, or Hertz (Hz), different patterns of synchronous activity have been assigned names corresponding to Greek letters.

One of the most common EEG rhythms is the **alpha** frequency, which varies from 8 to 13 Hz and has wave amplitudes ranging from 25 to 100 microvolts (µV). It has been observed most frequently from electrodes situated over the occipital and parietal lobes of the cortex (see Chapter 2, Figure 2.5 for an illustration of the lobes of the human brain). Alpha activity occurs in the EEG patterns of healthy individuals when they are awake but in a quiet, resting state with their eyes shut. During sensory stimulation or attentive mental activity, alpha activity is reduced or replaced by desynchronized activity.

Beta waves occur at frequencies between 14 and 30 Hz; their amplitudes seldom exceed 20 µV. Such activity is often called "low-voltage, fast" beta activity. Beta activity is recorded most commonly from the parietal and frontal cortical regions. The beta wave is characteristic of wakefulness or arousal (Schneider & Tarshis, 1986).

Among the less frequent patterns of synchronous brain-wave activity are **theta** and **delta** patterns. Theta rhythm was described initially by Walter and Dovey (1944) and includes waves in the range of 4 to 7 Hz, with moderately large amplitudes of less than 20 µV. Theta activity is a common pattern seen in EEG recordings of children under the age of 10, when recorded from frontal and temporal cortical sites. The appearance of midline frontal theta in humans under such conditions as simulated diving, chemical intoxication, sleep, and meditation suggests a relationship between such wave forms and various states of consciousness (Matsuoka, 1990). In people between ages 11 and 20, theta waves decrease in both amplitude and frequency. Delta activity is usually defined as large-amplitude EEG waves of 0.5 to 4 Hz. The presence of delta waves in the EEG of waking adults is considered abnormal.

As we noted earlier, Loomis, Harvey, and Hobart (1935) observed that these cortical brain-wave patterns could be used to identify different stages of consciousness. On the basis of these findings, and using EEG patterns as one criterion, these investigators were able to identify five stages that they believed represented increasing depths of sleep (or consciousness). A classification scheme that is used more frequently, and the one used in this chapter, was developed by Dement and Kleitman (1957). The Dement-Kleitman system identifies four stages of sleep depth and a fifth stage, Stage REM (see Figure 7.1).

Studying Your Sleep

Imagine that you have agreed to participate as a research subject in a sleep and dream study and that this is the second night of participation. The second night has been selected for purposes of this discussion because sleep researchers have observed that the data gathered during a subject's first night of participation in such a study are generally atypical. This is the so-called first-night effect (Antrobus, Fein, Jordan, Ellman, & Arkin, 1978). Once you have arrived at the sleep laboratory and completed your nightly ritual of preparing for bed, the researcher attaches surface electrodes to detect brain waves, eye movement, and muscle activity. The standard hook-up for studying sleep activity in the laboratory is shown in Figure 7.3.

Now you can get into bed, get comfortable, relax, and close your eyes. During this state of relaxed wakefulness, brain-wave activity will change from the desynchronized beta type that is commonly observed in the waking, alert individual to the synchronous, alpha type of 8–13 Hz. Should you hap-

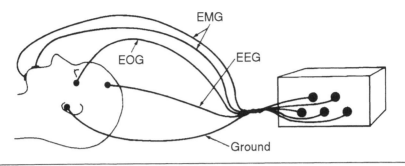

FIGURE 7.3   Recording Sites for Sleep Research

pen to open your eyes in response to a sudden stimulus or begin to think about some problem of the day at this point, the desynchronized activity will return. On the other hand, should you happen to fall asleep at this time, you will enter the first stage of sleep.

"Drifting off to sleep" and other similar colloquial expressions imply that the process of going to sleep is gradual. While this is the popular view of the onset of sleep, it is far from the truth. Actually, the onset of sleep is instantaneous. One second you are aware, and the next you are not. It is as though someone threw a switch that immediately put the portion of the brain that controls awareness on standby. With the onset of Stage 1 sleep, your body begins to show signs of relaxation; muscle tonus diminishes, heart rate slows, and breathing becomes deeper and more regular. In this stage, brain-wave activity is desynchronous, showing low-voltage, mixed frequencies; 12 to 17 Hz is the most prominent frequency. This stage represents a transition in consciousness between wakefulness and the deeper stages of sleep to follow. During this relatively brief stage, it would be very easy to awaken you.

Against this background of desynchronized EEG activity, brief bursts of sleep spindles and k-complexes begin to occur, signaling the onset of Stage 2 sleep. A *sleep spindle* is a sinusoidal wave with a frequency of between 12 and 14 Hz. The appearance of sleep spindles is associated with the loss of perceptual awareness, and for many researchers the appearance of the first sleep spindle during Stage 2 signals that the individual has truly fallen asleep (Steriade, McCormick, & Segnowski, 1993).

A *k-complex* is a biphasic wave form beginning with an initial, sharp negative wave followed by positive components. Although you are soundly asleep by this stage, you could still be awakened easily. In light of this, it is interesting to note that if you were to be awakened as soon as four minutes into this stage, you would most probably report that you had been asleep (Bonnet & Moore, 1982).

By Stage 3 sleep your physiological signs, such as muscle tonus, heart rate, blood pressure, and body temperature, all show signs of decreasing. You are now soundly asleep, and it would take a relatively strong stimulus to awaken you. The onset and termination of this stage are defined by the percentage of delta wave activity on the EEG recording. Against the background of desynchronous cortical brain-wave activity, punctuated by the k-complexes and sleep spindles of Stage 2, delta waves begin to appear. Stage 3 sleep begins when at least 20 percent of the EEG is composed of delta-wave activity.

During Stage 3 the frequency of delta wave activity continues to increase until more than 50 percent of the EEG consists of these slow waves. When this occurs, you have entered Stage 4 sleep. You are now in a very deep state of sleep, and you would be extremely difficult to awaken. If aroused during this stage, you would appear somewhat disoriented, and it would take a little time for you to become conscious of your surroundings. If allowed to sleep uninterrupted, you would begin to drift from Stage 4 into Stage 3 and then into Stage 2.

About every 30 to 90 minutes throughout the night, the sleeping subject passes from Stage 2 into REM sleep, and this passage is announced by both EEG and physiological changes. The EEG during this stage consists of relatively low-voltage, mixed frequencies, punctuated by occasional bursts of alpha activity. If you think that this description of EEG activity sounds familiar, you are correct. In fact, because the EEG of REM sleep resembles that of Stage 1 so closely, this stage of sleep is often called *paradoxical* sleep. Although the EEG pattern is similar to that of Stage 1 sleep, it would be much more difficult to arouse you from Stage REM than it would be from Stage 1.

The term **REM sleep** coined first by Dement, refers to the fact that the sleeper's eyes can be seen darting back and forth beneath closed eyelids at a rate of approximately 50–60 times per minute (Dement & Kleitman, 1957). Since this rapid eye movement occurs during dreaming, one might expect that the eye movements are linked to the visual aspects of the dream. It is almost as if the dreamer were viewing a private movie. Some researchers, however, now believe that rapid eye movements simply reflect the overflow of the individual's activated nervous system (Chase & Morales, 1983).

In addition to changes in the EEG and the *electrooculogram* (EOG), a record of eye movement, other bodily changes also occur during REM sleep. Respiration and pulse rates increase and become irregular during this stage. Blood pressure also increases. Finally, male subjects often experience penile erections during Stage REM sleep. The sleeper shows a profound loss of muscle tonus, although twitches or spasms in the limbs are often observed. That terrifying sensation of being frozen to the spot while someone is chasing you, or of opening your mouth to scream but being unable to utter a sound, may have a basis in the reality that we are, in fact, unable to move our muscles while we are dreaming.

This "dreamer's paralysis" may be due to a brain chemical that inhibits the motor neurons that ordinarily cause our muscles to contract (Chase, 1981a, 1981b). Quite probably, this paralysis is what prevents us from acting out our dream activity, which might be very dangerous (Moore-Ede, Sulzman, & Fuller, 1982). The sleeper's movement, of which all of us who have shared a bed with another are very much aware, takes place between these

REM periods. This movement occurs about every 15 minutes, or between 20 and 40 times each night. Although we might think the opposite to be true, poor sleepers tend to move less and spend more time on their backs than do good sleepers (De Koninck, Gagnon, & Lallier, 1983).

Earlier, we mentioned what has come to be one of the most fascinating characteristics of REM sleep: *dreaming*. Having observed that during the course of a night's sleep the subject's eyes periodically moved back and forth rapidly, Aserinsky and Kleitman (1953) began to awaken and question subjects during both REM and non-REM (NREM) sleep. The investigators observed that 74 percent of the subjects reported detailed accounts of their dreams when awakened during REM sleep, while only 7 percent were able to report their dreams when awakened during any other sleep stage. Foulkes (1962b) reported that when people in sleep laboratories were awakened from REM periods, they reported dreaming on the average of 80 percent of the time; in some cases, the percentage was closer to 100.

More recently, Hong, Potkin, Callaghan, and Gillin (1997) provided further support for the relationship between REM sleep eye movements and dream visual imagery. They propose that the scanning of the visual imagery in dreams is accomplished in a manner similar to the scanning of real objects during waking visual perception and, as in the case of wakefulness, is an automatic process that normally does not give rise to awareness of the direction of the gaze. Farthing (1992) states that not only are dreams more frequent during REM sleep, they are also more vivid, emotional, and storylike.

While these findings forced the conclusion that dreaming does occur during REM periods, they did not negate the possibility that dreaming could occur during NREM periods as well. Foulkes (1962a) and Rechtschaffen, Verdone, and Wheaton (1963) have provided results indicating that dreaming does in fact occur during NREM states but that these dreams are more difficult to recall on awakening than those that occur during REM periods. EEG records obtained during each of the sleep stages are shown in Figure 7.4.

A number of investigators have suggested that the diverging function, physiology, and mentation of REM and NREM sleep may be related to cortical lateralization, which we discussed in Chapter 2 (Goldstein, Stolzfus, & Gardocki, 1972; Gruzelier & Flor-Henry, 1979; McCarley & Hobson, 1979). In an early EEG study, Goldstein et al. (1972) obtained results that were interpreted as indicating greater right-hemisphere involvement in REM sleep and greater left-hemisphere activation during NREM sleep. However, attempts to further substantiate unihemispheric predominance during sleep have been for the most part unsuccessful.

Armitage, Hoffmann, Loewy, and Moffitt (1989) found significant differences between slow-wave, Stage 2, and REM sleep, demonstrating that slow-wave sleep evidenced more asymmetrical activity than either Stage 2 or REM sleep. Also, REM sleep was associated with the smallest asymmetries. Such results do not support the notion of a right-hemisphere REM/left-hemisphere

**FIGURE 7.4   EEG
Recordings from the
Frontal Lobe of Stages of
Wakefulness and Sleep**

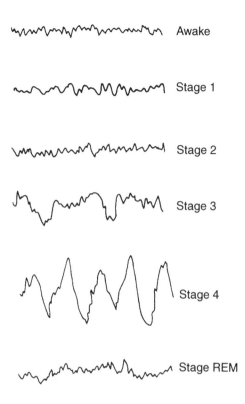

Awake

Stage 1

Stage 2

Stage 3

Stage 4

Stage REM

NREM relationship. The finding of significant differences in hemispheric asymmetry between Stage 2 and slow-wave sleep may also indicate functional differences within NREM sleep stages.

There are wide, individual variations in patterns of sleep, but most adults complete a full cycle of sleep stages every 90–120 minutes. If a night's sleep in the laboratory is a typical one, most deep sleep (Stages 3 and 4) occurs during the first third of the sleep period, while the bulk of the REM sleep occurs during the final third of the night (Hartmann, 1973). As the night progresses, the length of each REM period increases, while Stages 3 and 4 diminish and all but disappear (see Figure 7.5).

More than 22 million Americans work a shift other than the regular day shift (American Sleep Disorders Association, 1994). Work schedules that include night work greatly interfere with the sleep/waking pattern. Both survey and EEG studies demonstrate that morning sleep after a night shift is short and unrefreshing (Torsvall, Akerstedt, Gillander, & Knutsson, 1989). A few survey studies have also examined compensatory naps during days with short main sleep periods (Akerstedt & Torsvall, 1985; Evans, Cooke, Orne, & Orne, 1977). These naps contained a large proportion of slow-wave sleep and were apparently caused by the sleep deficit after the short main sleep period (Torsvall et al., 1989).

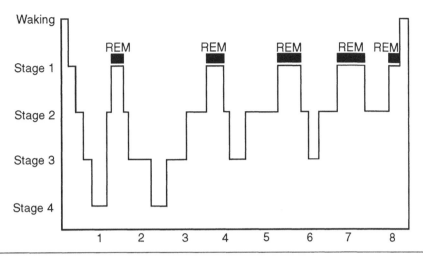

FIGURE 7.5   A Typical Night's Sleep

Another major negative effect of night work is the increase in perceived sleepiness, particularly during work. This sleepiness, which is normally at its maximum during the last half of the night shift (Akerstedt, Torsvall, & Gillberg, 1982), can lead to deterioration of performance (Mitler et al., 1988; Torsvall et al., 1989). The latter is of special importance in work situations in which the individual must take responsibility for human lives or for objects of great economic value.

Sleep patterns have also been noted to vary with age. Morewitz (1988), for example, has observed that age-related changes contribute to the excessive daytime sleepiness often observed in the elderly. Despite the fact that they represent only 12 percent of the population, it has recently been observed that the elderly in the United States receive 35–40 percent of the sedative-hypnotic drugs that are prescribed (Moran, Thompson, & Neis, 1988). Webb and Agnew (1971), however, found that the percentage of total time spent in Stage 4 sleep decreases as a function of age. Also, other investigators (Korner, 1968; Roffwarg, Muzio, & Dement, 1966) have observed similar decreases in percentage of total time spent in Stage REM sleep as the individual grows older. Monk, Reynolds, Buysse, and Hoch (1991) compared 34 healthy older adults, aged 80–91 years, who were self-described good sleepers with 30 young controls with regard to sleep habits. Using such measures as the Horne and Ostberg Morningness Questionnaire, the Circadian Type Questionnaire, the Eysenck Personality Questionnaire, a two-week sleep diary, and polysomnographic (e.g., EEG, EOG, and EMG measures), these investigators found that by almost all laboratory measures, the older group slept poorly compared with the young. They also found that compared with the younger subjects, the older subjects evidenced earlier habitual times of waking up and a lack of flexibility in sleep patterns. Correlations between sleep and health status, however, suggested that at least some of these differences might be attributed to illness rather than age. Moran et al. (1988) suggest that before drug intervention is initiated with this particular age group, both physicians and patients need to be made aware of the normal sleep changes that occur as a function of aging.

Finally, it is also known that the sleep pattern can be dramatically altered by ischemic strokes. In 1988, Rakhindzhanov, Gafurov, and Matkhalikov demonstrated that the structure of nocturnal sleep in stroke victims differs significantly from that of normal people in a number of parameters, including greater amounts of dream-state sleep, shorter REM-sleep latency periods, and a shortened sleep-spindle stage. What happens, however, if we are totally deprived of the altered state of consciousness we call sleep? Let us discuss this topic briefly.

SLEEP DEPRIVATION

Most of us try to allow ourselves between six and ten hours of sleep per night; only about 5 percent of us can get by with fewer than six hours sleep each night (Broughton, 1984). *Sleep deprivation* occurs when we have gone without sleep for 24 hours or so.

If we miss a night's sleep or greatly reduce the amount of sleep for any reason, we feel ill used and tend to express such feelings the next day in the form of irritability, inattentiveness, and generally lackluster performance. If we can agree that this is a common experience when we have been deprived of a single night's repose, then the next question might well be: What are the consequences of more prolonged periods of sleep deprivation?

Sleep deprivation studies with both human and animal subjects were performed as early as the 1890s. However, it was not until the 1950s that sleep researchers began to focus attention on this problem. Certainly, one major impetus to this sudden surge of research had to be newly acquired knowledge that in certain countries, prolonged periods of sleep deprivation, combined with emotional and physical abuse, were being used to induce personality disorders in noncooperative prisoners of the state.

Can prolonged periods of "sleep starvation" actually alter our normal state of consciousness? If such effects do occur, what is their nature? Are they relatively transitory or permanent? These are the sorts of questions that the sleep researchers tried to answer in a variety of ways.

A frequently cited example of sleep deprivation is Peter Tripp's bid in the early 1960s to stay awake for 200 consecutive hours to raise money for the March of Dimes. Tripp, a New York disk jockey, made daily broadcasts from his booth at Times Square, where crowds gathered to watch him. During the course of his self-imposed sleep starvation, Tripp was given medical and neurological examinations, performance tests, and psychological tests. He was watched closely by a number of sleep researchers, including Dement, Lubin, and Wolff. Almost from the beginning, Tripp had to fight off a strong tendency to go to sleep. As he neared the halfway mark (100 hours), it became evident that he was experiencing great difficulty in terms of memory, attention, and even simple mental tasks. He also had visual hallucinations. Luce (1965) described the last day of Tripp's 200-hour sleepless period:

> *By 170 hours the agony had become almost unbearable to watch. At times Tripp was no longer sure he was himself, and frequently tried to gain proof of his identity. Although he behaved as if he were awake, his brain patterns resembled those of sleep. In his psychotic delusions he was convinced that the doctors were in a conspiracy against him to send him to jail. On the last morning of his wakeathon, Tripp was examined by Dr. Wolff of Cornell. The late Dr. Wolff had a somewhat archaic manner of dress, and to Tripp he must have appeared funereal. Tripp undressed, as requested, and lay down on the table for medical examination, but as he gazed up at the doctor he came to the gruesome decision that the man was actually an undertaker, about to bury him alive. With this grim insight, Tripp leapt for the door, and tore into the Astor hall with several doctors in pursuit. At the end of the 200 sleepless hours, nightmare, hallucination, and reality had merged, and he felt he was the victim of a sadistic conspiracy among the doctors.*
>
> *With some persuasion, Tripp managed to make a final appearance in the glass-windowed booth in Times Square, and after his broadcast he went to sleep for 13 hours. (pp. 19–20)*

When Tripp awoke from his recovery sleep, the terrors, hallucinations, and mental deterioration had vanished. A three-month mild depression was the only residual effect he experienced.

Five years later, a 17-year-old high school student, Randy Gardner, made an effort to break the record for consecutive hours of wakefulness. He was highly motivated and in excellent health. The attempt was made in the familiar confines of his own home, and he had the aid of two schoolmates and Dr. William Dement. Under these conditions, Gardner was able to exceed the *Guinness Book of World Records* listing of 260 hours by four hours. Although Randy experienced some memory lapses, irritability, and difficulty in concentrating, he demonstrated no psychotic behavior or serious emotional change during the entire period. Dement and his colleagues did note that Randy experienced some neurological difficulties, including blurred vision, involuntary eye movements, and an EEG pattern that resembled a sleeping person, regardless of whether his eyes were open or closed (Johnson, Slye, & Dement, 1965).

Having set his record, Randy held a press conference and then went to bed, where he spent the next 14½ hours in a sleep dominated by Stages 4 and REM. On awakening, he appeared to have suffered no ill effects from his ordeal.

Why the differences in the effects of sleep deprivation between Peter Tripp and Randy Gardner? The lack of experimental controls in these observations makes it extremely difficult to pinpoint any single factor. However, a list of possible explanations would include age, physical health, prestudy psychological make-up, setting, and the kinds of demands placed on the subjects during their ordeals.

Laboratory research suggests that during total sleep deprivation, subjects may evidence decrements in performance. To account for such performance deficits, Williams and Lubin (1959) proposed a lapse hypothesis. They suggested that a subject under total sleep deprivation demonstrated an uneven slowing of performance that led to an eventual absence of the appropriate task-related response. Edwards (1941) observed that highly motivated sleep-deprived subjects were able to maintain an acceptable level of task performance, but only with tremendous difficulty. Goleman (1982) observed that when confronted with complex and interesting tasks, sleep-deprived subjects may evidence a very small drop in performance level.

While the underlying mechanisms still are not fully understood, it is clear from laboratory findings that sleep starvation is accompanied by impairment of memory. Though it generally has been accepted that sleep deprivation affects short-term memory (Lubin, Moses, Johnson, & Naitoh, 1974), Vojtechovsky, Safratova, Votava, and Feit (1971) have presented evidence to suggest that long-term memory also may be impaired.

It has been known for a long time that retention of recently learned information is generally better when learning is followed by a brief period of sleep rather than a period of wakefulness (Benson & Feinberg, 1977). Once paradoxical sleep was discovered, a strong interest developed in its possible role. A large body of evidence now establishes relations between paradoxical sleep and memory. It has been demonstrated in a variety of animals that increases in paradoxical sleep over normal levels occur following successful learning (Bloch, Hennevin, & Leconte, 1979; Gisquet-Verrier, & Smith, 1989; Hennevin, Hars, & Bloch, 1989; Smith, 1985). Also, deprivation of paradoxical sleep, at the times of extraparadoxical sleep following training, result in learning deficits (Gisquet-Verrier, & Smith, 1989; Hennevin et al., 1989; Pearlman, 1979; Smith, 1985). Unfortunately, any such theory attempting to explain the function of REM sleep must be able to adequately explain why *tricyclic antidepressant drugs* do not severely disrupt behavior. A class of drugs that is commonly prescribed for the treatment of depression and for some REM-sleep-related disorders, tricyclic antidepressants prevent the individual from experiencing REM sleep for months at a time, yet no side effects are experienced that can be explained by REM sleep loss (Pinel, 1997).

Finally, laboratory research (Hartmann, Baekeland, Zwilling, & Hop, 1971; Webb & Agnew, 1974) has shown that when total sleep time is reduced, the amount of time actually spent in Stage 4 does not decrease. In fact, if the reduction is severe, Stage 4 time may actually increase (Dement & Greenberg, 1966; Johnson & MacLeod, 1973). Therefore it should not be surprising to find that the better predictor of slow-wave sleep rebound following sleep reduction is not the amount of slow-wave sleep lost but rather the total duration of sleep (Lucidi, Devoto, Violani, Mastraceli, & Bertini, 1997).

Until now, we have dealt with the effects of total sleep loss. One might also ask what would be the effects of a more selective deprivation—say, deprivation of a single stage of sleep. Dement (1960) was one of the first researchers to deprive subjects selectively of Stage REM sleep. In his research, adults were allowed to sleep normally in the laboratory, except that whenever a subject entered Stage REM, he or she was awakened by the investigator, then allowed to return to sleep. Dement continued this procedure for five successive nights. He observed that with the passage of time, subjects had to be awakened more frequently, indicating that progressive deprivation of REM sleep increases the tendency to enter REM sleep. During their first normal night's sleep the REM-deprived subjects spent approximately 60 percent more time in REM sleep than they had during a comparable prestudy baseline period. This phenomenon was called the **REM-rebound effect**, since it appeared as though subjects were trying to make up for the lost Stage REM sleep. The REM-rebound effect has since been replicated many times (Brunner, Kijk, Tobler, & Borbely, 1990; Clemes & Dement, 1967; Dement, Greenberg, & Klein, 1966; Sampson, 1966).

Fisher (1966) noted that penile erections, which normally occur during Stage REM sleep, begin to occur during NREM sleep in REM-sleep-deprived male subjects. Tilley and Empson (1978) found that human memory may be affected subtly by Stage REM deprivation. Nevertheless, Webb (1974) suggested that, contrary to early studies (Dement & Greenberg, 1966), REM-sleep-deprivation studies have failed to demonstrate any harmful psychological effects.

SLEEP LEARNING

Passing from a conscious state of wakefulness to one of sleep does not mean a sudden cessation of brain activity. It has been demonstrated that we are not completely unaware of our environment during sleep (Arkin & Antrobus, 1978; Goodenough, Witkin, Koulack, & Cohen, 1975).

This knowledge that the brain still functions during sleep was probably all the impetus researchers needed to explore the possibility of learning during sleep, **hypnopedia**. Wouldn't it be wonderful if you could turn on a cassette by your bed at night and wake up the next morning with a head full of facts? While a great many claims have been made for the effectiveness of sleep learning, laboratory findings have failed to offer much support for such claims (Emmons & Simon, 1956). Webb and Cartwright (1978) observed that "no study has been able to show convincingly an ability to learn complex verbal material during sleep" (p. 227). Reviewing the research literature on hypnopedia, Aarons (1976) and Webb and Cartwright (1978) observed that many of these studies were poorly controlled. Adequately controlled studies do indicate, however, that while the subject does not actually learn material that is presented during sleep (with accompanying sleep brain-wave patterns), learning such material when awake (beta waves) appears to be facilitated slightly as compared with the rate at which similar, but new, material is learned. In short, there appears to be a positive savings score on learning similar material.

SLEEP DISORDERS

Before closing this discussion of sleep, we need to take a sample from what is, perhaps, the most dramatic aspect of this phenomenon: sleep disorders; that is, disorders of consciousness.

One of the most common of the sleep disorders is insomnia. On the average, 33 percent of American adults complain of insomnia to some degree and 17 percent believe that their symptoms are serious (Pressman, 1991). Dement (1972) refers to insomnia as "an illness that is caused by the treatment." The very sleeping pill the doctor prescribes to regulate the patient's sleep may well produce the sleep disturbance. Initially, the sleep medication may cause a suppression of REM sleep; but if the dosage is not increased, this effect will eventually habituate. As you might expect, once medication is discontinued, the individual experiences a tremendous REM-rebound effect. The sudden increase in REM sleep leads to sleeplessness that is often accompanied by vivid nightmares (Oswald, 1968). Now the patient is convinced that he or she has a bad case of insomnia and so returns to the sleeping pill, and the cycle begins once more. Over-the-counter drugs do no more good than sugar-coated pills and are only as effective as people's faith that they will help (Webb & Bonnet, 1979). The danger with these drugs is that people who regularly use sleeping pills also run the risk of psychological and physical drug dependence (Spielman & Herrera, 1991). Because they may not produce the desired effect, the frustrated insomniac may take more than what is recommended. This can lead to very serious medical problems.

While insomnia may take several forms, each form results in the same thing: a loss of sleep. The individual may experience great difficulty in initially falling asleep. This is sometimes referred to as a *sleep-onset disorder.* Other forms of insomnia include a tendency to wake up repeatedly during the night and to wake up very early in the morning, then be unable to go back to sleep. Regardless of the form, people with insomnia typically feel very sleepy during the daytime, and many sufferers consider this the most serious aspect of their problem (Coleman et al., 1982).

Approximately 25 percent of all insomniacs complain that they get little sleep, even though when they are brought into the sleep laboratory, their EEGs show normal sleep patterns. These patients suffer from a condition called *subjective insomnia.* If these people are aroused during Stage 2 sleep, they are more likely to say that they were awake when called than sound sleepers are (Borkovec, Lane, & VanDot, 1981; Trinder, 1988). They are able to give detailed accounts of their thoughts during sleep and often can describe accurately any sounds that occurred while they were sleeping (Engle-Friedman, Baker, & Bootzin, 1985). It seems clear that these insomniacs monitor the environment as normal sleepers do, but they are unable to shut these stimuli out of their sleeping consciousness.

As we have already observed, problems arise when sleeping pills are used to treat insomnia. It is only logical, then, that investigators would eventually begin the search for a more effective therapy with fewer side effects. Comparing the effectiveness of various behavioral therapies, Espie, Lindsay, Brooks, & Hood (1989) discovered that the techniques of progressive relaxation and stimulus control both produced significant improvement; however, the nature of the treatment gains varied. Stimulus control procedures improved the patient's sleep pattern, whereas progressive relaxation affected the patient's perception of the quality of his or her sleep.

Morawetz (1989), in a controlled study designed to evaluate a commercially available self-help treatment for insomnia based on stimulus control and progressive relaxation principles, observed that for individuals who were not taking sleep medication, this self-help program was clinically effective. However, for those taking sleep medication, the program had to be supplemented by professional assistance to be fully effective. Other investigators have demonstrated that various behavioral strategies are effective in alleviating insomnia (Lacks & Powlishta, 1989).

Another sleep disorder, *sleep apnea,* was identified first by Gastaut and Broughton (1965) in patients who complained of hypersomnia. Sleep apnea has been found to occur in about 40 percent of elderly people but is less common in younger adults (Coleman et al., 1981). As the name suggests, sleep apnea is characterized by brief periods during which the sleeping person stops breathing. These periods generally last from 15 to 60 seconds.

For the person who suffers from sleep apnea, the change from the waking to the sleeping state has the effect of turning off the respiratory centers of the brain. This causes the muscles necessary for breathing, the diaphragm and the intercostal muscle, to stop working. Under such conditions there can be no exchange of oxygen and carbon dioxide, so the amount of oxygen carried by the red blood cells decreases to extremely low levels while the carbon dioxide in the blood continues to increase. In response to these changes in blood-gas levels, the respiratory centers of the central nervous system and the respiratory muscles begin to function once more.

However, there is yet another problem. Because the loss of muscle tonus that normally accompanies sleep is exaggerated in sleep apnea, the throat collapses, effectively cutting off the flow of air to the lungs. Thus, oxygen levels continue to decrease and carbon dioxide levels increase until they reach dangerous levels and the individual is briefly aroused. After a series of gasping breaths, during which time the blood gases return to normal levels, the patient goes back to sleep, and the cycle begins again (Dement, 1972). The specific cause of sleep apnea is as yet unknown. Major treatments may include a *tracheotomy* (a surgical opening in the windpipe), major weight loss, and drugs (Kalat, 1992).

Narcolepsy is another common sleep disorder. It is estimated that 100,000 adults in the United States suffer from the symptoms of this disorder which is more technically known as *disorder of excessive somnolence* (Levinthal, 1990). Generally, narcolepsy shows up for the first time between ages 10 to 25 and may last throughout life. There are approximately 250,000 narcoleptics in the United States (Dement & Baird, 1977; Fenton, 1975). The individual suffering from narcolepsy experiences sudden and recurrent attacks of sleep and the desire to sleep during the waking hours. Many narcoleptics have difficulty differentiating between sleep and waking states (Browman & Mitler, 1988), and most experience other periodic disorders that occur frequently enough to be included as part of the narcolepsy syndrome. These disorders include cataplexy, sleep paralysis, and hypnogogic hallucinations.

Cataplexy refers to a sudden loss of muscle tonus and postural reflexes. During these seizures the patient is fully awake and aware of what is happening in the environment. *Sleep paralysis* is an inability to move that occurs while falling asleep or awakening. *Hypnogogic hallucinations* are very vivid, often frightening dreams that occur at the onset of sleep. Some three to four hours after waking, the narcoleptic feels overcome by sleepiness and often falls asleep while talking, standing, or simply moving about. Initially, a number of episodes that might be described as microsleep, or sleep periods lasting from five to fifteen seconds, will be experienced, but eventually, the narcoleptic is forced to take a nap.

Earlier in this chapter, we noted that the normal onset of sleep is characterized by NREM brain-wave activity. Laboratory studies have demonstrated that narcoleptics begin their night's sleep with a REM phase (Rechtschaffen, Wolpert, Dement, Mitchell, & Fisher, 1963). These results led Rechtschaffen and colleagues to predict that the narcoleptic's daytime sleep attacks may well be attacks of REM sleep—a prediction that was later confirmed in the laboratory (Rechtschaffen & Dement, 1969). The exact cause of this condition is unknown. However, findings such as those cited above led Dement, Holman, and Guilleminault (1976) to suggest that narcolepsy may be a physiological defect in the REM sleep-control mechanism. Although we do not at present know the precise cause of or the adequate treatment for narcolepsy, we do know that it is not associated with any kind of emotional disorder, runs in families, and may be a genetic disturbance.

Nocturnal panic, another sleep disorder, involves a sudden awakening from sleep in a state of panic characterized by various somatic sensations of sympathetic arousal and intense subjective fear (Craske & Barlow, 1989). Despite the fact that approximately 18 percent of all spontaneous panic attacks occur from a sleeping state, the phenomenon of nocturnal panic has received little research attention (Taylor, Sheikh, & Agras, 1986). Empirical evidence of this phenomenon has been based largely on accidental findings from the examination of naturally occurring panic attacks over 24-hour periods (Margraf, Taylor, & Ehlers, 1987; Taylor et al., 1986) and from sleep laboratory studies (Hauri, 1985; Lesser, Poland, Holcomb, & Rose, 1985). Nocturnal panics have been found to occur during light, non-REM sleep (Gastaut, Dongier, Broughton, & Tassinari, 1964) and during delta sleep (Hauri, Friedman, Ravaris, & Fisher, 1985; Lesser et al., 1985).

Several sleep disorders predominantly affect children, including sleepwalking, bed-wetting, and night terrors. Some 15 percent of all children between the ages of 5 and 12 sleepwalk at least once, and some 1 to 6 percent do it regularly (Anders, Carskado, & Dement, 1980). Children who suffer from sleepwalking, or *somnambulism,* usually go to sleep normally, but sometime during the night, they arise and walk in their sleep. Because the skeletal muscles are paralyzed during REM sleep, sleepwalkers do not actually act out their dreams. Instead, sleepwalking occurs during Stage 3 and Stage 4 sleep and therefore is more likely to occur during the first third of the night (Kefauver & Guilleminault, 1994). If unchecked, sleepwalkers may go from room to room, leave the house, and even perform rather complex tasks. During sleepwalking the child's eyes are partially or fully open, and he or she is able to avoid obstacles, listen when spoken to, and obey commands. After 15 to 30 minutes of such behavior, the sleepwalker will return to bed on his or her own. In the morning the child usually remembers none of these nocturnal events. Children of somnambulists are likely to have the same problem, a finding suggesting that this sleep disturbance has a hereditary component (Abe, Amatomi, & Oda, 1984).

Although we have been discussing sleep disorders that affect children, *REM- sleep behavior disorder* (RBD), which is very similar to sleepwalking, occurs primarily in older men, the average age of onset being approximately 50 (Schenck, Hurwitz, & Mahowald, 1993). This syndrome consists of injurious or disruptive behavior that occurs during REM sleep (Schenck & Mahowald, 1990).

Nocturnal enuresis, or bed-wetting, is a childhood sleep problem that affects some five million children in the United States. Sleep specialists do not consider bed-wetting a disorder if the child is under the age of five (Friman & Warzak, 1990). This sleep disorder is often associated with dreams in which the child is urinating into a toilet. The child awakens to discover that he or she has wet the bed. Turner and Taylor (1974) estimate that as many as four to five million children and adolescents in the United States suffer from this embarrassing condition. Because about 15 percent per year pass through this and become continent, the older the child is, the more important treatment becomes. The guilt and shame that often accompany enuresis are also important factors in determining whether or not to treat the condition (Scharf & Jennings, 1988).

Night terrors, or *incubus attacks,* normally occur during the early part of the night and leave a child in an apparent state of terror, thrashing and screaming, unable to communicate what is wrong and completely incon-solable. Concomitant with the night terror attack is a severe physiological upheaval. Kahn, Fisher, and Edwards (1978) suggest that during severe attacks, the heart rate may almost triple. Increases in heart rate, magnitude of respiration, and skin conductance are also observed. Such episodes are gen-erally short in duration, and the child characteristically returns to sleep once the attack passes. Despite the apparent intensity of the experience, the child often forgets it by morning.

Because at least some dream content is associated with these night ter-rors, it may come as a surprise that they normally occur near the end of one of the first Stage 4 (deep sleep) periods. Although the exact causes of these disorders remain unknown, a review of the literature suggests at least two hypotheses. Since night terrors are most common among children between three and eight years old, Hartmann (1981) suggests that they are linked with the development of the nervous system and may indicate a mild neurologi-cal disorder due to faulty maturation in the brainstem. Since these episodes generally disappear by adolescence, other sleep researchers (Mitler et al., 1975) recommend that when night terrors in children have no apparent cause, they should be allowed to run their course. Still other investigators say that the behavior observed in such disorders may be an expression of emotional conflicts that the child represses during the waking hours (Freud, 1933).

Night terrors and somnambulism seem to be present in young children and some adults under extreme stress. For this reason, patience, support, and reassurance at the time of sleep disruption are the treatment of preference (Arkin, 1991).

THEORIES OF SLEEP

In discussing sleep as the lowest state in our hierarchy of consciousness, we need to ask: Why do we sleep? This question has long puzzled both the layperson and the researcher. Theoretical responses to the question why we sleep have been many and varied. Rather than attempt to identify each theo-retical explanation that has been offered—a task that is well beyond the scope of this chapter—we have attempted to classify these explanations into five representational categories.

With the advent of new data about, and increased interest in, hematology (the study of blood) came the first categories of sleep theory, the *humoral the-ories*. Such theories suggest that some substance in the blood causes a dys-function in the central nervous system that results in sleep. One theory that is representative of this category, the *circulatory theory*, suggests that sleep is a result of the brain being deprived of its normal amount of oxygen.

Several investigators, such as Bartley and Chute (1947), proposed a *repar-ative theory* of sleep, arguing that cortical activity that occurs during the waking period brings about cortical cellular changes. Since such cortical functions as processing sensory information, processing memory, and thinking diminish or cease during sleep, the investigators conclude that the necessary cellular repairs are made during the sleep period. A study in the early 1980s, which found an increase in slow-wave sleep and in total sleep time after running a 92-kilometer road race, seems to support this theory (Shapiro, Bortz, Mitchell, Bartel, & Jooste, 1981). Because sleep research has shown continual brain and body activity during sleep, this is probably not the entire picture.

More recently, naturally occurring chemicals in the central nervous system have been studied to determine their possible effects on waking and sleeping. However, a "sleep toxin" has not yet been discovered (Groves & Schlesinger, 1982).

A number of years ago, sleep was described simply as a cessation of the active condition of wakefulness, not unlike the state of unconsciousness. This view of sleep has been incorporated into some modern theories. Of the modern *passive theories* of sleep, perhaps one of the best known is Lindsley's (1961) *reticular hypothesis.* According to this explanation, sleep results from the cessation of ascending impulses in the ascending reticular activating system.

In sharp contrast to the passive theories stand the *active theories* of sleep, which suggest that sleep is an active process produced by the activation of a sleep-producing system. All active theories of sleep contend that different neural mechanisms are involved in the control of wakefulness and sleeping.

Finally, some theories suggest that sleep is an evolved mechanism that has a particular survival function. One such evolutionary theory, proposed by Zepelin and Rechtschaffen (1974), contends that the sleep process evolved as a system of conserving energy. Studies of brain metabolism during sleep show that people use less energy while asleep than while awake (Madsen, 1993).

From the foregoing discussion, it should be obvious that there are many suggested explanations of why we sleep. However, none of the theories that have been offered to date has been clearly substantiated by the rigors of laboratory research. Thus, the question remains unanswered.

ON DREAMS AND DREAMING

When we dream, what do we dream about? Research has demonstrated that dream content is infinitely varied. Obviously, dream content is also a very private experience. Through EEG and EOG recordings it may be possible for the experimenter to determine whether a sleeping subject is dreaming. However, the only way researchers can discover what subjects are dreaming about is to ask them.

Although it presents certain methodological problems (Schwartz, Weinstein, & Arkin, 1978), *daytime dream recall* is one way of studying dream content. As its name suggests, the subject, on awakening, is requested to give an account of the dream or dreams he or she had during the previous night's sleep. The procedure is a bit like keeping a dream diary. Another approach to the study of dream content involves using EEG and EOG recordings to determine when the subject is dreaming, awakening him or her immediately after the dream period, and asking for a verbal report of the dream. One advantage of this research technique over daytime dream recall is that it eliminates dependency on the subject's memory.

Some researchers (Hall, 1951; Hall & Van de Castle, 1966; Snyder, 1970), using the dream logs of a large number of college students as their database, have tabulated the themes of these dreams to analyze dream content. Most dreams involve two or three people, usually strangers, and one or two familiar objects. Men dream about other men almost twice as often as they dream about women; women dream about men and other women with equal frequency.

Despite what your friends may have told you about their dreams, the probability is very low that their dreams are populated by such famous figures as Bill Clinton, Whitney Houston, or David Duchovny. Animals appear in dreams; however, the ever-popular dream monster is almost never encountered. Generally, some kind of activity, most frequently a form of movement, is found in dreams. The second most common activity is talking, followed in frequency by sitting, watching, socializing, and playing. Dream themes more often portray bad news, misfortune, and failure than success; aggressive encounters are slightly more frequent than friendly ones. Although sex-related dream themes are certainly not uncommon, their observed frequency of approximately 10 percent is far less than one might predict in view of the importance attached to sex by Freudian psychoanalysts. In fact, we rarely dream about sexual encounters and almost never about sexual intercourse (Kiester, 1980).

Evans and Evans (1983) suggest that about 50 percent of our dreams are in color; the percentage for women is a few points higher than it is for men. Kahn, Dement, Fisher, and Barmack (1962) obtained results that suggest that all dreams are in color. The researchers explain that only a small number of dreams are reported to have been in color because color is forgotten between the time of the dream experience and recall. The database for this study was obtained by awakening the subject immediately after the dream and carefully questioning him or her about the color content of the dream.

Finally, it would appear that the cognitive processing involved in dream production is not unique to the sleeping state. Cavallero and Natale (1988) first collected 36 mental activity reports provided by six subjects during experimental sessions, then collected an equal number of invented dreams from awake subjects. Next, three groups of 30 judges were asked to distinguish real from artificial dreams on the basis of seven structural dimensions: self-involvement, continuity, temporal attributes, implausibility, and three types of bizarreness. The judges were unable to distinguish real from artificial reports at a rate greater than chance.

In discussing the topic of dreams and dreaming in my psychology classes, I often ask students to estimate the frequency with which they dream.

In almost every class, I have found one or two students who swear that they never dream. Such a claim must fly in the face of the REM evidence, which makes it clear that everyone dreams every night (Faraday, 1972). However, as in the case of almost all human behavior, there are individual differences in the clarity with which we recall our dreams. Dreams may be difficult to recall because of some characteristic of the dream's content. Thus, exciting dreams are easier to recall than dull ones, and bizarre dreams are easier to recall than ordinary ones. It is also possible that some property of sleep that distinguishes it from other levels of consciousness, can explain why dream recall is so difficult (Goodenough, 1978).

Webb and Kersey (1967) have suggested that habitual dream recallers tend to wake up from REM sleep, whereas those who rarely recall dreams generally awaken from NREM sleep. Finally, it appears that the individual's presleep mood may affect dream recall. In a study designed to examine the relationship between depression and dream reporting, negative moods were related to an increase in dream recall (Cohen, 1979). This finding is probably due to the fact that the subject's unpleasant mood before sleep leads to poor sleep, which, in turn, results in the sleeper's awakening from REM sleep instead of NREM sleep. More recently, Robbins and Tanck (1988) obtained results that supported the earlier study. They discovered that it more frequently happened that subjects had been depressed before the nights in which they had dreams they were able to recall and describe than before the nights in which they had no memory of dreaming.

Most of you have probably experienced a dream that occurs over and over again with little or no change. The *recurrent dream* is typically one in which the dreamer is being threatened or pursued and is trying to hide. These anxiety dreams may be reported more often than others because they are so disturbing and therefore more likely to be remembered (Robbins & Houshi, 1983).

Recent lines of research suggest close parallels between dreaming and wakefulness. Foulkes (1982) carried out a longitudinal study of some 42 children from the time they were 3 until they were 15 years of age. Every year, each child spent nine nights in Foulkes's sleep laboratory, where dream reports from both ordinary and REM sleep were obtained. Foulkes discovered that the nature of children's dreams at different ages closely paralleled cognitive development, as described by Piaget (1970). Thus, the dreams of a preoperational child were very egocentric, those of a five- to seven-year-old were increasingly more concrete, and those of the adolescent were more abstract.

A second line of research attempted to gain awareness and control of dreams. Some people report having dreams in which they become aware that they are dreaming; such dreams are referred to as *lucid dreams*. By experimenting with a number of self-suggestive techniques, LaBerge, Nagel, Dement, and Zarcone (1981) demonstrated that it was possible to develop a self-suggestive technique called MILD (mnemonic induction of lucid dreams), by which subjects were able to increase the frequency of lucid dreams by some 400 percent to a maximum of approximately 26 lucid dreams a month over a three-year period. More recently, LaBerge (1992) reported on a training technique in which sleepers are trained to signal when they are dreaming by voluntarily moving their eyes and clenching their fists. The importance of this technique is that it provides researchers with the possibility of immediate rather than after-the-fact reporting. Some lucid dreamers report that once they become aware that they are dreaming, they are able to change the course of the dream (LaBerge, 1992; Weinstein, Schwartz, & Arkin, 1991).

Along the same lines, Carpenter (1988) presented data suggesting that presleep stimuli may have an effect on the dream experience. She found that simply having her college students look at pictures that produced positive, neutral, or negative effects before going to bed would produce corresponding dream effects as reported in their morning dream reports. She also observed that the physical elements of the dreams and pictorial stimuli were not related.

THEORIES OF DREAM ACTIVITY

Similar to the question posed earlier—Why do we sleep?—we can also ask: Why do we dream? Two prominent individuals who addressed this issue were Sigmund Freud and Carl Jung. Through their clinical observations, they each suggested a possible answer.

Sigmund Freud

Freud suggested that the function of dreams is twofold. First, dreams prevent the sleeper from being awakened by minor environmental disturbances. In this regard, Freud wrote, "The dream is the guardian of sleep" (Freud, 1913). Freud's theory seems to be supported by the fact that many disturbances during the night often find their way into dreams. For example, once I dreamed of being chased through the desert by bandits who were shooting at me. In my dream, I was hot and thirsty. When I awoke the next morning, I was indeed hot and thirsty. I had forgotten to turn down the thermostat before retiring, and the indoor thermometer read almost 80°. I have not yet determined the source of the gunshots. Perhaps they were produced by the window blinds slapping against the wall. Possibly you can recall having a similar dream experience.

Wish fulfillment is the second function proposed by Freud. He believed that unconscious impulses were responsible for dreams and that the goal of dreams was to gratify some drive. Thus, the hungry person dreams of food; the student, of graduating; and the failure, of success. According to Freud, dreaming is unconscious and reflects sexual and aggressive instincts that cannot be expressed during waking hours. These impulses are always pressing for activation, and dreams provide an occasion for their expression. In its final form, the dream is seen as a distorted and symbolic version of the impulses that triggered it. In fact, Freud (1900) put great emphasis on the symbolism contained in dreams, especially those related to repressed sexual desires. For example, when a woman dreamed about straight objects, this was interpreted as symbolic representation of the male penis. Similarly, a male dreaming about round objects was symbolically representing the female vagina. In addition to phallic representations in dreams, the raw materials the individual used to construct dreams were traces of prior perceptual experiences, particularly those of the day preceding the dream. Additionally, dreams contained repressed memories of infancy or childhood.

Dreams are not logically organized, but rather appear as a strange patterning of the aforementioned elements. The bizarre patterning is believed to occur so that the repressed impulses can be successfully disguised. Freud referred to this transformation as *dream work*, and because of it, the dream becomes progressively detached from sensory memory and less intelligible to waking consciousness. This strange organization of elements makes up the dream's *manifest content*—namely, what you remember and are able to convey to others—and disguises the dreamer's unconscious desires that give the dream its meaning. The unconscious component of the dream is called the *latent content*. It often rises from unresolved early emotional conflicts regarded by the dreamer as too evil or too frightening to be openly expressed (Fisher & Greenberg, 1977).

Carl Jung

Jung, as discussed by Hall and Lindzey (1978), also believed that dreams had several functions, but he suggested that dreams were more than unconscious wishes. First, he believed that dreams are *prospective*, or that they help the dreamer prepare for events anticipated in the immediate future. For instance, the test you must take tomorrow or the next day may be the main feature of your dream tonight. A second aspect of Jung's proposed function of dreams is closely tied to his theory of personality, which suggests that personality is composed of a number of subsystems. The goal of personality development is to unify these parts into an integrated whole. For this to be accomplished, Jung believed that all the parts of the personality had to develop fully. If the development of any one subsystem is neglected, it will find expression in the form of dreams.

Other Theories

We all encounter various problems during the course of the day. Some of these problems lend themselves to immediate solutions, while others require considerably more thought. French and Fromm (1964) suggested that dreams are simply the individual's attempts to solve such problems. The function of dreams is to help the dreamer define the problem more clearly.

A **cognitive** or **problem-solving theory** of dreaming was proposed by Cartwright (1977). On the basis of studies in sleep laboratories, Cartwright suggested that the several dreams that occur during a single night are related and may deal with the same theme or problem. The night's first dream is the most realistic; the middle dreams are the most distorted and fantastic; and the last dream is often focused on the solution of the problem. This led Cartwright to propose that dreams may have two major functions. First, the dream appears to afford the individual an opportunity to solve daily problems. Whether the solution that is arrived at in the dream carries over into waking life is as yet unknown. Second, dreams appear to provide the dreamer with an opportunity to attend to fantasy and to personal impulses. Cartwright argued that this opportunity enables the subject to focus more clearly on the world of reality during the waking hours.

The **activation-synthesis hypothesis** of Hobson and McCarley (1977) represents a radical departure from those theories of dreaming previously discussed. Rather than viewing dreams as problem-solving mechanisms or as a vehicle to express sexual and aggressive instincts, this hypothesis suggests that dreams have no inherent meaning at all. Rather, they reflect efforts of the cortex to make sense out of the neural activity ascending from the brainstem during REM sleep. According to this theory, during sleep, cholinergic (acetylcholine) stimulation of the REM sleep regulatory center, the paramedian pontine reticular formation, sends impulses to the cerebral cortex via the thalamus. This activates the cortical neurons, which elicit well-known images or emotions, and the cortex then tries to synthesize the disparate images into a meaningful whole. As one might expect, the dream product may be quite strange, even nonsensical, because it is triggered by the semirandom activity of the pons (Hobson, 1993). Evidence for this activation-synthesis is at best mixed (Bear, Conners, & Paradiso, 1996).

Building on the Hobson and McCarley theory, Crick and Mitchison (1983) proposed that REM sleep and the dreams that accompany it are part of an active process of "unlearning" that the brain requires to prevent becoming overloaded. The firing of the cortical neurons that occurs during the dream period serves to erase various random memory associations that may have been formed during the day. This ensures that the brain will have sufficient neural capacity to meet its waking needs. According to this theory, then, dreams are meant to be forgotten.

In an attempt to place dreams into an even broader theoretical perspective, Gabel (1989) suggested that dreams can be considered as dissociated systems of awareness within the context of current views of personality organization, based on dissociation theory. He argued that under the conditions of sleep, generally REM sleep, memories, emotions, information processing, and judgments about internal and external events can occur relatively independently of the usual waking conscious system's information processing. These distinct goals, viewpoints, or reactions are depicted metaphorically in the dream.

Bosinelli (1995) proposed a model of dream generation in which mnemonic materials are activated from long-term memory and entered into a dream production system using a bottom-up process, and these materials are elaborated and interpreted by a top-down process to produce the dream. Finally, a circular feedback system operating between these two processes is able to activate additional mnemonic materials.

As with sleep theories, dream theories differ widely. The classical theories, such as those of Freud and Jung, are so vague that subjecting them to experimental scrutiny would be extremely difficult. Attempts to test more recently developed theories in the research laboratory have generally produced results that are contradictory and often confounded by uncontrolled variables. In summary, then, the questions of why we sleep and why we dream must, for now, remain unanswered.

DAYDREAMING: ANOTHER LEVEL OF CONSCIOUSNESS

In addition to night dreams or those generated during sleep, we also experience so-called daydreams. How many times have you caught yourself thinking about the great weekend party you and your friends are planning, while sitting in class listening to the definitive lecture on "Epigone—The Seven Against Thebes?" Whether it is "woolgathering," "castles in Spain," or "looking into the middle distance," **daydreaming** is an activity that everyone appears to engage in almost daily (Singer, 1975).

Undoubtedly, you are very much aware of the highly private nature of this process. It is this characteristic that makes daydreaming so difficult to research and define. Perhaps the single most acceptable definition of day dreaming is as follows:

> Daydreaming represents a shift of attention away from some primary physical or mental task we have set for ourselves, or away from directly looking at or listening to something in the external environment, toward an unfolding sequence of private responses made to some internal stimulus. (Singer, 1975, p. 3)

In terms of our taxonomy of consciousness, as presented in Chapter 1, daydreaming is an example of a differentiated waking state (Kokoszka, 1988). Thus, such activity lies between our active consciousness and the dreams we have while we are asleep. During daydreams, as our awareness is turned inward, we lose awareness of our external world. For a very large number of people, daydreams take the form of fairly clear visual images of people, objects, or ongoing events.

Singer (1975) observed that daydreams fall into one of two general categories. The first group includes the dramatic, recurrent, self-consistent, and fairly elaborate fantasies that persist from early childhood. The second category consists of the individual's ongoing stream of consciousness, the private interior monologues and sometimes more elaborate fantasies, all of which seem to occur spontaneously in association with events observed in the outside world or in the chains of sequence to early memories. This latter type of daydream can be further categorized (Singer, 1975):

1. *Self-recriminating*: Daydreams are initiated by the statement, "What I should have done (or said) . . . "
2. *Well-controlled and thoughtful*: Planning daydreams in which the day is planned, a party is organized, and so forth.
3. *Autistic*: Material usually associated with night dreams breaks through and disrupts consciousness.
4. *Neurotic or self-conscious*: Fantasy daydreams: "How I can guess the winning lottery number and retire to Tahiti?" or "How I can be elected President of the United States?"

Despite the common belief that daydreams are often romantic, sexual, and violent, this is simply not the case. Although most people have such daydreams at times, they make up a very small proportion of the total.

Although you might expect men's and women's daydreams to be quite different, they are remarkably similar in frequency, vividness, spontaneity, and realism. The differences usually reflect contrasts in women's and men's concerns and stereotypical roles in our society (Klinger, 1987).

Daydreams usually occur when events in the external environment become boring or unchanging. When this happens, there is a tendency for our consciousness to turn toward the inner or private world. Our need for what Fiske and Maddi (1961) have called *varied experience* demands that when novel stimuli are absent in the external environment, we create our own.

Most people report that daydreaming occurs chiefly when they are alone, although some individuals indicate that they find themselves daydreaming even when they are engaged in conversation with others. Results of early studies suggest that late adolescence is a peak period for daydreaming frequency and that there is a very gradual decline with age through the fifties. There are also indications that elderly people, even into their eighties, daydream.

Daydreaming probably occurs most often when people are preparing to go to sleep at night. Under these circumstances, as we settle down for the night, consciously excluding varied external stimulation by shutting our eyes, there is probably increased awareness of innerworld activity. This increase in imagery and fantasy at this time may be so vivid and varied as to maintain alertness, even when sleep is much desired.

Consider the following situation, which I am certain many of you have experienced. It is the day before a major examination. You have spent most of the day in heavy study and preparation, and now, at 11:30 P.M., you decide that it is time to go to bed and get a good night's sleep. You get ready for bed, cover up, and get into that favorite sleeping position. You close your eyes and begin to daydream about all the possible questions that might appear on the test the next day. All of a sudden, you find yourself caught up in a stream of visual images. Even though you are tired and desperately want to go to sleep, chances are good that you will stay awake for hours.

What are the functions of this mental process that causes us to lose consciousness of the external world and, in so doing, become less effective in our work and study? Until recently, psychologists turned to the psychoanalytic model for answers to this question. According to this model, the daydream acts as a kind of safety valve; it allows for a socially acceptable expression of sexual needs or aggressive tendencies before they create severe psychological or psychosomatic symptoms. Thus, even the most socially accepted daydreams, such as seeing oneself as a servant of the poor and the downtrodden, can be reduced to basic sexual or aggressive tendencies that must be defended against and thus expressed in more socially acceptable forms (Freud, 1933).

Offering an alternative explanation, Singer (1975) suggests that daydreams may be more than just wishful explorations. Some simply create diversion and lower the levels of tension and distress occasioned by frustrating or anger-provoking circumstances. Others may provide us with an alternative environment to one that is boring or holds reminders of failures or insults. To some extent, however, daydreams also represent rehearsals for future actions. They may suggest new and alternative ways of dealing with situations. In the course of fairly extensive fantasizing, we may also encourage ourselves to further action in the pursuit of a particular goal. Thus, our daydreams may have motivational characteristics, encouraging us to try new kinds of experiences or at least to look for ways of reaching some compromise approach.

SEXUAL FANTASIES

Fantasies or daydreams appear to play an important role in human sexual functioning. According to a National Health and Social Life Survey, 19 percent of women and 54 percent of men spend at least a part of each day fantasizing about sex (Laumann, Gagnon, Michael, & Michaels, 1994). Studies have demonstrated that these self-created fantasies afford their creator the ability to control their sexual excitement or arousal as well as to spice up and add novelty to a relationship (Kelly, 1996).

Meuwissen and Over (1991) have suggested that on the basis of their theme, fantasies fall into one of the following four groups:

1. *Exploratory sexual fantasies:* Includes fantasies which have as their major theme group sex, mate-swapping, and homosexual behavior.
2. *Intimate sexual fantasies:* These fantasies have themes such as passionate kissing, oral sex, and mutual masturbation.

3. *Impersonal sexual fantasies:* Looking at pornography, having sex with a stranger, and watching others engage in sex represent the kinds of themes of fantasies belonging to this category.
4. *Sadomasochistic sexual fantasies:* Fantasies with themes such as whipping, spanking, and forceful sex are included in this category.

The most common sexual imagery in the above fantasies involve having sex with a past, new, or imaginary partner or having sex in various settings and positions. Both men and women show fewer fantasies of the impersonal and sadomasochistic type (Leitenberg & Henning, 1995).

Many questions concerning the study of sleep and dreams have not been answered, either by theory or by research. This is the present state of the science. However, we have discovered much information concerning sleep and dreams as states of consciousness. For example, we know that sleep is not one state of consciousness but rather several states, or at least, sleep consists of several levels. These levels are defined by differences in recorded brain-wave activity (EEG) that correspond to each stage of sleep. We know that each stage is different, not only in terms of EEG activity, but also in terms of consciousness experiences. For example, one stage may correspond to light sleep, while another may correspond to deep sleep. While in these stages, we have distinctly different experiences of consciousness or awareness. During another stage of sleep, dreams generally occur.

Therefore, when we discuss sleep and dreams as states of consciousness, it is clear that we do not simply have a wakeful state of consciousness and a sleep state of consciousness. The process is much more complex. We hope that, in time, science will help to reduce some of the complexity and help us better understand the role of sleep and dreams, not only as physiological events, but also as unique experiences that comprise altered states of consciousness.

FOR FURTHER READING

Barrett, D. (Ed.). (1996). *Trauma and dreams.* Cambridge, MA: Harvard University Press.

Dement, W. C. (1972). *Some must watch while some must sleep: Exploring the world of sleep.* San Francisco: Freeman.

Hobson, J. A. (1995). *Sleep.* New York: Freeman.

Lavie, P., & Berris, A. (1996). *The enchanted world of sleep.* New Haven, CT: Yale University Press.

Singer, J. L. (1975). *The inner world of daydreaming.* New York: Harper & Row.

Webb, W. B. (1975). *Sleep: The gentle tyrant.* Englewood Cliffs, NJ: Prentice-Hall.

8

SENSORY DEPRIVATION

Sitting here looking out the window of my study, I can see my seven-year-old daughter providing two of her playmates with an explanation, complete with elaborate gestures and gory details, of her most recent loss—her two upper front teeth. This backyard drama is being played out against a background of rock music that emanates from my teenage son's bedroom. I have yet to discover a way of shutting out sound waves. The day is clear and sunny, and the sunshine pouring through the study window feels warm and pleasant on my back. Since noon, I have been nursing along with great care the main course for this evening's dinner: stuffed cabbage rolls. Only now has the aroma begun to escape the confines of the kitchen to stimulate my sense of smell. Being the chef in our home carries certain advantages. The one I exercise most frequently is that of official taster. On my last trip to the kitchen to coax my creation, I paused long enough to satisfy my taste buds with the cream sauce. The movement of my arm as I write, the noise of the cars driving past the house, the light touch of my shirt against my skin, and the hunger pangs I feel are among the many environmental stimuli, both internal and external, of which I am currently aware.

In large part this stimulation will govern my behavior. The stimuli serve to initiate, maintain, or sustain certain physiological processes and bring about certain behavioral consequences. If the noise of my son's latest rock music becomes too loud, I will cease writing, open the doors of my study, and, in my stern, fatherly voice, explain to him the imminent danger his CD and stereo system face if the sound is not immediately diminished.

The environment I have described fairly teems with stimulation, but the important point to remember is that it is a brief and incomplete description of a typical environment. This will become evident if you put down your book for a minute and make a partial list of stimuli in your present environment. Now imagine that you are transported to another kind of environment, one that does not contain any of the stimulation that you normally encounter in your daily life.

Consider the small life raft of a lone crash survivor, adrift under a cloudless sky with nothing but endless ocean in sight. Or think of the small, dark, quiet cell of a prisoner in isolation or the water tank in a sensory deprivation laboratory in which the subject, blindfolded and nude, is immersed. These environments all have at least one thing in common: The normal daily exposure to stimulation is absent. After several days in such a strange new environment, how might you function? Can an environment so devoid of stimulation actually affect your level of consciousness and thus your perceptual judgments, learning, and problem-solving behavior? These questions, as well as others you may have thought of, will be addressed in this chapter.

Before we plunge into a discussion of sensory deprivation, it is necessary to have a clear understanding of what this term means. Actually, it is impossible to create a situation of complete sensory deprivation for a human subject. Even by using a well-ventilated, soundproof, and lightproof room, we would not be able to eliminate all possible stimulation. Our nude subject would still hear the pounding of the heart, the sounds generated by breathing, and perhaps an occasional growl of the stomach. Additional sensory stimulation may come from muscle activity involved in movement, body odors, and skin contact with another surface. In a sense, then, the term **sensory deprivation** is a misnomer; it implies that none of the senses can be stimulated at all.

The term *sensory deprivation* is not only scientifically imprecise, but through repeated associations with such notions as stress and brainwashing, it has come to carry a connotation of threat, disturbance, and adversiveness. For these reasons, Suedfeld (1980) has suggested that it is time to deemphasize this term, and to this end he proposes **Restricted Environmental Stimulation Technique (REST)** as an alternative. Throughout the remainder of this chapter we will adopt Suedfeld's terminology to indicate that the level of stimulation has been reduced or altered in such a way as to no longer conform to an individual's normal variety or range of exposure.

SENSORY DEPRIVATION AND CONSCIOUSNESS

In Chapter 6 we observed that certain meditative techniques involve the use of some external stimulus upon which the meditator learns to focus attention to exclude from consciousness all other external forms of stimulation. In the case of REST, an altered state of consciousness also appears to be achieved through a reduction in perceived external stimulation. However, unlike meditation, this reduction is not brought about by a mental process; rather it is accomplished by the direct experimental manipulation of the environment. Research data to date make it clear that manipulation in restricted environmental stimulation technique leads to an altered state of awareness. For example, REST may produce visual sensations (Zuckerman, 1969b) like those occurring just before dreams or increased proneness to being persuaded of something. These changes occur only under certain conditions (Suedfeld & Vernon, 1966; Myers, Murphy, & Smith, 1963). Many of these changes will be described in detail in this chapter.

We have noted that, in general, individuals enter situations that typically produce an altered state of consciousness to achieve a desired goal. For example, a person may enter a biofeedback training program to heighten his or her awareness of specific bodily responses to develop conscious control over them. For the person who can master a technique, meditation affords an opportunity to enter an altered state of consciousness and, in doing so, bring about a mystical experience. Finally, a person who experiences chronic pain may choose to undergo hypnosis or biofeedback in hopes of reducing the pain.

What can REST offer the individual? Why would a person decide to enter a sensory-deprived situation? At first glance your response to both of these questions might be negative. Certainly, any review of the literature on sensory deprivation, both natural observations and experimental research data, prior to 1975 would suggest very little to be gained by individuals who undergo such an experience. In the final section of this chapter, however, we will focus on some of the therapeutic possibilities that are a positive outgrowth of research on sensory deprivation and the altered state of awareness it establishes. Before discussing the ways in which REST changes states or levels of consciousness, let us trace the development of this manipulation.

HISTORICAL BACKGROUND

The topic of sensory deprivation certainly is not new to those interested in human behavior. The Bible provides a number of references to such isolation experiences. Moses, withdrawing from the multitudes, ascended Mount Sinai, where he spent 40 days and nights alone; there he received the Commandments from God. John the Baptist spent much of his early life in the isolation of the desert, where he developed the mystical qualities he would need to fulfill his ministry. Jesus, after being baptized by John, went out into the wilderness alone, where he overcame the temptations of the devil.

More detailed descriptions of the experiences of prisoners, writers, explorers, mystics, and others under conditions of extreme isolation have been made public. For example, Admiral Richard Byrd (1938) chronicled his experiences of being isolated for six months in a small hut buried beneath the snows of the Antarctic. The small, unchanging surroundings of his hut, combined with the quiet of the seemingly unending polar nights that served as Byrd's environment for this period, can best be described as monotonous, confining, and unchanging.

Although he undertook the ordeal voluntarily, Byrd soon discovered that life under such conditions was anything but peaceful and serene. His early reactions centered on a fear that his rescuers would not reach him in time; these fears gave way to an overwhelming apathy. It took an almost Herculean effort for Byrd to attend to life-sustaining necessities of eating, drinking, and keeping warm. He also experienced hallucinations. By the fourth month he had entered severe depression. He reported an extremely strong need for the kinds of stimulation we normally take for granted—sounds, odors, human touch, and so on. During this time, Byrd also reported feelings of loss of identity and of floating freely though space. Such descriptions undoubtedly served to attract the interest of psychological researchers as well as the general public.

Shurley (1961) has suggested that the experimental approach to sensory deprivation resulted from the convergence of three major lines of influence. First, the developments in neurophysiological techniques provided an avalanche of new findings and led to a revised model of the central nervous system. Instead of viewing the brain as a switchboard for connecting an appropriate response to a stimulus, the new model, using new electrophysiological methods, took into account such phenomena as reverberating circuits, neural feedback systems, and arousal centers (Hebb, 1949).

The second major influence was based on numerous investigations by psychological researchers into the effects of sensory deprivation on the developmental processes and learning of nonhuman subjects. The impetus for this research came, at least in part, from the many case reports of feral humans. Carl von Linnaeus (1707–1778) first introduced the term *feral man* in his 1758 edition of the *Systema Naturae*. He used it to describe cases in which a human child had been cared for, in complete social isolation from other human beings, either by animals or by only indirect contact with human caretakers. One of the best known of these cases is that of the Wild Boy of Aveyron (Itard, 1932).

By the early 1950s it had become apparent that, for the sake of national security, American researchers needed to investigate and attempt to understand the factors involved in thought-reform movements, indoctrination programs, and brainwashing techniques. This became the third push toward sensory deprivation research. Disturbing newspaper accounts of captured U.S. soldiers defecting to the enemy and confessing to all sorts of war atrocities began to appear. The publication of General William F. Dean's (1954) account of his own experiences at the hands of his Communist captors, combined with the newspaper reports, served to heighten public as well as government interest and speculation that the enemy had developed a new, secret method of breaking the mind.

It was at Canada's McGill University in 1953 that these three major influences—development of neurophysiological techniques and electrophysiological methods, research in sensory deprivation effects on subhumans, and the need to combat a threat to national security—finally brought about the development of a research program conducted by Donald O. Hebb and his students, focusing on stimulus reduction and decreased sensory variability. Besides formalizing the question of sensory deprivation, which they labeled *perceptual isolation,* the McGill University studies opened a whole new track for psychological research, theory, and speculation (Brownfield, 1965).

THE McGILL STUDIES

Historically, there have been any number of recorded natural observations of REST experiences. However, the initial, experimentally controlled attack on this problem was carried out in the 1950s at McGill University (Bexton, Heron, & Scott, 1954; Doane, Mahatoo, Heron, & Scott, 1959; Heron, Bexton, & Hebb, 1953; Heron, Doane, & Scott, 1956; Scott, Bexton, Heron, & Doane, 1959). Because this series of studies defined the problem and set the tone for future research in this area, it is important to review some of the details here.

In these studies, the researchers' goal was to reduce or alter the patterns or relationships in the sensory input from the environment by providing an experimental setting much like the one described in the section "Experimental Procedures" later in this chapter. Brief time-out periods were allowed for meals and going to the restroom, but subjects otherwise remained in this very restricted environment until they asked to end the experience. As an incentive, each was offered $20 each day they remained in this strange environment. (This might not seem like much money, but in the 1950s, $20 had much greater buying power than it does today.) Despite the potential financial gains, the experimental conditions were so intolerable that most subjects asked to get out within four days.

Most subjects spent the early part of the test period asleep. Later they slept less, became bored, and seemed to need some stimulation. To this end they began singing and talking to themselves, tapping together the cylinders in which their arms and legs were placed, or using the cylinders to explore the cubicle. They became restless and engaged in a great deal of random movement. When the experiment ended, subjects described their experience as extremely unpleasant. Upon leaving, they reported a number of aftereffects, including disturbances in visual perception, confusion, headaches, mild nausea, and fatigue.

Subjects reported some cognitive and perceptual disturbances during their time in the cubicle. Many were unable to concentrate on a single topic for any length of time. Some subjects, desperate for stimulation, attempted to review their studies or solve self-initiated intellectual problems. However, they found such activity extremely difficult and soon gave it up, lapsing instead into daydreaming and simply allowing their minds to wander. Several subjects reported blank periods during which they were unable to think of anything at all.

Reports such as these prompted some members of the McGill group to try to measure the cognitive and perceptual effects of sensory deprivation. Some 28 perceptual and cognitive tasks were administered to subjects before, during, and after their deprivation experience. While the group results suggested that certain of the tested functions were impaired after sensory deprivation, some subjects appeared to be completely unaffected. Certainly, one interpretation of these findings is that the REST experience causes deterioration of certain perceptual and cognitive skills. However, these same results can also be accounted for, at least in part, by a decrease in the subject's motivation.

Several of these researchers (Scott et al., 1959) found that with the passage of time, their subjects became extremely persuasible. For example, they requested to hear normally boring and childish passages over and over again. After hearing a message supporting the reality of psi (psychical research), they indicated substantially greater acceptance of this possibility than did control subjects hearing the same material.

During the experimental sessions the researchers observed an unusual degree of emotional fluctuation on the part of most subjects. In the early phase of the session, subjects reported being elated; however, as time passed, they became irritable. Perhaps the most interesting and certainly the most widely reported finding of the McGill studies was the occurrence of hallucinations. Visual hallucinations varied considerably in their degree of complexity, ranging from simple light flashes and geometric forms to much more complex, dreamlike scenes, such as "a procession of squirrels with sacks over their shoulders marching purposefully across a snow field and out of the field of vision" (Bexton et al., 1954). The hallucinatory experiences were not all visual. Subjects also reported auditory, kinesthetic, and somesthetic hallucinations. For example, one subject described a "miniature rocketship" shooting pellets at his arm; another reported hearing a music box. Finally, feelings of "otherness" and bodily "strangeness" were also reported. One subject indicated that his mind seemed to be a ball of cotton wool floating above his body.

SENSORY DEPRIVATION RESEARCH AFTER McGILL

The McGill research was followed by a number of studies that can best be described as exploratory rather than rigorous and authoritative (Zuckerman, 1969a, 1969b). These studies typically used relatively few subjects, who were drawn from restricted populations. They also introduced such variations as placing the subject in a small box with no room to move or having the subject sit in a reclining chair, lie in an inoperative iron lung, or lie on a bed in a dark, soundproof room. Or a subject might be entirely submerged in water using underwater breathing apparatus. Because of the introduction of these different research techniques, the term *perceptual isolation* gave way to a new term: *sensory deprivation* (Rossi, 1969). Finally, to explain the findings of this research, theories ranging from the psychoanalytic to the neurological were adopted (Brownfield, 1965).

As the second decade of research in sensory deprivation dawned in the mid-1960s, it had become clear that things were not always as they appeared.

Put another way, the effects attributed to sensory deprivation during the previous decade were not nearly as clear-cut and replicable as had been thought at first. For example, although it was one of the most widely cited results, visual sensations continued to be reported. Zuckerman (1969b), having surveyed 33 separate reports, concluded that the number of subjects reporting any visual sensation in any given experiment was most frequently zero. Suedfeld and Vernon (1964) suggested that if we define hallucinations as perceptions that the subject thought were real and over which he or she had no control, then they were practically a nonexistent finding in such research.

Other early findings had to be substantially modified as a result of new findings (Myers, Murphy, & Smith, 1963; Suedfeld & Vernon, 1966; Robertson & Walter, 1963; Zubek, Sansom, & Prysianiuk, 1960). For example, it had been supposed that sensory deprivation had a negative impact on cognition and that subjects undergoing sensory deprivation were more susceptible to persuasion than in normal circumstances.

It is also important to note that a few studies were published during this decade that explored the applicability of the effect of sensory deprivation in the context of clinical treatment (Adams, Robertson, & Cooper, 1963; Gibby & Adams, 1961).

Some methodological changes also were made during this second decade of REST research. Of the many techniques that were tried in the first 10 years, only two survived in active research programs: sensory reduction in a dark, soundproof chamber and the original perceptual isolation technique used at McGill. Even these were modified by instituting set durations of sessions, removing panic buttons, and orienting the subjects to the environment before initiating the session. These changes were effected to minimize the confounding effects of expectancy, uncertainty, and stress (Suedfeld, 1980).

As the second decade of research continued, it became evident that the popularity of sensory deprivation research was waning. Suedfeld (1980) suggested several reasons for this change. First, many scientists working in the field had only a limited interest in the dramatic phenomena associated with REST research and either had exhausted their concern or had decided to move on to other questions. Second, REST research is quite expensive, and any systematic program in this area would require substantial funding at a time when research support generally had begun to erode. Third, researchers in the area had failed to integrate the results of their research. Therefore, specialists in clinical psychology, perception, cognition, and so on were generally unaware of the relevance of sensory deprivation findings to these areas.

Finally, between the late 1960s and the early 1970s, a period of great political unrest, several sensory deprivation investigators came under attack from political activists who viewed sensory deprivation as analogous to solitary confinement and torture. These attacks ranged from hostile publications in both the popular media and professional journals, in which the deleterious effects reported during the first years of research were emphasized and exaggerated, to actual physical attack against these researchers. As a result some investigators left while others probably avoided the field. There is also anecdotal evidence to suggest that journal editors and perhaps even grant reviewers were not very receptive to sensory deprivation research and proposals (Suedfeld & Coren, 1989).

In addition to the reasons put forth by Suedfeld, Reed (1962) suggested at least one more reason for the decline of research on reduced environmental stimulation. He suggested that workers in the area became increasingly aware of the complexity of the variables involved and the even greater complexity of their interactions. It was frustrating to generate exact hypotheses to be tested.

Thus, for whatever reason, as the second decade (roughly mid-1960s to mid-1970s) came to a close, there were only three major research centers carrying out programmatic research in sensory deprivation with another few laboratories producing occasional papers. This represented a substantial decrease from the 20 such centers that were identified during the first decade of research (Suedfeld, 1969).

As the third decade opened, it was very clear that something had to happen to rekindle attention and attract researchers back to the area of sensory deprivation. While researchers began to focus their attention on further extension and application of the best established basic findings, two major events occurred that went a long way toward reestablishing sensory deprivation as a major research area.

First, there was the discovery that stimulus reduction, either alone or combined with other techniques, was a highly effective treatment in giving up smoking (Best & Suedfeld, 1982; Suedfeld & Ikard, 1974). The second was the discovery and publication by John C. Lilly (1977) of the method of floating in a warm solution of Epsom salts. This technique was generally reported to induce deep relaxation and enjoyment. This was completely contrary to the then prevalent notion that immersion in water and stimulus reduction led to extreme stress. The increased number of research projects in sensory deprivation focused on applications of this altered environment to modify habits. The flotation method was quickly adopted as a component of stress management and the treatment of stress-related disorders (Fine & Turner, 1982; Jacobs, Heilbronner, & Stanley, 1985; Koula, Kemp, Keane, & Belden, 1987; Suedfeld, Ballard, & Murphy, 1983; Suedfeld & Kristeller, 1982).

There were also some changes in methodology. While the darkened, soundproof chamber continued to be used, the use of the flotation tank replaced the perceptual isolation technique employed in the McGill studies. It was also during this decade that Suedfeld (1980) coined the term REST to which we have previously referred, *Restricted Environmental Stimulation Technique* (or *Therapy*, depending on the context).

Both the public and the professional image of this research area improved greatly between the mid-1970s and the mid-1990s. The release of the highly successful science fiction movie *Altered States,* which presents an exciting, although inaccurate, picture of flotation, did much to bring about an increased public interest and awareness of REST. Additionally, in response to public demand, commercial flotation centers charging about $20 per hour in the tank sprang up across North America. These pay-to-float facilities were extremely popular and offered both enjoyment and a way to beat the day's stresses. In light of this public response it was difficult to maintain the notion, popular during the previous decade, of sensory deprivation or REST as an aversive, damaging form of torture (Suedfeld & Coren, 1989). Professional acceptance of this technique also began to increase, and as we have already seen, there was a substantial increase in the number of scientific publications. The International REST Investigators' Society (IRIS) was formed in 1983 in Denver, Colorado, to disseminate information to researchers and therapists through its bulletin and conferences.

EXPERIMENTAL PROCEDURES

Although the specific conditions of REST vary from experiment to experiment, it is possible to identify at least three distinct, basic procedures that researchers use to reduce sensory input. The first of these approaches attempts to achieve an absolute reduction of sensory stimulation. To accomplish this, researchers, such as Lilly (1956) and Shurley (1960), used a large tank filled with continuously flowing water maintained at a temperature of 93.5° F (34.5° C). Shurley (1963) labeled his water-immersion technique a *hydro-hypodynamic environment.* The subject, nude except for a blacked-out face mask attached to breathing tubes, was immersed in the tank. This technique substantially diminishes gravity, light, and temperature stimuli. The tank itself is usually located in a room constructed so that light, sound, vibration, odor, and taste sensations are markedly reduced. The overall system provides a constant environment with maximal reduction of ambient physical stimuli. Once the subject is immersed in the tank, he or she is requested to get comfortable and to remain motionless for several hours. Either during or after the study, a subject may be requested to report on his or her experiences. Subjects were allowed to terminate their participation in the study at any time and for any reason.

The movie *Altered States,* which we have mentioned, and the popularity of commercial centers that employ a variation of the flotation tank technique have undoubtedly made this technique the most generally known of the sensory reduction methods.

The use of a dark, silent chamber is also a sensory reduction technique and dates back to the first decade (1955–1965) of REST investigation (Suedfeld & Coren, 1989). This technique employs a completely dark, sound-attenuated room that is typically furnished with a bed, a chemical toilet, an intercom for communication with the experimenter in the next room, and a food box containing thermos bottles of water and liquid diet food. Before entering this experimental environment, the subject is instructed to lie as still as possible on the bed and to refrain from getting up and walking about, singing, talking, or making any other kind of unnecessary noise. Once in the room, the subject remains there until the end of the session or until he or she requests that the session be terminated prematurely (Suedfeld, Ballard, Baker-Brown, & Borrie, 1986).

The second major approach employed by researchers in stimulus deprivation (e.g., Bexton et al., 1954) is to reduce or alter the patterns and relationships in sensory input from the environment. This technique, which was used by the McGill University group, was originally labeled *perceptual isolation*, was later called *pattern reduction*, and now is commonly referred to as **perceptual monotony**. The techniques employed do not decrease the absolute levels of stimulation and, in fact, may even increase them. Rather, they interfere with normal pattern perception.

The McGill subjects were required to lie on a comfortable bed located in a lighted, semisoundproof cubicle. Subjects wore translucent goggles that allowed the passage of only a diffuse light. Auditory stimulation was held constant by placing the subject's head on a U-shaped pillow of foam rubber and by using the sound of an exhaust fan located in the ceiling directly above the subject's head to provide a continuous masking noise. Each subject was required to wear gloves, and his or her hands and arms were encased in cardboard tubes to reduce the possibility of tactile stimulation. To allow subjects to communicate their needs to the experimenter, a two-way speaker system was embedded in the foam rubber pillow. Subjects were fed and permitted to go to the restroom when necessary and were able to terminate their participation in the experiment whenever they desired.

The third, and least commonly used, approach to the study of sensory deprivation is to impose highly structured or monotonous conditions in the sensory environment rather than reduce the levels of stimulation. It is termed *variation reduction* (Suedfeld, 1968). The subject, with arms and legs encased in rigid but comfortable cylinders to limit movement and tactile stimulation, is placed in a tank respirator (iron lung) containing a specially built mattress. Although the subject breathes normally, the respirator motor is turned on to provide a dull, monotonous masking noise. Room lighting is kept at a minimum. A large hood placed around the respirator prevents the subject from seeing anything but the front of the tank and the blank white walls and ceiling. Food in the form of an eggnog mixture is available through a tube placed near the subject's mouth, and a bedpan or urinal is provided upon request. This technique probably provides an environment that is closer to normal than any we have discussed so far. However, the mechanical elimination of bodily movement introduces a new dimension of deprivation that is far more stringent than the equivalent in other methods (Zubek, Bayer, Milstein, & Shephard, 1969).

In summary, the investigator is faced with the selection of one of the following major methodological approaches: (1) absolute reduction of sensory stimulation, (2) reduction or change in the patterns and relationships in the sensory input, or (3) imposition of highly structured or monotonous conditions in the sensory environment. Whichever approach is selected, an extremely complex experimental environment is required. Having reviewed the common experimental methodologies employed in the study of sensory deprivation, we are now ready to determine what effects, if any, this phenomenon may have upon consciousness or arousal.

RESTRICTED ENVIRONMENTAL STIMULATION THEORY

The preceding sections of this chapter have referred to both naturalistic and experimental observations of the effects of REST on human behavior. At some point in such a discussion, it is reasonable to expect that the curious student will question how these effects can best be explained within the framework of psychology. To account for these findings, investigators of this phenomenon have posited a number of interesting theoretical statements.

Concentrating on the hallucinatory experiences reported by some REST subjects, Rosenzweig (1959) suggested that the condition of sensory deprivation is somewhat analogous to that of schizophrenia. Rosenzweig contends that the schizophrenic's symptoms are brought about by disruptions in internal processes that, in turn, destroy the orderly associations of sensory and perceptual material. Thus, even though the schizophrenic may experience considerable stimulation, he or she simply is unable to establish the relevance of such input to ongoing cognitive processes.

Subjects of REST studies also find it extremely difficult to attach meaning to sensory input. In this case, however, the problem does not stem from any disruption of internal processes, but rather from the manipulation of external environmental conditions such that sensory stimuli are restricted, depatterned, or redundant. To Rosenzweig, then, it is not the lack of external stimuli, but rather that they are not relevant or meaningful, that leads to the effects, especially hallucinations, observed. Because of its concentration on the hallucinatorylike experiences reported by REST subjects, the current status of this theory is very much in question. As we have already seen in this chapter, the idea that REST leads to hallucinations has been pretty well exploded.

Robertson (1961) assumes that under normal conditions an individual's response is a result of the interaction between external and internal stimuli. As we use the terms here, *external stimuli* refer to those that the senses experience (e.g., sights, sounds, tastes); *internal stimuli* refer to feelings, memories, images, and thoughts. It follows that under conditions of restricted environmental stimulation technique, the hypothesized interaction between external and internal stimuli is substantially reduced, and behavior is determined almost completely by various internal stimuli. This leads to preoccupation, during which the subject's perceptual and cognitive activities are considerably restricted and internally directed. Robertson suggests that, faced with diminished external stimulation and with internal stimuli for which there is no normal background of external stimulation, the subject experiences a heightened suggestibility, and the behavioral effects of sensory deprivation are manifested.

To provide a somewhat different explanation for the effects of REST, Lindsley (1961) looked to the neurophysiology of the organism and, more specifically, to the functioning of the **ascending reticular activating system (ARAS).** Under normal conditions, two major functions are subserved by the neurons of the lower brainstem that make up the ARAS. First, the ARAS acts as a kind of relay station. It receives information in the form of neural impulses from each of the sensory receptors and in turn transmits messages centrally to other structures of the brain, especially the cortex. The ARAS neural impulses alert or arouse the cortex, which plays an essential role in the occurrence of normal perception. If for any reason the ARAS is not functioning, sensory information from the receptors will still reach the appropriate cortical projection centers. However, the cortex will not be sufficiently activated to allow the processes of sensory discrimination and perception to occur.

The second major function of the ARAS, under normal conditions, can best be described as a self-regulating or adjustive function. On the basis of its own neural activity and that of the cortex, which it monitors, the ARAS regulates the amount of its own sensory input. Put another way, the ARAS is functionally capable of monitoring its own input-output levels of neural excitation.

This regulatory function led Lindsley to the concept of an adaptation level. According to this concept, the ARAS, on the basis of the amount of input from various sensory receptors, adjusts the neural output of the cortex so as to establish a correspondingly high, neutral, or low level of arousal. As you might expect, under conditions of sensory deprivation, this level of arousal decreases markedly, with attendant boredom, inactivity, and finally sleep. A characteristic of the compensatory adjustment process is that it is limited. If these limits are exceeded, as they most certainly are in the case of REST, behavior deteriorates and becomes disorganized.

Finally, Ziskind (1965) suggests that the psychological symptoms that occur during the restricted environmental stimulation technique do not result from reduced sensory input per se, but rather from the reduced level of arousal that is also present during such an experience. Ziskind sees this reduction in awareness level as the condition necessary for the development of sensory-deprived mental symptoms. The reduction in awareness occurs in conjunction with internal and external stimuli and goal-directed actions, which Ziskind calls the *sufficient condition*. The sufficient condition apparently is related, in part at least, to the instructions and psychological set or demand characteristics of the experiment (Orne, 1959, 1979).

Taking a slightly different approach, Steel and Suedfeld (1994) recognized that there are certain natural working environments that closely resemble the restricted environment (e.g., the polar regions of the earth). Using a standardized personality test, they attempted to ascertain what effects, if any, such an environment would have upon personality. Comparing a group of polar workers with a normal sample of workers, they reported that polar workers were less conscientious, less extroverted, less agreeable, and more open to experiences than their normal counterparts were.

As you might have surmised, there certainly is no lack of theoretical speculation and explanation for the behavioral phenomena associated with the sensory deprivation experience. The major problem is one of accumulating critical evidence in support of one or more of these theoretical positions.

SENSORY DEPRIVATION AND ALTERED STATES OF CONSCIOUSNESS

Traditionally, seekers of a transcendental or spiritual experience have used solitude and stimulus restriction as means to that end. From the beginning, both Eastern and Western religious traditions have maintained that spiritual experiences are best sought in solitude. The uniformity that underlies many of the practices of yoga, Zen, Tao, Sufism and Christian monasticism reinforces this idea (Goleman, 1977; Pelletier & Garfield, 1976). Not only did Moses and Jesus first achieve the insights that led to their ministries while isolated in the wilderness, but so did Mohammed and the Buddha. Thus, there is a noteworthy similarity among the founders of the four great religions of the world. Today, modern mystics use periods of isolation in the desert or in other remote locations to achieve altered states of consciousness and transcendence. Religious retreats for laity and clergy also frequently incorporate periods of solitude for the same purpose (Havens, 1969; Lilly, 1972).

A second example is to be found in the initiation rites of countless societies. As Tyre (1978) has observed, one of the six defining characteristics of this ritual of passage is solitude. The anthropological literature suggests that a period of solitude or isolation has been a central feature of the initiation rite of societies in North America, the Middle East, Africa, Asia, and Australia. Such a finding suggests a universal appreciation of the possible values of being alone in a natural environment. Accounts of these culturally imposed periods of solitude also suggest that the participants often experienced what could best be described as an altered state of consciousness. Whether such experiences were due to long periods of fasting, use of drugs, or self-inflicted pain—often a part of the initiation rite—or solely to the isolation experience is impossible to determine.

Researchers using REST typically have not concerned themselves with the question of altered states of consciousness. Probably the one major exception to this is John C. Lilly. Lilly's original starting point was a logical one: He concluded that the appropriate way to study the body-brain-mind system was to isolate it from the influences of the external world, thus permitting examination of the system by itself. His early work in the area includes the description of his own spiritual experiences while undergoing water immersion. Frequently, these early experiences in the tank occurred while he was under the influence of LSD (Lilly, 1960, 1972).

Lilly's later work is characterized by the concept that the current view of the mind, as essentially contained within the brain, is inadequate and that the tank immersion environment, more than any other setting, has the potential for allowing the mind to operate at a much higher level of freedom.

The subjects involved in this work were volunteers who requested an opportunity to experience the tank and who often paid for the use of the facilities as a part of a workshop in self-exploration. The isolation tank, which was much smaller than the rather large ones used in the original immersion research, was located in a dark, soundproof environment, with body-temperature water mixed with Epsom salts to make it easier to float. No monitors were provided, so each tank was completely isolated. After the immersion session, each person was asked to write a report concerning the phenomena encountered during isolation.

According to Lilly, the immersion tank has two major uses, depending on the individual's orientation. If the individual is satisfied and thoroughly tied into Western concepts about the relationship between the external world and the individual, the isolation tank can be used as a place to rest and relax as well as to think over problems and work out solutions with a minimum of distraction. For those who do not find that much distinction between the external world and internal processes, the isolation environment is useful because it minimizes interactions with external reality and allows the internal process to be more fully explored.

As Lilly says, "The tank experience is a very refreshing one, a resting one. If one wants to push further than this, one can do so to the limits of one's mental discipline and to the limits of one's imagination" (Lilly, 1977, p. 31).

Lilly argues that the tank enables a person to separate the mind from the body and to become aware of many other states of being in which consciousness is unimpaired and apparently disconnected from the brain and body. These states include dream travel to other worlds, the appearance of extraterrestrial organisms, and the transformation of individuals into such organisms. Although the experiences are dreamlike, awareness, consciousness, and participation are much more vivid than usual.

Some 78 postimmersion reports are presented in Lilly's (1977) book *The Deep Self*. These indicate that in the beginning, subjects concentrate on the environment and on their own physical and psychological reactions. However, as tank time increases, the participants become more aware of relaxation, feelings of love and warmth, and vivid and novel imagery. The aftereffects appear to be very positive, consisting primarily of vivid memories, deep relaxation, restfulness, and pleasant sleep. Many, but not all, of the participants wanted to repeat the experience.

Clearly, the changes reported by Lilly and his subjects match our definition of an altered state of consciousness. Such events have also been reported in the course of more traditional research using REST. Altered states of consciousness develop gradually in such an environment (Taylor, 1973). The initial reaction is heightened alertness to features of the environment and to bodily sensations. For some subjects, the focus of attention then switches to internal cognitive and emotional experiences. Some subjects go further and develop vivid images that Taylor calls "visual translation and projection of cognitive and emotional states" (Taylor, 1973, p. 125).

Suedfeld and Mocellin (1987) report that subjects in the REST condition report experiencing the *sensed presence,* the perception or feeling that another person is present. This phenomenon can be explained in terms of Jaynes's bicameral mind (see Chapter 1). Beyond this phase comes a state of flowing imagery, interspersed with mental blankness and eventually a state of detachment, serenity, tranquillity, and unity with the infinite (Suedfeld, 1980; Suedfeld et al., 1986).

CLINICAL POTENTIAL OF SENSORY DEPRIVATION

Earlier in this chapter we posed the question: Are there any positive aspects of the sensory deprivation experience? Now that we have reviewed the effects of a sensory-deprived environment as observed under controlled experimental conditions, you may find it difficult to view this phenomenon positively. Keep in mind, however, that these studies have demonstrated that by limiting or modifying environmental stimuli, it is possible to produce marked changes in consciousness levels, and subsequently in behavior, without the use of drugs or other medical techniques.

From our earlier discussion you should remember that as far back as the early 1960s there was some research to determine whether or not REST might have a future as a therapeutic technique. It remained for Suedfeld and Ikard (1974) to provide a major demonstration of the effectiveness of REST as a treatment for cigarette smoking. In this study, four groups of subjects were used: a group in which the restricted environmental stimulation therapy was combined with the presentation of substantive messages and reinforcers, a group that received REST only, another that received messages only, and a control group. All subjects were psychologically addicted smokers; that is, their smoking habit was more than nicotine addiction. Eisinger (1972) notes that such subjects are the least likely to quit smoking.

Smoking rates of subjects in all four groups were compared over a two-year follow-up period. These findings not only pointed to the efficacy of

REST in the treatment of cigarette smoking, but also led the investigators to make several other significant observations. They noted that even though the messages were more elaborate and appeared more helpful than the previously used messages of Suedfeld, Landon, Pargament, and Epstein (1972), they had only a minimal additive effect when combined with REST. In other words, there was no significant difference between the REST-plus-message group and the REST-only group.

One major problem that is constantly found in literature on how to stop smoking is that while almost any treatment can reduce smoking rate for a while, almost none has resulted in significant reductions over a long period (Levenberg & Wagner, 1976). Suedfeld and Ikard (1974) found that almost every subject abstained completely for at least the first week following REST but that the number of cigarettes smoked per day later increased as it does in all smoking cessation techniques.

However, subjects who had received REST as part of a smoking cessation program frequently reported long-term maintenance of smoking rates that were significantly below their baseline, even though they were not able to abstain completely. This contrasts with the experience of many smoking-control clinics, which show that baseline smoking rate levels are rapidly reattained if the subject begins smoking again after treatment. Many of these findings have been replicated by more recent studies employing REST alone or in conjunction with hypnosis (Barabasz, Baer, Sheehan, & Barabasz, 1986; Suedfeld & Baker-Brown, 1986). Such research has spurred other researchers to look at other habitual problems for which REST therapy may be useful.

Precisely how REST is able to bring about this substantial reduction in cigarette smoking rate is a question, the answer to which must await more definitive research. We do know, however, that sensory deprivation induces an altered state of consciousness. Perhaps this state helps the subject learn to relax in certain anxiety-inducing situations or to come to grips with a habit, such as smoking.

Barabasz and Barabasz (1989) have demonstrated that REST can be used to enhance hypnotic susceptibility in patients suffering pain. Not only were they able to demonstrate increased hypnotic susceptibility using REST but also that subjects then were able to use hypnosis daily to reduce pain with a substantial decrease in pain medication.

More recently, Ramirez, Suedfeld, and Remick (1993) investigated the effect of electroconvulsive shock therapy (ECT) and environmental stimulation on memory complaints of clinically depressed patients. After recovering from ECT, patients were randomly assigned to spend time in a REST condition (lying on a bed in a sparsely furnished, dimly lit, quiet room), or a control condition (free to go to anyplace accessible to patients after receiving ECT). Objective and subjective measures of memory were taken before the first ECT session, after the last, and at one-week and one-month follow-ups. Subjective and objective memory measures showed significant memory improvements from baseline to last follow-up in both groups. However, the control group reported significantly less improvement in subjective memory over time than did the REST patients.

Clearly, we are a long way from being able to explain fully how REST can bring about a reduction in smoking or the enhancement of hypnotic susceptibility. Substantial clinical research will be required before we are able to provide answers to these questions. For now we can only accept the data that suggest that REST has a future as a part of the behavior therapist's arsenal.

As a technique for helping us understand the psychology of consciousness, REST has staged a significant comeback, and as it becomes more popular with the research community, we can expect that it may well provide us with new insights into consciousness. Clearly, REST does produce a change in the states or levels of consciousness. Earlier, we saw that sleep and "sensed presence" may be produced when persons are deprived of changes in sensory input. Therefore, although historically REST has had its ups and downs as a research technique, it still has much to offer.

FOR FURTHER READING

Brownfield, C. A. (1965). *Isolation: Clinical and experimental approaches.* New York: Random House.

Dean, W. F. (1954). *General Dean's story.* New York: Viking Press.

Lilly, J. C. (1977). *The deep self.* New York: Simon and Schuster.

Suedfeld, P. (1980). *Restricted environmental stimulation: Research and clinical applications.* New York: Wiley-Interscience.

Zubek, J. P. (Ed.). (1969). *Sensory deprivation: Fifteen years of research.* New York: Appleton-Century-Crofts.

9

PARAPSYCHOLOGY

Historically, parapsychology, or **psychical research (psi),** has been one of the most interesting and controversial areas of study in the realm of consciousness. Many individuals who are not psychologists admit to an interest in this area. The topic is often written about in popular magazines and discussed on television and radio programs. Many people would like nothing better than to be able to "read minds" or to make objects move in space by mental control. Can you imagine how nice it might be to read someone's mind, such as the brightest student's during an exam? Or your boyfriend's or girlfriend's? However, few admit to being able to perform these feats, although many believe that some people possess such abilities. Among scientists, especially psychologists and other behavioral scientists, a very small minority admit to the possibility of **extrasensory perception (ESP)** or **psychokinetic (PK) abilities** (McClenon, 1982). In fact, to express a belief in such possibilities is often to risk being labeled a scientific heretic, a believer in the occult.

Why is the study of parapsychology so controversial? Is there any scientific evidence to support some people's claims that they can read minds or perform other such feats? If so, do such claims indicate that these people possess a special ability to control mind over matter? These issues as well as others will be discussed here.

PARAPSYCHOLOGY AND CONSCIOUSNESS

Parapsychology literally means "alongside psychology." As this root definition implies, this area of interest is not within the mainstream of psychological study. However, those who conduct scientific investigations in psi claim that some people on some occasions are capable of processing information without relying on the five senses (vision, hearing, taste, smell, and touch). Such people supposedly can relate information to an investigator in ways beyond the normal limits of consciousness or awareness. Although you and I may not be able to sense or detect consciously a phenomenon or event, people with this ability theoretically can experience it. If such abilities do exist and can be isolated and controlled for scientific study, they may help us to understand yet another piece of information within the workings of the human system. These abilities supposedly enable one to consciously control or alter behavior that we once believed could not be so controlled. If some behavior can be manipulated or controlled outside the normal limits of our senses, the discovery would be remarkable indeed and might enable us to tighten our grasp on the limits of our abilities and potentialities. As we discuss psi as an area of investigation within the psychology of consciousness, we shall discover whether this is possible.

HISTORICAL DEVELOPMENT

Although stories about the ability to read minds or move objects by thought have circulated for centuries, it was not until 1882 that scientists organized to study parapsychology. In that year the Society for Psychical Research was founded in London by F. W. H. Myers (1843–1901), Edmund Gurney (1847–1888), and Henry Sidgwick (1838–1900), who became the first president of the organization. One of the most notable members of the society was Sir Arthur Conan Doyle (1859–1930), author of the Sherlock Holmes detective stories. An American version of this society was organized in Boston in 1885 with the purpose of investigating claims of telepathy, clairvoyance, precognition, and other forms of paranormal cognition (Mauskopf, 1989). Some prominent members of the Boston society were psychologists Gardner Murphy (1895–1980) and William James (1842–1910). The two societies later merged, and James eventually became president.

The most prevalent investigation in the early scientific years of parapsychology centered around **mediumship**, or communication with the dead. In fact, several very prominent psychologists were attracted to parapsychology because of their interest in communicating with a dead person. These individuals included William James (Murphy & Ballou, 1969), who played a major role in the early development of the psychology of consciousness (see Chapter 1), and William McDougall (1871–1938).

James believed that psychic research was an important and little understood area of the human mind and its powers. He thought it necessary that this area be investigated by "any means at our disposal if progress in understanding was to be achieved" (Murphy & Ballou, 1969, p. 12). He further believed that a phenomenon was not necessarily untrue simply because it conflicted with known principles of science. (Many people view parapsychology as conflicting with such principles.)

McDougall probably played the most important role in developing the scientific investigation of parapsychology in the United States. In 1927, while at Duke University, McDougall set up the first laboratory devoted to the investigation of psi—specifically to study telepathy, clairvoyance, precognition, and psychokinesis. McDougall was also at the time a very influential force in the council of the Society for Psychical Research.

McDougall brought to Duke two botanists, Joseph B. Rhine (1895–1980), who is often credited with coining the term *parapsychology* (Wallechinsky & Wallace, 1975), and his wife, Louisa E. Rhine (1891–1983), who had been experimenting with psi at Harvard University.

The Rhines' major area of interest did not fall within the categories of study for which McDougall had organized his laboratory. Rather, they were interested in the area that was the impetus for the development of psi research, the question of survival after death. Their research involved having a medium in one room try to read the thoughts of a subject in another room; they could not deduce how such thought transference could take place. They hypothesized that either a dead person was communicating with the medium by acting as an intermediary to relay information or telepathy was taking place between the medium and the subject. The latter hypothesis seemed more reasonable to them (and far easier to test experimentally) than the former. Thus, they commenced their investigation of mental telepathy with the aid of research support from the Rockefeller Foundation and the U.S. Navy. They published the first formal report of their findings in a book titled *Extrasensory Perception* (1934). This important publication, reprinted in 1964 (see the References), described the Rhines' many experiments with subjects' abilities to deduce symbols on a deck of cards. These cards were called *Zener cards* after the originator of the deck, Karl Zener (1903–1964).

A Zener deck consisted of 25 cards with 5 identical cards in each of five different suits (see Figure 9.1). The suits consisted of crosses, circles, stars, wavy lines, and squares. The probability of guessing the correct suit of a particular card was 1 in 5. Thus, a typical subject would correctly guess the suit of 5 cards out of 25 presented. The odds of guessing all 25 correctly were 298,023,223,876,953,125 to 1. According to the Rhine report, one subject named Hubert Pearce, a divinity student at Duke, remarkably beat those odds and guessed all 25 cards correctly. Unfortunately, he was unable to repeat his phenomenal performance.

FIGURE 9.1   The Five Suits Depicted on Zener ESP Cards

Ever since scientists began to investigate parapsychological phenomena, card-guessing ability has been one of the most researched areas. The technical term for this ability is *telepathy*. This term is used when the experimenter can see the cards while the subject tries to guess their identity.

Precognition is the attempt by the subject to guess the order in which the cards will be arranged before the experimenter arranges them. When the experimenter does not know the identity or order of the cards but the subject nevertheless guesses their identity, the subject's ability is known as *clairvoyance*. Each of these powers will be discussed under the general heading of "Extrasensory Perception." Extrasensory perception is distinguished from psychokinesis, which describes the ability to move objects by thought. Both ESP and PK have been scientifically investigated by many researchers (Moss & Butler, 1978; Rao, 1966, 1979; Rao & Palmer, 1987; J. B. Rhine, 1964; L. E. Rhine, 1964, 1970; Rhine & Pratt, 1957); many positive as well as negative findings have been reported (Alcock, 1987; Rao & Palmer, 1987).

EXTRASENSORY PERCEPTION

Extrasensory perception, or ESP, generally refers to the phenomena of clairvoyance, precognition, and telepathy. Each of these will now be described.

Clairvoyance

Clairvoyance, broadly defined, is the ability to experience the occurrence of an event without physically perceiving it (without using the senses)—in other words, in an "extrasensory" manner. Pratt (1973a, 1973b) reports an example of an individual who claimed to have such an ability. His name was Pavel Stepanek, and he lived in Prague, Czechoslovakia. In an experiment designed to test clairvoyant abilities, Stepanek was requested to guess on many trials whether a given card placed in a covered container was white or colored. Before the testing session, all of the cards and covers were ordered randomly so that in no event did the experimenter know what type of card was in a given container. Thus, the experimenter could not convey any information regarding the card's identity to the subject. This procedure is necessary for conducting a scientific experiment in clairvoyance.

After examining Stepanek's guesses over a series of trials, researchers discovered that he significantly exceeded chance in correctly identifying the color of cards hidden from both himself and the experimenter. Pratt mentions that this ability was not random or spurious, for Stepanek was able to demonstrate this feat over and over again, not only for Pratt but for other investigators as well (Beloff, 1968).

The case of Pavel Stepanek is interesting. Here is a demonstration of the ability of an individual to experience an event accurately (above chance) without relying on his five senses. Does this finding scientifically establish the existence of an ESP component in clairvoyance? Although the evidence seems to be convincing in the case of Stepanek, it is still unclear how he performed his feat. Learning as a function of trials cannot be totally discounted as an alternative to the possibility of ESP. For example, if one guesses (correctly or incorrectly) the same color of a card for a series of responses, one probably will switch to another color after a while.

In a similar manner, if someone is flipping a coin and asks you if you wish to pick "heads" or "tails," you have a 50 percent chance of being correct on each and every flip of the coin. However, let us say that by coincidence or chance, a "head" appears three times in a row. Might you switch to saying "tails" on the fourth trial simply because "heads" appeared on the previous trials? Might you do this even if you know that the probability of a "head" has remained the same?

In essence, subjects often develop a strategy for performing or guessing, often in the face of probability. Could it be that Stepanek became very skilled in developing a strategy for producing accurate guesses? After all, it is known that some card players often develop strategies that help them to win more money than would be the case if they had not developed a winning strategy. With regard to Stepanek, it is not possible to determine whether he developed a successful strategy for performing in a clairvoyance task because Pratt did not discuss this issue. However, this is not unusual, since investigators in this area generally tend to ignore alternatives to psi as an explanation for results. Perhaps future investigators will make a greater effort to consider such explanations.

Precognition

Another area of ESP is *precognition*, the ability to predict a future event. Did you ever predict a future occurrence? Do you remember how shocked or surprised you were when the event really happened? Did it occur by coincidence, or is precognition possible? Such a possibility formed the basis of an experiment by Friedman, Schmeidler, and Dean (1976). Subjects were asked to predict which of 5 possible targets would be selected by an experimenter on each of 20 calls or trials. This assignment differs from the one employed in clairvoyance experiments because the experimenter knows the identity of the targets to be guessed. Also, the subject predicts what an experimenter *will do* rather than saying what he or she *did*. In this experiment, subjects scored significantly above chance, but only if they were in a nonaggressive mood and didn't need social affection. Mood states were determined before the experiment by having subjects complete the Nowlis (1965) Mood Adjective Checklist.

It is not clear why these mood states were necessary for subjects to score above chance. There seems to be no logical reason why precognition would require these states. There also is no definitive evidence that the data of Friedman and associates support the existence of precognitive abilities. Perhaps, as we discussed in the case of clairvoyance, subjects became skillful at developing a strategy for guessing on the basis of a learning experience over 20 trials. Obviously, there is no way to resolve the controversy over whether Friedman and associates really demonstrated precognition. However, they did make a scientific attempt to determine the possible existence of the phenomenon. It is hoped that, with many more such attempts, science will be able to give us some clues as to whether precognition is a bona fide phenomenon.

Telepathy

The third major area of ESP, *telepathy,* is the ability to read someone's mind and to tell others the thoughts perceived in this fashion. As with precognition and clairvoyance, the possible existence of telepathic skills has been scientifically investigated. But telepathy differs from both clairvoyance and precognition in that it requires the experimenter to look at a target while the subject tries to guess the target's identity (see Figure 9.2). Therefore, telepathy is akin to mind reading.

Tart (1966, 1977b) researched telepathy in a manner similar to Rhine's experiments with Zener cards (1964). Tart hypothesized that giving a subject immediate feedback in a repeated card-guessing task would stabilize psi per-

---

FIGURE 9.2 A Person Reading Another's Mind

formance by permitting talented individuals to develop a strategy for learning which cards had a greater chance of appearing on subsequent guesses. This strategy of research was based in part on a memory theory of ESP proposed by Roll (1966). Roll suggested that ESP responses are in fact revived memory traces that are activated by an external ESP target stimulus.

According to Tart, Palmer, and Redington (1979a, 1979b), such learning could take place via internal processes that enable the subject to gain conscious control of ESP functioning. In essence, the subject makes "mental snapshots" in reaching a response decision, stores such snapshots in memory along with the feedback knowledge of the success or failure of each response, and then examines the stored data to determine which internal events constituted a guide for a useful ESP guessing strategy.

Although their results are not as impressive as those produced by Hubert Pearce in the Rhine report (1964), the experiments conducted by Tart and colleagues do present evidence that card-guessing above chance definitely is possible. The question is whether this skill requires ESP. It seems that Tart's data can easily be explained in nonparapsychological terms, namely, that good subjects have the ability to memorize card sequences, much as good poker players can remember which cards have been played previously in an expended deck.

Because of the feedback manipulation, the assertion that ESP was necessary for above-chance performance is at best tenuous. As Irwin (1978a, 1978b) and Kennedy (1980) have demonstrated in their card-guessing experiments, and as Vitulli (1983) has demonstrated in a computer-assisted psi test, the ability to be an above-chance guesser may relate more to the subject's ability to process available information, as in a perception or cognition task (see Kahneman, 1973; Lindsey and Norman, 1977), than to possession of ESP abilities.

Remote Viewing

Related to the phenomena of clairvoyance, precognition, and telepathy is a reported experience referred to as *remote viewing* (Targ & Puthoff, 1974a; 1977). This refers to the ability of subjects to describe places being visited by other people without having any normal form of communication with the visitors. Unfortunately, attempts at replicating this phenomenon have been unsuccessful (Marks & Kammann, 1978; 1980). The major reason given for a failure to replicate concerns the judging procedure used by Targ and Puthoff.

In the Targ and Puthoff studies, judges were asked to match a series of subject responses to a set of target responses. ("Target responses" means those that were determined before the experiment to be the ones most likely to be given by subjects.) Marks and Kammann argued that the transcripts of the subjects' reports should have been edited to remove cues that would assist the judges in identifying the target responses. Since this was not done, the judging procedure was biased and produced above-chance matching of transcripts with targets. As a result, Marks and Kammann and, later, Marks and Scott

(1986) argued that remote viewing is only another example of a psi phenomenon that can be explained by experimenter bias.

FACTORS INFLUENCING EXPERIMENTAL FINDINGS

Ganzfeld Controls

In an attempt to partially address the issue of experimenter bias, some researchers have studied psi phenomena in a *ganzfeld*. This term refers to a condition of reduced sensory stimulation that can, for example, be produced by applying halved Ping-Pong balls to a subject's eyes and shining a light onto them while playing white noise (a combination of all sound frequencies) into the subject's ears via headphones. Some researchers have indicated that this control procedure, when applied, produces about a 50 percent replication rate of psi experiments (Blackmore, 1980).

However, in an exhaustive analysis of virtually all psi ganzfeld research between 1974 and 1981, Hyman (1985) concluded that the replication rate was really close to chance, primarily because of detected experimental flaws in all studies examined. Honorton (1985) argued that Hyman's conclusion was inaccurate and that many of the studies, in which so-called flaws were detected, were really free of such experimenter error or bias. In a joint paper, Hyman and Honorton (1986) finally agreed that a conclusion on the viability of the ganzfeld as a control procedure for psi experiments was premature and that the value of this procedure could be determined only by continuing its use in future research.

Individual Differences

Regardless of the type of ESP experiment a researcher is conducting, subjects are classified into two types—*sheep* (believers in ESP) and *goats* (disbelievers or doubters). Research has tended to show that sheep generally score better than chance on ESP tasks, while goats tend to score at or below random chance (Palmer, 1971; Schmeidler & McConnell, 1958). However, such differences between sheep and goats are not always found. For example, Smith (1992) investigated belief in the paranormal and how this affects the observation of a "psychic" demonstration. Individuals were shown a videotaped demonstration of ostensible psychic ability. Subjects were told that the demonstration was authentic or that it involved trickery. Sheep and goats did not differ in their observation and subsequent report of the demonstration.

Interestingly, belief in paranormal phenomena has been correlated with manic-depressive illness (Thalbourne & French, 1995), with neurotic disorders (Thalbourne, Dunbar, & Delin, 1995), and with childhood trauma (Irwin, 1994). Also, Snel, van der Sijde, and Wiegant (1995) found that believers (sheep) are more field-dependent (influenced by external stimuli) than nonbelievers (goats). As a result, they concluded that believers tend to interpret paranormal phenomena and information in the context in which they are presented, while nonbelievers tend to abstract the context and interpret paranormal phenomena and information analytically.

Besides being a sheep or goat, are other factors important in demonstrating ESP abilities? This is not an easy question to answer. However, L. E. Rhine (1961) and J. B. Rhine (1964) have reported that subjects who demonstrated ESP in their experiments did not fall into one particular age group. Their subjects have ranged in age from 4 to 60 years. For college students who have served as subjects, grades have not been a predictive factor in determining who can demonstrate ESP. In addition, no evidence exists to demonstrate that ESP ability is related to gender.

Factors that appear to improve ESP abilities include one's level of confidence (people who are more confident demonstrate greater abilities) and concentration. Krippner, Hickman, Auerhahn, and Harris (1972) also discovered that for some subjects, ESP abilities were improved when there was a full moon. We can only speculate why any of these factors influence ESP abilities. Does a person's level of consciousness change when he or she is more confident about performing a certain task and concentrates on the task? In Chapter 4 we learned that both these factors appeared to be important in determining who was hypnotizable. Therefore, it is also conceivable that these factors play a role in determining who can demonstrate certain ESP abilities. However, this is only a matter of conjecture.

As for the influence of moon phase on ESP abilities, a physical force may be working on behavior and consciousness in a manner similar to that which controls tide levels. Because this suggestion is highly speculative and is supported by no evidence, a scientific conclusion is not possible. However, would it not be interesting if such a phenomenon were taking place?

Hypnotic Influences

Is hypnotic susceptibility related to ESP performance or belief? Pekala, Kumar, and Cummings (1992) investigated hypnotic susceptibility in relation to a variety of parapsychological and anomalous feelings, beliefs, and experiences. Over 500 students completed the Harvard Group Scale of Hypnotic Susceptibility (see Chapter 4) and two questionnaires that dealt with altered state and cognitive experiences. Individuals with high hypnotic susceptibility endorsed far more psi-related items and anomalous beliefs and experiences than did those with low hypnotic susceptibility.

In reviewing the literature on hypnotic suggestions and ESP performance, Honorton and Krippner (1969) and Hinds (1995) reported some very interesting findings. Some of the studies reviewed were those by Grela (1945), Fahler and Cadoret (1958), and Casler (1962, 1967), in which hypnosis appears to be a facilitator in clairvoyance and telepathy.

Grela (1945) undertook the first systematic investigation of the effects of hypnosis on ESP performance. In this study, one group of subjects, who were judged high in hypnotic responsiveness, were hypnotized and asked to guess symbols displayed on a deck of cards that were visible only to an experimenter. While hypnotized, they were told that they possessed ESP abilities and that these abilities would be displayed more than adequately when they were asked to guess the symbols. A second group of subjects, who were judged low in hypnotic susceptibility and therefore not hypnotized, was asked to perform the same task with the same instructions. Although Grela's results did not prove to be statistically significant, a trend was exhibited in which hypnosis tended to facilitate card-guessing accuracy.

In a related card-guessing study by Fahler and Cadoret (1958), subjects who were judged high in hypnotic susceptibility participated in an ESP experiment during a waking state and again during a state of hypnosis. During the waking state, the number of correct guesses did not exceed chance. However, in the hypnotized state, a very high level of performance was achieved, statistically exceeding chance.

Casler (1962, 1967) also found that subjects demonstrated ESP card-guessing abilities that were significantly better with hypnotic facilitation than during the waking state. In these studies, subjects were asked to generate, during hypnosis, whatever suggestions of their own they felt would help them perform better in an ESP task. Results indicated that self-induced suggestions during hypnosis significantly improved card-guessing performance.

In addition to the studies we have discussed, Krippner (1968) reported a study concerned with the effects of hypnotic imagery on ESP performance. When subjects were instructed to concentrate on an image that they could not physically see but that the experimenter could, Krippner found that hypnotized subjects were better able to accurately report the content of the image. He concluded that hypnosis may have served to accelerate the processing of the extrasensory material.

Clairvoyant dreams have also been examined by Honorton (1972). In this study, subjects who were judged highly susceptible to hypnotization were hypnotized and given suggestions to dream about the contents of an envelope. Results indicated that content guessing was significantly improved in subjects experiencing clairvoyant dreams under hypnosis. However, such a finding is not consistently reported in the literature (e.g., Honorton & Stump, 1969). Unfortunately, when positive findings are reported in one laboratory, they are soon met with negative or disconfirming findings from another laboratory (see Alcock, 1987). Thus, although hypnosis would appear to facilitate ESP abilities, especially telepathy and clairvoyance, results are far from conclusive.

In general, despite many failures to replicate a variety of phenomena labeled extrasensory perception, and despite the continuing controversy over whether ESP even exists, many reports continue to be published that demonstrate that clairvoyance, telepathy, and precognition can be produced in a laboratory situation (e.g., Radin, 1988; Schmeidler, 1985; Sondow, 1988).

PSYCHOKINESIS

In addition to telepathy, precognition, and clairvoyance, another interesting area of research in parapsychology is what is referred to as **psychokinesis (PK)**, or the ability to make an object move by mind control—that is, without being in physical contact with it. We have witnessed such an occurrence in a number of movies using the film industry's expertise in special effects, but can people actually demonstrate such an ability? We shall now examine this possibility in terms of reported laboratory findings.

There are several examples of PK in the parapsychology literature. One classic case was reported by Aylesworth (1975). An Englishman, Harry Price, observed a young girl who appeared to be able to depress a telegraph key without touching it. Doubting the girl's PK abilities, Price had her repeat the performance under some very stringent controls. He blew a soap and glycerin bubble over the telegraph key and placed the setup in a glass enclosure. After this, he further enclosed the apparatus in a wire cage. He hoped that all of these precautions would guarantee the girl's not having physical contact with the telegraph key. Price was astonished to see that she nonetheless depressed the telegraph key.

Other examples of PK have been reported in the Duke University laboratories of the Rhines (L. E. Rhine, 1970). Basically, the Rhines' (J. B. and L. E.) study of PK grew out of their concern for methodological control during investigations of parapsychological phenomena. They wondered, for example, whether the number of Zener cards a subject could accurately report, in excess of chance guessing, might be due to clairvoyant or telepathic abilities. Or could it be that the subject used PK to control the order in which the cards were presented? To help answer these questions, the Rhines used as a subject in a PK experiment a man who had previously demonstrated clairvoyant abilities with the Zener cards. This time, instead of having the subject report the symbol on each card, he was to report the exact order of the cards before and after they were shuffled. The researchers observed no difference between these two sessions; in both instances the subject exceeded chance guessing. As a result, it appeared that the ability to name Zener card symbols might be multidetermined. That is, it could be attributed to clairvoyance, telepathy, PK, or perhaps just good guessing.

It was obvious to the Rhines that isolating the various ESP and PK phenomena in the card-guessing task would not be possible. Although several subjects in the Duke experiments demonstrated the ability to guess Zener cards accurately above the chance guessing level, no conclusion could be made concerning the reasons for their ability to do so.

Therefore, the Rhines began another experiment to determine whether PK could exist. This was a dice-throwing task. In one such experiment (Rhine & Brier, 1968), subjects were asked to throw two dice and attempt to have their sum total greater than 7. Of a possible 36 combinations of 2 dice, 15 are greater than 7. Subjects threw the dice a total of 6,744 times, and managed to accumulate 3,110 throws in which the total of the dice exceeded 7. The odds against doing so are about a billion to 1 when 2,810 throws of the dice totaling more than 7 are expected by chance. Again, however, a question arose regarding whether subjects were controlling the dice by PK or whether they knew via precognition how the dice would land. This question frequently arises in experiments like this and must be dealt with if such experiments are to be conducted in a controlled fashion.

Although Rhine and colleagues have studied PK in the laboratory for many years, examples of PK phenomena also happen in the natural environment. Pratt and Roll (1958) report the case of the James H. Herrmann family of Seaford, New York. For several weeks this family complained of rather strange occurrences in their home. Objects moved for no apparent reason: a figurine flew through the air and a bottle of shampoo moved across the bathroom shelf. Sixty-seven such events occurred before the Herrmanns sought assistance.

Poltergeist Phenomena

Poltergeist is a German word meaning "noisy spirit" and generally refers to strange happenings such as objects moving in space (see Figure 9.3) and other things that occurred in the Herrmann home. Pratt and Roll discovered that objects never moved in the home when it was unoccupied. However, when

---

FIGURE 9.3   Objects Floating in Space

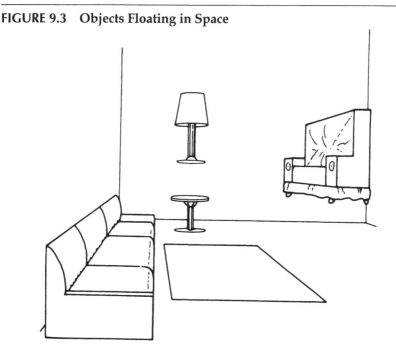

the Herrmann son, James, Jr., was present, objects began to move. Pratt and Roll observed five of these so-called PK movements, and they did not believe that trickery or deception was involved.

In fact, Pratt (1973a) reported several additional instances of poltergeist events similar to the Herrmann example. In one case a court reporter from Oakland, California, named James Hazlewood reported some strange happenings in his office. A Dictaphone foot pedal moved from a cabinet; light bulbs in a fixture became unscrewed, fell, and broke; and the metal top of a typewriter went through an open window and fell to the street below.

Are these poltergeist phenomena examples of PK in the real world? This question is not easy to answer, because many of the PK or poltergeist events are reported after the fact and therefore cannot be verified scientifically. However, similar examples continue to be reported and therefore cannot be dismissed lightly. Until more examples can be demonstrated under controlled laboratory settings, the scientific community will not accept the poltergeist phenomenon.

Some of the most interesting demonstrations of PK were exhibited by Uri Geller. Geller claimed to be able to break metal rings simply by concentration and to start broken clocks by concentrating on them. As reported by Aylesworth (1975), Geller demonstrated bending a ring that belonged to Friedbert Karger of the Max Planck Institute in Berlin. While Geller visited the space scientist Werner von Braun, von Braun's calculator ceased functioning. This also happened at the Stanford Research Institute in California when Geller appeared as a subject for an experiment by two physicists, Russell Targ and Harold Puthoff.

Targ and Puthoff (1974b) conducted several experiments on Geller. All the experiments were filmed or videotaped to ascertain that the scientists would not miss anything, such as a sleight-of-hand trick or other deception. In one experiment, Geller unbalanced a precision scientific scale. He also bent a steel band to an angle that would have required about 100 pounds of pressure. Geller accomplished this without coming into physical contact with the objects.

Needless to say, the PK demonstrations by Geller and others are highly controversial. Can some or all of the feats performed by Geller be magic? In other words, could a magician replicate the so-called PK demonstrations? One magician, the Amazing Randi, says yes. In fact, Randi (1975, 1982) has written two books in which he detailed exactly how Geller performed his so-called feats. As an example, it is possible to demonstrate the bending of forks or spoons on television if one uses utensils made of sterling silver. With the heat generated by the lights required for television cameras, silver will begin to bend, especially if exposed to intense light for a prolonged period. Thus, the research in the area of PK, especially the feats demonstrated by Geller, does not appear to have a sound methodological base. It is difficult to take research on the aforementioned PK phenomena seriously when magicians can replicate the demonstrated feats.

Kirlian Photography

Another PK phenomenon is called **Kirlian photography**. This process was discovered by two Russian scientists, Semyon and Valentina Kirlian (Krippner & Rubin, 1974; Moss & Johnson, 1974). The notion behind this phenomenon is that a form of energy flows, or can be made to flow, by PK from acupuncture points on the human body. The Kirlians believe they have discovered a process that can photograph this energy. (Such photography has also been demonstrated with plants.)

The actual Kirlian process involves the use of an electric tesla coil (a type of transformer) that is connected to two metal plates. An object (usually a finger) is then placed between the plates, where a piece of film touches the object. Electricity is then turned on, generating a high-energy frequency that causes the film to record an "aura" or "halo." Variations in the color and form of the halo are considered descriptors of mood states. For example, a red, blotchy halo is indicative of anxiety; a glowing halo indicates relaxation (the greater the glow, the more relaxed the person is). Since the energy flow does not appear to be controlled by the five senses, parapsychologists believe that it is controlled by PK.

Whether this is really the case cannot be stated at this time. Montandon (1977), however, believed that Kirlian photography and the resultant auras were related to palmar sweating. If so, such photography has a physical basis that is autonomically controlled. That is, it is controlled involuntarily by the autonomic nervous system (ANS) (see Chapter 5). If this is the case, and if Kirlian photography is an accurate recording of ANS activity, the potential uses of Kirlian photography are limitless. For example, the technique might someday serve as a lie detector in recording levels of anxiety or nervousness. Or it might be used to help individuals understand their level of anxiety and subsequently decrease or control this level, much as in biofeedback training. Of course, these suggestions are speculative and are based on the assumption that Kirlian photography is not an illustration of PK. Only time will help us to understand this process more fully.

Random Event Generation

A final example of PK is illustrated by Schmidt, Morris, and Rudolph (1986) and by Schmidt (1970a, 1970b, 1973) in their random-event generator studies. Their method basically involved asking subjects to predict or influence the radioactive emission of subatomic particles. While Schmidt reported positive results indicating that subjects can have control over such particles, Alcock (1987) argued that Schmidt's procedure suffered from less than optimal experimental control. For example, subjects were usually unsupervised, and the control of experimental conditions was not rigorous. In addition, Alcock argued that Schmidt's random-event generator was not truly random and that, since subjects were provided with immediate feedback concerning their performance, it was possible that they learned how to respond on subsequent performances.

Needless to say, Schmidt (1987) disagreed with Alcock's assessment. Thus, as with other psi phenomena, results concerning conclusive evidence for the control of subatomic particles is inconclusive.

In general, as with clairvoyance, precognition, and telepathy, many people question the existence of PK as a scientific phenomenon. However, as with the phenomena we have mentioned, published reports continue to demonstrate PK abilities (e.g., Braud & Schlitz, 1983; Schmeidler, 1984; Schmidt et al., 1986).

THE OUT-OF-BODY EXPERIENCE

In addition to the study of clairvoyance, precognition, telepathy, and PK, parapsychologists have also developed an interest in what are referred to as the **out-of-body experience (OBE)** and the **near-death experience (NDE).** The OBE is the experience of a subject who has been separated from his or her physical body (Alvarado, 1992). The NDE refers to a number of experiences, including an out-of-body experience, reported by individuals who have been pronounced clinically dead and then resuscitated. What they say they perceived or witnessed while "dead" is the NDE.

The OBE, the feeling that one has been separated from one's body, is generally accompanied by a number of other phenomena. For example, some subjects, who have reported that they have experienced leaving their bodies or have seen themselves as a type of spirit floating above their physical bodies (see Figure 9.4), also report that they have experienced accompanying physical paralysis or catalepsy (Morris, Harary, Janis, Hartwell, & Roll, 1978; Muldoon & Carrington, 1977). Others have reported that separation from the body is frequently accompanied by strong vibrational sensations (Monroe, 1971). A pronounced clarity of consciousness also seems to be common among those reporting OBEs (Crookall, 1966; Fox, 1962; Monroe, 1971). Other separation experiences include hearing unexplained noises (Crookall, 1966; Monroe, 1971) and a heightened sexual arousal (Monroe, 1971). And some of these experiences seem to be associated with REM or rapid eye movement activity (see Chapter 7), indicating that perhaps the person is asleep and dreaming in a conscious state (Salley, 1982).

How common is it for individuals to report that they have been separated from their physical body? In a survey of college students, Blackmore (1982) reported that around 13 percent had such experiences. Before her report, a number of investigators reported OBEs ranging from around 8 percent (Haraldsson, Gudmundsdottir, Ragnarsson, Loftsson, & Jonsson, 1977) to around 34 percent (Green, 1967).

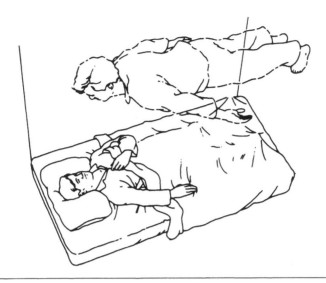

FIGURE 9.4   An Out-of-Body Experience

What produces this strange experience? Salley (1982) has suggested that OBEs may merely be vivid hallucinatory dreams and that the paralysis and sexual arousal simply reflect the physiology of REM sleep. (Incidentally, the other symptoms also seem to fall into what might be considered typical symptomology of dream or REM activity). However, Tart (1968) reported that during an OBE some subjects are capable of demonstrating extrasensory perception. Needless to say, this cannot be accounted for by the REM hypothesis.

Exactly what OBEs are, and what produces them, is not known. As we mentioned, Salley believes that they are related to the onset of REM activity. Blackmore (1982) has likewise reported that OBEs appear to be related to lucid dreams. Whether they are related to sleep, dreams, or whatever cannot be answered at this time. Some have speculated that they result from a blockage in the perception of body-relevant stimulation at a sensory level and that they are emotionally neutral or even pleasant experiences (Irwin, 1988; Nash, Lynn, & Stanley, 1984).

However, this is not the case. In fact, Nash et al. have shown that OBEs are reported to be troubling and unpleasant. Also, they found little support for their own contention that they are the result of a sensory blockage. Clearly, more controlled laboratory experiments than have been reported thus far are needed to answer the question of what produces OBEs. It is clear, however, that they are interesting experiences, and regardless of what they are and what produces them, they continue to be reported in the scientific literature (e.g., Alvarado, 1984).

Related to the out-of-body experience is the so-called near-death experience (NDE). In fact, as previously mentioned, one near-death experience is an out-of-body report. What exactly are NDEs? Are these potential indicators that there is life after death? These are some of the issues we shall now consider.

THE NEAR-DEATH EXPERIENCE

The scientific study of the NDE began with the appearance of two books on the subject by Moody (1975, 1988). In these books, Moody reported a number of interviews he conducted with individuals who had narrowly escaped death or who had been brought back to life after experiencing clinical death. These people reported a variety of happenings, including the following (see Figure 9.5):

1. Seeing oneself leave one's physical body, often from a distance (the out-of-body experience)
2. Seeing spirits of relatives and friends who had already died
3. Seeing light or an illuminated apparition

FIGURE 9.5 A Near-Death Description of "Entering the Light"

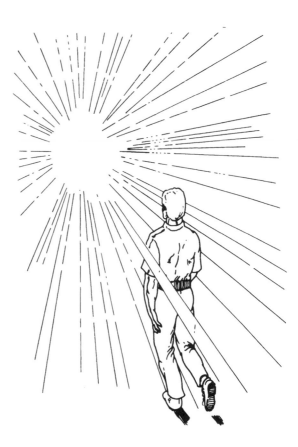

4. Seeing what appeared to be a review of the major events of one's life
5. Feeling warmth, joy, happiness, and peace
6. Having psi experiences, especially precognition

After these reports, a number of scientific studies were conducted to determine how universal these experiences were and to what, if anything, they were related. Foremost among the studies on the NDE were those of Ring (1980, 1985, 1993, 1995), who studied a number of individuals who had been brought back to life after experiencing clinical death. From his sample, half had reported NDEs that were practically identical to those reported by Moody. Ring subsequently categorized the NDEs as follows:

60 percent reported feeling at peace.
53 percent reported "entering the darkness."
37 percent had experienced leaving one's body.
33 percent "saw the light" (of this percentage, 20 percent actually entered it).
33 percent reported that they had chosen or willed themselves back to life.
25 percent reviewed the highlights of their life.

As further evidence for the universality of NDEs, Kellehear (1996) has indicated that reports garnered by researchers such as Ring are remarkably similar all over the world. Individuals in India, China, Guam, Australia, and New Zealand report experiences very similar to those obtained in the United States and Canada.

Several explanations have been offered concerning the NDE. Palmer (1978) believed that sensory deprivation (see Chapter 8) and stress, which can produce hallucinations, might, to some extent, be involved in producing NDEs. If one conceives that being near death is a state of sensory deprivation and that dying is a stressful event, then Palmer's explanation may have some validity.

Another explanation for the NDE was proposed by McHarg (1978). He believed that the NDE resulted from cerebral anoxia or a shortage of oxygen in the brain metabolism and temporal lobe or epileptic seizures. Cerebral anoxia involves symptoms of anxiety, disorientation, and distortions of perception; temporal lobe seizures are sometimes associated with seeing visions of objects or people not physically present. While such visions may be associated with the anoxia and temporal lobe seizures, it is difficult to imagine that all NDE reports are associated with the combination of these two events. Also, as Grosso (1981) pointed out, the match between symptoms associated with NDE and those associated with anoxia, temporal lobe, and epileptic seizures was not sufficiently similar. One study (Audette, 1979) also indicated that many NDE reports come from individuals who displayed flat EEGs. This, of course, precludes the possibility of universal temporal lobe involvement.

Palmer (1978) suggested that religious expectations may influence the NDE. That is, highly religious individuals who are dying may expect to see or to be taken away by an apparition. However, many individuals who report NDEs are not religious in any sense of the term (Moody, 1975, 1977, 1985, 1988; Ring, 1980, 1985, 1993, 1995). As Grasso (1981) has nicely summarized, "the empirical findings across the board so far indicate that religious beliefs influence the *interpretation,* not the *content,* of experiences of this nature" (p. 48).

Attribution has also been offered as an explanation for the NDE (Norton & Sahlman, 1995). In essence, it is argued that personal belief systems influence coding and interpreting NDEs. Thus, individuals who report experiencing an NDE might first simplify the experience to help interpret its meaning. Ambiguities are then resolved, and the NDE is eventually attributed to a cause. While this may be going on during an NDE, attribution, in and of itself, cannot be argued as the sole cause for such an experience.

To date, there is really no universal explanation for the NDE (Corcoran, 1988; Perry, 1988; Schroter-Kunhardt, 1993). It is an interesting phenomenon, and many of us have heard of individuals who have had this type of experience. Some have even interpreted the NDE as an indication that there is life after death or as evidence to confirm the existence of a deity. Unfortunately, these, like other explanations, must fall into the category of speculations.

PSYCHIC HEALING

Another topic that has sparked the interest of many in the area of parapsychology is *psychic healing,* or what is also sometimes referred to as faith healing. With this phenomenon, we generally envision a type of mystical or religious ceremony in which someone is helping an afflicted person to overcome a disease or medical problem. Those who seek a faith cure generally do so either when a medical cure has failed or when this may be their only means of treatment. Does this form of healing really work? Is it possible that an altered state of consciousness accompanies the psychic healing process? These are some of the questions we will address here.

Although psychic or faith healing is generally associated with some sects of Protestant Christianity, it is also found in various forms in Catholicism, Judaism, and even societal organizations that do not adhere to an organized religion. As examples, exorcism was and still is practiced to some extent by some Catholics. This form of healing requires the presence of a priest to rid the person's body of a supposed evil spirit that possesses it. In Judaism, psychic healing has been employed in what has been referred to as Jewish Science (Meyer, 1965), a counterpart to Christian Science. In both Jewish and Christian Science, believers feel that a variety of maladies can be treated through prayer to a deity who has power to cure them of their affliction. Strong prayer may induce the person to experience a change in the normal, waking state of consciousness.

Those who seek cures primarily with prayer often report that, during such prayer, they felt removed from their normal, waking state. This distance helped them come closer to their deity, who helped to cure their illness or problem. In all likelihood, major physical illnesses could not be treated successfully with psychic healing alone, although many adherents to such beliefs would disagree with us (Ricalla, 1975). However, a variety of psychosomatic problems can be alleviated, and many individuals find relief from their troubles through the power of prayer and a strong belief in psychic healing as a way to deal with illness and other problems.

The most popularized form of psychic healing is the type we often see on Sunday morning television or at revival meetings at which a religious leader "lays hands" on an afflicted believer and tries to cure him or her of a malady. In a stereotyped example, a physically incapacitated person confined to a wheelchair is brought to a stage, where a preacher lays his hands on the individual's head or sometimes another part of the body. The preacher then begins to pray and asks the invalid to pray along with him. He may then ask whether the person believes in Jesus and believes that Jesus can cure the person's problems. After receiving an affirmative response, the preacher applies some pressure through the laying on of hands as a gesture of transferring psychic healing power from Jesus to the afflicted individual.

While continuing to pray and while experiencing the pressure being applied to his or her body, the believer then is observed to experience either a sense of euphoria or, in many instances, a loss of waking consciousness. If the believer does not faint, he or she appears to at least have experienced some transformation in consciousness from the normal, waking state. The audience may then sometimes observe the afflicted individual beginning to walk after being confined to the wheelchair for many years. Of course, this produces a definite religious high, both for the afflicted person and for those observing this miracle example of psychic healing.

Did psychic healing really occur? Was there a change in consciousness by which healing was achieved? Believers in psychic healing may experience relief from an affliction or, in some instances, a bona fide cure (Whitlock, 1978). However, most who have experienced a psychic cure probably suffered from a psychosomatic illness. Therefore, if they truly believed that Jesus, through the aid of the psychic healer, could help them, it is very possible that they indeed were helped.

What about those who truly believed that Jesus could help them and yet were not cured? Often, they are simply accused of not being true believers. Since Jesus could detect lack of true faith, the cure did not come about. A more realistic suggestion is that their illness was not psychosomatic. Therefore, a psychic cure could not be as effective for them.

Although there are numerous informal reports of psychic healing, there has virtually been no scientific research into this area of parapsychology. This is unfortunate, since there appears to be some promise that this form of healing may be beneficial for some individuals. No doubt, as interest in this area continues, research will be forthcoming.

GENERAL THEORIES
OF PARAPSYCHOLOGY

For science to progress in a particular area of concern, it is essential that theories either exist or can be established to explain the various phenomena considered. In an area such as psi, which has many critics and doubters, this requisite is especially crucial. Some researchers (Moss & Butler, 1978; Scriven, 1976) have argued that there exist no bona fide theories of parapsychology. There is surely an absence of a general, comprehensive theory that is considered scientifically adequate to integrate and explain some psi phenomena; this matter is elaborated upon at length by Rao (1977). Some general, theoretical accounts of psi include those by Walker (1975, 1984), Stanford (1974, 1977a, 1977b), and Schmidt (1975).

Walker

Walker's theory was based on the notion that ESP and PK are products of hidden variables in quantum mechanics. He stated that this is possible because the mathematical formalism of quantum mechanics does not specify exactly what constitutes an observation or measurement of an event. Because of this deficiency, hidden variables are conceived that are essentially inaccessible to physical measurement. These variables function independently of space and time constraints.

Walker believed that hidden variables exist in consciousness as a part of one's "will" and, as a result, may not be directly observable or measurable. The hidden variables could then produce physical changes in the environment that cannot be accounted for by any physical variables. Thus, phenomena such as ESP and PK could take place even though science is unable to determine their physical or biological loci.

The attempt to explain psi as a function of physics, specifically a measurement problem of quantum mechanics, is an interesting avenue in parapsychology. Unfortunately, Walker's theory is not scientifically testable because of the impossibility of locating these hidden variables for manipulation. Also, Walker's assumption that ESP and PK are the result of physical events remains unproven. Furthermore, to argue that something occurs as a result of something "hidden" is like trying to catch a ghost with an invisible net. To look for psi by proposing "hidden variables" is a very poor approach to explaining a supposed scientific relationship.

Stanford

Stanford (1974, 1977a, 1977b) proposed a theory of psi that appears to incorporate and elaborate on the idea of mind projection (Rhine, 1945, 1953). Specifically, in addition to using other sense modalities, the individual also employs psi to scan the environment. In this way, psi may be considered a "sixth sense." In a particular need situation, an individual uses ESP as well as other senses to gather necessary information about the world. When the individual obtains extrasensory information, he or she may use it to satisfy a need or what Stanford calls the *psi-mediated instrumental response* (PMIR). Stanford explained PK as "a response mode for PMIR." Thus, PMIR may be a kind of goal-relevant response that comes about as a result of extrasensory means via PK.

Basically, Stanford proposed that all psi responses are mediated, are instrumental, and serve to satisfy a need. Unfortunately, as with Walker's theory, there is no scientific basis or evidence for his conclusions. If psi functions as Stanford has predicted, it should be possible to test his assumptions with basic instrumental learning techniques, such as shaping and extinction. This is not possible, however, because we do not know what behavior to shape or extinguish. Until Stanford can define this "sixth sense" more operationally and explain how it functions, his theory will not help to advance our knowledge of parapsychology.

Schmidt

Probably the most sophisticated attempt to develop a theory of psi was made by Schmidt (1975). He proposed a mathematical explanation that postulates the existence of "psi sources." These mathematically derived sources, according to Schmidt, act similarly to the behavior exhibited by successful PK subjects. His theory proposes a psi axiom that leads mathematically to the spatial and temporal independence of psi. Also, the different forms of psi, such as PK, precognition, and clairvoyance, appear as logical consequences of one psi axiom.

Although Schmidt's theory sounds very impressive, Schmidt applied mathematics to things we cannot observe. There is nothing intrinsically wrong with doing so, except that mathematical models of behavior often do not have a basis in the real world. To date, Schmidt has not shown such a basis; until he does, his model will remain interesting but not scientifically predictive.

For the time being, it is safe to say that all existing theories of psi have received little or no experimental support. This unfortunate state in the science of parapsychology is undoubtedly one of the major reasons why a large number of scientists, especially psychologists, do not take research in parapsychology very seriously.

General Problems

Alcock (1987) and Moss and Butler (1978) summarized the major problems that haunt parapsychology as an area of study in the psychology of consciousness. These include:

1. Inadequate reporting of test procedures and experimental designs
2. Failure to replicate most parapsychology experiments
3. Absence of psychological, predictive laws and theories of psi
4. Lack of harmony between psi and established physical and biological laws and theories
5. Absence of generally observable (i.e., by most of us) psi phenomena in the real world and, therefore, an absence of practical applications of psi
6. General absence of scientific evidence in the laboratory to establish the existence of psi phenomena
7. Absence of internal consistency (Berkowitz, 1986) essential to convince other scientists that extraneous variables did not influence the outcome of the experiment

In response to these criticisms, Rao (1979) and Rao and Palmer (1987) accused Moss, Butler, and Alcock of bias in reaching their conclusions. They believe that an accumulation of evidence reported in two scientific publications for psi research, the *Journal of Parapsychology* and the *Journal of the American Society for Psychical Research,* basically contradicted each of the points made by these critics. Rao and Palmer went on to say that although the critics' points might be true for a small number of psi experiments, they were no less true for psychology experiments in general. For example, Rao and Palmer stressed that most experimental psychologists do not attempt to replicate their studies (see Bozarth and Roberts, 1972), and, as a result, it is often not known whether they are replicable. Psi experiments, however, are often replicated successfully (Honorton, 1978).

Despite Rao and Palmer's arguments in defense of psi and psi research, there are problems with their defense. For instance, it is simply not true that experimental psychologists do not attempt to replicate their findings. Also, other problems face investigators in the field of parapsychology in addition to those enumerated by the critics (and many of these are still valid, despite Rao and Palmer's defense). There is the problem of the inability of good ESP and PK subjects to replicate their own performance. On one day or trial they exhibit an above-chance performance, while on another day or trial the performance is below chance. This has been dubbed the "decline effect" (Anderson, 1959; Pratt, 1973b; Pratt & Woodruff, 1939; Woodruff & Rhine, 1942). Does this observation indicate that ESP and PK performances are spurious or occur by coincidence? Many believe so (see Tart, 1996). However, those who defend psi findings (e.g., Rao, 1979) believe that it is not possible to set up controls for psi performances, and therefore they are not predictable. Thus, it is not unusual to discover an individual manifesting strong psi abilities on some occasions and reduced or nonexistent abilities on others. As Stanford (1974) has theorized, psi is a sixth sense; sometimes we use it and sometimes we do not.

In the final analysis the study of parapsychology may simply reveal that strange things happen in the laboratory and in the real world that cannot be explained by traditional laws and theories of science. Such investigators as Stanford, Schmidt, Walker, the Rhines, and others have proposed explanations for these happenings. Some believe that these explanations may help us ultimately to understand these occurrences; others believe that such happenings are spurious events that might be attributable to physical, biological, or psychological laws that we have not yet been able to discover. And some (Randi, 1975, 1982) believe that there simply are no real strange happenings that cannot be explained by a magician.

As you can see, a conclusion concerning the validity of psi is not possible. As with many areas of consciousness we have discussed (e.g., hypnosis, meditation, biofeedback), there will always be critics and disbelievers. With regard to parapsychology, most researchers today maintain a fairly healthy skepticism (see Krippner, 1995). While they keep an open mind, they have many doubts about the likelihood of this area becoming an important part of psychological study. Also, the other areas of consciousness have provided us with practical applications, regardless of whether scientists believe the manipulations are totally valid. This has not been the case with parapsychology, and until this happens, the study of psi will remain as controversial as it is now.

FOR FURTHER READING

Edge, H. L., Morris, R. L., Palmer, J., & Rush, J. H. (1986). *Foundations of parapsychology.* London: Routledge & Kegan Paul.

Hansel, C. E. M. (1980). *ESP and parapsychology: A critical evaluation.* Buffalo: Prometheus.

Kane, B., Millay, J., & Brown, D. H. (Eds.). (1993). *Silver threads: 25 years of parapsychology research.* Westport, CT: Praeger.

Kellehear, A. (1996). *Experiences near death: Beyond medicine and religion.* New York: Oxford University Press.

Moody, R. A., Jr. (1988). *The light beyond.* New York: Bantam.

Rhine, J. B., & Brier, R. (Eds.). (1968). *Parapsychology today.* New York: Citadel Press.

Tart, C. T., Puthoff, H. E., & Targ, R. (Eds.). (1979). *Mind at large.* New York: Praeger.

Wolman, B. B. (Ed.). (1977). *Handbook of parapsychology.* New York: Van Nostrand Reinhold.

10

CONCLUSION

Having discussed the psychology of consciousness, we wish to spend a few pages summarizing the status of this field of inquiry. Although much of what you read here will be our own opinions, remember that this area of psychology is timely. This is most exemplified by the presence of a chapter on consciousness in most introductory psychology textbooks. In fact, in many textbooks designed for the first course in psychology, consciousness is given equal treatment along with the most traditional areas of psychology (e.g., perception, social psychology, learning). And we believe that the popularity of the study of consciousness undoubtedly will spread to many other areas of psychology and related behavioral sciences. With this thought in mind we will try to put the study of consciousness in its proper perspective.

As we mentioned in Chapter 1, our approach in this book has been to show that consciousness is a multilevel or multistate phenomenon. One of these levels, obviously, is our normal, unaltered state of awareness. This level is our baseline for comparison with other levels of consciousness that may arise (e.g., levels of sleep) or that may be produced (e.g., drug-altered states). We can all relate easily to the baseline level or state. It is easy to compare our wakeful level of consciousness with that of someone else's. Likewise, another person can relate to your experiences of wakefulness.

However, when consciousness shifts to a different level, communication may break down. Even though we have all experienced the different levels of sleep (discussed in Chapter 7), can one individual compare his or her Stage 3 with another person's? In terms of brain-wave activity, Stage 3 sleep is fairly similar from one individual to another. Unfortunately, this level of consciousness cannot be compared verbally or in a psychological sense because we generally cannot recall our Stage 3 experiences. Hence, this level of consciousness is not capable of being compared in the same sense that our experiences of wakefulness can be compared.

This example may not be as easy to identify with as, perhaps, that of Stage REM, the level of consciousness associated with dream production. Yet how easy is it to compare your Stage REM experiences to those of your friends? Try it. You will find that such comparisons are not easy. First, individuals vary in their ability to recall dreams. Second, all dreams are qualitatively different. Finally, dreams vary within the same individual. What a person dreams at one time may differ considerably from what that person dreams on another occasion.

Even induced levels of consciousness create interesting dilemmas. After meditating, a group of individuals may all share a common experience, such as relaxation. Yet each person may have experienced meditation at a different level (jhana) or may have experienced the same level of consciousness in a different way. One person may have had a tension-relieving experience, while another may have had a so-called religious experience.

The point we are trying to make is that, although consciousness is a phenomenon that can be studied by experience and observation, both in and outside the laboratory, it is necessary for science to come to grips with problems facing this speciality in psychology. These include the development of methods for summarizing the vast individual differences in levels of experience or states of consciousness. Developing adequate procedures for assessing and describing levels of consciousness is also necessary. Finally, it is mandatory that scientifically testable theories be developed for the areas of investigation under what we call consciousness so that experiments can be derived. This has been accomplished to some extent (see Chapter 1), but many of the theories discussed throughout this book are not strong. Some are not based on generalizable data collected in a scientific manner, and others fail to define terms and concepts operationally so as to make the theory scientifically testable. Without strong and empirically testable theories of consciousness this area of study cannot progress to become and remain an important area within psychology and related behavioral sciences.

We realize that all the topics in this book represent controversial areas of study. Yet these areas are what many people believe psychology is all about. This observation can be verified by reading certain popular magazines and weekly tabloids. If most people believe such notions, which are known to be distortions of the total picture, investigators must put to rest these misconceptions through empirical experimentation. In the scientific community, a strong bias still exists that prevents researchers from engaging in such investigations. However, the psychology of consciousness has much to offer, and perhaps the development of strong theories and experiments will break down this bias.

FUTURE APPLICATIONS
OF CONSCIOUSNESS

The future of each area we have discussed will depend on many factors. We would like to indicate what we see happening in these areas.

As we tried to make clear in Chapter 3, consciousness-altering drugs have been used for a variety of beneficial purposes. This was the reason they were originally produced. However, many of these drugs are abused. One would not think that good could come of abused drugs, but in fact this has happened in several instances. The misuse of marijuana has led to two important applications. One has been in the treatment of excessive eye pressure, or glaucoma. An individual who suffered from this condition discovered that after he smoked marijuana, his eye condition improved, as verified by ophthalmologic examination. Reporting this to his ophthalmologist led to several laboratory experiments that verified that marijuana can be beneficial in treating glaucoma (Cohen, 1981; Green, 1979; Helper & Frank, 1971).

Similarly, several cancer patients receiving chemotherapy reported that marijuana reduced their experiences of nausea after such treatment. This discovery has been verified in the laboratory (Borison, McCarthy, & London, 1981; McCarthy & Borison, 1977). Marijuana has also had beneficial effects on symptoms of asthma, epilepsy, depression, and alcoholism (Cohen, 1981). These discoveries might not have been made so quickly had it not been for the drug's misuse by patients suffering from these conditions. Although we by no means advocate the use of marijuana, it is not too speculative to predict that several more discoveries of the beneficial effects of using the substance will be made in the near future. Such discoveries may also be forthcoming for other drugs of abuse that were discussed in Chapter 3.

Regarding future applications of hypnosis (Chapter 4), Wallace (1979) has speculated that this manipulation could be employed to help individuals with poor concentration. For example, students from elementary grades through college who have difficulty studying might be taught to focus their attention on the material they must study and to attenuate distractions that interfere with their task. Similarly, hypnosis could be employed to help athletes concentrate better during sports activities and thereby improve their game. Such applications have received little attention from investigators in the field of the psychology of consciousness.

Other applications of hypnosis will include its continued and expanded use in habit control, especially for controlling smoking, weight, and stress. We would not be surprised to see a proliferation of professional clinics in which individuals could be helped to control a specific habit with the aid of hypnosis.

Law enforcement has also used hypnosis to help solve crimes. Specifically, it has been used to assist witnesses to a crime recall information that is not easy to retrieve. Although use of this application appears to be in the future, it has already come under considerable scrutiny. Loftus (1979, 1980) believes that hypnosis helps people to relax, concentrate, and cooperate with the questions of a hypnotist. Unfortunately, for this reason, she believes that the suggestibility of a witness is so heightened that the person "recalls" events that may never have occurred. There is little doubt that such confabulation takes place. However, in a number of instances, information retrieved by hypnotizing an eyewitness to a crime has helped to solve that crime. And although information retrieved through hypnosis is not allowed as evidence in most courtroom situations, we will probably see an expanded use of hypnosis by law enforcement agencies in the years to come. The information retrieved through such uses will undoubtedly not produce court-admissible evidence, but law enforcement agencies may derive information through hypnosis that will lead to other evidence that is admissible in court.

We envision hypnosis being used increasingly as an analgesic manipulation for helping individuals to overcome experienced pain. This application was discussed in Chapter 4, and we believe it will be used more commonly in future years, especially to control the pain of arthritis, rheumatism, and various forms of cancer (Hilgard & Hilgard, 1983).

We see the use of biofeedback (Chapter 5) expanding greatly in the future. As with hypnosis, we may well see the development and proliferation of biofeedback clinics. There, people can be helped to control tension and migraine headaches, anxiety, hypertension, and other problems that have been shown to be alleviated with biofeedback training (this claim is by no means universal; e.g., Blanchard & Epstein, 1978; Kewman & Roberts, 1979). We also believe that biofeedback will be used more widely for treating such problems as stuttering (Lanyon, Barrington, & Newman, 1976), epilepsy, teeth grinding, muscle spasms, and backaches (Carson, Butcher, & Coleman, 1988). One note of caution: For the potential of biofeedback to be assessed thoroughly as a clinical intervention, more carefully controlled experiments must be undertaken in the next few decades.

As with hypnosis and biofeedback, we see the continuing development of meditation clinics—or "societies," as they often refer to themselves. Perhaps we will see the development of centers, under the auspices of physicians or psychologists, devoted to the use of consciousness-altering techniques as a whole. In such places, hypnosis, biofeedback, meditation, and other interventions will be offered to assist people who have problems that can be alleviated with consciousness-altering techniques. We also envision the continued use of meditation techniques (Chapter 6) to help people control stress and anxiety through relaxation. Like hypnosis, meditation will also be used to help with problems of concentration.

Future years will also produce much research that will help us better to understand sleep and dreams (Chapter 7). We would not be surprised to see great strides in finding nonchemical methods for treating sleep disorders, such as those described in Chapter 7. Several consciousness-altering techniques (e.g., hypnosis and meditation) have already been shown to be helpful in dealing with insomnia. We still do not fully understand the physiological processes underlying sleep and dreams. Perhaps the coming decades will help to shed light on these areas of study as they relate to consciousness.

Future applications of sensory deprivation (Chapter 8, "Experimental Procedures") include its use in a technique called *tank therapy* (Daniel, 1981).

In tank therapy, a person lies down in a tank of water and Epsom salts (similar to that used by Lilly, 1956, 1977), that is heated to 93° F (33.9° C). After a few minutes the person begins to feel weightless from the buoyancy and relaxation that ensue. Some patients of such therapy (which may include traditional talk therapy while in the tank) report beneficial effects in helping them with a variety of psychological problems, including anxiety and habit control (Suedfeld, 1980; Suedfeld & Coren, 1989).

Sensory deprivation will also continue to be explored in the various manned space projects of the United States and Russia. With astronauts and cosmonauts up in space for increasingly longer periods of time, the isolation of space and being in a space suit, shuttle, or other confined environment approximate the conditions described in sensory deprivation environments. Our guess is that sensory deprivation and its effects will become an increasingly important topic for research as countries attempt to explore new worlds in space.

Parapsychology (Chapter 9) is an area of consciousness that will continue to interest laypeople. However, we do not see this area advancing beyond its present state. For advancement to occur, reliable and valid tests of so-called psi phenomena must be established, and empirical theories must be produced. Despite the many years of investigating these phenomena, such tests and theories have not been developed, and we doubt that this situation will change. Therefore, most scientists will continue to hold this topic in low regard and esteem, and the area will remain at the bottom of the scientific ladder. While the University of Edinburgh established (in 1986) an endowed chair in the area of parapsychology (thanks to the generosity of the late author Arthur Koestler), we do not perceive this will necessarily improve the lot or status of the study of psi phenomena.

The psychology of consciousness has much to accomplish in the years to come. Many areas under the rubric of consciousness have much to offer science, and we expect research in these areas to progress and flourish. Other areas will remain low in scientific prestige. It is hoped that the psychology of consciousness, a facet neglected since the advent and growth of behaviorism in the early 1900s, will become a major area of concern and study by psychologists and other behavioral scientists.

REFERENCES

Aarons, L. (1976). Sleep-assisted instruction. *Psychological Bulletin, 83*, 1–40.

Abe, K., Amatomi, M., & Oda, N. (1984). Sleepwalking and recurrent sleeptalking in children of childhood sleepwalkers. *American Journal of Psychiatry, 141*, 800–801.

Abelson, H. I., & Fishburne, P. M. (1976). *Nonmedical use of psychoactive substances.* Princeton, NJ: Response Analysis Corporation.

Abou Nader, T. M., Alexander, C. N., & Davies, J. L. (1990). The Maharishi Technology of the Unified Field and reduction of armed conflict: A comparative longitudinal study of Lebanese villeges. In R. A. Chalmers, G. Clements, H. Schenkluhn, & M. Weinless (Eds.), *Scientific research on the Transcendental Mediation and TM-Sidhi program: Collected papers* (Vol. 4). Vlodrop, Netherlands: Maharishi Vedic University Press.

Abraham, H. D. (1983). Visual phenomenology of the LSD flashback. *Archives of General Psychiatry, 40*, 884–889.

Achmon, J., Granek, M., Golomb, M., & Hart, J. (1989). Behavioral treatment of essential hypertension: A comparison between cognitive therapy and biofeedback of heart rate. *Psychsomatic Medicine, 51*, 152–164.

Adams, H. B., Robertson, M. H., & Cooper, G. D. (1963). Facilitating therapeutic personality changes in psychiatric patients by sensory deprivation methods. Paper read at the International Congress of Psychology, Montreal.

Adams, H. E., Brantley, P. J., & Thompson, K. (1982). Biofeedback and headache: Methodological issues. In L. White and B. Tursk (Eds.), *Clinical biofeedback: Efficacy and mechanisms* (pp. 358–367). New York: Guilford.

Akelaitis, A. J. (1941). Studies on the corpus callosum. II. The higher visual functions in each homonymous field following complete section of the corpus callosum. *Archives of Neurology and Psychiatry, 45*, 789–796.

Akelaitis, A. J. (1944). The study of gnosis, praxis, and language following section of the corpus callosum and the anterior commissure. *Journal of Neurosurgery, 1*, 94–102.

Akerstedt, T., & Torsvall, L. (1985). Napping in shift work. *Sleep, 8*, 105–109.

Akerstedt, T., Torsvall, L., & Froberg, J. (1983). A questionnaire study of sleep/wake disturbances and irregular work hours. *Sleep Research, 12*, 358.

Akerstedt, T., Torsvall, L., & Gillberg, M. (1982). Sleepiness and shift work: Field studies. *Sleep, 5*, 95–106.

Akil, H., Watson, S., Sullivan, S., & Barchas, J. D. (1978). Enkephalin-like material in normal human cerebrospinal fluid: measurement and levels. *Life Science, 23*, 121–126.

Akil, H., Watson, S. J., Young, E., Lewis, M. E., Khachaturian, H., & Walker, J. M. (1984). Endogenous opioids: Biology and function. *Annual Review of Neuroscience, 7*, 223–235.

Alcock, J. E. (1987). Parapsychology: Science of the anomalous or search for the soul? *Behavioral and Brain Sciences, 10*, 553–643.

Aloe, L., Collings, B., Wauqwer, A., McGrady, A., & Gerard, G. (1994). Effect of biofeedback-assisted relaxation on migraine headaches and changes in cerebral blood flow velocity. Paper presented at the 25th annual meeting of the Association for Applied Psychophysiology and Biofeedback, Atlanta.

Alvarado, C. S. (1984). Phenomenological aspects of out-of-body experiences: A report of three studies. *Journal of the American Society for Psychical Research, 78*, 219–240.

Alvarado, C. S. (1992). The psychological approach to out-of-body experiences: A review of early and modern developments. *Journal of Psychology, 126*, 237–250.

American Society for Pharmacology and Experimental Therapeutics and Committee on Problems of Drug Dependence. (1987). Scientific perspectives on cocaine abuse. *The Pharmacologist, 29*, 20–27.

Anand, B. K., Chhina, G. S., & Singh, B. (1961a). Some aspects of electroencephalographic studies in yogis. *Electroencephalography and Clinical Neurophysiology, 13*, 452–456.

Anand, B. K., Chhina, G. S., & Singh, B. (1961b). Studies on Shri Ramanand Yogi during his stay in an air-tight box. *Indian Journal of Medical Research, 49*, 82–89.

Anders, T. F., Carskado, M. A., & Dement, W. C. (1980). Sleep and sleepiness in children and adolescents. *Pediatric Clinics of North America, 27*, 29–43.

Andersen, M. S. (1985). Hypnotizability as a factor in the hypnotic treatment of obesity. *International Journal of Clinical and Experimental Hypnosis, 33*, 150–159.

Anderson, M. (1959). A precognition experiment comparing time intervals of a few days and one year. *Journal of Parapsychology, 23*, 81–89.

Andreychuck, T., & Skriver, C. (1975). Hypnosis and biofeedback in the treatment of migraine headaches. *International Journal of Clinical and Experimental Hypnosis, 23*, 172–183.

Antrobus, J. S., Fein, G., Jordan, L., Ellman, S. J., & Arkin, A. M. (1978). Measurement and design in research on sleep reports. In A. M. Arkin, J. S. Antrobus, & S. J. Ellman (Eds.), *The mind in sleep: Psychology and psychophysiology.* Hillsdale, NJ: Erlbaum.

Appenzeller, O. (1973). Getting a sore head from banging it on the wall. *Headache, 13*, 131–132.

Arkin, A. M. (1991). Sleeptalking. In S. A. Ellman & J. S. Antrobus (Eds.), *The mind in sleep: Psychology and psychophysiology* (2nd ed., pp. 415–436). New York: Wiley.

Arkin, A. M., & Antrobus, J. S. (1978). The effects of external stimuli applied to and during sleep on sleep experience. In A. M. Arkin, J. S. Antrobus, & S. J. Ellman (Eds.), *The mind in sleep: Psychology and psychophysiology.* Hillsdale, NJ: Erlbaum.

Armitage, R., Hoffman, R., Loewy, D., & Moffitt, A. (1989). Variations in period-analysed EEG asymmetry in REM and NREM sleep. *Psychophysiology, 26*, 329–336.

Ascher, L. M., Barber, T. X., & Spanos, N. P. (1972). Two attempts to replicate the Parrish-Lundy-Leibowitz experiment on hypnotic age regression. *American Journal of Clinical Hypnosis, 14*, 178–185.

Aserinsky, E., & Kleitman, N. (1953). Regularly occurring periods of eye motility and concomitant phenomena during sleep. *Science, 118*, 273–274.

Ashley, R. (1976). *Cocaine: Its history, uses, and effects.* New York: Warner Books.

Audette, J. R. (1979). Denver cardiologist discloses findings after 18 years of near-death research. *Anabiosis, 1*, 1–2.

Aylesworth, T. G. (1975). *ESP.* New York: Watts.

Baars, B. J. (1983). Conscious contents provide the nervous system with coherent, global information. *Consciousness and Self-Regulation, 3*, 45–76.

Baars, B. J. (1988). *A cognitive theory of consciousness.* Cambridge, UK: Cambridge University Press.

Baars, B. J. (1997). *Consciousness regained: The new science of human experience.* Oxford, UK: Oxford University Press.

Bachman, J. G., Johnston, L. D., & O'Malley, P. M. (1990). Explaining the recent decline in cocaine use among young adults: Further evidence that perceived risks and disapproval lead to reduced drug use. *Journal of Health and Social Behavior, 31*, 173–184.

Bachman, J. G., Johnston, L. D., O'Malley, P. M., & Humphrey, R. H. (1988). Explaining the recent decline in marijuana use: Differentiating the effects of perceived risks, disapproval, and general lifestyle factors. *Journal of Health and Social Behavior, 29*, 92–112.

Bakan, P. (1969). Hypnotizability, laterality of eye movements, and functional brain asymmetry. *Perceptual and Motor Skills, 28*, 927–932.

Baker, E. L., & Nash, M. R. (1987). Applications of hypnosis in the treatment of anorexia nervosa. *American Journal of Clinical Hypnosis, 29*, 185–193.

Banks, W. P. (1993). Problems in the scientific pursuit of consciousness. *Consciousness & Cognition, 2*, 255–263.

Barabasz, A. F., Baer, L., Sheehan, D. V., & Barabasz, M. (1986). A three-year follow-up of hypnosis and restricted environmental stimulation therapy for smoking. *International Journal of Clinical and Experimental Hypnosis, 34*, 169–181.

Barabasz, A. F., & Barabasz, M. (1989). Effects of restricted environmental stimulation: Enhancement of hypnotizability for experimental and chronic pain control. *International Journal of Clinical and Experimental Hypnosis, 36*, 217–231.

Barber, J., & Adrian, C. (1982). *Psychological approaches to the management of pain.* New York: Brunner-Mazel.

Barber, T. X. (1962). Hypnotic age regression: A critical review. *Psychosomatic Medicine, 24*, 286–299.

Barber, T. X. (1969). *Hypnosis: A scientific approach.* Princton, NJ: Van Nostrand.

Barber, T. X. (1970). *LSD, marihuana, yoga, and hypnosis.* Chicago: Aldine.

Barber, T. X., & Glass, L. B. (1962). Significant factors in hypnotic behavior. *Journal of Abnormal and Social Psychology, 64*, 222–228.

Barber, T. X., Spanos, N. P., & Chaves, J. F. (1974). *Hypnotism, imagination, and human potentialities.* New York: Pergamon.

Barkley, R. A., Hastings, J. E., & Jackson, T. L., Jr. (1977). The effects of rapid smoking and hypnosis in the treatment of smoking behavior. *Journal of Clinical and Experimental Hypnosis, 25*, 7–17.

Barron, F., Jarvik, M. E., & Bunnell, S. (1964). The hallucinogenic drugs. *Scientific American, 210*, 29–37.

Bartley, S. H., & Chute, E. (1947). *Fatigue and impairment in man.* New York: McGraw-Hill.

Baruss, I. (1987). Metanalysis of definitions of consciousness. *Imagination, Cognition and Personality, 6*, 321–329.

Beahrs, J. O. (1988). Hypnosis can not be fully nor reliably excluded from the court-room. *American Journal of Clinical Hypnosis, 31*, 18–27.

Bear, M. F., Conners, B. W., & Paradiso, M. A. (1996). *Neuroscience: Exploring the brain.* Baltimore: Williams & Wilkins.

Beatty, J. (1982). Biofeedback in the treatment of migraine: Simple relaxation or specific effects? In L. White and B. Tursky (Eds.), *Clinical biofeedback: Efficacy and mechanisms* (pp. 211–221). New York: Guilford.

Beaty, T., & Haynes, S. (1979). Behavioral intervention with muscle-contraction headache: A review. *Psychosomatic Medicine, 41*, 165–180.

Belick, L., Elfner, L., & May, J. (1982). Biofeedback treatment of dysmenorrhea. *Biofeedback and Self-Regulation, 7*, 499–520.

Beloff, J. (1968). ESP: Proof from Prague? *New Scientist, 40*, 76–77.

Benson, H., & Friedman, R. (1985). A rebuttal to the conclusions of David S. Holmes's article: "Meditation and somatic arousal reduction." *American Psychologist, 40*, 725–728.

Benson, H., Rosner, B. A., & Marzetta, B. R. !1973). Decreased blood pressure in hypertensive subjects who practiced meditation. *Journal of Clinical Investigation, 52*, 8a–11a.

Benson, H., & Wallace, R. K. (1972). Decreased drug abuse with transcendental meditation: A study of 1862 subjects. In C. Zarafonetis (Ed.), *Drug abuse: Proceedings of the International Conference* (pp. 239–252). Philadelphia: Lea and Febiger.

Benson, K., & Feinberg, I. (1977). Beneficial effect of sleep in an extended Jenkins and Dallenbach paradigm. *Psychophysiology, 14*, 375–384.

Berkowitz, L. (1986). *A survey of social psychology* (3rd ed.). New York: Holt, Rinehart & Winston.

Best, J. A., & Suedfeld, P. (1982). Restricted environmental stimulation therapy and behavioral self-management in smoking cessation. *Journal of Applied Social Psychology, 12*, 408–419.

Bexton, W. H., Heron, W., & Scott, T. H. (1954). Effects of decreased variation in the sensory environment. *Canadian Journal of Psychology, 8*, 70–76.

Birk, L., Crider, A., Shapiro, D., & Tursky, B. (1966). Operant electrodermal conditioning under partial curarization. *Journal of Comparative and Physiological Psychology, 62*, 165–166.

Black, A. H. (1966). The operant conditioning of heart rate in curarized dogs: Some problems of interpretation. Paper presented at the meetings of the Psychonomic Society, St. Louis.

Blacker, K. H., Jones, R. T., Stone, G. C., & Pfefferbaum, D. (1968). Chronic users of LSD: The acidheads. *American Journal of Psychiatry, 125*, 97–107.

Blackmore, S. J. (1980). The extent of selective reporting of ESP ganzfeld studies. *European Journal of Parapsychology, 3*, 213–219.

Blackmore, S. J. (1982). Out-of-body experiences, lucid dreams, and imagery: Two surveys. *Journal of the American Society for Psychical Research, 76*, 301–317.

Blackwell, B., Hanenson, I. B., Bloomfield, S. S., Magenheim, N. G., Nidich, S. I., & Gartside, P. (1975). Effects of transcendental meditation on blood pressure: a controlled pilot experiment. *Psychosomatic Medicine, 37*, 86.

Blanchard, E. B., Ahles, T., & Shaw, E. (1979). Behavioral treatment of headaches. In M. Hersen, R. Eisler, and P. Miller (eds.), *Progress in behavior modification*. New York: Academic Press.

Blanchard, E. B., Andrasick, F., Evans, D. D., Neff, D. F., & Appelbaum, K. A. (1985). Individual predictors of self-regulating treatment outcome in tension headache. Paper presented at the annual meeting of the Biofeedback Society of America, New Orleans.

Blanchard, E. B., & Epstein, L. H. (1978). *A biofeedback primer.* Reading, MA: Addison-Wesley.

Bloch, V., Hennevin, E., & Leconte, P. (1979). Relationship between paradoxical sleep and memory processes. In M. A. B. Brazier (Ed.), *Brain mechanisms in memory and learning: From the single neuron to man* (pp. 329–343). New York: Raven.

Block, R. I., Farinpour, R., & Braverman, K. (1992). Acute effects of marijuana on cognition: Relationships to chronic effects and smoking techniques. *Pharmacology Bulletin, 43,* 907–917.

Block, R. I., & Ghoneim, M. M. (1993). Effects of chronic marijuana use on human cognition. *Psychopharmacology, 110,* 219–228.

Blum, G. S., & Porter, M. L. (1974). Effects of the restriction of conscious awareness in a reaction-time task. *International Journal of Clinical and Experimental Hypnosis, 22,* 335–345.

Boller, J., & Flam, B. (1979). Treatment of the common migraine: Systematic application of biofeedback and autogenic training. *American Journal of Clinical Biofeedback, 2,* 63–64.

Bonnet, M. H., & Moore, S. E. (1982). The threshold of sleep: Perception of sleep as a function of time asleep and auditory threshold. *Sleep, 5,* 267–276.

Borgeat, F., Hade, B., Larouche, L., & Bedwant, C. (1980). Effect of therapist's active presence on EMG biofeedback training of headache patients. *Biofeedback and Self-Regulation, 5,* 275–282.

Borgeat, F., Hade, B., Larouche, L., & Gauthier, B. (1984). Psychophysiological effects of therapist's active presence during biofeedback as a simple psychotherapeutic situation. *Psychiatric Journal of the University of Ottawa, 9,* 132–137.

Boring, E. G. (1929). *A history of experimental psychology.* New York: Appleton-Century-Crofts.

Borison, H. L., McCarthy, L. E., & London, S. W. (1981). Cannabinoids and emesis. *New England Journal of Medicine, 298,* 1480–1481.

Borkovec, T. D., Lane, T. W., & VanDot, P. H. (1981). Phenomenology of sleep among insomniacs and good sleepers: Wakefulness experience when cortically asleep. *Journal of Abnormal Psychology, 90,* 607–609.

Bosinelli, M. (1995). Mind and consciousness during sleep. Special Issue: The function of sleep. *Behavioural Brain Research, 69,* 195–201.

Boudreau, L. (1972). Transcendental meditation and yoga as reciprocal inhibitors. *Journal of Behavior Therapy and Experimental Psychiatry, 3,* 97–98.

Bowers, K. S. (1976). *Hypnosis for the seriously curious.* New York: Norton.

Bozarth, J. D., & Roberts, R. R. (1972). Signifying significant significance. *American Psychologist, 27,* 774–775.

Braud, W., and Schlitz, M. (1983). Psychokinetic influence on electrodermal activity. *Journal of Parapsychology, 47,* 95–120.

Brecher, E. M., & the Editors of Consumer Reports. (1972). *Licit and illicit drugs.* Mount Vernon, NY: Consumers Union.

Bremer, F. (1937). L'activite cerebrale au cours du sommeil et de la narcose: Contribution a l'etude du mecanisme du sommeil. *Bulletin de l'Academie Royale de Belgique, 4,* 68–86.

Broughton, R. (1984). Quoted in "Is sleep a waste of time?" *Science Digest, 92,* 4.

Browman, C. P., & Mitler, M. M. (1988). Hypersomnia and the perception of sleep-wake states: Some preliminary findings. *Perceptual and Motor Skills, 66,* 463–470.

Brown, B. B. (1970). Recognition of aspects of consciousness through association with EEG alpha activity represented by a light signal. *Psychophysiology, 6,* 442–452.

Brown, H. (1971). Some anticholinergic-like behavioral effects of trans(-)-delta^8 tetrahydocannabinol. *Psychopharmacologia, 21,* 294–301.

Brown, H. (1972). Possible anticholinesterase-like effects of trans(-)-delta^8 and -delta^9 tetrahydrocannabinol as observed in the general motor activity of mice. *Psychopharacologia, 27,* 111–116.

Brownfield, C. A. (1965). *Isolation: Clinical and experimental approaches.* New York: Random House.

Bruner, J. (1965). *On knowing: Essays for the left hand.* New York: Atheneum.

Brunner, D. P., Kijk, D. J., Tobler, I., & Borbely, A. A. (1990). Effect of partial sleep stages and EEG power spectra: Evidence for non-REM and REM sleep homeostasis. *Electroencephalography and Clinical Neurophysiology, 75,* 492–499.

Budzynski, T. H. (1978). Biofeedback strategies in headache treatment. In J. V. Basmjian (Ed.), *Biofeedback: Principles and practice for clinicians* (pp. 132–152). Baltimore: Williams and Wilkins.

Budzynski, T. H. (1979). Biofeedback and the twilight states of consciousness. In D. Goleman and R. J. Davidson (Eds.), *Consciousness: Brain states of awareness and mysticism.* New York: Harper and Row.

Budzynski, T. H., Stoyva, J. M., & Adler, C. (1970). Feedback-induced muscle relaxation: Application to tension headache. *Journal of Behavioral Therapy and Experimental Psychiatry, 1,* 205–211.

Budzynski, T. H., Stoyva, J. M., Adler, C., & Mullaney, B. J. (1973). EMG biofeedback and tension headache: A controlled outcome study. *Psychosomatic Medicine, 35,* 484–496.

Burns, P. A., Clesse-Desotelle, P.M., Nochajski, T., & Pranikoff, K. (1990). Biofeedback procedure for stress urinary incontinence. *Clinical Gerontologist, 10,* 51–54.

Byrd, R. E. (1938). *Alone.* New York: Putnam.

Campbell, K. A., Foster, T. C., Hampson, R. E., & Deadwyler, S. A. (1986). Effects of delta-9-tetrahydrocannabinol on sensory-evoked discharges of granule cells in the dentate gyrus of behaving rats. *Journal of Pharmacology and Experimental Therapeutics, 239,* 941–945.

Carlson, N. R. (1998). *Physiology and behavior* (6th ed.). Boston: Allyn and Bacon.

Carpenter, K. A. (1988). The effects of positive and negative pre-sleep stimuli on dream experiences. *Journal of Psychology, 122,* 33–37.

Carrington, P. (1977). *Freedom in meditation.* New York: Doubleday.

Carrington, P. (1978). The uses of meditation in psychotherapy. In A. A. Sugarman & R. E. Tarter (Eds.), *Expanding dimensions of consciousness.* New York: Springer.

Carson, R. C., Butcher, J. N., & Coleman, J. C. (1988). *Abnormal psychology and modern life* (8th ed.). Glenview, IL: Scott Foresman.

Carter, J. L., & Russell, H. L. (1985). Use of EMG biofeedback procedures with learning disabled children in a clinical and an educational setting. *Journal of Learning Disabilities, 18,* 213–216.

Cartwright, R. D. (1977). *Nightlife: Explorations in dreaming.* Englewood Cliffs, NJ: Prentice-Hall.

Casler, L. (1962). The improvement of clairvoyance scores by means of hypnotic suggestion. *Journal of Parapsychology, 26,* 77–87.

Casler, L. (1967). Self-generated hypnotic suggestions and clairvoyance. *International Journal of Parapsychology, 9,* 125–128.

Cavallero, C., & Natale, V. (1988). Was I dreaming or did it really happen? A comparison between real and artificial dream reports. *Imagination, Cognition and Personality, 8,* 19–24.

Chagas, C. (1959). Studies on the mechanisms of curarization. *Annals of New York Academy of Sciences, 81,* 345–357.

Chalsma, A. L., & Boyum, D. (1994). *Marijuana situation assessment.* Washington, DC: Office of National Drug Control Policy.

Chase, M. H., & Morales, F. R. (1983). Subthreshold excitatory activity and motoneuron discharage during REM periods of active sleep. *Science, 221,* 1195–1198.

Chien, I., Gerard, D. L., Lee, R. S., & Rosenfeld, E. (1964). *The road to H: Narcotics, delinquency, and social policy.* New York: Basic Books.

Chin, J. H., & Goldstein, D. B. (1977). Drug tolerance in biomembranes: A spin label study of the effects of ethanol. *Science, 196,* 684–685.

Christie, M. J., & Todd, J. L. (1975). Experimenter-subject-situational interactions. In P. H. Venables & M. J. Christie (Eds.), *Research in Psychophysiology.* London: Wiley.

Cicero, T. J. (1978). Tolerance to and physical dependence on alcohol: Behavioral and neurobiological mechanisms. In M. A. Lipton, A. DiMascio, & K. F. Killman (Eds.), *Pharmacology,* New York: Raven.

Clemes, S. R., & Dement, W. C. (1967). Effects of REM sleep deprivation on psychological functioning. *Journal of Nervous and Mental Disease, 144,* 488–491.

Coe, W. C. (1978). The credibility of posthypnotic amnesia: A contextualist's view. *International Journal of Clinical and Experimental Hypnosis, 26,* 218–245.

Coe, W. C., & Sarbin, T. R. (1977). Hypnosis from the standpoint of a contextualist. In W. E. Edmonston (Ed.), *Conceptual and investigative approaches to hypnosis and hypnosic phenomena. Annals of the New York Academy of Science, 296,* 2–13.

Cohen, D. (1979). Remembering and forgetting dreaming. In J. F. Kihlstrom & F. J. Evans (Eds.), *Functional disorders of memory.* Hillsdale, NJ: Erlbaum.

Cohen, S. (1971). Statement before the Subcommittee to Investigate Juvenile Delinquency of the U.S. Senate Committee on the Judiciary on Drug Abuse, December 15.

Cohen, S. (1981). *The substance abuse problems.* New York: Haworth.

Coleman, R. M., Miles, L. E., Guillemineult, C. C., Zarcone, V. P., Jr., Vanden Hoed, J., & Dement, W. C. (1981). Sleep-wake disorders in the elderly: A polysomnographic analysis. *Journal of the American Geriatrics Society, 29,* 289–296.

Coleman, R. M., Roffwag, H. P., Kennedy, S. J., Guillemineult, C. C., Cinque, J., Cohn, M. A., Karacan, I., Kupfer, D. J., Lemmi, H., Miles, L. E., Orr, D., & Dement, W. C. (1982). Sleep-wake disorders based on a polysomnographic diagnosis. *Journal of the American Medical Association, 247,* 997–1003.

Conn, J. H., and Conn, R. N. (1967). Discussion of T. X. Barber's 'Hypnosis as a causal variable in present-day psychology': A critical analysis. *International Journal of Clinical and Experimental Hypnosis, 16,* 106–110.

Corcoran, D. K. (1988). Helping patients who've had near-death experiences. *Nursing 88, 18,* 34–39.

Cornish, P. J., Blanchard, E. B., & Wittrock, D. (1989). Relation of subjective experiences to clinical outcome in the thermal biofeedback treatment of essential hypertension. Paper presented at the meetings of the Association of Applied Psychophysiology and Biofeedback, San Diego.

Costin, F., & Draguns, J. G. (1989). *Abnormal psychology: Patterns, issues, interventions.* New York: Wiley.

Cowen, R. (1990, April 14). Cocaine and the nervous system. *Science News, 56,* 449–456.

Craig, A. R., & Cleary, P. J. (1982). Reduction of stuttering by young male stutterers using EMG feedback. *Biofeedback and Self-Regulation, 7,* 241–255.

Craske, M. G., & Barlow, D. H. (1989). Nocturnal panic. *Journal of Nervous and Mental Disease, 177,* 160–167.

Crawford, H. J. (1981). Hypnotic susceptibility as related to gestalt closure tasks. *Journal of Personality and Social Psychology, 40,* 376–383.

Crawford, H. J. (1982). Hypnotizability, daydreaming style, imagery vividness, and absorption: A multidimensional study. *Journal of Personality and Social Psychology, 42,* 915–926.

Crawford, H. J. (1983). Enhanced visual memory during hypnosis as mediated by hypnotic responsiveness and cognitive strategies. *Journal of Experimental Psychology: General, 112,* 662–685.

Crawford, H. J. (1996). Cerebral brain dynamics of mental imagery: Evidence and issues for hypnosis. In R. G. Kunzendorf, N. P. Spanos, & B. Wallace (Eds.), *Hypnosis and imagination* (pp. 253–282). Amityville, NY: Baywood.

Crawford, H. J., Brown, A. M., & Moon, C. E. (1993). Sustained attentional and disattentional abilities: Differences between low and highly hypnotizable persons. *Journal of Abnormal Psychology, 102,* 534–543.

Crawford, H. J., Crawford, K., & Koperski, B. J. (1983). Hypnosis and lateral cerebral function as assessed by dichotic listening. *Biological Psychiatry, 18,* 415–427.

Crawford, H. J., Gur, R. C., Skolnick, B., Gur, R. E., and Benson, D. M. (1993). Effects of hypnosis on regional cerebral blood flow during ischemic pain with and without suggested hypnotic analgesia. *International Journal of Psychophysiology, 15,* 181–195.

Crawford, H. J., Macdonald, H., and Hilgard, E. R. (1979). Hypnotic deafness: A psychophysiological study of responses to tone intensity as modified by hypnosis. *American Journal of Psychology, 92,* 193–214.

Crawford, H. J., Wallace, B., Nomura, K., and Slater, H. (1986). Eidetic-like imagery in hypnosis: Rare but there. *American Journal of Psychology, 99,* 527–546.

Crick, F., and Mitchison, G. (1983). The function of dream sleep. *Nature, 304,* 111–114.

Crider, A., Schwartz, G. E., and Shnidman, S. R. (1969). On the criteria for instrumental autonomic conditioning: A reply to Katkin and Murray. *Psychological Bulletin, 71,* 455–461.

Critchlow, B. (1986). The powers of John Barleycorn: Beliefs about the effects of alcohol on social behavior. *American Psychologist, 41,* 751–763.

Crookall, R. (1966). *The study and practice of astral projection.* Secaucus, NJ: University Books.

Cunningham, K. A., & Appel, J. B. (1987). Neuropharmacological reassessment of the discriminative stimulus properties of d-lysergic acid diethylamide (LSD). *Psychopharmacology, 91,* 67–73.

Cutter, H. S. G., O'Farrell, T. J., Whitehouse, J., & Dentch, G. M. (1986). Pain changes among men from before to after drinking: Effects of expectancy set and dose manipulations with alcohol and tonic as mediated by prior experience with alcohol. *International Journal of the Addictions, 21,* 937–945.

Dackis, C. A., & Gold, M. S. (1985). New concepts in cocaine addiction: The dopamine depletion hypothesis. *Neuroscience and Biobehavioral Reviews, 9,* 469–477.

Dahl, J., & Melin, L. (1989). The psychological treatment of epilepsy: A behavioral approach. Paper presented at the meetings of the Association of Applied Psychophysiology and Biofeedback, San Diego.

Dale, H. H. (1938). Acetylcholine as a chemical transmitter substance of the effects of nerve impulses. The William Henry Welch Lectures, 1937. *Journal of Mount Sinai Hospital, 4*, 401–429.

Daniel, A. (1981, January 12). Off the couch and into the tub. *Time*, p. 45.

Davenport-Slack, B. (1975). A comparative evaluation of obstetrical hypnosis and antenatal childbirth training. *International Journal of Clinical and Experimental Hypnosis, 23*, 266–281.

Davies, J. L., & Alexander, C. N. (1989). Alleviating political violence through reduction of collective stress: Impact assessment analysis of the Lebanon war. Paper presented at the annual meeting of the American Political Science Association, Atlanta.

Davis, S. M., & Drichta, C. E. (1980). Biofeedback theory and application in allied health speech pathology. *Biofeedback and Self-Regulation, 5*, 159–174.

Dean, W. F. (1954). *General Dean's story.* New York: Viking Press.

Deepak, K. K., Manchanda, S. K., & Maheshwari, M. C. (1994). Meditation improves clinicoelectroencephalographic measures in drug-resistant epileptics. *Biofeedback & Self-Regulation, 19*, 25–40.

Deikman, A. J. (1966). Deautomatization and the mystic experience. *Psychiatry, 29*, 324–338.

Deikman, A. J. (1971). Bimodal consciousness. *Archives of General Psychiatry, 45*, 481–489.

De Koninck, J., Gagnon, P., & Lallier, S. (1983). Sleep positions in the young adult and their relationship with the subjective quality of sleep. *Sleep, 6*, 52–59.

Delmonte, M. M. (1984). Physiological responses during meditation and rest. *Biofeedback and Self-Regulation, 9*, 181–200.

Dement, W. C. (1960). The effect of dream deprivation. *Science, 131*, 1705–1707.

Dement, W. C. (1972). *Some must watch while some must sleep.* San Francisco: Freeman.

Dement, W. C., & Baird, W. P. (1977). *Narcolepsy: Care and treatment.* Stanford, CA: American Narcolepsy Association.

Dement, W. C., & Greenberg, S. (1966). Changes in total amount of stage four sleep as a function of partial sleep deprivation. *Electroencephalography and Clinical Neurophysiology, 20*, 523–526.

Dement, W. C., Greenberg, S., & Klein, R. (1966). The effect of partial REM sleep deprivation and delayed recovery. *Journal of Psychiatric Research, 4*, 141–152.

Dement, W. C., Holman, R. B., & Guilleminault, C. (1976). Neurochemical and neuropharmacological foundations of the sleep disorders. *Psychopharmacology Communications, 2*, 77–90.

Dement, W. C., & Kleitman, N. (1957). Cyclic variations in EEG during sleep and their relation to eye movement, body motility, and dreaming. *Electroencephalography and Clinical Neurophysiology, 9*, 673–690.

Dengrove, E. (1976). *Hypnosis and behavior therapy.* Springfield, IL: Charles C. Thomas.

Denkowski, K. M., Denkowski, G. C., & Omizo, M. M. (1984). Predictors of success in the EMG biofeedback training of hyperactive male children. *Biofeedback and Self-Regulation, 9*, 253–264.

Denton, K., & Krebs, D. (1990). From the scene to the crime: The effect of alcohol and social context on moral judgment. *Journal of Personality and Social Psychology, 59*, 242–248.

DePascalis, V., Silveri, A., & Palumbo, G. (1988). EEG asymmetry during covert mental activity and its relationship with hypnotizability. *International Journal of Clinical and Experimental Hypnosis, 36,* 38–52.

Deutsch, M., Canavan, D., & Rubin, J. (1971). Effects of size of conflict and sex of experimenter upon interpersonal bargaining. *Journal of Experimental Social Psychology, 7,* 258–267.

Devane, W. A., Hanus, L., Brauer, A., Pertwee, R. G., Stevenson, L. A., Griffin, G., Gibson, D., Mandelbaum, A., Etinger, A., & Mechoulam, R. (1992). Isolation and structure of a brain constituent that binds to the cannabinoid receptor. *Science, 258,* 1946–1949.

Dewan, E. D. (1967). Occipital alpha rhythm, eye position, and lens accommodation. *Nature, 214,* 975–977.

Dhanens, T. P., and Lundy, R. M. (1975). Hypnotic and waking suggestions and recall. *International Journal of Clinical and Experimental Hypnosis, 23,* 68–79.

Diamond, M. J. (1974). Modification of hypnotizability: a review. *Psychological Bulletin, 81,* 180–198.

Diamond, M. J. (1977). Hypnotizability is modifiable: an alternative approach. *International Journal of Clinical and Experimental Hypnosis, 25,* 147–166.

Diamond, S., Diamond-Falk, J., and Deveno, T. (1978). Biofeedback in the treatment of vascular headache. *Biofeedback and Self-Regulation, 3,* 385–408.

DiCara, L., & Miller, N. E. (1968). Instrumental learning of vasomotor responses by rats: Learning to respond differentially in the two ears. *Science, 159,* 1485–1486.

Dienstfrey, H. (1991). Neal Miller, the dumb autonomic nervous system, and biofeedback. *Advances, 7,* 33–44.

Dillbeck, M. C., Assimakis, P. D., Raimondi, D., Orme-Johnson, D. W., & Rowe, R. (1986). Longitudinal effects of the Transcendental Meditation and TM-Sidhi program on cognitive ability and cognitive style. *Perceptual and Motor Skills, 62,* 731–738.

Dillbeck, M. C., Cavanaugh, K. L., Glenn, T., Orme-Johnson, D. W., & Mittlefehldt, V. (1987). Consciousness as a field: The Transcendental Meditation and TM-Sidhi program and changes in social indicators. *Journal of Mind and Behavior, 8,* 67–104.

Dillbeck, M. C., & Orme-Johnson, D. (1987). Physiological differences between transcendental meditation and rest. *American Psychologist, 42,* 879–881.

Dixit, S. P., Agrawal, A., & Dubey, G. P. (1994). Management of essential hypertension by using biofeedback technique. *Pharmacopsychoecologia, 71,* 17–19.

Doane, B. K., Mahatoo, W., Heron, W., & Scott, T. H. (1959). Changes in perceptual function after isolation. *Canadian Journal of Psychology, 13,* 210–219.

Doyle, A. C. (1938). The Sign of the Four. In *The Complete Sherlock Holmes.* New York: Garden City Publishing.

Drury, R., DeRisi, W., & Liberman, R. (1979). Temperature biofeedback treatment for migraine headache: A controlled multiple baseline study. *Headache, 19,* 278–284.

Dusek, D., & Girdano, D. A. (1980). *Drugs: A factual account.* Reading, MA: Addison-Wesley.

Duvall, H., Locke, B., &Brill, L. (1963). Follow-up study of narcotic drug addicts five years after hospitalization. *Public Health Service Reports, 78,* 185–193.

Dworetzky, J. P. (1997). *Psychology* (6th ed.). Pacific Grove, CA: Brooks Cole.

Dywan, J., & Bowers, K. S. (1983). The use of hypnosis to enhance recall. *Science, 222,* 184–185.

Earle, J. (1981). Cerebral laterality and meditation: A review of the literature. *Journal of Transpersonal Psychology, 13,* 155–173.

Eccles, J. C. (1977). *The understanding brain.* New York: McGraw-Hill.

Edmonston, W. E., Jr. (1986). *The induction of hypnosis.* New York: Wiley.

Edwards, A. S. (1941). Effects of the loss of one hundred hours of sleep. *American Journal of Psychology, 54,* 80–91.

Ehrlichman, H., & Weinberger, A. (1979). Lateral eye movements and hemispheric asymmetry: A critical review. *Psychological Bulletin, 85,* 1080–1101.

Eiseman, B., Lam, R., & Rush, B. (1964). Surgery on the narcotic addict. *Annals of Surgery, 159,* 748–757.

Eisinger, R. A. (1972). Psychosocial predictors of smoking behavior change. *Social Sciences and Medicine, 6,* 137–144.

Eliseo, T. S. (1974). The Hypnotic Induction Profile and hypnotic susceptibility. *International Journal of Clinical and Experimental Hypnosis, 22,* 320–326.

Ellinwood, E. H. (1969). Amphetamine psychosis: a multi-dimensional process. *Seminars in Psychiatry, 6,* 208–226.

Ellinwood, E. H., Kilbey, M. M., Castellani, S., & Khoury, C. (1977). Amygdala hyperspindling and seizures induced by cocaine. In E. H. Ellinwood & M. M. Kilbey (Eds.), *Cocaine and other stimulants.* New York: Plenum.

Emmons, W. H., & Simon, C. W. (1956). The non-recall of material presented during sleep. *American Journal of Psychology, 69,* 79–81.

Engel, J. M., & Rapoff, M. A. (1990). Biofeedback-assisted relaxation training for adult and pediatric headache disorders. *Occupational Therapy Journal of Research, 10,* 283–299.

Engle-Friedman, M., Baker, E. A., and Bootzin, R. R. (1985). Reports of wakefulness during EEG identified stages of sleep. *Sleep Research, 14,* 152.

Erickson, M. H. (1973). Psychotherapy achieved by a reversal of the neurotic processes in a case of ejaculatio precox. *American Journal of Clinical Hypnosis, 15,* 217–222.

Espie, C. A., Lindsay, W. R., Brooks, D. N., & Hood, E. M. (1989). A controlled comparative investigation of psychological treatments for chronic sleep-onset insomnia. *Behavior Research and Therapy, 27,* 79–88.

Evans, C., & Evans, P. (Eds.). (1983). Landscapes of the night. New York: Viking.

Evans, F., Cook, M., Cohen, H., Orne, E., & Orne, M. (1977). Appetitive and replacement naps: EEG and behavior. *Science, 197,* 687–689.

Evans, F. J. (1979a). Hypnosis and sleep: Techniques for exploring cognitive activity during sleep. In E. Fromm & R. E. Shor (Eds.), *Hypnosis: Developments in research and new perspectives.* New York: Aldine.

Evans, F. J. (1979b). Contextual forgetting: posthypnotic source amnesia. *Journal of Abnormal Psychology, 88,* 556–563.

Eysenck, M. W., & Keane, M. T. (1995). *Cognitive psychology: A student's handbook.* Hillsdale, NJ: Erlbaum.

Fackelmann, K. A. (1993). Marijuana and the brain. *Science News, 143,* 88–94.

Fahler, J., & Cadoret, R. J. (1958). ESP card tests of college students with and without hypnosis. *Journal of Parapsychology, 22,* 125–136.

Faraday, A. (1972). *Dream power.* New York: Coward, McCann and Geoghagen.

Farthing, G. W. (1992). *The psychology of consciousness.* Englewood Cliffs, NJ: Prentice-Hall.

Feinstein, A. D., & Morgan, R. M. (1986). Hypnosis in regulating bipolar affective disorders. *American Journal of Clinical Hypnosis, 29,* 29–38.

Fenton, G. W. (1975). Clinical disorders of sleep. *British Journal of Hospital Medicine, August,* 120–144.

Fine, T. H., & Turner, J. W., Jr. (1982). The effect of brief restricted environmental stimulation therapy in the treatment of essential hypertension. *Behavior Research and Therapy, 20,* 567–570.

Fischman, M. W., Schuster, C. R., Javid, J., Hatano, Y., & Davis, J. (1985). Acute tolerance development to the cardiovascular and sujective effects of cocaine. *Journal of Pharmacology and Experimental Therapeutics, 235,* 677–682.

Fisher, C. (1966). Dreaming and sexuality. In L. Lowenstein, M. Newman, M. M. Schur, & A. Solnit (Eds.), *Psychoanalysis: A general psychology.* New York: International University Press.

Fisher, L. E., & Kotses, H. (1973). Race differences and experimenter race effect in galvanic skin response. *Psychophysiology, 10,* 578–582.

Fisher, S. (1962). Problems of interpretation and controls in hypnotic research. In G. H. Estabrooks (Ed.), *Hypnosis: Current problems.* New York: Harper and Row.

Fisher, S., & Greenberg, R. P. (1977). *Scientific credibility of Freud's theory and therapy.* New York: Basic Books.

Fiske, D. W., & Maddi, S. R. (1961). *Functions of varied experience.* Homewood, IL: Dorsey.

Foltin, R. W., Brady, J. V., & Fischman, M. W. (1986). Behavioral analysis of marijuana effects on food intake in humans. *Pharmacology, Biochemistry, and Behavior, 25,* 577–582.

Forgione, A. G. (1988). Hypnosis in the treatment of dental fear and phobia. *Dental Clinics of North America, 32,* 745–761.

Foulkes, D. (1962a). Cognitive processes during sleep: Evolutionary aspects. In A. Mayes (Ed.), *Sleep mechanisms and functions.* Wokingham, England: Van Nostrand Reinhold.

Foulkes, D. (1962b). Dream reports from different stages of sleep. *Journal of Abnormal and Social Psychology, 65,* 14–25.

Foulkes, D. (1982). *Children's dreams: Longitudinal studies.* New York: Wiley.

Fowler, R. L., & Kimmel, H. D. (1962). Operant conditioning of the GSR. *Journal of Experimental Psychology, 63,* 563–567.

Fox, O. (1962). *Astral Projection: A record of out-of-the-body experiences.* Secaucus, NJ: University Books. (Originally published 1939).

Frankel, F. J., & Orne, M. T. (1976). Hypnotizability and phobic behavior. *Archives of General Psychiatry, 33,* 1259–1261.

Fredericks, L. E. (1980). The value of teaching hypnosis in the practice of anesthesiology. *International Journal of Clinical and Experimental Hypnosis, 28,* 6–15.

Freedman, D. X., & Halaris, A. E. (1978). Monoamines and the biochemical mode of action of LSD at synapses. In M. A. Lipton, A. DiMascio, & K. F. Killam (Eds.), *Psychopharmacology.* New York: Raven.

Freedman, R., Ianni, P., & Wenig, P. (1985). Beta-adrenergic vasodilating mechanisms in biofeedback. Paper presented at the annual meeting of the Biofeedback Society of America, New Orleans.

Freedman, R., Lynn, S., Ianni, P., & Hale, P. (1981). Biofeedback treatment of Raynaud's phenomenon. *Biofeedback and Self-Regulation, 6,* 355–365.

French, S. N. (1980). Electromyographic biofeedback for tension control during fine motor skill acquisition. *Biofeedback and Self-Control, 5,* 221–228.

French, T., & Fromm, E. (1964). *Dream interpretation: A new approach.* New York: Basic Books.

Freud, S. (1900). *The interpretation of dreams.* London: Hogarth.

Freud, S. (1913). *Totem and taboo.* London: Penguin.

Freud, S. (1933). *New introductory lectures on psychoanalysis.* London: Hogarth.

Freud, S. (1970). On the general effect of cocaine. Lecture given at Psychiatric Union, March 5, 1885. Reprinted in *Drug Dependence, 5,* 17.

Frezza, M., di Padova, C., Pozzato, G., Terpin, M., Baraona, E., & Lieber, C. S. (1990). High blood alcohol levels in women: The role of decreased gastic alcohol dehydrogenase activity and first-pass metabolism. *New England Journal of Medicine, 322,* 95–99.

Fridlund, A. J., Fowler, S. C., & Pritchard, D. A. (1980). Striate muscle tension patterning in frontalis EMG biofeedback. *Psychophysiology, 17,* 47–55.

Fried, F., Lamberti, J., & Sneed, P. (1977). Treatment of tension and migraine headaches with biofeedback techniques. *Missouri Medicine, 74,* 253–255.

Friedman, A. (1979). Characteristics of tension headache: A profile of 1420 cases. *Psychosomatic Medicine, 20,* 451–461.

Friedman, R. M., Schmeidler, G. R., and Dean, E. D. (1976). Ranked-target scoring for mood and intragroup effects in precognitive ESP. *Journal of the American Society for Psychical Research, 70,* 195–206.

Friman, P. C., & Warzak, W. J. (1990). Nocturnal enuresis: A prevalent, persistant, yet curable parasomnia. *Pediatrician, 1,* 38–45.

Frischholz, E. J., Spiegel, D., Trentalange, M. J., & Spiegel, H. (1987). The Hypnotic Induction Profile and absorption. *American Journal of Clinical Hypnosis, 30,* 87–93.

Fromm, E., & Shor, R. E. (Eds.). (1979). *Hypnosis: Developments in research and new perspectives.* New York: Aldine.

Fromm, E., Brown, D. P., Hurt, S. W., Oberlander, J. Z., Boxer, A. M., & Pfeifer, G. (1981). The phenomena and characteristics of self-hypnosis. *International Journal of Clinical and Experimental Hypnosis, 29,* 189–246.

Frumkin, L. R., Ripley, H. S., & Cox, G. B. (1978). Changes in cerebral lateralization with hypnosis. *Biological Psychiatry, 13,* 741–750.

Fuchs, K., Hoch, Z., & Kleinhauz, M. (1976). Hypno-desensitization therapy of vaginismus. Paper presented at the International Congress of Hypnosis and Psychosomatic Medicine, Philadelphia.

Fuchs, K., Hoch, Z., Paldi, E., Abromovici, H., Brandes, J. M., Timor-Tritsch, I., & Kleinhauz, M. (1973). Hypno-desentization therapy of vaginismus. I. In vitro method. II. In vivo method. *International Journal of Clinical and Experimental Hypnosis, 21,* 144–156.

Fuller, G. D. (1978). Current status of biofeedback in clinical practice. *American Psychologist, 33,* 39–48.

Gaarder, K. R., and Montgomery, P. S. (1977). *Clinical biofeedback: A procedural manual.* Baltimore: Williams and Wilkins.

Gabel, S. (1989). Dreams as a possible reflection of a dissociated self-monitoring system. *Journal of Nervous and Mental Disease, 177,* 560–568.

Galin, D., & Ornstein, R. E. (1972). Lateral specialization of cognitive mode: An EEG study. *Psychophysiology, 9,* 412–418.

Gallois, P. (1984). Modifications neurophysiologiques et respiratoires lors de la pratique des techniques de relaxation. *L'Encephale, 10,* 139–144.

Gannon, L., and Sternbach, R. A. (1971). Alpha enhancement as a treatment for pain: A case study. *Behavior Therapy and Experimental Psychiatry, 2,* 209–213.

Garrett, J. B., & Wallace, B. (1975). A novel test of hypnotic anesthesia. *International Journal of Clinical and Experimental Hypnosis, 23*, 139–147.

Gastaut, H., & Broughton, R. (1965). A clinical polygraphic study of episodic phenomena during sleep. In J. Wortis (Ed.), *Recent Advances in Biological Psychiatry*, (Vol. 7), New York: Plenum.

Gastaut, H., Dongier, M., Broughton, R., & Tassinari, C. A. (1964). Electroencephalographic and clinical study of diurnal and nocturnal anxiety attacks. *Electroencephalography and Clinical Neurophysiology, 17*, 475–481.

Gawin, F. H., & Kleber, H. D. (1986). Abstinence symptomatology and psychiatric diagnosis in cocaine abusers. *Archives of General Psychiatry, 43*, 107–113.

Gazzaniga, M. S. (1983). Right hemisphere language following brain bisection: A 20 year perspective. *American Psychologist, 38*, 525–537.

Gazzaniga, M. S., Bogen, J. E., & Sperry, R. W. (1965). Observations on visual perception after disconnection of the cerebral hemispheres in man. *Brain, 8*, 221–236.

Gazzaniga, M. S., Volpe, B., Smylie, C., Wilson, D. H., & LeDoux, J. E. (1979). Plasticity in speech organization following commissurotomy. *Brain, 102*, 805–816.

Gazzaniga, M. A., & LeDoux, J. E. (1978). *The integrated mind*. New York: Plenum.

Gazzaniga, M. A., & Sperry, R. W. (1967). Language after section of the cerebral commissures. *Brain, 90*, 131–148.

Gelderloos, P. (1987). *Valuation and transcendental meditation*. Lelystad, Netherlands: Soma Scientific Publishers.

Gelderloos, P., Walton, K. G., Orme-Johnson, D, & Alexander, C. N. (1991). Effectiveness of the transcendental meditation program in preventing and treating substance misuse: A review. *International Journal of the Addictions, 26*, 293–325.

Giannelli, P. C. (1995). The admissibility of hypnotic evidence in U.S. courts. *International Journal of Clinical and Experimental Hypnosis, 43*, 212–233.

Gibbs, F. A., Davis, H., & Lennox, W. G. (1935). The electroencephalogram in epilepsy and in conditions of impaired consciousness. *Archives of Neurology and Psychiatry, 34*, 1133–1148.

Gibby, R. G., & Adams, H. B. (1961). Receptiveness of psychiatric patients to verbal communication: An increase following partial sensory deprivation. *Archives of General Psychiatry, 5*, 366–370.

Girodo, M. (1974). Yoga meditation and flooding in the treatment of anxiety neurosis. *Journal of Behavior Therapy and Experimental Psychiatry, 5*, 157–160.

Gisquet-Verrier, P., & Smith, C. (1989). Avoidance performance in rats enhanced by postlearning paradoxical sleep deprivation. *Journal of Behavioral and Neural Biology, 52*, 152–169.

Glaus, K. D., Happ, A., & Kotses, H. (1976). Airway resistance changes associated with conditioned frontalis and bronchioradiolis EMG. Paper presented at the meeting of the Society for Psychophysiological Research, San Diego.

Glaus, K. D., & Kotses, H. (1976). Conditioned frontalis muscle tension effects on airway resistance. Paper presented at the meeting of the Society for Psychophysiological Research, San Diego.

Glaus, K. D., & Kotses, H. (1983). Facial muscle tension influences lung airway resistance: Limb muscle tension does not. *Biological Psychology, 17*, 105–120.

Glueck, B. (1973, May 27). Quoted in the *Hartford Courant*, p. 6.

Glueck, B. C., & Stroebel, C. F. (1975). Biofeedback and meditation in the treatment of psychiatric illnesses. *Comprehensive Psychiatry, 16,* 303–321.

Goldman, M. S. (1983). Cognitive impairment in chronic alcoholics: Some cause for optimism. *American Psychologist, 38,* 1045–1054.

Goldstein, L., Stolzfus, N., & Gardocki, J. (1972). Changes in interhemispheric amplitude relations in the EEG during sleep. *Physiology and Behavior, 8,* 811–815.

Goleman, D. (1971). Meditation as a meta-therapy: Hypotheses toward a proposed fifth state of consciousness. *Journal of Transpersonal Psychology, 3,* 1–25.

Goleman, D. (1977). *The varieties of the meditative experience.* New York: Dutton.

Goleman, D. (1982). Staying up: The rebellion against sleep's gentile tyranny. *Psychology Today, 16,* 24–35.

Goleman, D. (1988). *The meditative mind: The varieties of the meditative experience.* New York: G. P. Putnam's Sons.

Goleman, D., & Davidson, R. J. (1979). *Consciousness: Brain, states of awareness, and mysticism.* New York: Harper and Row.

Goodenough, D. R. (1978). Dream recall: History and current status of the field. In A. M. Arkin, J. S. Atrobus, & S. J. Ellman (Eds.), *The mind in sleep: Psychology and psychophysiology.* Hillsdale, NJ: Erlbaum.

Goodenough, D. R., Witkin, H. A., Koulack, D., & Cohen, H. (1975). The effects of stress filds on dream affect and on respiration and eye movement during rapid-eye movement sleep. *Psychophysiology, 15,* 313–320.

Gordon, H. W., & Sperry, R. W. (1968). Olfaction following surgical disconnection of the hemisphere in man. Paper presented at the annual meetings of the Psychonomic Society, Austin, TX.

Grabowski, J., & Dworkin, S. E. (1985). Cocaine: An overview of current issues. *International Journal of the Addictions, 20,* 1065–1088.

Graffin, N. F., Ray, W. J., & Lundy, R. (1995). EEG concomitants of hypnosis and hypnotic susceptibility. *Journal of Abnormal Psychology, 104,* 123–31.

Graham, C., & Evans, F. J. (1977). Hypnotizability and the development of waking attention. *Journal of Abnormal Psychology, 86,* 631–638.

Graham, C., & Leibowitz, H. W. (1972). The effect of suggestion on visual acuity. *International Journal of Clinical and Experimental Hypnosis, 20,* 169–186.

Graham, G. W. (1975). Hypnotic treatment for migraine headaches. *International Journal of Clinical and Experimental Hypnosis, 23,* 165–171.

Graham, K. R. (1977). Perceptual processes and hypnosis: Support for a cognitive-state theory based on laterality. In W. E. Edmonston (Ed.), *Conceptual and investigative approaches to hypnosis and hypnotic phenomena. Annals of the New York Academy of Science, 296,* 274–283.

Graham, K. R., & Pernicano, K. (1979). Laterality, hypnosis, and the autokinetic effect. *American Journal of Clinical Hypnosis, 22,* 79–84.

Graham, R. B. (1990). *Physiological psychology.* Belmont, CA: Wadsworth.

Gravitz, M. A. (1988). Early uses of hypnosis as surgical anesthesia. *American Journal of Clinical Hypnosis, 30,* 201–208.

Gravitz, M. A. (1993). Étienne Felix d'Henin de Cuvilleres: A founder of hypnosis. *American Journal of Clinical Hypnosis, 36,* 7–11.

Gravitz, M. A., & Gerton, M. I. (1984). Origins of the term hypnotism prior to Braid. *American Journal of Clinical Hypnosis, 27,* 107–110.

Green, C. E. (1967). Ecsomatic experiences and related phenomena. *Journal of the American Society for Psychical Research, 44,* 111–131.

Green, E., & Green, A. (1979). General and specific applications of thermal biofeedback. In J. Basmajian (Ed.), *Biofeedback: Principles and practice for clinicians.* Baltimore: Williams and Wilkins.

Green, K. (1979). *The ocular effects of cannabinoids: Vol. 1. Current topics in eye research.* New York: Academic Press.

Greenberg, R., & Pearlman, C. (1967). Delirium tremens and dreaming. *American Journal of Psychiatry, 124,* 37–46.

Greenwood, P., Wilson, D. H., & Gazzaniga, M. S. (1977). Dream report following commissurotomy. *Cortex, 13,* 311–316.

Grela, J. J. (1945). Effect on ESP scoring of hypnotically induced attitudes. *Journal of Parapsycholgy, 9,* 194–202.

Grilly, D. M. (1981). People's views on drugs and driving: An update. *Journal of Psychoactive Drugs, 13,* 377–379.

Grilly, D. M. (1998). *Drugs and human behavior* (3rd ed.). Boston: Allyn and Bacon.

Grinspoon, L. (1969). Marihuana. *Scientific American, 221,* 17–25.

Grinspoon, L., & Bakalar, J. (1979). A kick from cocaine. *Psychology Today, 12,* 36–39, 77–78.

Grinspoon, L., & Bakalar, J. (1993). *Marihuana, the forbidden medicine.* New Haven, CT: Yale University Press.

Grosso, M. (1981). Toward an explanation of near-death phenomena. *Journal of the American Society for Psychical Research, 75,* 37–60.

Groves, P. M., & Schlesinger, K. (1982). *Biological psychology.* Dubuque, IA: William C. Brown.

Gruzelier, J., & Flor-Henry, P. (Eds.). (1979) *Hemisphere asymmetries of functin in psychopathology.* Amsterdam: Elsevier.

Guerra, F. (1971). *The pre-Columbian mind.* New York: Seminar Press.

Guglielmi, R. S., Roberts, A. H., & Patterson, R. (1982). Skin temperature biofeedback for Raynaud's disease: A double-blind study. *Biofeedback and Self-Regulation, 7,* 99–120.

Gunn, J. (1979). Drugs in the violence clinic. In M. Sandler (Ed.), *Psychopharmacology of aggression.* New York: Raven.

Gur, R. C., & Gur, R. E. (1974). Handedness, sex, and eyedness as moderating variables in the relation between hypnotic susceptibility and functional brain asymmetry. *Journal of Abnormal Psychology, 83,* 635–643.

Gur, R. E., Gur, R. C., & Harris, L. J. (1975). Cerebral activation as measured by subjects' lateral eye movements is influenced by experimenter location. *Neuropsychologia, 13,* 35–44.

Guze, S. B., Cloninger, C. R., Martin, R., & Clayton, P. J. (1986). Alcoholism as a medical disorder. *Comprehensive Psychiatry, 27,* 501–510.

Haber, R. N. (1979). Twenty years of haunting eidetic imagery: Where's the ghost? *Behavioral and Brain Sciences, 2,* 583–629.

Haber, R. N., & Haber, R. B. (1964). Eidetic imagery. I. Frequency. *Perceptual and Motor Skills, 19,* 131–138.

Haber, R. N., & Hershenson, M. (1980). *The psychology of visual perception.* New York: Holt, Rinehart, and Winston.

Hageman-Wenselaar, L. H. (1988). Hypnosis for pain control during lumbar puncture and bone marrow aspirations in children with cancer. *Tijdschr Kindergeneeskd, 56,* 120–123.

Hall, C. S. (1951). What people dream about. *Scientific American, 184,* 60–63.

Hall, C. S., & Lindzey, G. (1978). *Theories of personality* (3rd ed.). New York: Wiley.

Hall, C. S., & Van de Castle, R. L. (1966). *The content analysis of dreams.* New York: Appleton-Century-Crofts.

Hall, J. R., & McGill, J. C. (1986). Hypnobehavioral treatment of self-destructive behavior: Trichotillomania and bulimia in the same patient. *American Journal of Clinical Hypnosis, 29,* 39–46.

Hall, J. S., & Crasilneck, H. B. (1970). Development of a hypnotic technique for treating chronic cigarette smoking. *International Journal of Clinical and Experimental Hypnosis, 18,* 283–289.

Hamilton, W. (1880). *Lectures on metaphysics.* New York: Sheldon.

Hansel, C. E. M. (1980). *ESP and parapsychology: A critical evaluation.* Buffalo: Prometheus.

Haraldsson, E., Gudmundsdottir, A., Ragnarsson, A., Loftsson, J., & Jonsson, S. (1977). National survey of psychical experiences and attitudes towards the paranormal in Iceland. In J. D. Morris, W. G. Roll, & R. L. Morris (Eds.), *Research in Parapsychology 1976.* Metuchen, NJ: Scarecrow Press.

Hart, J. T. (1967). Autocontrol of EEG alpha. Paper presented at the annual meeting of the Society for Psychophysiological Research, San Diego.

Hart, J. T., & Cichanski, K. (1981). A comparison of frontal EMG biofeedback and neck EMG biofeedback in the treatment of muscle-contractin headache. *Biofeedback and Self-Regulation, 6,* 63–74.

Hartmann, E. L. (1973). *The functions of sleep.* New Haven: Yale University Press.

Hartmann, E. L. (1981). The strangest sleep disorder. *Psychology Today, 15,* 14–18.

Hartmann, E., Baekeland, F., Zwilling, G., & Hop, P. (1971). Sleep need: How much sleep and what kind? *American Journal of Psychiatry, 127,* 1001–1008.

Harver, A., Kotses, H., Segreto, J., & Creer, T. L. (1984). Impact of facial relaxation training on asthma symptoms. Paper presented at the Fifth International Symposium on Respiratory Psychophysiology, Nijmegen, The Netherlands.

Harvey, S. C. (1985). Hypnotics and sedatives. In A. G. Gilman, L. S. Goodman, T. W. Rall, & F. Murad (Eds.), *The pharmacological basis of therapeutics.* New York: Macmillan.

Harwood, C. W. (1962). Operant heart rate conditioning. *Psychological Record, 12,* 279–284.

Hashtroudi, S., Parker, E. S. Yablick, L., DeLisi, L. E., & Wyatt, R. J. (1981). Generation is a better "antidote" for alcohol amnesia than semantic elaboration. Paper presented at the meetings of the Psychonomic Society, Philadelphia.

Hatch, J. P. (1981). Voluntary control of sexual responding in men and women: Implicatins for the etiology and treatment of sexual dysfunctions. *Biofeedback and Self-Regulation, 6,* 191–206.

Hauri, P. J. (1985). Primary sleep disorders and insomnia. In T. Riley (Ed.), *Clinical aspects of sleep and sleep disturbance.* Boston: Butterworth.

Haut, J. S., Beckwith, B. E., Petros, T. V., & Russell, S. (1989). Gender differences in retrieval from long-term memory following acute intoxication with ethanol. *Physiology and Behavior, 45,* 1161–1165.

Havens, J. (1969). Psychology and religious retreats. *Pastoral Psychology, 20,* 45–52.

Hebb, C. (1970). CNS at the cellular level: Identity of transmitter agents. *Annual Review of Physiology, 32,* 165–192.

Hebb, D. O. (1949). *The organization of behavior.* New York: Wiley.

Heilman, K. M., Rothi, L., & Kertesz, A. (1983). Localization of apraxia-producing lesions. In A. Kertesz (Ed.), *Localization in neuropsychology* (p. 381). New York: Academic Press, p. 381.

Helper, R. S., & Frank, I. M. (1971). Marijuana smoking and intraocular pressure. *Journal of the American Medical Association, 217,* 1392.

Hennevin, E., Hars, B., & Block, V. (1989). Improvement of learning by mesencephalic reticular stimulation during postlearning paradoxical sleep. *Journal of Behavioral and Neural Biology, 51,* 291–306.

Heron, W., Bexton, W. H., & Hebb, D. O. (1953). Cognitive effects of decreased variation to sensory environment (abstract). *American Psychologist, 8,* 366.

Heron, W., Doane, B. K., & Scott, T. H. (1956). Visual disturbances after prolonged perceptual isolation. *Canadian Journal of Psychology, 10,* 13–18.

Hess, W. R. (1944). Das Schlafsyndrom als Folgedienzephaler Reizung. *Helvetica Physiologica et Pharmacologica Acta, 2,* 305–344.

Hilgard, E. R. (1965). *The experience of hypnosis.* New York: Harcourt, Brace and World.

Hilgard, E. R. (1973). A neodissociation interpretation of pain reduction in hypnosis. *Psychological Review, 80,* 396–411.

Hilgard, E. R. (1976). Neodissociation theory of multiple cognitive controls. In G. E. Schwartz & D. Shapiro (Eds.), *Consciousness and self-regulation: Advances in research.* New York: Plenum.

Hilgard, E. R. (1977a). Controversies over consciousness and the rise of cognitive psychology. *Australian Psychologist, 12,* 7–27.

Hilgard, E. R. (1977b). *Divided consciousness: Multiple controls in human thought and action.* New York: Wiley.

Hilgard, E. R. (1979). Divided consciousness in hypnosis: The implications of the hidden observer. In E. Fromm & R. E. Shor (Eds.), *Hypnosis: Developments in research and new perspectives.* New York: Aldine.

Hilgard, E. R. (1987). Research advances in hypnosis: Issues and methods. *International Journal of Clinical and Experimental Hypnosis, 35,* 248–264.

Hilgard, E. R., & Hilgard, J. R. (1994). *Hypnosis in the relief of pain* (2nd ed.). Los Altos, CA: Kaufmann.

Hilgard, E. R., Morgan, A. H., & MacDonald, H. (1975). Pain and dissociation in the cold pressor test: a study of hypnotic analgesia with "hidden reports" through automatic keypressing and automatic talking. *Journal of Abnormal Psychology, 84,* 280–289.

Hilgard, J. R., & LeBaron, S. (1982). Relief of anxiety and pain in children and adolescents with cancer: Quantitative measures and clinical observations. *International Journal of Clinical and Experimental Hypnosis, 30,* 418–442.

Hilgard, J. R., & LeBaron, S. (1984). *Hypnosis in the treatment of pain and anxiety in children with cancer: A clinical and quantitative investigation.* Los Altos, CA: Kaufmann.

Hindman, M. H. (1979, Fall). Family violence: An overview. *Alcohol Health and Research World* (NIAAA, Public Health Administration, Department of Health, Education, and Welfare), p. 4.

Hinds, J. (1995). A model of the mind that explains subject and experimenter expectancy effects. *Journal of the American Society for Psychical Research, 89,* 51–72.

Hirsch, C. (1972). The dermatopathology of narcotic addiction. *Human Pathology, 3,* 45–52.

Hjelle, L. A. (1974). Transcendental meditation and psychological health. *Perceptual and Motor Skills, 39,* 623–628.

Hobson, J. A. (1993). Sleep and dreaming. *Current Opinion in Neurobiology, 10,* 371–382.

Hobson, J. A. (1995). *Sleep.* New York: Freeman.

Hobson, J. A., & McCarley, R. W. (1977). The brain as a dream state generator: An activation-synthesis of the dream process. *American Journal of Psychiatry, 134,* 1335–1348.

Hobson, J. A., & Strickgold, R. (1995). The conscious state paradigm: A neurocognitive approach to waking, sleeping, and dreaming. In M. S. Gazzaniga (Ed.), *The cognitive neurosciences.* Cambridge, MA: MIT Press, pp. 1373–1389.

Hofmann, F., & Hofmann, A. (1975). *A handbook on drug and alcohol abuse.* New York: Oxford.

Hogue, D. R., & Hunter, R. E. (1988). The use of hypnosis in orthopaedic surgery. *Contemporary Orthopaedics, 16,* 65–68.

Hollister, L. (1971). Marihuana in man: Three years later. *Science, 172,* 21–29.

Hollister, L. E. (1986). Health aspects of cannabis. *Pharmacological Reviews, 38,* 1–20.

Holmes, D. S. (1984). Meditation and somatic arousal reduction: A review of the experimental evidence. *American Psychologist, 39,* 1–10.

Holroyd, J. (1980). Hypnosis treatment for smoking: An evaluative review. *International Journal of Clinical and Experimental Hypnosis, 28,* 341–357.

Hong, C. C., Potkin, J. S., Antrobus, M. D., Callaghan, G. M., & Gillin, C. (1997). REM sleep eye movement counts correlate with visual imagery in dreaming: A pilot study. *Psychophysiology: The International Journal of the Society for Psychophysiological Research, 34,* 377–381.

Honorton, C. (1972). Significant factors in hypnotically induced clairvoyant dreams. *Journal of the American Society for Psychical Research, 66,* 86–102.

Honorton, C. (1978). Replicability, experimenter influence, and parapsychology: An empirical context for the study of mind. Paper presented at the Annual Meeting of the American Association for the Advancement of Science, Washington, D.C.

Honorton, C. (1985). Meta-analysis of psi ganzfeld research: A response to Hyman. *Journal of Parapsychology, 49,* 51–91.

Honorton, C., & Krippner, S. (1969). Hypnosis and ESP performance: A review of the experimental literature. *Journal of the American Society for Psychical Research, 63,* 214–253.

Honorton, C., & Stump, J. P. (1969). A preliminary study of hypnotically induced clairvoyant dreams. *Journal of the American Society for Psychical Research, 63,* 175–184.

Honsberger, R. (1973). The effect of transcendental meditation upon bronchial asthma. *Clinical Research, 21,* 368.

Hooker, W. D., & Jones, R. T. (1987). Increased susceptibility to memory intrusions and the stroop interference effect during acute marijuana intoxication. *Psychopharmacology, 91,* 20–24.

Hoon, E. F. (1980). Biofeedback-assisted arousal in females: A comparison of visual and auditory modalities. *Biofeedback and Self-Regulation, 5,* 175–191.

Hoppe, K. D. (1977). Split brains and psychoanalysis. *The Psychoanalytic Quarterly, 46,* 220–224.

Horowitz, M. J. (1969). Flashbacks: Recurrent intrusive images after the use of LSD. *American Journal of Psychiatry, 126,* 147–151.

Hothersall, D., & Brener, J. (1969). Operant conditioning of changes in heart rates in curarized rats. *Journal of Comparative and Physiological Psychology, 68*, 338–342.

Hubel, D. H., & Wiesel, T. N. (1979). Brain mechanisms of vision. In *The Brain (Scientific American Reprints)*. San Francisco: Freeman.

Hughes, J., Smith, T. W., Kosterlitz, H. W., Fothergill, L. A., Morgan, B. A., & Morris, H. R. (1975). Identification of two related pentapeptides from the brain with potent opiate agonist activity. *Nature, 258*, 577–579.

Hull, J. G., & Bond, C. F. (1986). Social and behavioral consequences of alcohol consumption and expectancy: A meta-analysis. *Psychological Bulletin, 99*, 347–359.

Humphrey, M. E., & Zangwill, O. L. (1951). Cessation of dreaming after brain injury. *Journal of Neurology, Neurosurgery and Psychiatry, 14*, 322–325.

Hunt, H. T. (1995). *On the nature of consciousness: Cognitive, phenomenological, and transpersonal perspectives*. New Haven, CT: Yale University Press.

Husain, S. (1989). Effects of delta-9-tetrahydrocannabinol on in vitro energy substrate metabolism in mouse and rat testes. *Physiology and Behavior, 46*, 65–68.

Husain, S., & Patra, P. B. (1989). Delta-9-tetrahydrocannabinol on spermatogenesis in mice. *Physiology and Behavior, 46*, 60–64.

Hyman, R. (1985). The ganzfeld/psi experiment: A critical appraisal. *Journal of Parapsychology, 49*, 3–49.

Hyman, R., & Honorton, C. (1986). A joint communique: The psi ganzfeld controversy. *Journal of Parapsychology, 50*, 351–364.

Irwin, H. J. (1978a). ESP and the human information processing system. *Journal of the American Society for Psychical Research, 72*, 111–126.

Irwin, H. J. (1978b). Psi, attention, and processing capacity. *Journal of the American Society for Psychical Research, 72*, 301–313.

Irwin, H. J. (1988). Out-of-body experiences and attitudes to life and dealth. *Journal of the American Society for Psychical Research, 82*, 237–251.

Irwin, H. J. (1994). Childhood trauma and the origins of paranormal belief: A constructive replication. *Psychological Reports, 74*, 107–111.

Istvan, J., & Matarazzo, J. D. (1984). Tobacco, alcohol, and caffeine use: A review of their interrelationships. *Psychological Bulletin, 95*, 301–326.

Itard, J. M. G. (1932). *The Wild Boy of Aveyron* (G. Humphrey & M. Humphrey, Trans.). New York: Appleton-Century-Crofts.

Jackson, J. H. (Ed.). (1958). *Selected writings of John Hughlings Jackson*. New York: Basic Books.

Jacob, P., Jones, R. T., Benowitz, N. L., & Shulgin, A. T. (1989). Cocaine smokers inhale a pyrolysis product: Anhydroecgonine methyl ester. Paper presented at the meetings of the American Society for Clinical Pharmacology and Therapeutics, Nashville.

Jacobs, B. L. (1987). How hallucinogenic drugs work. *American Scientist, 75*, 386–392.

Jacobs, G. D., Heilbronner, R. L., & Stanley, J. M. (1985). The effects of short term flotation REST on relaxation: A controlled study. In T. H. Fine & J. W. Turner, Jr. (Eds.), *Proceedings of the First International Conference on REST and Self-Regulation* (pp. 86–102). Toledo, OH: IRIS.

Jacobson, E. (1938). *How to relax and have your baby: Scientific relaxation in childbirth*. New York: McGraw-Hill.

Jaffe, J. H . (1985). Drug addiction and drug abuse. In A. G. Gilman, L. S. Goodman, T. W. Rall, & F. Murad (Eds.), *The pharmacological basis of therapeutics*. New York: Macmillan.

James, W. (1890). *Principles of psychology* (Vol. 1). New York: Holt.

James, W. (1904). Does consciousness exist? *Journal of Philosophy, Psychology, and Scientific Methods, 1,* 477–491.

Jarvik, M. E. (1967). The psychopharmacological revolution. *Psychology Today, 1,* 51–58.

Jaynes, J. (1976). *The origin of consciousness in the breakdown of the bicameral mind.* Boston: Houghton Mifflin.

Jaynes, J. (1986a). Hearing voices and the bicameral mind. *Behavioral and Brain Sciences, 9,* 526–527.

Jaynes, J. (1986b). Consciousness and voices of the mind. *Canadian Psychology, 27,* 128–148.

Jeffcoat, R. A., Perez-Reyes, M., Hill, J. M., Sadler, B. M., & Cook, E. (1989). Cocaine disposition in humans after intravenous injection, nasal insufflation (snorting), or smoking. *Drug Metabolism and Disposition, 17,* 153–159.

Jeffrey, T. B., Jeffrey, L. K., Greuling, J. W., & Gentry, W. R. (1985). Evaluation of a brief group treatment package including hypnotic induction for maintenance of smoking cessation: A brief communication. *International Journal of Clinical and Experimental Hypnosis, 33,* 95–98.

Jevning, R., Wallace, R. K., & Beidebach, M. (1992). The physiology of meditation: A review: A wakeful hypometabolic integrated response. *Neuroscience & Biobehavioral Reviews, 16,* 415–424.

John, R., Hollander, B., & Perry, C. (1983). Hypnotizability and phobic behavior: Further supporting data. *Journal of Abnormal Psychology, 92,* 390–392.

Johnson, L. C., & MacLeod, W. L. (1973). Sleep and awake behavior during gradual sleep reduction. *Perceptual and Motor Skills, 36,* 87–97.

Johnson, L. C., Slye, E., & Dement, W. C. (1965). EEG and autonomic activity during and after prolonged sleep deprivation. *Psychosomatic Medicine, 27,* 415–423.

Johnson, L. S. (1981). Current research in self-hypnotic phenomenology: The Chicago paradigm. *International Journal of Clinical and Experimental Hypnosis, 29,* 247–258.

Johnson, R. F. Q., Maher, B. A., & Barber, T. X. (1972). Artifact in the "essence of hypnosis": An evaluation of trance logic. *Journal of Abnormal Psychology, 79,* 212–220.

Johnson, W. G., and Turin, A. (1975). Biofeedback treatment of migraine headache: A systematic case study. *Behavior Therapy, 6,* 394–397.

Jones, E. (1953–1957). *The life and work of Sigmund Freud* (3 vols.). New York: Basic Books.

Jones-Witters, P., & Witters, W. L. (1983). *Drugs and society: A biological perspective.* Belmont, CA: Wadsworth.

Julesz, B. (1971). *Foundations of cyclopean perception.* Chicago: University of Chicago Press.

Julien, R. M. (1997). *A primer of drug action* (8th ed.). New York: Freeman.

Jurek, I. E., Higgins, J. T., & McGrady, A. (1992). Interaction of biofeedback-assisted relaxation and diuretic in treatment of essential hypertension. *Biofeedback & Self-Regulation, 17,* 125–141.

Kahn, E., Dement, W. C., Fisher, C., & Barmack, J. L. (1962). The incidence of color in immediately recalled dreams. *Science, 137,* 1054.

Kahn, E., Fisher, C., & Edwards, A. (1978). Night terrors and anxiety dreams. In A. M. Arkin, J. S. Antrobus, and S. J. Ellman (Eds.), *The mind in sleep: Psychology and psychophysiology.* Hillsdale, NJ: Erlbaum.

Kahneman, D. (1973). *Attention and effort.* Englewood Cliffs, NJ: Prentice-Hall.

Kalat, J. W. (1992). *Biological psychology* (4th ed.). Belmont, CA: Wadsworth

Kamiya, J. (1968). Conscious control of brain waves. *Psychology Today, 1,* 57–60.

Kamiya, J. (1969). Operant control of the EEG alpha rhythm and some of its reported effects on consciousness. In C. T. Tart (Ed.), *Altered states of consciousness.* New York: Wiley.

Kane, B., Millay, J., & Brown, D. H. (Eds.) (1993). *Silver threads: 25 years of parapsychology research.* Westport, CT: Praeger.

Karlin, R. A. (1979). Hypnotizability and attention. *Journal of Abnormal Psychology, 88,* 92–95.

Karniol, J. G., & Carlini, E. A. (1972). The content of delta-9-trans-tetrahydrocannabinol (delta-9-THC) does not explain all biological activity of some Brazilian marihuana samples. *Journal of Pharmacy and Pharmacology, 24,* 833–835.

Kasamatsu, A., & Hirai, T. (1963). Science of Zazen. *Psychologia, 6,* 86–91.

Kasamatsu, A., & Hirai, T. (1966). An electroencephalographic study on the Zen meditation. *Folia Psychiatrica et Neurologia Japonica, 20,* 315–336.

Kasamatsu, A., & Hirai, T. (1969). An electroencephalographic study of the Zen meditation (Zazen). *Psychologia, 12,* 205–225.

Katkin, E. S., & Murray, E. N. (1969). Instrumental conditioning of autonomically mediated behavior: Theoretical and methodological issues. *Psychological Bulletin, 70,* 52–68.

Katkin, E. S., Murray, E. N., & Lachman, R. (1969). Concerning instrumental autonomic conditioning: A rejoinder. *Psychological Bulletin, 71,* 462–466.

Katz, M. M., Waskow, E. E., & Olsson, J. (1968). Characteristics of the psychological state produced by LSD. *Journal of Abnormal Psychology, 73,* 1–14.

Kay, J., Shively, M., & Kilkenny, J. (1978). Training of sensorimotor rhythm in developmentally disabled children through EEG biofeedback. *Biofeedback and Self-Regulation, 3,* 197–198.

Kefauver, J. S. P., & Guilleminault, C. (1994). Sleep terrors and sleepwalking. In M. Kyger, T. Roth, & W. C. Dement (Eds.), *Principles and practices of sleep medicine* (2nd ed.). Philadelphia: Saunders, pp. 567–573.

Kellehear, A. (1996). *Experiences near death: Beyond medicine and religion.* New York: Oxford University Press.

Keller, M. (1966). Alcohol in health and disease. *Annals of the New York Academy of Science, 133,* 820.

Kelly, G. F. (1996). Using meditative techniques in psychotherapy. *Journal of Humanistic Psychology, 36,* 49–66.

Kennedy, J. E. (1980). Learning to use ESP: Do the calls match the targets or do the targets match the calls? *Journal of the American Society for Psychical Research, 74,* 381–393.

Kewman, D., & Roberts, A. H. (1979). Skin temperature biofeedback and migraine headaches. Paper presented at the annual conference of the Biofeedback Society of America, San Diego.

Kewman, D. G., & Roberts, A. H. (1980). Skin temperature biofeedback and migraine headaches: A double-blind study. *Biofeedback and Self-Regulation, 5,* 327–345.

Kewman, D. G., & Roberts, A. H. (1983). An alternative perspective on biofeedback efficacy studies: A reply to Steiner and Dince. *Biofeedback and Self-Regulation, 8,* 487–503.

Kiester, E., Jr. (1980). Images of the night. *Science 80, 1,* 36–43.

Kihlstrom, J. F. (1980). Posthypnotic amnesia for recently learned material: Interactions with episodic and semantic memory. *Cognitive Psychology, 12,* 227–251.

Kihlstrom, J. F. (1985). Hypnosis. *Annual Review of Psychology, 36,* 385–418.

Kihlstrom, J. F. (1994). The rediscovery of the unconscious. In H. Morowitz & J. L. Singer (Eds.), *The mind, the brain, and complex adaptive systems* (pp. 123–143). Reading, MA: Addison-Wesley.

Kihlstrom, J. F. (1996). Unconscious processes in social interaction. In S. R. Hameroff, A. W. Kaszniak, & A. C. (Eds.), *Toward a science of consciousness* (pp. 93–104). Cambridge, MA: MIT Press.

Kimmel, H. D. (1967). Instrumental conditioning of autonomically mediated behavior. *Psychological Bulletin, 67,* 337–345.

Kimmel, H. D. (1974). Instrumental conditioning of autonomically mediated responses in human beings. *American Psychologist, 29,* 325–335.

Kimmel, H. D., & Hill, F. A. (1960). Operant conditioning of the GSR. *Psychological Reports, 7,* 555–562.

Kimura, D. (1977). Acquisition of a motor skill after left hemisphere damage. *Brain, 100,* 527–542.

Kirsch, I., & Barton, R. D. (1988). Hypnosis in the treatment of multiple personality. *British Journal of Clinical and Experimental Hypnosis, 5,* 131–137.

Klinger, E. (1987). The power of daydreams. *Psychology Today, 21,* 36–44.

Klonoff, H. (1974). Marijuana and driving in real-life situations. *Science, 186,* 317–324.

Kluft, R. P. (1988). The simulation and dissimulation of multiple personality disorder. *American Journal of Clinical Hypnosis, 30,* 104–118.

Knapp, T. J., & Wells, L. A. (1978). Behavior therapy for asthma: A review. *Behaviour Research and Therapy, 16,* 103–115.

Knox, V. J., Crutchfield, L., & Hilgard, E. R. (1975). The nature of task interference in hypnotic dissociation: An investigation of hypnotic behavior. *International Journal of Clinical and Experimental Hypnosis, 23,* 305–232.

Kokoszka, A. (1988). An integrated model of the main states of consciousness. *Imagination, Cognition, and Personality, 7,* 285–294.

Kokoszka, A. (1992). An evolutionary-psychodynamic model of the main states of consciousness. *Imagination, cognition, and personality, 12,* 387–394.

Kondo, C., & Canter, A. (1977). True and false electromyographic feedback: Effect on tension headache. *Journal of Abnormal Psychology, 36,* 93–95.

Korner, A. F. (1968). REM organization in neonates: Theoretical implications for development and the biological functions of REM. *Archives of General Psychiatry, 19,* 330–340.

Kotses, H., & Glaus, K. (1981). Applications of biofeedback to the treatment of asthma: A critical review. *Biofeedback and Self-Regulation, 6,* 573–594.

Kotses, H., Glaus, K. D., Bricel, S. K., Edwards, J. E., & Crawford, P. L. (1978). Operant muscular relaxation and peak expiratory flow rate in asthmatic children. *Journal of Psychosomatic Medicine, 22,* 17–23.

Kotses, H., Glaus, K. D., Crawford, P. L., Edwards, J. E., & Scherr, M. S. (1976). Operant reduction of frontalis EMG activity in the treatment of asthma in children. *Journal of Psychosomatic Medicine, 20,* 453–459.

Kotses, H., Hindi-Alexander, M., & Creer, T. L. (1989). A reinterpretation of psychologically induced airway changes. *Journal of Asthma, 26,* 53–63.

Koula, G. M., Kemp, J. C., Keane, K. M., & Belden, A. D. (1987). Replication of a clinical outcome study on a hospital-based stress management and behavioral medicine program utilizing flotation REST (Restricted Environmental Stimulation Technique) and biofeedback. In T. H. Fine & J. W. Turner, Jr. (Eds.), *Proceedings of the Second International Conference on REST* (pp. 127–135). Toledo, OH: IRIS.

Krauss, H. H., Katzell, R., & Krauss, B. J. (1974). Effect of hypnotic time distortion upon free-recall learning. *Journal of Abnormal Psychology, 83,* 140–144.

Krippner, S. (1968). Experimentally induced telepathic effects in hypnosis and non-hypnosis groups. *Journal of the American Society for Psychical Research, 62,* 387–398.

Krippner, S. (1995). Psychical research in the postmodern world. *Journal of the American Society for Psychical Research, 89,* 1–18.

Krippner, S., Hickman, J., Auerhahn, N., & Harris, R. (1972). Clairvoyant perception of target material in three states of consciousness. *Perceptual and Motor Skills, 35,* 439–446.

Krippner, S., & Rubin, D. (Eds.). (1974). *The Kirlian aura.* New York: Anchor Books.

Kroger, W. S. (1977). *Clinical and experimental hypnosis.* Philadelphia: Lippincott.

Kumano, H., Horie, H., Shidara, T., Kuboki, T., Suematsu, H., & Yasushi, M. (1996). Treatment of a depressive disorder patient with EEG-driven photic stimulation. *Biofeedback & Self-Regulation, 21,* 323–334.

Kumar, V. K., & Pekala, R. J. (1988). Hypnotizability, absorption, and individual differences in phenomenological experience. *International Journal of Clinical and Experimental Hypnosis, 36,* 80–88.

Kunzendorf, R. G., Spanos, N. P., & Wallace, B. (Eds.). (1996). *Hypnosis and imagination.* Amityville, NY: Baywood.

Kus, R. J. (1995). Prayer and meditation in addiction recovery. In R. J. Kus, *Spirituality and chemical dependency* (pp. 101–115). New York: Harrington Park Press.

LaBerge, S. P. (1992). *Physiological studies of lucid dreaming.* Hillsdale, NJ: Erlbaum.

LaBerge, S. P., Nagel, L. E., Dement, W. C., & Zarcone, V. (1981). Lucid dreaming verified by volitional communication during REM sleep. *Perceptual and Motor Skills, 52,* 727–732.

Lacks, P., & Powlishta, K. (1989). Improvement following behavioral treatment for insomnia: Clinical significance, long-term maintenance, and predictors of outcome. *Behavior Therapy, 20,* 117–134.

Lang, P. J., and Lazovik, A. D. (1963). Experimental desensitization of a phobia. *Journal of Abnormal and Social Psychology, 66,* 519–525.

Langenbucher, J. W., & Nathan, P. E. (1983). Psychology, public policy, and the evidence for alcohol intoxication. *American Psychologist, 38,* 1070–1077.

Langton, P. A. (1991). *Drugs and the alcohol dilemma.* Boston: Allyn and Bacon.

Lanyon, R. I., Barrington, C. C., & Newman, A. C. (1976). Modification of stuttering through EMG biofeedback: A preliminary study. *Behavior Therapy, 7,* 96–103.

Latha, K. K. V. (1991). Yoga, pranayama, thermal biofeedback techniques in the management of stress and high blood pressure. *Journal of Indian Psychology, 9,* 36–46.

Laumann, E. O., Gagnon, J. H., Michael, R. T., & Michaels, S. (1994). *The social organization of sexuality.* Chicago: University of Chicago Press.

Laurence, J. R., & Perry, C. (1983). Hypnotically created memory among highly hypnotizable subjects. *Science, 222,* 523–524.

Lavie, P., & Berris, A. (1996). *The enchanted world of sleep.* New Haven, CT: Yale University Press.

Leavitt, F. (1995). *Drugs and behavior* (3rd ed.). Newbury Park, CA: Sage.

LeDoux, J. E., Wilson, D. H., & Gazzaniga, M. S. (1977). Manipulo-spatial aspects of cerebral lateralization: Clues to the origin of lateralization. *Neuropsychologia, 15,* 743–750.

Leitenberg, H., & Henning, K. (1995). Sexual fantasy. *Psychological Bulletin, 117,* 469–496.

Leo, J. (1986). How cocaine killed Leonard Bias. *Time, 128,* 52.

Leskowitz, E. (1988). The "third eye": A psychoendocrine model of hypnotizability. *American Journal of Clinical Hypnosis, 30,* 209–215.

Lesser, I. M., Poland, R. E., Holcomb, C., & Rose, D. E. (1985). Electrocephalographic study of nighttime panic attacks. *Journal of Nervous and Mental Disorders, 173,* 744–746.

Levenberg, S. B., & Wagner, M. K. (1976). Smoking cessation: Long-term irrelevance of mode of treatment. *Journal of Behavior Therapy and Experimental Psychiatry, 7,* 93–95.

Levine, B. A. (1984). Effects of depression and headache type on biofeedback for muscle-contraction headaches. *Behavioral Psychotherapy, 12,* 300–307.

Levine, J. (1969). LSD: A chemical overview. In P. Black (Ed.), *Drugs and the brain.* Baltimore: Johns Hopkins Press.

Levine, J. L., Kurtz, R. M., & Lauter, J. L. (1984). Hypnosis and its effects on right and left hemisphere activity. *Biological Psychiatry, 19,* 1461–1475.

LeVine, W. R., & Irvine, J. K. (1984). In vivo EMG biofeedback in violin and viola pedagogy. *Biofeedback and Self-Regulation, 9,* 161–168.

Levinthal, C. F. (1990). *Introduction to physiological psychology.* Englewood Cliffs, NJ: Prentice-Hall.

Levy, J. Trevarthen, C., & Sperry, R. W. (1972). Perception of bilateral chimeric figures following hemispheric disconnection. *Brain, 95,* 61–78.

Li, X., & Shen, Z. (1985). Positive electron emission layer scanning technique and its application in psychological research. *Information on Psychological Sciences, 3,* 54–58.

Lichtenfeld, P. J., Rubin, D. B., & Feldman, R. S. (1984). Subarachnoid hemorrhage precipitated by cocaine snorting. *Archives of Neurology, 41,* 223–224.

Lilly, J. C. (1956). Mental effects of reduction of ordinary levels of physical stimuli in intact, healthy persons. *Psychiatric Research Reports, 5,* 1–28.

Lilly, J. C. (1960). Discussion of paper by J. T. Shurley. Profound experimental sensory isolation. *American Journal of Psychiary, 117,* 544–545.

Lilly, J. C. (1972). *Center of the cyclone: An autobiography of inner space.* New York: Julian.

Lilly, J. C. (1977). *The deep self.* New York: Simon and Schuster.

Linden, M., Habib, T., & Radojevic, V. (1996). A controlled study of the effects of EEG biofeedback on cognition and behavior of children with attention deficit disorder and learning disabilities. *Biofeedback & Self-Regulation, 21,* 35–49.

Lindsey, P. H., & Norman, D. A. (1977). *Human information processing: An introduction to psychology* (2nd ed.). New York: Academic Press.

Lindsley, D. B. (1961). Common factors in sensory deprivation, sensory distortion, and sensory overload. In P. Solomon, P. Kubzansky, P. Leiderman, J. Mendelson, R. Trumbull, & D. Wexler (Eds.), *Sensory deprivation: A symposium.* Cambridge: Harvard University Press.

Lindsley, D. B., Bowden, J., & Magoun, H. (1949). Effect upon the EEG of acute injury to the brain stem activating system. *Electroencephalography and Clinical Neurophysiology, 1,* 475–486.

Lingeman, R. (1974). *Drugs from A to Z: A dictionary.* New York: McGraw-Hill.

Lisina, M. I. (1965). The role of orientation of the transformation of involuntary reactions into voluntary ones. In L. G. Veronin, A. H. Leontiev, A. R. Luria, C. N. Sokolov, & O. S. Vinogradova (Eds.), *Orienting reflex and exploratory behavior.* Washington, DC: American Institute of Biological Sciences.

Locke, J. (1975). *An essay concerning human understanding.* Oxford: Oxford University Press. (Originally published 1690)

Loftus, E. F. (1979). *Eyewitness testimony.* Cambridge, MA: Harvard University Press.

Loftus, E. F. (1980). *Memory.* Reading, MA: Addison-Wesley.

London, P., Hart, J. T., & Leibovitz, M. P. (1968). EEG alpha rhythms and susceptibility to hypnosis. *Nature, 219,* 71–72.

Loomis, A. L., Harvey, E. N., & Hobart, G. A. (1935). Potential rhythms of the cerebral cortex during sleep. *Science, 81,* 597–598.

Loomis, A. L., Harvey, E. N., & Hobart, G. A. (1937). Cerebral states during sleep, as studied by human brain potentials. *Journal of Experimental Psychology, 21,* 127–144.

Lubin, A., Moses, J., Johnson, L. C., & Naitoh, P. (1974). The recuperative effects of REM sleep and stage 4 sleep on human performance after complete sleep loss: experiment 1. *Psychophysiology, 2,* 125–132.

Luce, G. G. (1965). *Research on sleep and dreams.* Bethesda, MD: National Institute of Mental Health.

Lucidi, F., Devoto, A., Violani, C., Mastraceli, P., & Bertini, M. (1997). Effects of different sleep duration on delta sleep in recovery nights. *Psychophysiology: The International Journal of the Society for Psychophysiological Research, 32,* 227–233.

Luria, A. R. (1966). *Higher cortical functions in man.* New York: Basic Books.

Lynch, J. J., & Paskewitz, D. A. (1971). On the mechanism of the feedback control of human brain wave activity. *Journal of Nervous and Mental Disease, 153,* 205–217.

Lynn, S. J., & Rhue, J. W. (1986). The fantasy-prone person: Hypnosis, imagination, and creativity. *Journal of Personality and Social Psychology, 51,* 404–408.

MacDonald, T. K., Zanna, M. P., & Fong, G. T. (1995). Decision making in altered states: Effects of alcohol on attitudes toward drinking and driving. *Journal of Personality and Social Psychology, 68,* 973–985.

MacLennan, B. J. (1995). The investigation of consciousness through phenomenoogy and neuroscience. In J. King & K. H. Pribram (Eds.), *Scale in conscious experience: Is the brain too important to be left to specialists to study?* (pp. 25–43). Mahwah, NJ: Erlbaum.

MacLeod-Morgan, C., & Lack, L. (1982). Hemispheric specificity: A physiological concomitant of hypnotizability. *Psychophysiology, 19,* 687–690.

Madsen, P. L. (1993). Bloodflow and oxygen uptake in the human brain during various states of sleep and wakefulness. *Acta Neurologica Scandinavica, 88,* 1–27.

Maharishi Mahesh Yogi. (1963). *The science of being and art of living.* London: Unwin.

Malcolm, N. (1964). Behaviorism as a philosophy of psychology. In T. W. Wann (Ed.), *Behaviorism and phenomenology: Contrasting bases for modern psychology.* Chicago: University of Chicago Press.

Malone, M. D., Kurtz, R. M., & Strube, M. J. (1989). The effects of hypnotic suggestion on pain report. *American Journal of Clinical Hypnosis, 31,* 221–230.

Mandler, G., Preven, D. W., & Kuhlman, C. K. (1962). Effects of operant reinforcement on the GSR. *Journal of the Experimental Analysis of Behavior, 62,* 552–559.

Mann, B. J., & Sanders, S. (1995). The effects of light, temperature, trance length, and time of day on hypnotic depth. *American Journal of Clinical Hypnosis, 37,* 43–53.

Marcus, E. M. (1972). Clinical considerations of the cerebral hemispheres and a general survey of neuropathology. In B. A. Curtis, S. Jacobson, & E. M. Marcus (Eds.), *An introduction to the neurosciences*. Philadelphia: Saunders.

Margraf, J., Taylor, C. B., & Ehlers, A. (1987). Panic attacks in the natural environment. *Journal of Nervous and Mental Disorders, 175*, 558–565.

Marks, D., & Kammann, R. (1978). Information transmission in remote viewing experiments. *Nature, 272*, 680–681.

Marks, D., & Kammann, R. (1980). *The psychology of the psychic*. New York: Prometheus.

Marks, D., & Scott, C. (1986). Remote viewing exposed. *Nature, 319*, 444.

Martin, B. (1986). Cellular effects of cannabinoids. *Pharmacological Reviews, 38*, 45–74.

Martindale, W. (1967). *Extrapharmacopoeia* (25th ed.). London: Pharmaceutical Press.

Marx, J. L. (1984). "Anxiety peptide" found in brain. *Science, 227*, 934.

Mathis, J. L. (1970). Sexual aspects of heroin addiction. *Medical Aspects of Human Sexuality, 4*, 98–109.

Matsuoka, S. (1990). Theta rhythms: State of consciousness. *Brain Topography, 3*, 203–208.

Mauskopf, S. H. (1989). The history of the American Society for Psychical Research: An interpretation. *Journal of the American Society for Psychical Research, 83*, 7–30.

McCarley, R., & Hobson, A. (1979). The form of dreams and the biology of sleep. In B. Wolman (Ed.), *Handbook of dreams*. New York: Van Nostrand Reinhold.

McCarthy, L. E., & Borison, H. L. (1977). Antiemetic activity of nabilone, a cannabinol derivative, reversed by naloxone in awake cats. *Pharmacologist, 19*, 230.

McClenon, J. (1982). A survey of elite scientists: Their attitudes toward ESP and parapsychology. *Journal of Parapsychology, 46*, 127–152.

McConkey, K. M. (1988). A view from the laboratory on the forensic use of hypnosis. *Australian Journal of Clinical and Experimental Hypnosis, 16*, 71–81.

McConkey, K. M., & Perry, C. (1985). Benjamin Franklin and mesmerism. *International Journal of Clinical and Experimental Hypnosis, 33*, 122–130.

McHarg, J. F. (1978). Review of At the hour of death by K. Osis and E. Haraldsson. *Journal of the American Society for Psychical Research, 49*, 885–887.

McKim, W. A. (1997). *Drugs and behavior: An introduction to behavioral pharmacology* (4th ed.). Englewood Cliffs, NJ: Prentice-Hall.

Melzack, R. (1990). The tragedy of needless pain. *Scientific American, 262*, 27–33.

Melzack, R., & Perry, C. (1975). Self-regulation of pain: The use of alpha-feedback and hypnotic training for the control of chronic pain. *Experimental Neurology, 46*, 452–469.

Merkel, J. (1979). A study of individual differences in eletromyograph feedback treatment for muscle contraction headache. *Dissertation Abstracts, 40*, 1904.

Meuwissen, I., & Over, R. (1991). Multidimensionality of the content of female sexual fantasy. *Behaviour Research and Therapy, 29*, 179–189.

Meyer, D. (1965). *The positive thinkers*. New York: Doubleday.

Michaels, R. R. Huber, M. J., & McCann, D. S. (1976). Evaluation of transcendental meditation as a method of reducing stress. *Science, 192*, 1242–1244.

Milkman, H. B., & Shaffer, H. J. (Eds.). (1985). *The addictions: Multidisciplinary perspectives and treatments*. Lexington, MA: Lexington.

Miller, J. J., Fletcher, K., & Kabat-Zinn, J. (1995). Three-year follow-up and clinical implications of a mindfulness meditation-based stress reduction intervention in the treatment of anxiety disorders. *General Hospital Psychiatry, 17*, 192–200.

Miller, L. L., & Branconnier, F. (1983). Cannabis: Effects on memory and the cholinergic limbic system. *Psychological Bulletin, 87,* 441–457.

Miller, L. L., McFarland, D., Cornett, T., Brightwell, D., & Wikler, L. (1977). Marijuana and memory impairment: Effect of free recall and recognition memory. *Pharmacology, Biochemistry, and Behavior, 7,* 99–103.

Miller, N. E., & DiCara, L. (1968). Instrumental learning of urine formation by rats: Changes in ural blood flow. *American Journal of Physiology, 215,* 677–683.

Miller, N. E., & Dworkin, B. R. (1974). Visceral learning: Recent difficulties with curarized rats and significant problems for human research. In P. A. Obrist, A. H. Black, J. Brener, & L. V. DiCara (Eds.), *Cardiovascular psychophysiology.* Chicago: Aldine.

Miller, S., & Konorski, J. (1928). On a particular type of conditioned reflex. *Proceedings of the Biological Society* (Polish Section, Paris), *99,* 1155–1157.

Milner, B. (1965). Visually guided maze learning in man: Effects of bilateral, frontal, and unilateral cerebral lesions. *Neuropsychologia, 3,* 317–338.

Miskiman, D. E. (1977a). The treatment of insomnia by the transcendental meditation program. In D. Orme-Johnson & J. Farrow (Eds.), *Scientific research on the transcendental meditation program* (Vol. 1, pp. 296–298). Los Angeles: Maharishi European Research University Press.

Miskiman, D. E. (1977b). Long-term effects of the transcendental meditation program in the treatment of insomnia. In D. Orme-Johnson & J. Farrow (Eds.), *Scientific research on the transcendental meditation program* (Vol. 1, pp. 299–300). Los Angeles: Maharishi European Research University Press.

Mitler, M. M., Carskadon, M. A., Czeisler, C. A., Dement, W. C., Dinges, D. F., & Graeber, R. C. (1988). Catastrophes, sleep, and public policy: Consensus report. *Sleep, 11,* 100–109.

Mokler, D. J., Stoudt, K. W., Sherman, L. C., & Rech, R. H. (1986). The effects of intracranial administration of hallucinogens on operant behavior in the rat. I. Lysergic acid diethylemide. *Pharmocology, Biochemistry, and Behavior, 25,* 717–725.

Monk, T. H., Reynolds, C. F., Buysse, D. J., & Hoch, C. C. (1991). Circadian characteristics of healthy 80-yr-olds and their relationship to objectively recorded sleep. *Journal of Gerontology, 46,* M171–M175.

Monroe, R. A. (1971). *Journeys out of the body.* Garden City, NY: Doubleday.

Montandon, H. E. (1977). Psychophysiological aspects of the Kirlian phenomenon: A confirmatory study. *Journal of the American Society for Psychical Research, 71,* 45–49.

Monteiro, K. P., & Zimbardo, P. G. (1987). The path from classroom seating to hypnotizability: A dead end. *International Journal of Clinical and Experimental Hypnosis, 35,* 83–86.

Moody, R. A., Jr. (1975). *Life after life.* Atlanta: Mockingbird.

Moody, R. A., Jr. (1977). *Reflections on life after life.* New York: Bantam.

Moody, R. A., Jr. (1985). *Reflections on life after life* (2nd ed.). Atlanta: Mockingbird.

Moody, R. A., Jr. (1988). *The light beyond.* New York: Bantam.

Moore-Ede, M. C., Sulzman, F. M., & Fuller, C. A. (1982). *The clocks that time us.* Cambridge, MA: Harvard University Press.

Moran, M. S., Thompson, T. L., & Neis, A. S. (1988). Sleep disorders in the elderly. *American Journal of Psychiatry, 145,* 1369–1378.

Morawetz, D. (1989). Behavioral self-help treatment for insomnia: A controlled evaluation. *Behavior Therapy, 20,* 365–379.

Morewitz, J. H. (1988). Evaluation of excessive daytime sleepiness in the elderly. *Journal of the American Geriatrics Society, 36*, 324–330.

Morrell, E. M. (1986). Meditation and somatic arousal. *American Psychologist, 41,* 712–713.

Morris, R. L., Harary, S. B., Janis, J., Hartwell, J. & Roll, W. G. (1978). Studies of communication during out-of-body experiences. *Journal of the American Society for Psychical Research, 72,* 1–21.

Moruzzi, G., & Magoun, H. W. (1949). Brainstem reticular formation and activation of the EEG. *Electroencephalography and Clinical Neurophysiology, 1,* 455–473.

Moss, S., & Butler, D. C. (1978). The scientific credibility of ESP. *Perceptual and Motor Skills, 46,* 1063–1079.

Moss, T., & Johnson, K. (1974). Bioplasma or corona discharge? In S. Krippner & D. Rubin (Eds.), *The Kirlian aura.* New York: Anchor Books.

Mowrer, O. H. (1938). Preparatory set (expectancy): A determinant in motivation and learning. *Psychological Review, 85,* 61–91.

Muldoon, S., & Carrington, H. (1977). *The projection of the astral body.* London: Rider. (Originally published 1929)

Murphy, G., & Ballou, R. O. (1969). *William James on psychical research.* New York: Viking Press.

Myers, T. I., Murphy, D. B., & Smith, S. (1963). The effect of sensory deprivation and social isolation on self-exposure to propaganda and attitude change. Paper read at the meetings of the American Psychological Association, Chicago.

Myers, R. E., & Sperry, R. W. (1958). Interhemispheric communication through the corpus callosum: Mnemonic carryover between the hemispheres. *Archives of Neurology and Psychiatry, 80,* 298–303.

Nanamoli, T. (1964). *Mindfulness of Breathing.* Kandy, Sri Lanka: Buddhist Publication Society.

Nanamoli, T. (1976). *Visuddhimagga: The Path of Purification.* Berkeley: Shambala.

Naranjo, C., & Ornstein, R. E. (1976). *On the psychology of meditation.* New York: Penguin.

Nash, J. M. (1997). The chemistry of addiction. *Time, 149,* 68–77.

Nash, M. R., Johnson, L. S., & Tipton, R. D. (1979). Hypnotic age regression and the occurrence of transitional object relationships. *Journal of Abnormal Psychology, 88,* 547–555.

Nash, M. R., Minton, A., & Baldridge, J. (1988). Twenty years of scientific hypnosis in dentistry, medicine and psychology. *International Journal of Clinical and Experimental Hypnosis, 36,* 198–205.

Nathan, R. G., Morris, D. M., Goebel, R. A., & Blass, N. H. (1987). Preoperative and intraoperative rehearsal in hypnoanesthesia for major surgery. *American Journal of Clinical Hypnosis, 29,* 238–241.

National Institute on Alcolol Abuse and Alcoholism. (1994). Alcohol and minorities. *Alcohol Alert, 23* (PA 347).

Natsoulas, T. (1978a). Consciousness. *American Psychologist, 33,* 906–914.

Natsoulas, T. (1978b). Toward a model for consciousness in the light of B. F. Skinner's contribution. *Behaviorism, 6,* 139–176.

Natsoulas, T. (1979). The unity of consciousness. *Behaviorism, 7,* 45–63.

Natsoulas, T. (1987). The six basic concepts of consciousness and William James's stream of thought. *Imagination, Cognition and Personality, 6,* 289–319.

Nauta, W. J. H. (1946). Hypothalamic regulation of sleep in rats: Experimental study. *Journal of Neurophysiology, 9,* 285–316.

Nelson, J. (1987). Cracking up. *Essence, 65–66*, 100–101.

Nelson, T. O., McSpadden, M., Fromme, K., & Marlatt, G. A. (1986). Effects of alcohol intoxication on metamemory and on retrieval from long-term memory. *Journal of Experimental Psychology: General, 115*, 247–254.

Nidich, S., Seeman, W., & Dreshin, T. (1973). Influence of transcendental meditation: A replication. *Journal of Counseling Psychology, 20*, 565–566.

Nigil, A. J. (1981). A comparison of binary and analog EMG biofeedback techniques in the treatment of low back pain. *American Journal of Clinical Biofeedback, 4*, 24–31.

Nigil, A. J. (1984). *Biofeedback and behavioral strategies in pain treatment.* Jamaica, NY: Spectrum.

Norton, M. C., & Sahlman, J. H. (1995). Describing the light: Attribution theory as an explanation of the near-death experience. *Journal of Near-Death Studies, 13*, 167–184.

Nowlis, D., & Kamiya, J. (1970). The control of electroencephalographic alpha rhythms through auditory feedback and the associated mental activity. *Psychophysiology, 6*, 476–484.

Nowlis, V. (1965). Research with the mood ajective checklist. In S. S. Tomkins & C. E. Izard (Eds.), *Affect, cognition and personality.* New York: Springer.

O'Beirne, M., Gurevich, N., & Carlen, P. L. (1986). Pentobarbital inhibits hippocampal neurons by increasing potassium conductance. *Canadian Journal of Physiological Pharmacology, 65*, 36–41.

O'Connell, D. N., Shor, R. E., & Orne, M. T. (1970). Hypnotic age regression: An empirical and methodological analysis. *Journal of Abnormal Psychology Monograph Supplement, 76*, 1–32.

Odajnyk, V. W. (1993). *Gathering the light: A psychology of meditation.* Boston: Shambhala.

Olness, K., & Kohen, D. P. (1996). *Hypnosis and hypnotherapy with children.* New York: Guilford.

Olton, D., & Noonberg, A. R. (1980). *Biofeedback: Clinical applications in behavioral medicine.* New York: Prentice-Hall.

Orme-Johnson, D. W. (1973). Autonomic stability and transcendental meditation. *Psychosomatic Medicine, 35*, 341–349.

Orme-Johnson, D. W. (1987). Medical care utilization and the Transcendental Meditation program. *Psychsomatic Medicine, 49*, 493–507.

Orme-Johnson, D. W., Dillbeck, M. C., & Alexander, C. N. (1989). Strategic interventions reducing international conflicts and terrorism: Time series analysis of coherence creating groups. Paper presented at the meetings of the American Political Science Association, Atlanta.

Orne, M. T. (1959). The nature of hypnosis: Artifact and essence. *Journal of Abnormal and Social Psychology, 58*, 277–299.

Orne, M. T. (1979). On the simulating subject as a quasi-control group in hypnosis research: Why, what and how. In E. Fromm & R. E. Shor (Eds.), *Hypnosis: Developments in research and new perspectives.* New York: Aldine.

Orne, M. T., Hilgard, E. R., Spiegel, H., Spiegel, D., & Crawford, H. J. (1979). The relation between the Hypnotic Induction Profile and the Stanford Hypnotic Susceptibility Scales, Forms A and C. *International Journal of Clinical and Experimental Hypnosis, 27*, 85–102.

Orne, M. T., & McConkey, K. M. (1981). Toward convergent inquiry into self-hypnosis. *International Journal of Clinical and Experimental Hypnosis, 29*, 313–323.

Ornstein, R. E. (1972). *The psychology of consciousness.* San Francisco: Freeman.

Ornstein, R. E. (1986). *The psychology of consciousness* (2nd ed.). New York: Penguin.

Osmond, H. (1957). A review of the clinical effects of psychotomimetic agents. Annals of the New York Academy of Scinece, 66, 418–434.

Oswald, I. (1968). Drugs and sleep. *Pharmacological Review, 20,* 272–303.

Oxford English Dictionary. (1933). Oxford: Oxford University Press.

Oystragh, P. (1988). Vaginismus: A case study. *Australian Journal of Clinical and Experimental Hypnosis, 16,* 147–152.

Pagano, R., & Frumkin, L. (1977). Effects of TM in right hemispheric functioning. *Biofeedback and Self-Regulation, 2,* 407–415.

Pagano, R. R., Akots, N. J., & Wall, T. W. (1988). Hypnosis, cerebral laterality and relaxation. *International Journal of Clinical and Experimental Hypnosis, 36,* 350–358.

Palace, E. M. (1995). Modification of dysfunctional patterns of sexual response through autonomic arousal and false physiological feedback. *Journal of Consulting and Clinical Psychology, 63,* 604–615.

Palmer, J. (1971). Scoring in ESP tests as a function of belief in ESP: 1. The sheep-goat effect. *Journal of the American Society for Psychical Research, 65,* 373–408.

Palmer, J. (1978). Correspondence: Deathbed apparitions and the survival hypothesis. *Journal of the American Society for Psychical Research, 72,* 392–395.

Parker, J. B., Chelone, G. J., Hamblin, D. K., & Kitchens, E. M. (1984). Verbal impairment in alcoholics. *Addictive Behavior, 9,* 287–290.

Pascual-Leone, A., Dhuna, A., Altafullah, I., & Anderson, D. C. (1990). Cocaine-induced seizures. *Neurology, 40,* 404–407

Paskewitz, D. A. (1975). Biofeedback instrumentation: Soldering closed the loop. *American Psychologist, 30,* 371–378.

Patel, D. H. (1975). Twelve-month follow-up of yoga and biofeedback in the management of hypertension. *Lancet, 1,* 62–65.

Pearlman, C. (1979). REM sleep and information processing: Evidence from animal studies. *Neuroscience and Biobehavioral Review, 3,* 57–68.

Pekala, R. J., Kumar, V. K., & Cummings, J. (1992). Types of high hypnotically-susceptible individuals and reported attitudes and experiences of the paranormal and the anomalous. *Journal of the American Society for Psychical Research, 86,* 135–150.

Pelletier, K. R., & Garfield, G. (1976). *Consciousness East and West.* New York: Harper and Row.

Penfield, W., & Roberts, L. (1959). *Speech and brain mechanisms.* Princeton, NJ: Princeton University Press.

Percival, G., & Striefel, S. (1994). Ethical beliefs and practices of A.A.P.B. members. *Biofeedback & Self-Regulation, 19,* 67–93.

Perez-Reyes, M., Guiseppi, S. D., Ondrusek, G., Jeffcoat, A. R., & Cook, C. E. (1982). Free-base cocaine smoking. *Clinical Pharmacology and Therapeutics, 32,* 459–465.

Perry, C., Gelfand, R., & Marcovitch, P. (1979). The relevance of hypnotic susceptibility in the clinical context. *Journal of Abnormal Psychology, 88,* 592–603.

Perry, C., & Mullen, G. (1975). The effects of hypnotic susceptibility on reducing smoking behavior treated by an hypnotic technique. *Journal of Clinical Psychology, 31,* 498–505.

Perry, C., Orne, M. T., London, R. W., & Orne, E. C. (1996). Rethinking per se exclusions of hypnotically elicited recall as legal testimony. *International Journal of Clinical and Experimental Hypnosis, 44,* 66–81.

Perry, P. (1988). Brushes with death. *Psychology Today, 22*, 14–17.

Pert, C. B., and Snyder, S. H. (1973). Opiate receptor: Demonstration in nervous tissue. *Science, 179*, 1011–1014.

Petersen, R. C. (Ed.). (1977). *Marijuana research findings*. National Institute of Drug Abuse Research Monograph No. 14, Rockville, MD: National Institute of Drug Abuse.

Petersen, R. C. (1979, July 24.) *Cocaine*. Statement of R. C. Petersen (NIDA, Alcohol, Drug Abuse, and Mental Health Administration Public Health Service, DHEW) Before the Select Committee on Narcotics Abuse and Control, House of Representatives.

Phelps, M. E., & Mazzietta, J. C. (1985). Positron emission tomography: Human brain function and biochemistry. *Science, 228*, 799–809.

Piaget, J. (1970). Piaget's theory. In P. H. Mussen (Ed.), *Carmichael's manual of child psychology* (Vol. 1). New York: Wiley.

Piccione, E., Hilgard, E. R., & Zimbardo, P. G. (1989). On the degree of stability of measured hypnotizability over a 25-year period. *Journal of Personality and Social Psychology, 56*, 289–295.

Pinel, J. P. J. (1997). *Biopsychology* (3rd ed.). Needham Heights, MA: Allyn and Bacon.

Plotkin, W. B., and Cohen, R. (1976). Occipital alpha and attributes of the "alpha experience." *Psychophysiology, 13*, 16–21.

Pope, H. G., & Yurgelun-Todd, D. (1996). The residual cognitive effects of heavy marijuana use in college students. *Journal of the American Medical Association, 275*, 521–527.

Post, R. M. (1975). Cocaine psychosis: A continuum model. *American Journal of Psychiatry, 132*, 225–231.

Powell, D. H. (1980). Helping habitual smokers using flooding and hypnotic desensitization techniques. *International Journal of Clinical and Experimental Hypnosis, 28*, 192–196.

Pratt, J. G. (1973a). *ESP research today: A study of developments in parapsychology since 1960*. Metuchen, NJ: Scarecrow Press.

Pratt, J. G. (1973b). A decade of research with a selected ESP subject: An overview and reappraisal of the work with Pavel Stepanek. *Proceedings of the American Society for Psychical Research, 30*, 1–78.

Pratt, J. G., & Roll, W. G. (1958). The Seaford disturbances. *Journal of Parapsychology, 22*, 79–124.

Pratt, J. G., & Woodruff, J. L. (1939). Size of stimulus symbols in extrasensory perception. *Journal of Parapsychology, 3*, 121–158.

Pressman, M. R. (1991). Whatever happened to insomnia (and insomnia research)? *American Journal of Psychiatry, 148*, 419–420.

Priebe, F. A., & Wallace, B. (1986). Hypnotic susceptibility, imaging ability and the detection of embedded objects. *International Journal of Clinical and Experimental Hypnosis, 34*, 320–329.

Proverbio, A. M., Zani, A., Gazzaniga, M. S., & Mangun, G. R. (1994). ERP and RT signs of a rightward bias for spatial orienting in a split-brain patient. *Neuroreport: An International Journal for the Rapid Communication of Research in Neuroscience, 5*, 2457–2461.

Putnam, W. H. (1979). Hypnosis and distortions in eyewitness memory. *International Journal of Clinical and Experimental Hypnosis, 27*, 437–448.

Pykett, I. L. (1982). NMR imaging in medicine. *Scientific American, 246*, 78–88.

Radin, D. I. (1988). Effects of a priori probability on psi perception: Does precognition predict actual or probable futures? *Journal of Parapsychology, 52,* 187–212.

Radnitz, C. L., & Blanchard, E. B. (1989). Bowel sound biofeedback as a treatment for irritable bowel syndrome: A 2-year follow-up study. Paper presented at the meetings of the Association for Applied Psychophysiology and Biofeedback, San Diego.

Raikov, V. L. (1980). Age regression to infancy by adult subjects in deep hypnosis. *American Journal of Clinical Hypnosis, 22,* 156–163.

Rakhindzhanov, A. R., Gafurov, V. G., & Matkhalikov, A. F. (1988). The pathogenesis of nocturnal and diurnal cerebral strokes. *Soviet Neurology and Psychiatry, 21,* 50–57.

Ramirez, C. E., Suedfeld, P., & Remick, R. (1993). Reducing post-ECT memory complaints by REST. Paper presented at the meetings of the 54th annual convention of Canadian Psychological Association, Montreal.

Randi, J. (1975). *The magic of Uri Geller.* New York: Ballatine.

Randi, J. (1982). *Truth about Uri Geller.* Buffalo, NY: Prometheus.

Rao, K. R. (1966). *Experimental parapsychology.* Springfield, IL: Charles C. Thomas.

Rao, K. R. (1977). On the Nature of psi: An examination of some attempts to explain ESP and PK. *Journal of Parapsychology, 41,* 294–351.

Rao, K. R. (1979). On "the scientific credibility of ESP." *Perceptual and Motor Skills, 49,* 415–429.

Ras, K. R., & Palmer, J. (1987). The anamoly called psi: Recent research and criticism. *Behavioral & Brain Sciences, 10,* 539–643.

Raskin, N. (1980). Migraine, tension Headache: Same disorder. *Clinical Psychiatric News,* May 15.

Ray, O., & Ksir, C. (1987). *Drugs, society, and human behavior.* St. Louis: Mosby.

Reading, C., & Mohr, P. D. (1976). Biofeedback control of migraine: A pilot study. *British Journal of Social and Clinical Psychology, 15,* 429–433.

Rech, R. H., & Commissaris, R. L. (1982). Neurotransmitter basis of the behavioral effects of hallucinogens. *Neuroscience and Biobehavioral Reviews, 6,* 521–528.

Rech, R. H., & Rosecrans, J. A. (1982). Review of mechanisms of hallucinogenic drug action. *Neuroscience and Biobehavioral Reviews, 6,* 481–482.

Rechtschaffen, A., & Dement, W. C. Narcolepsy and hypersomnia. (1969). In A. Kales (Ed.), *Sleep: Physiology and pathology.* Philadelphia: Lippincott.

Rechtschaffen, A., Verdone, P., & Wheaton, J. (1963). Reports of mental activity during sleep. *Canadian Psychiatric Association Journal, 8,* 409–414.

Rechtschaffen, A., Wolpert, E. A., Dement, W. C., Mitchell, S. A., & Fisher, C. (1963). Nocturnal sleep of narcoleptics. *Electroencephalography and Clinical Neurophysiology, 15,* 599–609.

Reed, G. K. (1962). Preparatory set as a factor in the production of sensory deprivation phenomena. *Proceeding of the Royal Society of Medicine, 55,* 1010–1014.

Reed, S. K. (1996). *Cognition: Theory and applications* (4th ed.). Monterey, CA: Brooks/Cole.

Reiman, E. M., Lane, R. D., Ahern, G. L., Schwartz, G. E., & Davidson, R. J. (1996). Positron emission tomography, emotion, and consciousness. In S. R. Hameroff, A. W. Kaszniak, & A. C. Scott (Eds.), *Toward a science of consciousness: The first Tucson discussions and debates* (pp. 311–320). Cambridge, MA: MIT Press.

Relman, A. S. (1982). Marijuana and health. *New England Journal of Medicine, 306,* 603–605.

Resnick, R. B., Kestenbaum, R. S., & Schwartz, L. K. (1977). Acute systematic effects of cocaine in man: A controlled study by intranasal and intravenous routs of administration. *Science, 195,* 696–698.

Restak, R. (1977, March 5). The brain makes its own narcotics. *Saturday Review,* pp. 8–11.

Reuter-Lorenz, P. A., Nozawa, G., Gazzaniga, M. S., & Hughes, H. C. (1995). Fate of neglected targets: A chronometric analysis of redundant target effects in the bisected brain. *Journal of Experimental Psychology: Human Perception and Performance, 21,* 211–230.

Rhine, J. B. (1945). Parapsychology and dualism (editorial). *Journal of Parapsychology, 9,* 225–228.

Rhine, J. B. (1953). *New world of the mind.* New York: William Sloan.

Rhine, J. B. (1964). *Extrasensory perception.* Boston: Bruce Humphries. (Originally published 1934)

Rhine, J. B., & Brier, R. (Eds.). (1968). *Parapsychology today.* New York: Citadel Press.

Rhine, J. B., & Pratt, J. G. (1957). *Parapsychology: Frontier science of the mind.* Springfield, IL: Charles C. Thomas.

Rhine, L. E. (1961). *Hidden channels of the mind.* New York: Sloan Associates.

Rhine, L. E. (1970). *Mind over matter.* New York: Macmillan.

Rhue, J. W., & Lynn, S. J. (1989). Fantasy proneness, hypnotizability and absorption: A reexamination. *International Journal of Clinical and Experimental Hypnosis, 37,* 100–106.

Ricalla, L. M. (1975). Healing by laying on of hands: Myth or fact? *Ethics in Science and Medicine, 2,* 167–171.

Ring, K. (1980). *Life at death: A scientific investigation of the near-death experience.* New York: Morrow.Ring, K. (1985). *Heading toward omega: In search of the meaning of the near-death experience.* New York: Morrow.

Ring, K. (1993). Near-death experiences: Implications for human evolution and planetary transformation. In B. Kane, J. Millay, & D. H. Brown (Eds.), *Silver threads: 25 years of parapsychology research* (pp. 242–257). Westport, CT: Praeger.

Ring, K. (1995). The impact of near-death experiences on persons who have not had them: A report of a preliminary study and two replications. *Journal of Near-Death Studies, 13,* 223–235.

Ritchie, J. M. (1985). The aliphatic alcohols. In A. G. Gilman, L. S. Goodman, T. W. Rall, & F. Murad (Eds.), *The pharmacological basis of therapeutics.* New York: Macmillan.

Robbins, P. R., & Houshi, F. (1983). Some observations on recrurrent dreams. *Bulletin of the Menninger Clinic, 47,* 262–265.

Robbins, P. R., & Tanck, R. H. (1988). Depressed mood, dream recall and contentless dreams. *Imagination, Cognition and Personality, 8,* 165–174.

Roberts, A. H. (1985). Biofeedback: Research, training, and clinical roles. *American Psychologist, 40,* 938–941.

Roberts, G., & McGrady, A. (1996). Racial and gender effects on the relaxation response: Implications for the development of hypertension. *Biofeedback & Self-Regulation, 21,* 51–61.

Robertson, M. H. (1961). Theoretical implications of sensory deprivation. *Psychological Records, 11,* 33–42.

Robertson, M. H., & Walter, D. J. (1963). The effect of sensory deprivation upon scores on the Wechsler Adult Intelligence Scale. *Journal of Psychology, 56,* 213–218.

Roffwarg, H. P., Muzio, J. N., & Dement, W. C. (1966). Ontogenetic development of the human sleep-dream cycle. *Science, 152,* 604–619.

Roll, W. G. (1966). ESP and memory. *International Journal of Neuropsychiatry, 2,* 505–521.

Rosenthal, R. (1966). *Experimenter effects in behavioral research.* New York: Appleton-Century-Crofts.

Rosenzweig, N. (1959). Sensory deprivation and schizophrenia: Clinical and theoretical similarities. *American Journal of Psychiatry, 116,* 326–329.

Rossi, A. M. (1969). General methodological considerations. In J. P. Zubek (Ed.), *Sensory deprivation: Fifteen years of research* (pp. 16–46). New York: Appleton-Century-Crofts.

Rossi, A. M., Kuehnle, J. C., & Mendelson, J. H. (1978). Marijuana and mood in human volunteers. *Pharmacology, Biochemistry, and Behavior, 8,* 447–453.

Rossi, E. L. (1982). Hypnosis and ultradian cycles: A new state(s) theory of hypnosis? *American Journal of Clinical Hypnosis, 25,* 21–32.

Sackheim, H. A., Paulus, D., & Weiman, A. L. (1979). Classroom seating and hypnotic susceptibility. *Journal of Abnormal Psychology, 88,* 81–84.

Salley, R. D. (1982). REM sleep phenomena during out-of-body experiences. *Journal of the American Society for Psychical Research, 76,* 157–165.

Sampson, H. (1966). Psychological effects of deprivation of dreaming sleep. *Journal of Nervous and Mental Disease, 143,* 305–317.

Sanders, G. S., & Simmons, W. L. (1983). Use of hypnosis to enhance eyewitness accuracy: Does it work? *Journal of Applied Psychology, 68,* 70–77.

Sarbin, T. R., & Coe, W. C. (1972). *Hypnosis: A social psychological analysis of influence communication.* New York: Holt, Rinehart, Winston.

Sarbin, T. R., & Coe, W. C. (1979). Hypnosis and psychopathology: Replacing old myths with fresh metaphors. *Journal of Abnormal Psychology, 88,* 506–526.

Sargent, J. D., Green, E. E., & Walters, E. D. (1973). Preliminary report on the use of autogenic feedback techniques in the treatment of migraine and tension headaches. *Psychosomatic Medicine, 35,* 129–135.

Sargent, J. D., Green, E. E., & Walters, E. D. (1977). The use of autogenic feedback training in a pilot study of migraine and tension headaches. *Headache, 12,* 120–124.

Sattler, J. M. (1970). Racial "experimenter effects" in experimentation, testing, interviewing and psychotherapy. *Psychological Bulletin, 73,* 137–160.

Saxby, E. (1995). Alpha-theta brainwave neurofeedback training: An effective treatment for male and female alcoholics with depressive symptoms. *Journal of Clinical Psychology, 51,* 685–693.

Scharf, M. B., & Jennings, S. W. (1988). Childhood enuresis: Relationship to sleep, etiology, evaluation, and treatment. *Annals of Behavioral Medicine, 10,* 113–120.

Schenck, C. H., Hurwitz, T. D., & Mahowald, M. W. (1993). REM sleep behaviour disorder: An update on a series of 96 patients and a review of the world literature. *Journal of Sleep Research, 2,* 224–231.

Schenck, C. H., & Mahowald, M. W. (1990). Polysomnographic, neurologic, psychiatric, and clinical outcome report on 70 consecutive cases with REM sleep behavior disorder (RBD). Sustained clonazepam efficiency in 84.5% of 57 treated patients. *Cleveland Clinic Journal of Medicine, 57* supplement, S9–S23.

Schlosberg, H. (1937). The relationship between success and the laws of conditioning. *Psychological Review, 44,* 379–394.

Schmeidler, G. R. (1984). Further analyses of PK with continuous termperature recording. *Journal of the American Society for Psychical Research, 78,* 355–362.

Schmeidler, G. R. (1985). Field and stream: Background stimuli and the flow of ESP responses. *Journal of the American Society for Psychical Research, 79*, 13–26.

Schmeidler, G. R., & McConnell, R. A. (1958). *ESP and personality patterns*. New Haven: Yale University Press.

Schmidt, H. (1970a). A PK test with electronic equipment. *Journal of Parapsychology, 34*, 175–181.

Schmidt, H. (1970b). A quantum mechanical random number generator for psi tests. *Journal of Parapsychology, 34*, 219–224.

Schmidt, H. (1973). PK tests with a high-speed random number generator. *Journal of Parapsychology, 37*, 105–118.

Schmidt, H. (1975). Toward a mathematical theory of psi. *Journal of the American Society for Psychical Research, 69*, 301–319.

Schmidt, H. (1987). Alcock's critique of Schmidt's experiments. *Behavioral and Brain Sciences, 10*, 609.

Schmidt, H., Morris, R. L., & Rudolph, L. (1986). Channeling evidence for a PK effect to independent observers. *Journal of Parapsychology, 50*, 1–15.

Schnarch, D., & Hunter, J. (1980). Migraine incidence in clinical and nonclinical populations. *Psychosomatic Medicine, 21*, 314–325.

Schneider, A. M., & Tarshis, B. (1986). *An introduction to physiological psychology*. New York: Random House.

Schneider, F., Elbert, T., Heimann, H., Welker, A., Stetter, F., Mattes, R., Birbaumer, N., & Mann, K. (1993). Self-regulation of slow cortical potentials in psychiatric patients: Alcohol dependency. *Biofeedback & Self-Regulation, 18*, 23–32.

Schroter-Kunhardt, M. (1993). A review of near death experiences. *Journal of Scientific Exploration, 7*, 219–239.

Schultz, J. H., & Luthe, W. (1969). *Autogenic therapy* (Vol. 1). New York: Grune and Stratton.

Schwartz, D. G., Weinstein, L. N., & Arkin, A. M. (1978). Qualitative aspects of sleep mentation. In A. M. Arkin, J. S. Antrobus, & S. J. Ellman (Eds.), *The mind in sleep: Psychology and psychophysiology*. Hillsdale, NJ: Erlbaum.

Schwartz, G. E., & Beatty, J. (1977). *Biofeedback theory and research*. New York: Academic Press.

Schwartz, M. S. (Ed.). (1995). *Biofeedback: A practitioner's guide* (2nd ed.). New York: Guilford.

Schwartz, S. P., Taylor, A. E., Scharf, L. P., & Blanchard, E. B. (1989). Behavioral treatment of irritable bowel syndrome: A 3- and 4-year follow-up study. Paper presented at the meetings of the Association for Applied Psychophysiology and Biofeedback, San Diego.

Scott, T. H., Bexton, W. H., Heron, W., & Doane, B. K. (1959). Cognitive effects of perceptual isolation. *Canadian Journal of Psychology, 13*, 200–209.

Scriven, M. (1976). The frontiers of psychology: psychoanalysis and parapsychology. In J. M. O. Wheatley & H. L. Edge (Eds.), *Philosophical dimensions of parapsychology*. Springfield, IL: Charles C. Thomas.

Searle, J. R. (1995). The problem of consciousness. In J. King & K. H. Pribram (Eds.), *Scale in conscious experience: Is the brain too important to be left to specialists to study?* Mahwah, NJ: Erlbaum, pp. 13–22.

Segalowitz, S. J. (1983). *Two sides of the brain: Brain lateralization explored*. Englewood Cliffs, NJ: Prentice-Hall.

Sepinwall, J., & Cook, L. (1980). Relationship of gamma-aminobutyric acid (GABA) to antianxiety effects of benzodiazepins. *Brain Research, 5,* 839–848.

Seymour, S. E., Reuter-Lorenz, P. A., & Gazzaniga, M. S. (1994). The disconnection syndrome: Basic findings reaffirmed. *Brain, 117,* 105–115.

Shah, I. (1970). *The way of the Sufi.* New York: Dutton.

Shapiro, C. M., Bortz, R., Mitchell, D., Bartel, P., & Jooste, P. (1981). Slow wave sleep: A recovery after exercise. *Science, 214,* 1253–1254.

Shapiro, D. H. (1976). Zen meditation and behavioral self-control strategies applied to a case of generalized anxiety. *Psychologia, 9,* 134–138.

Shapiro, D. H. (1980). *Meditation: Self-regulation strategy and altered state of consciousness.* New York: Aldine.

Shapiro, D. H. (1985). Clinical use of meditation as a self-regulation strategy: Comments on Holmes's conclusions and implications. *American Psychologist, 40,* 719–722.

Shapiro, D. H., & Walsh, R. (Eds.). (1984). *Meditation: Classic and contemporary perspectives.* New York: Aldine.

Sharpless, S. K. (1970). Hypnotics and sedatives. In J. Goodman & A. Gilman (Eds.), *The pharmacological basis of therapeutics.* New York: Macmillan.

Shearn, D. W. (1960). *Operant conditioning of heart rate.* Unpublished doctoral dissertation, Indiana University.

Sheehan, E. P., Smith, H. V., & Forrest, D. W. (1982). A signal detection study of the effects of suggested improvement on the monocular visual acuity of myopes. *International Journal of Clinical and Experimental Hypnosis, 30,* 138–146.

Sheehan, P. W. (1979). Hypnosis and the process of imagination. In E. Fromm & R. E. Shor (Eds.), *Hypnosis: Developments in research and new perspectives.* Chicago: Aldine.

Sheehan, P. W. (1982). Imagery and hypnosis: Forging a link, at least in part. *Research Communication in Psychology, Psychiatry, and Behavior, 7,* 257–272.

Sheehan, P. W. (1988). Memory distortion in hypnosis. *International Journal of Clinical and Experimental Hypnosis, 36,* 296–311.

Sheehan, P. W., Donovan, P., & MacLeod, C. M. (1988). Strategy manipulation and the Stroop effect in hypnosis. *Journal of Abnormal Psychology, 97,* 455–460.

Sheehan, P. W., & McConkey, K. M. (1982). *Hypnosis and experience: The exploration of phenomena and process.* Hillsdale, NJ: Erlbaum.

Sheehan, P. W., & Tilden, J. (1983). Effects of suggestibility and hypnosis on accurate and distorted retrieval from memory. *Journal of Experimental Psychology: Learning, Memory and Cognition, 9,* 283–293.

Sheer, D. E. (Ed.). (1961). *Electrical stimulation of the brain.* Austin: University of Texas Press.

Shor, R. E. (1979). The fundamental problem in hypnosis research as viewed from historic perspectives. In E. Fromm & R. E. Shor (Eds.), *Hypnosis: Developments in research and new perspectives.* New York: Aldine.

Shor, R. E., & Orne, E. C. (1962). *The Harvard Group Scale of Hypnotic Susceptibility: Form A.* Palo Alto, CA: Consulting Psychologists Press.

Shouse, M. N., & Lubar, J. F. (1977). Management of the hyperkinetic syndrome with methylphenidate and SMR biofeedback training. *Biofeedback and Self-Regulation, 2,* 290.

Shurley, J. T. (1960). Profound experimental sensory isolation. *American Journal of Psychiatry, 117,* 539–545.

Shurley, J. T. (1961). Problems and methods in experimental sensory input alteration and variance. Unpublished paper.

Shurley, J. T. (1963). The hydro-hypodynamic environment. *Proceedings of the Third World Congress of Psychiatry, Vol. 3.* Toronto: University of Toronto.

Siegel, R. K. (1977). Hallucinations. *Scientific American, 237,* 132–140.

Siegel, R. K. (1985). Quoted in Cocaine use: Disturbing signs. *Science News,* 128.

Silling, S. M. (1980, January). LSD flashbacks: An overview of the literature for counselors. *American Mental Health Counselors Association Journal, 39–*45.

Silver, B., & Blanchard, E. (1978). Biofeedback and relaxation training in the treatment of psychophysiological disorders: Or are the machines really necessary? *Journal of Behavioral Medicine, 1,* 217–239.

Silver, B., Blanchard, E., Williamson, D., Theobald, D., & Brown, D. (1979). Temperature biofeedback and relaxation training in the treatment of migraine headaches. *Biofeedback and Self-Regulation, 4,* 359–366.

Silverman, K., Evans, S. M., Strain, E. C., & Griffiths, R. R. (1992). Withdrawal syndrome after the double-blind cessation of caffeine consumption. *New England Journal of Medicine, 327,* 1109–1114.

Simantov, R., Goodman, R., Aposhian, D., & Snyder, S. H. (1976). Phylogenetic distribution of a morphine-like ligand "enkephalin." *Brain Research, 111,* 204–211.

Simon, D. B., Oparil, S., & Kimball, C. P. (1977). The transcendental meditation program and essential hypertension. In D. Orme-Johnson & J. Farrow (Eds.), *Scientific research on the transcendental meditation program* (Vol. 1). Los Angeles: Maharishi European Research University Press.

Singer, J. L. (1975). *The inner world of daydreaming.* New York: Harper & Row.

Skinner, B. F. (1964). Behaviorism at fifty. In T. W. Wann (Ed.), *Behaviorism and phenomenology: Contrasting bases for modern psychology.* Chicago: University of Chicago Press.

Skinner, B. F. (1974). *About behaviorism.* New York: Knopf.

Skolnick, P., Noncada, V., Barker, J. L., & Paul, S. M. (1981). Pentobarbital: Dual actions to increase brain benzodiazepine receptor affinity. *Science, 211,* 1448–1450.

Slaughter, J., Hahn, W., & Rinaldi, R. (1970). Instrumental conditioning of heart rate in the curarized rat with varied amounts of pretraining. *Journal of Comparative and Physiological Psychology, 72,* 356–359.

Sloan, M. C. (1981). A comparison of hypnosis vs. waking state and visual vs. nonvisual recall instructions for witness/victim memory retrieval in actual major crimes. Unpublished doctoral disseration, Florida State University.

Smith, C. (1985). Sleep states and learning: A review of the animal literature. *Neuroscience and Biobehavioral Review, 9,* 157–168.

Smith, D. E., & Rose, A. J. (1967–1968). LSD: Its use, abuse, and suggested treatment. *Journal of Psychelic Drugs, 1,* 117–123.

Smith, J. (1964). Do drugs have religious import? In D. Soloman (Ed.), *LSD: The consciousness-expanding drug.* New York: Putnam's Sons.

Smith, J. C., Ellenberger, H. H., Ballanyi, K., Richter, D. W., & Feldman, J. L. (1991). Pre-Botzinger complex: A brainstem region that may generate respiratory rhythm in mammals. *Science, 254,* 726–729.

Smith, J. T., Barabasz, A., & Barabasz, M. (1996). Comparison of hypnosis and distraction in severely ill children undergoing painful medical procedures. *Journal of Counseling Psychology, 43,* 187–195.

Smith, M. D. (1992). The effect of belief in the paranormal and prior set upon the observation of a "psychic" demonstration. *European Journal of Parapsychology, 9,* 24–34.

Smith, P. F. (1995). Cannabis and the brain. *New Zealand Journal of Psychology, 24,* 5–12.

Smith-Donals, L., & Klitzner, M. D. (1985). Self-reports of youthful drinking and driving! Sensitivity analyses of sensitive data. *Journal of Psychoactive Drugs, 17,* 179–190.

Snel, F. W. J. J., van der Sijde, P. C., & Wiegant, F. A. C. (1995). Cognitive styles of believers and disbelievers in paranormal phenomena. *Journal of the Society for Psychical Research, 60,* 251–257.

Snodgrass, M., & Lynn, S. J. (1989). Music absorption and hypnotizability. *International Journal of Clinical and Experimental Hypnosis, 37,* 41–54.

Snyder, F. (1970). The phenomenology of draming. In H. Madlow & L. H. Snow (Eds.), *The psychodynamic implications of the physiological studies on dreams.* Springfield, IL: Charles C. Thomas.

Snyder, S. H. (1971). Cannabis. *Psychology Today, 4,* 37–40.

Snyder, S. H. (1977). The brain's own opiates. *Chemical and Engineering News, 55,* 26–35.

Sokolov, E. N. (1963). *Perception and the conditioned reflex.* New York: Pergamon.

Sondow, N. (1988). The decline of precognized events with the passage of time: Evidence from spontaneous dreams. *Journal of the American Society for Psychical Research, 82,* 33–52.

Soulairac, A., & Soulairac, M. (1965). Effects of certain steroid hormones on the sexual behaviour of the male rat and an analysis of their effect on the central nervous system. *Hormonal steroids, biochemistry, pharmacology and therapeutics: Proceedings of the First International Congress on Hormonal Steroids* (Vol. 2). New York: Academic Press.

Spanos, N. P. (1982). A social psychological approach to hypnotic behavior. In G. Weary & H. Mirels (Eds.), *Integration of clinical and social psychology.* New York: Oxford University Press.

Spanos, N. P. (1986). Hypnosis and the modification of hypnotic susceptibility: A social psychological perspective. In P. Naish (Ed.), *What is hypnosis? Current theories and research.* (pp. 85–120). Philadelphia: Open University Press.

Spanos, N. P., Ansari, F., & Stam, H. J. (1979). Hypnotic age regression and eidetic imagery: A failure to replicate. *Journal of Abnormal Psychology, 88,* 88–91.

Spanos, N. P., Cross, W. P., & de Groh, M. M. (1987). Measuring resistence to hypnosis and its relationship to hypnotic susceptibility. *Psychological Reports, 60,* 67–70.

Spanos, N. P., Gorassini, D. R., & Petrusic, W. (1981). Hypnotically induced limb anesthesia and adaptation to displacing prisms: A failure to confirm. *Journal of Abnormal Psychology, 90,* 329–333.

Spanos, N. P., Ham, M. W., & Barber, T. X. (1973). Suggested ("hypnotic") visual hallucinations: Experimental and phenomenological data. *Journal of Abnormal Psychology, 81,* 96–106.

Spanos, N. P., Radtke, H. L., & Dubreuil, D. L. (1982). Episodic and semantic memory in posthypnotic amnesia. *Journal of Personality and Social Psychology, 43,* 565–573.

Spanos, N. P., Radtke, H. L., Hodgins, D. C., Bertrand, L., Stam, H. J., & Dubreuil, D. L. (1983). The Carleton University Responsiveness to Suggestion Scale: Stability, reliability, and relationships with expectancy and hypnotic experience. *Psychological Reports, 53,* 555–563.

Spanos, N. P., Radtke, H. L., Hodgins, D. C., Stam, H. J., & Bertrand, L. (1983). The Carleton University Responsiveness to Suggestion Scale: Normative data and psychometric properties. *Psychological Reports, 53,* 523–535.

Spanos, N. P., Radtke, H. L., Hodgins, D. C., Stam, H. J., & Noretti, P. (1983). The Carleton University Responsiveness to Suggestion Scale: Relationships with other measures of susceptibility, expectancies, and absorption. *Psychological Reports, 53,* 723–734.

Sperry, R. W. (1966). Brain bisection and consciousness. In J. Eccles (Ed.), *Brain and conscious experience.* New York: Springer-Verlag.

Sperry, R. W. (1974). Lateral specialization in the surgically separated hemispheres. In F. O. Schmitt & F. G. Wordon (Eds.), *The neurosciences: Third study program,* Cambridge: MIT Press.

Spiegel, D., & Barabasz, A. F. (1988). Effects of hypnotic instructions on P_{300} event-related-potential amplitudes: Research and clinical implications. *American Journal of Clinical Hypnosis, 31,* 11–17.

Spiegel, D., Bierre, P., & Rootenberg, J. (1989). Hypnotic alteration of somatosensory perception. *American Journal of Psychiatry, 146,* 749–759.

Spiegel, H. (1970). An eye-roll sign for hypnotizability. Paper presented at the annual meeting of the Society for Clinical and Experimental Hypnosis, Philadelphia, October.

Spiegel, H. (1979a). The Hypnotic Induction Profile (HIP): A review of its development. In W. E. Edmonston (Ed.), *Conceptual and investigative approaches to hypnosis and hypnotic phenomena. Annals of the New York Academy of Science, 296,* 129–142.

Spiegel, H. (1979b). A single-treatment method to stop smoking using ancillary self-hypnosis. *International Journal of Clinical and Experimental Hypnosis, 18,* 235–250.

Spielman, A., & Herrera, C. (1991). Sleep disorders. In S. A. Ellman & J. S. Antrobus (Eds.), *The mind in sleep: Psychology and psychophysiology* (2nd ed., pp. 25–80). New York: Wiley.

Spotts, J., & Schontz, F. (1976). *The life styles of nine American cocaine users.* Washington, DC: Department of Health, Education, and Welfare.

Springer, S. P., & Deutsch, G. (1997). *Left brain/right brain: Perspectives from cognitive neuroscience* (5th ed.). New York: Freeman.

Stambaugh, E. E., & House, A. E. (1977). Multimodality treatment of migraine headache: A case study utilizing biofeedback, relaxation, autogenic and hypnotic treatments. *American Journal of Clinical Hypnosis, 19,* 235–240.

Stanford, R. G. (1974). An experimentally testable model for spontaneous psi events. I. Extrasensory events. *Journal of the American Society for Psychical Research, 68,* 34–57.

Stanford, R. G. (1977a). Are parapsychologists paradigmless in psiland? In B. Shapin & L. Coly (Eds.), *The Philosophy of parapsychology.* New York: Parapsychology Foundation.

Stanford, R. G. (1977b). Conceptual frameworks of contemporary psi research. In B. Wolman (Ed.), *Handbook of Parapsychology.* New York: Van Nostrand Reinhold.

Stanton, H. E. (1975). Weight loss through hypnosis. *American Journal of Clinical Hypnosis, 18,* 34–38.

Steiner, S., & Dince, W. (1981). Biofeedback efficacy study: A critique of critiques. *Biofeedback and Self-Regulation, 6,* 275–288.

Steel, G. D., & Suedfeld, P. (1994). The "big five" personality dimensions in polar sojourners. Paper presented at the meetings of the 55th annual convention of the Canadian Psychological Association, Penticton, BC.

Stephens, R. C. (1987). *Mind-altering drugs.* Newbury Park, NY: Sage.

Steriade, M., McCormick, D. A., & Segnowski, T. J. (1993). Thalmocortical oscillations in sleeping and aroused brain. *Science, 262,* 679–685.

Sterling-Smith, R. S. (1976). A special study of drivers most responsible in fatal accidents. *Summary for Management Report,* Contract DOT HS 310-3-595. Washington, DC: Department of Transportation.

Sterman, M. B. (1973). Neurophysiological and clinical studies of sensorimotor EEG biofeedback training: Some effects on epilepsy. *Seminars in Psychiatry, 5,* 507–525.

Stern, D. B., Spiegel, H., & Nee, J. C. (1979). The Hypnotic Induction Profile: Normative observations, reliability, and validity. *American Journal of Clinical Hypnosis, 21,* 109–133.

Stern, W., & Morgane, P. (1974). Theoretical view of REM sleep functions: Maintenance of catecholamine systems in the central nervous system. *Behavioral Biology, 11,* 1–32.

Sternberg, R. J. (1996). *Cognitive psychology.* Ft. Worth, TX: Harcourt Brace.

Stroebal, C., & Ford, M. (1981). Quieting response training: Five-year evaluation of a clinical biofeedback practice. *Proceedings of the Biofeedback Society of America, 8,* 78–81.

Stromeyer, C. F., & Psotka, J. (1970). The detailed texture of eidetic images. *Nature, 225,* 346–349.

Sudsuang, R., Chentanez, V., & Veluvan, K. (1991). Effect of Buddhist meditation on serum cortisol and total protein levels, blood pressure, pulse rate, lung volume and reaction time. *Physiology & Behavior, 50,* 543–548.

Suedfeld, P. (1968). Anticipated and experienced stress in sensory deprivation as a function of orientation and ordinal position. *Journal of Social Psychology, 76,* 259–263.

Suedfeld, P. (1969). Changes in intellectual performance and in susceptibility to influence. In J. P. Zubek (Ed.), *Sensory deprivation: Fifteen years of research.* New York: Appleton-Century-Crofts.

Suedfeld, P. (1980). *Restricted environmental stimulation: Research and clinical applications.* New York: Wiley.

Suedfeld, P., & Baker-Brown, G. (1986). Restricted environmental stimulation therapy and aversive conditioning in smoking cessation. *Behavior Research and Therapy, 24,* 421–428.

Suedfeld, P., Ballard, E. J., Baker-Brown, G., & Borrie, R. A. (1986). Flow of consciousness in restricted environmental stimulation. *Imagination, Cognition, and Personaltiy, 5,* 219–230.

Suedfeld, P., Ballard, E. J., & Murphy, M. (1983). Water immersion and flotation: From stress experiment to stress treatment. *Journal of Environmental Psychology, 3,* 147–155.

Suedfeld, P., & Coren, S. (1989). Perceptual isolation, sensory deprivation, and REST: Moving introductory psychology texts out of the 1950s. *Canadian Psychology, 30,* 17–29

Suedfeld, P., & Ikard, F. F. (1974). The use of sensory deprivation in facilitating the reduction of cigarette smoking. *Journal of Consulting and Clinical Psychology, 42,* 888–895.

Suedfeld, P., & Kristeller, J. L. (1982). Stimulus reduction as a technique in health psychology. *Health Psychology, 1,* 337–357.

Suedfeld, P., Landon, P. B., Pargament, R., & Epstein, Y. M. (1972). An experimental attack on smoking: Attitude manipulation in restricted environments. III. *International Journal of the Addictions, 7,* 721–733.

Suedfeld, P., & Mocellin, J. S. P. (1987). The sensed presence in unusual environments. *Environment and Behavior, 19*, 33–52.

Suedfeld, P., & Vernon, J. (1964). Visual hallucinations during sensory deprivation: A problem of criteria. *Science, 145*, 412–413

Suedfeld, P., & Vernon, J. (1966). Attitude manipulation in restricted environments. II. Conceptual structure and the internalization of propaganda received as a reward for compliance. *Journal of Personality and Social Psychology, 3*, 586–589.

Sugi, Y., & Akutsu, K. (1964). *Science of Zazen—Energy metabolism*. Tokyo: University Press of Tokyo.

Surwit, R. S. (1982). Biofeedback and the behavioral treatment of Raynaud's disease. In L. White & B. Tursky (Eds.), *Clinical biofeedback: Efficacy and mechanisms* (pp. 222–232). New York: Guilford.

Suzdak, P. D., Glowa, J. R., Crawley, J. N., Schwartz, R. D., Skolnick, P., & Paul, S. M. (1986). A selective imidazobenzodiazepine antagonist of ethanol in the rat. *Science, 234*, 1243–1248.

Switras, J. E. (1974). A comparison of the eye-roll test for hypnotizability and the Stanford Hypnotic Susceptibility Scale: Form A. *American Journal of Clinical Hypnosis, 17*, 54–55.

Targ, R., & Puthoff, H. (1974a). Information transfer under conditions of sensory shielding. *Nature, 251*, 602–607.

Targ, R., & Puthoff, H. (1974b). ESP experiments with Uri Geller. In W. G. Roll, R. L. Morris, & J. D. Morris (Eds.), *Research in parapsychology*. Metuchen, NJ: Scarecrow Press.

Targ, R., & Puthoff, H. (1977). *Mind-read*. New York: Delacorte.

Tart, C. T. (1966). Card guessing tests: Learning paradigm or extinction paradigm? *Journal of the American Society for Psychical Research, 60*, 46–55.

Tart, C. T. (1968). A psychophysiological study of out-of-the-body experiences in a selected subject. *Journal of the American Society for Psychical Research, 62*, 3–27.

Tart, C. T. (Ed.). (1972). *Altered states of consciousness*. Garden City, NY: Doubleday.

Tart, C. T. (1975). *States of consciousness*. New York: Dutton.

Tart, C. T. (1977a). Putting the pieces together: A conceptual framework for understanding discrete states of consciousness. In N. E. Zinberg (Ed.), *Alternate states of consciousness: Multiple perspectives on the study of consciousness*. New York: Free Press.

Tart, C. T. (1977b). Toward conscious control of psi through immediate feedback training: some considerations of internal processes. *Journal of the American Society for Psychical Research, 71*, 375–407.

Tart, C. T. (1996). Parapsychology and transpersonal psychology. In B. W. Scotton, A. B. Chinen, & J. R. Battista (Eds.), *Textbook of transpersonal psychiatry and psychology* (pp. 186–194). New York: Basic Books.

Tart, C. T., Palmer, J., and Redington, D. J. (1979a). Effects of immediate feedback on ESP performance: A second study. *Journal of the American Society for Psychical Research, 73*, 151–165.

Tart, C. T., Palmer, J., & Redington, D. J. (1979b). Effects of immediate feedback on ESP performance over short time periods. *Journal of the American Society for Psychical Research, 73*, 291–301.

Tart, C. T., Puthoff, H. E., & Targ, R. (Eds.). (1979). *Mind at large*. New York: Praeger.

Taylor, C. B., Sheikh, J., & Agras, W. S. (1986). Self report of panic attacks: Agreement with heart rate changes. *American Journal of Psychiatry, 143*, 478–482.

Taylor, E. I. (1973). Psychological suspended animation. Unpublished master's thesis, Southern Methodist University.

Taylor, N. (1949). *Flight from reality*. New York: Duell, Sloan and Pearce.

Tellegen, A., & Atkinson, G. (1974). Openness to absorbing and self-altering experiences ("absorption"), a trait related to hypnotic susceptibility. *Journal of Abnormal Psychology, 83*, 268–277.

Thalbourne, M. A., Dunbar, K. A., & Delin, P. S. (1995). An investigation into correlates of belief in the paranormal. *Journal of the American Society for Psychical Research, 89*, 215–231.

Thalbourne, M. A., & French, C. C. (1995). Paranormal belief, manic-depressiveness, and magical ideation: A replication. *Personality and Individual Differences, 18*, 291–292.

Tibbetts, V., & Pepper, E. (1989). Follow-up study on EMG/incentive inspirometer training to reduce asthmatic symptoms. Paper presented at the meetings of the Association for Applied Psychophysiology and Biofeedback, San Diego.

Tilley, A. J., & Empson, J. A. C. (1978). REM sleep and memory consolidation. *Biological Psychology, 6*, 293–300.

Tinklenberg, J. R., & Stillman, R. (1970). Drug use and violence. In D. Daniels, M. Gilula, & F. Ochberg (Eds.), *Violence and the struggle for existence*. Boston: Little, Brown.

Tinklenberg, J. R., & Woodrow, K. M. (1974). Drug use among youthful assultive and sexual offenders. In S. H. Frazier (Ed.), *Aggression research publication*. Association for Research in Nervous and Mental Disease.

Titchener, E. B. (1909). *Experimental psychology of the thought process*. New York: Macmillan.

Tomori, Z., & Widdicombe, J. G. (1969). Muscular bronchomotor, and cardiovascular reflexes elicited by mechanical stimulation of the respiratory tract. *Journal of Physiology, 200*, 25–49.

Torsvall, L., Akerstaedt, T., Gillander, K., & Knutsson, A. (1989). Sleep on the night shift: 24-hour EEG monitoring of spontaneous sleep/wake behavior. *Psychophysiology, 26*, 352–358.

Treisman, A., & Geffen, G. (1967). Selective attention: Perception or response? *Quarterly Journal of Experimental Psychology, 19*, 1–18.

Trinder, J. (1988). Subjective insomnia without objective findings: A pseudo diagnostic classification? *Psychological Bulletin, 103*, 87–94.

Trowill, J. A. (1967). Instrumental conditioning of heart rate in curarized rat. *Journal of Comparative and Physiological Psychology, 63*, 7–11.

Tulpule, T. E. (1971). Yogic exercises in the management of ischaemic heart disease. *Indian Heart Journal, 23*, 259–264.

Turk, D. C., Meichenbaum, D., & Berman, W. H. (1979). Application of biofeedback for the regulation of pain: A critical review. *Psychological Bulletin, 86*, 1322–1338.

Turner, R. K., & Taylor, P. D. (1974). Conditioning treatment of nocturnal enuresis in adults: Preliminary findings. *Behavioral Research and Therapy, 12*, 41–52.

Tyre, R. H. (1978). Teaching "The Lord of the Rings." *Media and Methods, 15*, 18–20.

U.S. Department of Health and Human Services. (1994). *Preliminary estimates for the 1993 National Household Survey on Drug Abuse*. Washington, DC: U.S. Government Printing Office.

Van Dyke, C., Jatlow, P., Ungerer, J., Barash, P., & Byck, R. (1978). Oral cocaine: Plasma concentrations and central effects. *Science, 200*, 211–213.

Van Wagenen, W., & Herren, R. (1940). Surgical division of commissure pathways in the corpus callosum. *Archives of Neurology and Psychiatry, 44*, 740–759.

Vitulli, W. F. (1983). Immediate feedback and target-symbol variation in computer-assisted psi test. *Journal of Parapsychology, 47*, 37–47.

Vojtechovsky, M., Safratova, V, Votava, Z., & Feit, V. (1971). The effects of sleep deprivation on learning and memory in healthy volunteers. *Activitas Nervosa Superior, 13*, 143–144.

Walker, E. H. (1975). Foundations of paraphysical and parapsychological phenomena. In L. Oteri (Ed.), *Quantum physics and parapsychology.* New York: Parapsychology Foundation.

Walker, E. H. (1984). A review of criticisms of the quantum mechanicial theory of psi phenomena. *Journal of Parapsychology, 48*, 277–332.

Walker, N. S., Garrett, J. B., & Wallace, B. (1976). Restoration of eidetic imagery via hypnotic age regression: A preliminary report. *Journal of Abnormal Psychology, 85*, 335–337.

Wall, V. J., & Womack, W. (1989). Hypnotic versus active cognitive strategies for alleviation of procedural distress in pediatric oncology patients. *American Journal of Clinical Hypnosis, 31*, 181–191.

Wallace, B. (1978a). Restoration of eidetic imagery via hypnotic age regression: More evidence. *Journal of Abnormal Psychology, 87*, 673–675.

Wallace, B. (1978b). Hypnotic susceptibility and the perception of afterimages and dot stimuli. *American Journal of Psychology, 92*, 681–691.

Wallace, B. (1979). *Applied hypnosis: An overview.* Chicago: Nelson-Hall.

Wallace, B. (1988). Hypnotic susceptibility, visual distraction, and reports of Necker cube apparent reversals. *Journal of General Psychology, 115*, 389–396.

Wallace, B. (1993). Day persons, night persons, and variability in hypnotic susceptibility. *Journal of Personality and Social Psychology, 64*, 827–833.

Wallace, B., & Fisher, L. E. (1982). Hypnotically induced limb anesthesia and adaptation to displacing prisms. *Journal of Abnormal Psychology, 91*, 390–391.

Wallace, B., & Fisher, L. E. (1984). Prism adaptation with hypnotically-induced limb anesthesia: The critical roles of head position and prism type. *Perception and Psychophysics, 36*, 303–306.

Wallace, B., & Garrett, J. B. (1973). Hypnotic susceptibility and autokinetic movement frequency. *Perceptual and Motor Skills, 36*, 1054.

Wallace, B., & Garrett, J. B. (1975). Perceptual adaptation with selective reductions of felt sensation. *Perception, 4*, 437–445.

Wallace, B., Garrett, J. B., & Anstadt, S. P. (1974). Hypnotic susceptibility, suggestion and reports of autokinetic movement. *American Journal of Psychology, 87*, 117–123.

Wallace, B., & Hoyenga, K. B. (1980). Reduction of proprioceptive errors with induced hypnotic anesthesia. *International Journal of Clinical and Experimental Hypnosis, 28*, 140–147.

Wallace, B., Knight, T. A., & Garrett, J. B. (1976). Hypnotic susceptibility and frequency reports to illusory stimuli. *Journal of Abnormal Psychology, 85*, 558–563.

Wallace, B., & Kokoszka, A. (1995). Fluctuations in hypnotic susceptibility and imaging ability over a 16-hour period. *International Journal of Clinical and Experimental Hypnosis, 43*, 20–33.

Wallace, B., & Patterson, S. L. (1984). Hypnotic susceptibility and performance on various attention-specific cognitive tasks. *Journal of Personality and Social Psychology, 47*, 175–181.

Wallace, R. K., & Benson, H. (1972). The physiology of meditation. *Scientific American,* *226,* 85–90.

Wallace, R. K., Benson, H., & Wilson, A. F. (1971). A wakeful hypometabolic physiological state. *American Journal of Physiology, 221,* 795–799.

Wallechinsky, D., & Wallace, I. (1975). *The people's almanac.* Garden City, NY: Doubleday.

Walsh, D. H. (1974). Interactive effects of alpha feedback and instructional set on subjective state. *Psychophysiology, 11,* 428–435.

Walsh, R. N. (1977). Initial meditative experiences. I. *Journal of Transpersonal Psychology, 9,* 151–192.

Walsh, R. N. (1978). Initial meditative experiences. II. *Journal of Transpersonal Psychology, 10,* 1–28.

Walsh, R. N. (1981). *Towards an ecology of brain.* Jamaica, NY: Spectrum.

Walsh, R. N. (1982). A model for viewing meditation research. *Journal of Transpersonal Psychology, 14,* 69–84.

Walter, W. G. (1936). The location of cerebral tumors by electroencephalography. *Lancet, 2,* 305–308.

Walter, W. G., & Dovey, V. J. (1944). Electro-encephalography in cases of subcortical tumour. *Journal of Neurology, Neurosurgery, and Psychiatry, 7,* 57–65.

Walton, K. G., & Levitsky, D. (1994). A neuroendocrine mechanism for the reduction of drug use and addictions by Transcendental Meditation. *Alcoholism Treatment Quarterly, 11,* 89–117.

Washburn, M. C. (1978). Observations relevant to a unified theory of meditation. *Journal of Transpersonal Psychology, 10,* 45–65.

Watson, J. B. (1913). Psychology as the behaviorist views it. *Psychological Review, 20,* 158–177.

Webb, W. B. (1973). Sleep research past and present. In W. B. Webb (Ed.), *Sleep: An active process.* Glenview, IL: Scott, Foresman.

Webb, W. B., & Agnew, H. W., Jr. (1971). Stage 4 sleep: Influence of time course variables. *Science, 174,* 1354–1356.

Webb, W. B., & Agnew, H. W., Jr. (1974). The effects of a chronic limitation of sleep length. *Psychophysiology, 11,* 265–274.

Webb, W. B., & Bonnet, M. H. (1979). Sleep and dreams. In M. E. Meyer (Ed.), *Foundations of contemporary psychology.* New York: Oxford University Press.

Webb, W. B., & Cartwright, R. D. (1978). Sleep and dreams. *Annual Review of Psychology, 29,* 223–252.

Webb, W. B., & Kersey, J. (1967). Recall of dreams and the probability of stage 1-REM sleep. *Perceptual and Motor Skills, 24,* 627–630.

Weil, A. T. (1972). *The natural mind: A new way of looking at drugs and the higher consciousness.* Boston: Houghton Mifflin.

Weil, A. T. (1996). Pharmacology of consciousness: A narrative of subjective experience. In S. R. Hameroff, A. W. Kaszniak, & A. C. Scott (Eds.), *Toward a science of consciousness* (pp. 677–689). Cambridge, MA: MIT Press.

Weil, A. T., Zinberg, N. E., & Nelson, J. N. (1968). Clinical and physiological effects of marihuana in man. *Science, 162,* 1234–1242.

Weiner, H. (1977). *Psychobiology and human disease.* New York: Elsevier.

Weinstein, L. N., Schwartz, D. G., & Arkin, A. M. (1991). Qualitative aspects of sleep mentation. In S. A. Ellman & J. S. Antrobus (Eds.), *The mind in sleep: Psychology and psychophysiology* (2nd ed., pp. 172–213). New York: Wiley.

Weishaar, B. B. (1986). A comparison of Lamaze and hypnosis in the management of labor. *American Journal of Clinical Hypnosis, 28,* 214–217.

Weitzenhoffer, A. M., & Hilgard, E. R. (1959). *Stanford Hypnotic Susceptibility Scale, Forms A and B.* Palo Alto: Consulting Psychologists Press.

Weitzenhoffer, A. M., & Hilgard, E. R. (1962). *Stanford Hypnotic Susceptibility Scale, Form C.* Palo Alto: Consulting Psychologists Press.

Welwood, J. (1977). Meditation and the unconscious. *Journal of Transpersonal Psychology, 9,* 1–26.

Wesson, D. R., & Smith, D. E. (1971). Barbiturate use as an intoxicant: A San Francisco perspective. Testimony given to the Subcommittee to investigate Juvenile Delinquency, San Francisco, December 15.

West, M. A. (Ed.). (1987). *The psychology of meditation.* New York: Oxford University Press.

West, V., Fellows, B., & Easton, S. (1995). The British Society of Experimental and Clinical Hypnosis: A national survey. *Contemporary Hypnosis, 12,* 143–147.

Wetii, C. V., & Wright, R. K. (1979). Death caused by recreational cocaine use. *Journal of the American Medical Association, 241,* 2519–2522.

Wheeler, L., Reis, H. T., Wolff, E., Grupsmith, E., & Mordkoff, A. M. (1974). Eye-roll and hypnotic susceptibility. *International Journal of Clinical and Experimental Hypnosis, 22,* 327–334.

White, L., & Tursky, B. (Eds.). (1982). *Clinical biofeedback: Efficacy and mechanisms.* New York: Guilford.

Whitlock, F. A. (1978). The psychiatry and psychopathology of paranormal phenomena. *Australian and New Zealand Journal of Psychiatry, 12,* 11–19.

Whitmer, P. G. (1978). EMG biofeedback manipulation of arousal and the test of the oversarousal and underarousal areas of childhood hyperactivity. *Disseratation Abstracts International, 38,* 3423.

Whitwell, J. R. (1936). *Historical notes on psychiatry.* London: H. K. Lewis.

Wickelgren, I. (1997). Marijuana: Harder than thought? *Science, 276,* 1967–1968.

Wickramasekera, I. E. (1972). Electromyographic feedback training and tension headache: Preliminary observations. *American Journal of Clinical Hypnosis, 15,* 83–85.

Wilber, K. (1980). *The Atman project.* Wheaton, IL: Quest.

Wilber, K. (1982). Odyssey: A personal inquiry into humanistic and transpersonal psychology. *Journal of Humanistic Psychology, 22,* 57–90.

Williams, H. L., & Lubin, A. (1959). *Impaired performance in a case of prolonged sleep loss.* Mimeographed paper. Washington, DC: Walter Reed Army Institute of Research.

Williams, J. M., & Hall, D. W. (1988). Use of single session hypnosis for smoking cessation. *Addictive Behavior, 13,* 205–208.

Wilson, A. F., Honsberger, R., Chiu, J. T., & Novey, H. S. (1975). Transcendental meditation and asthma. *Respiration, 32,* 74–80.

Winkel, G. H., & Sarason, I. G. (1964). Subject, experimenter and situational variables in research on anxiety. *Journal of Abnormal and Social Psychology, 68,* 601–608.

Wolkove, N., Kreisman, H., Darragh, D., Cohen, C., & Frank, H. (1984). Effect of Transcendental Meditation on breathing and respiratory control. *Journal of Applied Physiology, 56,* 607–612.

Wolman, B. B. (Ed.). (1977). *Handbook of parapsychology.* New York: Van Nostrand Reinhold.

Wolman, B. B., & Ullman, M. (Eds.) (1986). *Handbook of states of consciousness.* New York: Van Nostrand Reinhold.

Wolpe, J. (1969). For phoria: A hair of the hound. *Psychology Today, 3,* 34–37.

Wood, D. M., & Emmett-Oglesby, M. W. (1986). Characteristics of tolerance, recovery from tolerance and cross-tolerance for cocaine used as a discriminative stimulus. *Journal of Pharmacology and Experimental Therapeutics, 237,* 120–125.

Woodruff, J. L., & Rhine, J. B. (1942). An experiment in precognition using dice. *Journal of Parapsychology, 6,* 243–262.

Woody, E. Z., Drugovic, M., & Oakman, J. M. (1997). A reexamination of the role of nonhypnotic suggestibility in hypnotic responding. *Journal of Personality and Social Psychology, 72,* 399–407.

Woolfolk, R. L. (1975). Psychophysiological correlates of meditation. *Archives of General Psychiatry, 32,* 1326–1333.

Worthington, T. S. (1979). The use in court of hypnotically enhanced testimony. *International Journal of Clinical and Experimental Hypnosis, 27,* 402–416.

Yapko, M. D. (1986). Hypnotic and strategic interventions in the treatment of anorexia nervosa. *American Journal of Clinical Hypnosis, 28,* 224–232.

Yates, A. J. (1980). *Biofeedback and the modification of behavior.* New York: Plenum.

York, J. L., & Welte, J. W. (1994). Gender comparisons of alcohol consumption in alcoholic and nonalcoholic populations. *Journal of the Study of Alcohol, 55,* 743–750.

Zarcone, V. (1973). Marijuana and ethanol: Effects on sleep. *Psychiatry and Medicine, 4,* 201–212.

Zelig, M., & Beidelman, W. B. (1981). The investigative use of hypnosis: A word of caution. *International Journal of Clinical and Experimental Hypnosis, 29,* 401–412.

Zepelin, H., & Rechtschaffen, A. (1974). Mammalian sleep, longevity, and energy metabolism. *Brain, Behavior, and Evolution, 10,* 425–470.

Zinberg, N. E. (1977). *Alternate states of consciousness: Multiple perspectives on the study of consciousness.* New York: Free Press.

Ziskind, E. (1965). An explanation of mental symptoms found in acute deprivation: Researches, 1958–1963. *American Journal of Psychiatry, 121,* 939–946.

Zlotogorski, Z., Hahnemann, L. E., & Wiggs, E. A. (1987). Personality characteristics of hypnotizability. *American Journal of Clinical Hypnosis, 30,* 51–56.

Zubek, J. P. (1969). *Sensory deprivation: Fifteen years of research.* New York: Appleton-Century-Crofts.

Zubek, J. P., Bayer, L., Milstein, S., & Shephard, J. M. (1969). Behavioral and physiological changes during prolonged immobilization plus perceptual deprivation. *Journal of Abnormal Psychology, 74,* 230–236.

Zubek, J. P., Sansom, W., & Prysianiuk, A. (1960). Intellectual changes during prolonged perceptual isolation (darkness and silence). *Canadian Journal of Psychology, 14,* 233–243.

Zuckerman, M. (1969a). Variables affecting deprivation results. In J. P. Zubek (Ed.), *Sensory deprivation: Fifteen years of research* (pp. 47–84). New York: Appleton-Century-Crofts.

Zuckerman, M. (1969b). Hallucinations, reported sensations, and images. In J. P. Zubek (Ed.), *Sensory deprivation: Fifteen years of research* (pp. 85–125). New York: Appleton-Century-Crofts.

AUTHOR INDEX

SUBJECT INDEX